DANCE OF THE DOLPHIN

Dance of the Dolphin

TRANSFORMATION AND DISENCHANTMENT IN THE AMAZONIAN IMAGINATION

CANDACE SLATER

The University of Chicago Press

Chicago and London

Candace Slater is professor of Spanish and Portuguese at the University of California, Berkeley. She is author of three previous books on South American folklore.

The University of Chicago Press, Chicago 60637
The University of Chicago Press, Ltd., London
© 1994 by The University of Chicago.
All rights reserved. Published 1994
Printed in the United States of America

03 02 01 00 99 98 97 96 95 94   1 2 3 4 5
ISBN: 0-226-76183-5 (cloth)
          0-226-76184-3 (paper)

Library of Congress Cataloging-in-Publication Data

Slater, Candace.
    Dance of the dolphin: transformation and disenchantment
in the Amazonian imagination / Candace Slater.
        p.   cm.
    Includes bibliographical references and index.
    1. Folklore—Brazil—Amazonas.   2. Tales—Brazil—
History and criticism.   3. Folklore—Brazil—Pará (State)
4. Dolphins—Brazil—Folklore.   5. Metamorphosis—
Folklore.   I. Title.
GR133.B62A527   1994
398'.369953—dc20   93-27472
                                                              CIP

Oh, minha filha, você está querendo uma coisa impossível. Quer pegar o encantado por meio dos estudos, e não pega, não. Pois você só pega ele por meio do pensamento, pela força da concentração. A pessoa corre muito risco de vida para chegar lá no Encante, tem que sofrer uma transformação.

(Oh, my dear, you want something impossible. You want to comprehend the Enchanted Beings through study, and that's not the way. Because you can capture them only through thought, through the force of concentration. A person has to risk his life to get to the Enchanted City, he has to undergo a transformation.)

—*Dona Marina, midwife, age 59, Parintins*

O Boto? Puxa vida, todo mundo conta.

(The Dolphin? Good grief, everybody tells the story.)

—*High school student (female), age 16, Parintins*

Por quê é que tudo é sempre difícil aqui em Amazônia? Talvez porque é o fim do mundo, e também o seu começo.

(Why is it that everything is always difficult here in Amazônia? Perhaps because it is the world's end, and also, its beginning.)

—*Gold miner, age 37, Porto Velho*

CONTENTS

ACKNOWLEDGMENTS

M y interest in the Amazon in general and the Dolphin in particular began with a request from students in a Brazilian civilization course at the University of California at Berkeley for something about the region. What I thought was going to be a quick trip to the library became an extended research project and ongoing passion. Intrigued by the shelves of studies on a part of Brazil about which I knew relatively little, I decided to see the Amazon for myself. This book is one result.

My former students, Ted Whitesell and Brent Millikan, and Ted's wife, Lucilene Lira, provided me with my first contacts in Amazônia (the Brazilian Amazon) and invited me to visit them in their respective research locations during my third trip to the region. In addition, as my research assistant back at Berkeley, Lucilene transcribed a number of the stories quoted in this book. I am grateful as well to my students in subsequent undergraduate and graduate courses on images of the Amazon, and to colleagues in the NEH Summer Seminar for College Teachers which I directed in 1992 for their questions and observations. Major financial backing for this project came from the National Endowment for the Humanities and the University of California President's Fellowships in the Humanities Program, with supplements from Berkeley's Committee on Research and its Joint Center for Latin American Studies. Good counsel and much-appreciated editorial assistance was provided by my editor, T. David Brent, copy editor Carol Saller, and their colleagues at the University of Chicago Press.

One of this project's greatest pleasures has been unexpected forays into areas of study previously all but unknown to me. The comments and helpful suggestions of Ellen Basso, Michael Brown, Janet Chernela, Marlene Dobkin de Rios, David Guss, Waud Kracke, Gerardo Reichel-Dolmatoff, Peter Roe, Michael Taussig, Charles Wagley, and Johannes Wilbert, as well as those of various participants at the Latin American Indigenous Literature

Association meetings in San Juan, Puerto Rico, greatly enriched my under-standing of South American Indian cosmology. I am similarly grateful to Dr. Vera M. F. da Silva and her colleague Mr. Fernando Rosas at the Projeto Peixe-Boi at the Instituto Nacional de Pesquisas Amazônicas in Manaus, and to Dr. Giorgio Pilleri for their detailed answers to my many questions about *Inia geoffrensis,* otherwise known as the *boto* or Amazonian red dol-phin. I also thank Marlene Prado, Ana Rita Alves, Deborah Magalhães Lima, Lúcio Flávio Pinto, Anaiza Vergolino, and (posthumously) Napoleão Figueiredo, for information that helped me in the initial stages of my research.

A number of friends and colleagues were kind enough to read parts of this manuscript. I am grateful to William Christian, Jr., Rachel Fretz, Ste-phen Greenblatt, Gwen Kirkpatrick, Steven Knapp, Francine Masiello, Nancy Scheper-Hughes, Tom Bogenschild, Madeline Kizer, and Maria Mas-solo for their contributions at various stages of this project; Márcio Souza, Jorge Bodanzky, and Lúcio Flávio Pinto were similarly helpful; and Thomas Gregor and Dell Hymes made a number of particularly useful suggestions. Patrick McIlrath helped devise the map and sketch of the two types of Amazonian dolphin that appear here, and Ana Maria Carvalho helped check my Portuguese transcriptions and English translations for accuracy. David Staebler printed and, often, improved the photographs I took.

In Amazônia, numerous people went out of their way to help me. I thank Eder and Patrícia Coelho in Santarém, Aracélia Farias in Belém, Sebastiana Medeiros in Bragança, Octávio Campos in Marajó, the Joaquim Ribeiro family in Macapá, the Samuel Bemerguy family in Itaituba, Sylvia Aguiar and Nilson Rodrigues in Porto Velho, Zé Seringueiro and D. Nené in the Cupuaí rubber settlement, and José Maria Barbosa da Silva, Luís Reis, and Rosita Araújo in Manaus, for taking me into their homes. I also am grateful to the families with whom I stayed in numerous communities of the Parintins interior, in Silêncio do Matá (Óbidos) and Seringal Mara-batá (Carauari). I have special debts of gratitude to representatives of the Roman Catholic church in Faro, Terra Santa, Oriximiná, Óbidos, Maués, and São Joaquim (Amapá), and, especially, Parintins. Marlicy Bemerguy, Antonio Zacarias de Souza Cruz, Tonzinho Saunier, Robert Tadheu, Eulália Ribeiro, and Lucila Campos and her family also helped me. In Amapá, I was able to make recordings that would otherwise have been impossible, thanks to the help of Helder Macedo, and to the state Ministry of Culture.

Special thanks go to my mother, Adelaide Nielsen Slater, and to my husband, Paul Zingg, who gave me, among other things, the title of this book. First and last, I am indebted to the several hundred storytellers, including the half dozen individuals in Parintins who appear throughout this book. Although, in the interest of their privacy, their real names do not appear here, their absence in no way indicates a lack of gratitude, as I am well aware that they took me places I could not have gone alone.

INVITATION TO THE DANCE

O Boto se transforma em gente e vai dançar na festa. A minha avó dançou com Boto uma vez, aí, eu tenho toda certeza que estas coisas acontecem. Pelo menos, aconteciam. Hoje, é mais difícil.

(Dolphins turn into people and show up to dance at parties. My own grandmother once danced with a Dolphin, so I know for sure that these things happen. At least, they used to happen. Today, it is more difficult.)

—*Young woman, interior of Parintins*

Transformation is this study's end, and also its beginning. The book, however, is about quite different sorts of change. On the most literal level, it is an examination of widely familiar folk stories involving the metamorphosis of Amazonian freshwater dolphins into human beings. Unlike in many other traditions, where these animals are viewed as highly intelligent fellow mammals, when not symbols of selfless charity or the immortal soul, dolphins in the Amazon are often *encantados,* supernatural entities in the guise of aquatic animals who turn into men and women in order to carry off the objects of their desire to an underwater city, or *Encante,* from which few ever return.[1]

And yet, if this book's immediate subject is Dolphins (I will use the capitalized form to indicate the more-than-animal being), it deals through them with other, far broader and more complex sorts of metamorphoses. Indirect, and for this reason, particularly vivid, reflections of the massive physical, social, and economic changes that the Amazon is currently undergoing, the stories—told by Portuguese-speaking individuals, often of mixed

1. There are actually two types of Amazonian freshwater dolphin. The reddish dolphin believed to be an enchanted being is the *boto vermelho* (*Inia geoffrensis*) while its smaller, dark-bodied counterpart, said to help fishermen and shipwrecks, is known as the *tucuxi* (*Sotalia fluviatilis*). Despite recent articles in the popular press that have underscored these animals' "dark side" (most notably, the males' tendency to gang up on fertile females), dolphins continue to attract overwhelmingly positive attention in the United States and Europe.

1

racial heritage—mediate and transmute experience into narrative. Seen against a backdrop of many-faceted encounters between a largely traditional regional culture and a development-minded national culture, they suggest how perpetual motion (the Dolphin's refusal to assume an assigned niche within a stable, outwardly imposed order) may constitute a potential way of standing firm. In so doing, they challenge and expand conventional definitions of resistance as conscious oppositional force.[2]

Although they reveal little or no militant capacity for action, the stories' stubborn faith in a world beyond everyday experience suggests an intricate web of ambivalences and ambiguities between dominant and dominated within Amazônia today. One of many sorts of narratives that deal with the supernatural, the Dolphin stories stand apart in their protagonists' difficult-to-fathom behavior. Unlike forest spirits or UFOs or Roman Catholic saints, whose actions obey a logic clear to storytellers, *encantados* in general and Dolphins in particular often act for no apparent reason. The unpredictability and instability that make them especially appealing to many of the people I encountered piqued my own interest in these stories. So did storytellers' propensity to use them, and not some other sort of narrative, as a framework for extended commentary on the profound changes the Amazon is presently undergoing.

Unlike previous writers who have judged the Dolphin to be a European import, I argue for these tales' ultimately non-Western vision of the world.[3] While the Dolphin stories unquestionably incorporate Iberian elements, as well as African Brazilian and numerous indigenous elements, they continue to reveal a nonanthropocentric perspective and a supremely fluid sense of self and other very different from imported images such as El Dorado, Paradise Lost, or Green Hell. This composite vision is less proof of the staying power of the past than of present-day Amazonians' ability to recuperate and continually reconfigure traditional forms for their own, dis-

2. Michael F. Brown ("Beyond Resistance") and Lila Abu-Lughod ("The Romance of Resistance"), among others, caution that the term "resistance" may cloud the intricacies and contradictions of power when used unreflectively, and I by no means suggest that all Dolphin tales reveal a single dynamic or that the storytellers necessarily have any sort of active political consciousness or engagement. In most cases, the resistance of which I am speaking is a half-conscious, though for this reason no less strong, reaction to a capitalist economic order that is making life in the countryside increasingly untenable and to an accompanying rationalistic vision of the world in which there is no place for the Dolphin's *mistério,* or enigmatic force.

3. Luís da Câmara Cascudo, one of Brazil's most influential folklore scholars, acknowledges the antiquity of the Dolphin cycle but insists that nothing "leads one to believe in its existence among the Indians of pre-colonial Brazil" (Cascudo, *Geografia dos mitos brasileiros,* p. 141).

tinctly contemporary, ends. Now funny, now frightening, frequently strange and beautiful, the tales demand a reexamination of the Judeo-Christian premises that shape, often unconsciously, not just literary representations, but also much contemporary scientific writing and policy debate. In the end, they offer an alternate way of looking at both the Amazon and human experience.

Conceived as the conclusion to a study of representations of the Amazon by outsider observers, what was to have been a chapter grew into a book. All too cognizant of the ironies and limits inherent in my own identity as a foreigner—"What you want is impossible," Dona Marina says flatly—I have focused as much as possible on the transformation of a people and a landscape as reflected through their own symbolic forms. The resulting study of the Amazonian imagination provides a complement and counterbalance to economic, ecological, and political analyses that tend to deal with impersonal forces in either very general or extremely narrow terms. Any narrative is in some way about its author, and I have tried to acknowledge my own involvement in the experiences that lie behind this study. At the same time, I have sought to go beyond the large collection of unabashedly impressionistic travel literature that describes the author's adventures in a vast unknown ("That night we camped beside the river and ate alligator stew!").

Because I began my fieldwork with the conviction that the close to ninety-nine percent of the Brazilian Amazonian population of some thirteen million that does not define itself as indigenous deserves far more attention, I was not looking for Amazonian Indian influences.[4] The Dolphin stories attracted me precisely because of their apparently unremarkable, extremely widespread character; their interest to many different kinds of people; and their presence in both the countryside and cities into which rural migrants continue to flood. Although, as time went on, I became increasingly interested in the stories' non-European aspects, including specific parallels in indigenous culture, this study is not intended as any sort of literary archaeology. Ultimately, I am far less concerned with what might be Amerindian—or African Brazilian or European—in these stories than

---

4. There is a large and growing body of scholarship on Amazonian Indian oral traditions. For studies specifically relating to narrative see Susan A. Niles, *South American Indian Narrative*. Articles concerning more recent research frequently appear in the *Latin Amerindian Literatures Journal,* published by the Latin American Indigenous Literatures Association, and the *Journal of Latin American Lore* (Center for Latin American Studies at UCLA). As Charles Wagley noted in his introduction to *The Amazon Caboclo* in 1985, there is dramatically less scholarship on mixed-ancestry or *caboclo* groups. A list of existing studies appears in Pennie L. Magee, "The Water Is Our Land,'" p. 4.

I am with the dynamics of symbolic transformation and resistance, and the present-day significance of a hybrid, and uniquely Amazonian, expressive form.

The tellers of the Dolphin stories vary in terms of age, sex, level of education, occupation, place of birth, and present residence. Most, however, are at least nominally Roman Catholic, and the great majority identify with not just Amazônia, but also Brazil. A growing number live in urban centers, but even those who continue to live in isolated hamlets are increasingly connected to a larger nation state and international, capitalist economic order through television and radio, visitors (missionaries, tourists, researchers), and public schools. Not only have they heard of the greenhouse effect, but many can provide detailed, first-hand illustrations of the results of deforestation in or near their own communities. In addition, rural inhabitants often either have resided, or have relatives residing, in the big cities of Belém and Manaus.

Although my focus here is the Brazilian Amazon, or Amazônia, stories similar to the Dolphin tales crop up in the rain forests of the Andean countries, much of the Orinoco river basin, and various parts of the Caribbean. Many of these stories tell of both male and female Dolphins who like nothing better than to dance till dawn in the often raucous *festas* that enliven a difficult existence in the interior. Dapper in straw hats, white suits, and shiny black shoes that are actually stingrays, the males are reported to father numerous half-human children. The females, for their part, take on the form of seductive women. Capable of provoking various afflictions, including madness, these enchanted beings also may help the shamanic healers called *pajés* who regularly invoke their assistance.[5]

The Dolphin's particularly widespread appeal as a symbol distinguishes the narratives from the many other stories of the supernatural told today in Amazônia. Although persons of limited means and education are most apt to recount these tales, Dolphins appear on municipal telephone book covers, in folklore festivals that involve a wide range of social classes, in movies aimed at an urban, middle-income audience, and in television ads for politicians. Because they mean quite different things to the fisherman in an isolated rural community, the small-town high-school student, and the country-born factory worker in a major urban center, they inspire discussion and, often, spirited debate.

Like my earlier research on Brazilian *cordel* or chapbook literature and

---

5. I will use the term "shamanic healer" in place of "shaman" throughout this discussion to underscore the difference between native Amazonian healers and generally mixed-heritage curers who often incorporate elements from more than one tradition into their healing practices.

tales of both Brazilian and southern Spanish folk saints, this book focuses on the present-day, largely commonplace symbolic expression of apparently ordinary people, relying heavily on fieldwork in its attempt to place the narratives within a broader context.[6] Although my training is in literature, and my ultimate allegiance is to narrative, I once again have tapped a range of disciplines—literary criticism, history, folklore, and cultural anthropology—in drawing out the larger social and metaphorical significance of individual stories. I have tried, however, to avoid repeating old solutions and to reframe familiar questions in a way that underscores the often alien underpinnings of these tales.

In its focus on a tradition that suggests an at least partially non-Western vision of the natural world and human beings' role within it, and its accompanying concern for issues of transculturation, this book stands apart from my earlier work on primarily Iberian-based folk forms.[7] Furthermore, despite the tendency of educated authors, artists, filmmakers, and musicians to look to them for inspiration, the *encantado* tales—in contrast to the chapbook or the saint's life, which rely in part on written sources—remain a distinctly oral, folk and popular, tradition.[8]

This book also differs from my earlier efforts in its consciously greater scope and sense of urgency. If the Dolphin stories suggest different sorts of transformations, they also reveal two quite separate varieties of disenchantment—one by definition humanizing, the other alienating. Most storytellers who speak here are well aware of how their already precarious existence is complicated, if not directly threatened, by the ongoing destruction of not only rivers and forests, but also of a distinctive, if not always just or easy, way of life. Often they assert that the *encantados* are abandoning the burnt fields and ever more crowded cities. ("Who, if they could, wouldn't leave a place like this?" one man asks ruefully.)[9] The Dolphin's insouciant

6. The studies are Candace Slater, *Stories on a String, Trail of Miracles,* and *City Steeple, City Streets.*

7. The term "transculturation," initially coined by Cuban sociologist Fernando Ortiz in the 1940s, and later reintroduced by Venezuelan literary critic Angel Rama, refers to the translation, or recasting in a native idiom, of one culture by another.

8. Probably the most celebrated work by an educated Brazilian author to draw on the *encantado* tradition is Raul Bopp's long lyric poem, "Cobra Norato." Other writers who have looked to the enchanted beings for inspiration include Inglês de Souza (*Contos Amazônicos*) and Márcio Souza (*A resistível ascenção do Boto Tucuxi*). The mass-market U.S. film *Where the Water Runs Black* and the Brazilian *Ele, o Boto* (*The Dolphin*) also utilize the *encantado* theme.

9. Man, age 51, born interior of Parintins, lives Manaus (5 years). Married, janitor, 2 years grade school. Here, and throughout this study, I identify the speakers by sex, age, and birthplace. I also give the present place of residence, indicating in parentheses how long the person has lived there, if this is different from the place of birth. A statement of marital status

5

disregard for an imported, increasingly pervasive social and economic order that marginalizes the great majority of the region's residents can be seen as the storytellers' response to the degradation of a cultural as well as physical environment, an attempt to modify the present through its description in a familiar language.

Finally, and perhaps most important, the present book stands apart from my other work in its deep sense of the *encantados'* fundamental mystery. Time and research have clarified many aspects of the stories which I have attempted to present here. Nevertheless, the stories remain strange to me in ways that the chapbooks and saints' lives do not. Each time I return to Amazônia, I am newly surprised by previously unsuspected aspects of the stories and by the larger, ever-shifting world of which they afford a brief, if radiant, glimpse. Although in a heterogeneous and complex culture like that of Amazônia, many images, traditions, and institutions offer competing views of human existence, the Dolphin stories provide a privileged understanding of the meanings and mystifications upon which worlds are built.

The experiences that underlie this book also remain in part enigmatic. Given the overtly sexual nature of the Dolphin stories, it is hardly surprising that my interest in them should have led to a number of situations charged with a certain sexual ambiguity. And yet, while, in retrospect, this ambiguity could easily have been predicted, I found myself caught off guard at times in ways not true of my earlier research. Once, for instance, when I was staying in a rubber colony on the Juruá River, I slipped away to a relatively secluded section of the river to take a bath. Leaving most of my clothes in a canoe moored at the riverbank, I slid into the water, delighted to escape momentarily the merciless gnats and mosquitoes and relieved, for once, to be totally alone.

I had not been splashing about in the river for more than a few minutes when a voice from the leafy overhang directly above me declared, "You should get out of the water now." Too surprised to react in any other way, I got dressed, and trudged back to the mosquitoes, not sure what to think. Later that day, a male neighbor started talking in my presence to my hosts about the large number of stingrays that had begun congregating at the point in the river where I had gone to bathe. "That's always been a dangerous place," everyone agreed. His comment made me feel frightened in

---

(the self-designation "married" does not necessarily imply any sort of formal union), present occupation, and years—if any—of formal schooling follows. Because years of schooling often do not reflect a person's degree of literacy (public schools were rare in the interior before the 1970s and those who learned to read and write often did so with relatives or private tutors), this information should be interpreted with caution. Also, although I have listed "farming" as an occupation, this term designates an activity often closer to intensive horticulture than agriculture.

retrospect, embarrassed at (and grateful for) his intervention, and at once irritated and amused that someone should be following around the crazy foreigner without her knowledge. ("Why," I asked myself, "didn't I expect this?") I also felt a sudden jolt of physical attraction for this man with no teeth, eleven children, and intensely brown eyes, which surprised me in the moment and gave me food for thought.

Not infrequently in the course of my research, I found myself in person-ally revealing conversations with both men and women. Sometimes, I got bewildered or visibly angry when people I thought I knew did things I did not understand. When a friend who composes exquisite love songs began publicly insulting his young wife after she begged to leave a party (their two-year-old was getting cranky), my own anger at him surprised both them and me. Then, when the young woman later laughed off the experi-ence ("It didn't mean a thing, Cândida, believe me! Men just have to talk like that!"), I both believed and disbelieved her. "You're from another planet!" I once informed a customarily reflective friend when he started gleefully impugning a particular woman's honor with no apparent cause or knowledge. "No, no, you're the one who's from another planet!" he assured me with equal conviction, and it occurred to me that he might be right. Every once in a while, people would ask me teasingly if I myself were a Bota, and I suspect that the thought really may have crossed more than one mind. Dolphin-women, after all, are said to be tall, fair-skinned and blue-eyed, and they always appear in the white clothing I favored in the relentless sun.

And yet, if my involvement with many of the people who told me stories sometimes threatened to transgress my own notions of proper fieldwork, much of what I know—or, at least, suspect—about the Dolphin owes directly to those moments in which I forgot who was self and who was other. Although I felt extremely close to many of the people in my earlier studies, the experiences that underlie them did not fill me with the same aching certainty of human limits and accompanying sense of the world's vastness.

Once, in a remote rubber settlement on the Juruá River, a shamanic healer named Seu Josias invited me to go with him to the river bottom where he and others believe there is an enchanted city. "We'll take the boat to the Remanso Cove at midnight—what do you say?" he asked. The truth is that I had to think about his offer for several minutes. The slippery logs that led from the dock to the house in whose kitchen we were standing were hard enough for me to scramble up at midday, and I wondered how I would keep from falling into the brackish water in the dark of night. I get seasick and I panic in the presence of caimans and piranhas—what would I do if the boat started rocking wildly or even capsized while this man I barely knew was enmeshed in some sort of trance? Besides, it was raining and there was, for once, a chill wind. When I finally took a deep breath and told him, "Yes," he said, "Good, then we will go there in your dream tonight." "My dream!" I exclaimed with a degree of indignation that led everyone to laugh.

The next morning when Seu Josias asked me how I had liked our visit to the river bottom, I replied somewhat sourly that I remembered nothing, and he laughed again. To this day, he insists that the two of us spent all night strolling about the Enchanted City ("We were there together, a turtle in fine clothes served us *cafezinho,* and you kept begging me to stay!"). I, for my part, tell him that while he may well have gone there, I spent the night—at least, I think I spent the night—in bed. I hope the following pages hint at a mystery familiar to Seu Josias and many other residents of the Amazon. I have tried to suggest something of a world beneath the waters that I may not have had the eyes to see but which they were generous enough to want to show me.

My pursuit of the *encantados*—or, as Seu Josias would say, their pursuit of me—builds on two important Brazilian studies. The first, *Santos e visagens,* by Eduardo Galvão, is based on fieldwork conducted with noted American anthropologist Charles Wagley in the late 1940s.[10] Set in a small river community in the state of Pará, the study compares attitudes and practices involving Roman Catholic saints and a variety of forest and water spirits, chief among them the *encantados.*

In many ways, Raymundo Heraldo Maués's *A ilha encantada: Medicina e xamanismo numa comunidade de pescadores (The Enchanted Island: Medicine and Shamanism in a Fishing Community)* takes up where Galvão leaves off.[11] Based on fieldwork conducted in 1977 in a fishing village on Pará's Atlantic coast, the book underscores the ideological bases of the traditional healing system and sheds light on the social role of the shamanic curer.[12]

Two other, shorter studies, Fernando Madriz Galindo's brief, primarily descriptive "Los Encantos, elementos del agua" ("The *Encantos,* Water Entities") and David Guss's longer and more analytical "The Encantados: Venezuela's Invisible Kingdom," focus on beliefs about Venezuelan water spirits.[13] Relying on his fieldwork in the Turimiquire region, Guss suggests

10. Eduardo Galvão, *Santos e visagens.* The work is a revised, Portuguese-language version of the author's 1954 Columbia University Ph.D. dissertation.

11. Raymundo Heraldo Maués, *A ilha encantada.*

12. Like Galvão, Maués and many of his colleagues in the Federal University of Pará's Núcleo de Altos Estudos Amazônicos (Center for Advanced Amazonian Studies), or NAEA, have a special interest in problems of social and cultural transformation.

13. See Fernando Madriz Galindo, "Los encantos, elementos del agua"; and David M. Guss, "The Encantados." The section on the *yacuruna,* or water people, of the Peruvian

links between present-day *criollo* ideas about the enchanted beings and far older indigenous patterns of reciprocity between human hunters and their prey.

At the same time that it draws on these and other analyses of Amazonian folk religion, the present study is different in its orientation and intent. Because I was considerably more interested in observing the dynamics of symbolic change as these emerge in the Dolphin stories than in using these tales to map out a particular set of religious beliefs and social relations (the two objectives, to be sure, are not wholly separable), I devoted particular attention to an urban site. Although Parintins, where I tape-recorded many of the stories that appear here, has only about 60,000 people, it is nonetheless the second or third most populous city in Amazonas, Brazil's largest state. (Parintins and Itacoatiara, about six hours downriver by boat from Manaus, have a running battle over which of the two is larger.) Not surprisingly, the often widely diverse tales I recorded there and in other parts of Amazônia are less likely to reflect the conscious, cosmological whole described by writers working in smaller, rural communities than they are to evoke the jumble of processes subsumed under the terms "modernization" and "acculturation."

Then too, although this study focuses on the *encantados,* it locates stories about these beings within a broader geographical and thematic framework. Like a growing number of literary scholars, anthropologists, and historians, I have been especially interested in the larger question of cultural confrontation and the subversive possibilities of apparently innocuous symbolic forms. Even while the *encantado* tales affirm a distinctively Amazonian past that has survived, piecemeal and continuously redeployed, into the present, the storytellers may be relative newcomers to the region, largely, if not wholly, unaware of regional traditions.

The first part of this book introduces the stories and their social, historical, and performative context. I then consider three separate and yet ultimately interrelated aspects of the Dolphin. Each of these identities—*encantado,* lover, and white man—hinges on a central paradox. In the first case, Dolphins appear as extensions of nature, and yet, people find them threatening precisely because of their all-too-human traits. In the second, they are both enforcers of a patriarchal social order and accomplished lovers whose exploits challenge prevailing gender definitions of active male and passive female. And in the third instance, these overbearing, devious,

Amazon in Jaime Regan, *Hacia la tierra sin mal,* pp. 173–85, provides an equally useful comparison. See also Regina Harrison's discussion of snake-lovers in her *Signs, Songs, and Memory in the Andes,* pp. 144–71; Seth Leacock and Ruth Leacock, *Spirits of the Deep;* and Napoleão Figueiredo and A. Vergolino e Silva, *Festas de santo e encantados.*

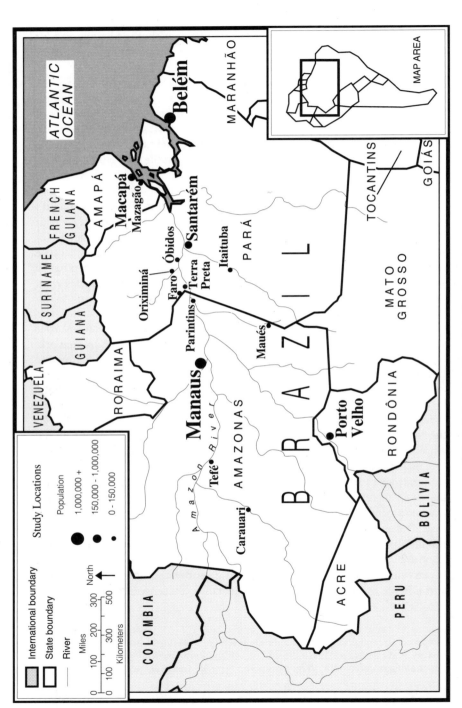

Principal study locations, Brazilian Amazon.

and insatiably greedy aliens increasingly appear as embodiments, and even champions, of specifically Amazonian beliefs and practices. Although largely separate and, on occasion, contradictory, all three of these identities offer resistance to established hierarchies.

The conclusion returns to the vision of the world underlying the Dolphin narratives and the idea of perpetual motion as a form of resistance to cultural and economic changes imposed from without. More protean than Proteus—who eventually tires and yields his secrets to pursuers—the Dolphin eludes domination through unwearying self-transformation.

My analysis is based on fourteen months of fieldwork conducted in four separate segments between 1988 and 1992. During this time, I recorded more than two hundred hours of Dolphin stories and related narratives. I traveled to the small city of Parintins during all four stays, but had somewhat different objectives on each occasion. I should make clear that I did not go to Amazônia with the express intention of studying the *encantados*. Although my second and third stays were full-fledged research trips for which I wrote grant proposals, the first was a gift to myself upon my promotion to full professor. My fourth trip, a return to the Amazon after this book was largely completed, helped me to become reacquainted with the people about whom I had been writing.

My initial impressions of Amazônia were really very negative. Manaus's lack of trees, acrid air, and teaming squatter settlements depressed me. Having imagined flocks of parrots, I could not get over the multitude of vultures. I also was stricken with a kind of in-country culture shock, and felt homesick for the Brazilian Northeast. In fact, I made my first, somewhat grudging trip to Parintins because of its widely known June festival called *Boi-Bumbá*, brought to Amazônia by northeastern settlers.

My attention soon shifted from the *Boi* to the less spectacular but, to my mind, considerably more enigmatic and thus intriguing *Boto*. Although the latter can be found in many places, I continued to use Parintins as a base of operations. Not only was I seeking an urban setting, but the city's location on the border of Pará and Amazonas, the two largest states in the Brazilian Amazon, was a definite attraction. Pará—which has more people than any other state in Amazônia—is known for its significant African Brazilian population; Amazonas—a state almost four times the size of California—for its strongly indigenous character.

Perhaps most important, I chose Parintins because I liked it. Every time I sailed, sunburnt, mosquito-pocked, and weary, into the city's harbor, I felt happy and, in a way, at home. When in town, I usually slept in a small, family-style hotel with much-welcome air-conditioning and moderately reliable plumbing. I spent the day, however, in the streets and private homes. In addition, I was lucky enough to have boat-owning friends whose work took them far into the interior, and who were gracious enough to allow me to accompany them on journeys that would have been very hard, if not impossible, for me to have made alone. One Roman Catholic priest, active in various church-related human rights movements, was of particular help to me during my initial stay in Parintins. Through him and his associates, I got to know and record conversations with the residents of more than a dozen small communities on the Mamuru and Uaicurapá rivers.

I also became acquainted with many people within the city, a number of whom were willing to speak at length about the Dolphin. During my first trip to Parintins, I tried to talk with as many different people as possible. Then, during subsequent stays, I focused on a small number of individuals and their friends and families. These persons included a shoemaker in his late sixties and his young assistant; a woman in her mid-forties and her fisherman husband; a rural migrant with dreams of a university education; a young manicurist; and a midwife who had once been a shamanic healer. Through interweaving references to Tô Pereira, Gerineldo, Alzira, Maurício, Dona Marina, and Kátia (not their real names), as well as their friends and families, I have tried both to create a sense of continuity and to suggest the place of these initially exotic-seeming stories in people's daily lives.

Accounts of the enchanted beings appealed to me in large part because they raised questions that other tales about supernatural figures—such as the forest guardians called *Curupiras* or the more universally known vanishing hitchhiker—did not. I sensed that these stories also puzzled many of the tellers and that this ability to puzzle was part of their creative force and continuing appeal. Many persons had trouble answering my questions about the *encantados*. ("Do they really fall in love?" "Why are they only vulnerable in human guise?" "Who decides their actions?") Some people had clearly never thought about these issues before my arrival, and looked at me strangely when I raised them. Others, however, admitted that they had often pondered the questions I was asking. Although a few individuals—usually the *pajés*—had ready answers, many others seemed to be thinking out loud in my presence. Precisely because of their apparent casualness and evanescence, the Dolphin tales allow people to affirm and explore areas of their own experience that might otherwise appear unfathomable and threatening.

While a good number of these stories arose spontaneously during extended, open-ended conversations, I elicited others through questions such as "Are Dolphins always as dangerous as people say?" or "Does the *pajé* who lives in Vila Bela *really* travel to the bottom of the river?" Often, people would respond to my queries with a statement to the effect that they had never seen or heard anything worth recounting. Once one person started telling stories, however, others often jumped in ("Ah, now that reminds me of the time . . ."). People themselves often observed that one tale prompts another ("Um caso puxa outro"). Thus, while my presence undoubtedly had some effect on people, it usually took very little for them to begin exchanging stories, and, not infrequently, they were still talking when I took my leave. ("You *knew* I knew these stories, didn't you!" they might demand in parting.)

Having transcribed and thought about the narratives from prior trips in the light of additional readings, I had many questions for the tellers on my succeeding visits to Parintins. I also was interested in hearing the individuals mentioned above repeat tales with which I was already familiar, as well as in their reactions to stories told by others both within and outside the city.

Quite often, storytellers asked me what I thought about the *encantados* and the Dolphin in particular. Initially, I dodged the issue, but as I increasingly came to respect these tales' metaphoric truth, I began to respond honestly that I found the events they were describing mysterious and hard to explain. On occasion, I struggled to voice my sense that the stories could be true on some level even if the particular occurrences they described were fictions. "No, no, I don't understand what you are saying," one older man with very white hair declared as we and his four daughters sat drinking small cups of sugary, home-roasted coffee. "But I do see you like my stories, and listen—here's a really good one."

I often registered surprise or obvious fascination, and occasionally I burst out laughing. (Some of the Dolphin stories are really very funny.) Fortunately, the tellers rarely took offense. Often, they and other listeners also started laughing. On other occasions they demanded to know what I had found so amusing. I quite often asked point-blank, "But how could that be?" in an attempt to get people to further clarify and defend their claims, as well as to indicate that I was aware when they tried to pull my leg. (Some persons took delight in obvious inventions that made others laugh or roll their eyes.)

I never said, however, that I did not believe their stories, not only because I did not want to anger or silence them, but because, as just noted, I found very few of these accounts to be fundamentally untrue. Certainly, it is hard for an outsider to imagine a dancing Dolphin in a suit "white as tapioca" and flashy, stingray shoes. It is, however, considerably less difficult to appreciate the stories' sense of a world in defiant motion, in which shifting surfaces conceal equally shifting depths.

During my second trip to Amazônia, I spent time not only in Parintins but also in the state capitals of Belém (Pará) and Manaus (Amazonas). In addition, for purposes of comparison, I visited a number of cities near

Parintins. By this time, however, I had heard many, many Dolphin tales, and was often less interested in amassing still more stories than in hearing what Kátia, Gerineldo, Alzira, Maurício, Tô, and Dona Marina had to say about particular narratives. I took the opportunity to learn all I could about their lives and to ask them questions I would have hesitated to ask strangers ("Is the Dolphin really a great lover like people say?" "How do they know for sure?"). Often, the six had scouted out new stories in my absence or had remembered stories that I had not yet heard, partly out of a desire to help me, but also partly because my questions had increased their curiosity about these tales. ("I've been waiting to tell you this for months now!" they more than once exclaimed.)

As part of my third stay in Amazônia, I visited three other widely different locations. The first was the small city of Carauari and its outlying rubber settlements or *seringais* on the still relatively remote Juruá River in southwestern Amazonas. The second was the city and surrounding countryside of Macapá, capital of the newly created state of Amapá, which borders French Guiana. The third was Porto Velho, capital of the state of Rondônia, which has experienced massive deforestation over the last two decades. I chose these places because of the striking differences among them. In all three cases, I was fortunate enough to have friends or friends of friends who took me into their homes—straw huts, wooden shacks, river view apartments—and who went out of their way to help me make the most of my time among them.

As will become clearer in the course of this discussion, there are significant regional differences among the stories. In the rubber settlements, for instance, many people continue to employ an elaborate hunting magic and speak of making pacts not with the devil but with the "Rubber Tree Mother" (*A Mãe da Seringueira*), an old woman with numerous gashes in her gnarled and barklike skin. Storytellers in Amapá, for their part, may attribute to the *encantados* natural phenomena such as the whirling current called the *pororoca,* unknown in many other parts of the Amazon, and are apt to introduce numerous Caribbean elements into their tales. The heavy influx of colonists from the Brazilian south into Rondônia has led to a notable intermingling and reconstellation of customarily separate narrative motifs.

And yet, despite various regional and local differences, I discovered stories about the *encantados* virtually everywhere I went. Often, they showed up in places I did not expect to find them—such as among the descendants of runaway slaves in the interior of Pará, the gold miners of Rondônia and Itaituba, and the sons and daughters of Japanese jute workers. Furthermore, although attitudes toward the Dolphin and his fellows are changing, belief in the *encantados* is by no means limited to older people, and a number of the most accomplished storytellers were teenagers and children, who had heard the tales from friends and family members.

The title of this book is meant to suggest the near-choreographic leaps of freshwater dolphins above the river's surface, as well as the widespread belief that Dolphins love to glide about the floor at parties. Above all, however, the "dance" refers to that universe in flux which the stories portray. Because the natural world, of which humans are just one part, is always changing, it can never be comprehended in its totality. And evading comprehension, it defies exploitation and control. "So then," a young carpenter in Parintins says, prying at a bent nail, "life has many things, both seen and unseen. And, in my opinion, the *encantado* is the mystery of this world."[14]

14. Man, age 22, born interior of Parintins (Semeão). Single, fisherman and farmer, 3 years school.

1

TIME AND PLACE

Por quê será que só aqui em Amazônia é que os botos gostam de dançar?

(Why, I wonder, is it only here in Amazônia that the dolphins like to dance?)

—*Sixty-year-old barber in Cachoeirinha (Manaus)*

In 1499, seven years after Columbus's discovery of a world new to Europeans, the Spanish captain, Vicente Yañez Pinzón, headed in toward the Brazilian coast, where he anchored in the mouth of a river so immense as to lead him to call it a *Mar Dulce,* or "Freshwater Sea." Disappointed to find nothing of immediate value, he consoled himself by capturing thirty-six Indians and one monkey before fleeing in astonishment the floodlike tides that threatened to sweep away his ship. Although hardly memorable in its own right, Yañez's expedition nonetheless set the stage for what would be a recurring drama of fearful wonder at the land and exploitation of its inhabitants.[1]

Amazônia—the Brazilian Amazon—comprises approximately half of the entire Amazon Basin. Distributed over seven countries, the river system drains about a third of the land surface of South America. By some estimates, this larger area of some 2.7 million square miles of savannah, bush, and wetlands contains approximately a million species of flora and fauna.[2] Four thousand miles long from source to sea, the river, which boasts a thousand tributaries, begins in a tiny lake high in the Andes. Between December and June, torrential rains deluge the rich floodplain known as the *várzea,* swelling the rivulets called *igarapés* and creating flooded meadows (*igapós*) that will vanish with the summer sun.

During the rainy season, the river may rise by as much as thirty feet,

1. For a discussion of the first explorers see Anthony Smith, *Explorers of the Amazon.*
2. For an introduction to the physical landscape see Mark Collins, ed., *The Last Rain Forests.*

sweeping away cows, pigs, and the thatched roofs of abandoned huts, together with whole chunks of land. Given the constant, often dramatic, changes in the land, the traveler who passes by a spot in July may fail to recognize it not only in December, but also the next summer. Although nineteenth-century naturalists joined earlier visitors to the region in extolling the Amazon's apparently limitless fecundity (the normally perspicacious Bates pronounced the soil "fertile in the extreme"), all but the top three or four inches of soil is poor in nutrients.[3] Once fire, chain saws, or bulldozers destroy the ground cover, rains wash away the topsoil in a matter of years.

Despite the fact that the official entity known as "legal Amazônia" occupies three-fifths of the national territory, it has long existed on the margins of Brazilian political and economic life.[4] During the colonial period, the ocean currents that made travel from Belém to Lisbon easier than from Belém to Rio de Janeiro cut off the region from settlements along the Atlantic coast. Largely as a result of the ensuing isolation, in 1621 the Portuguese Crown created the state of Maranhão, as separate from the state of Brazil.[5] Although Amazônia became part of Brazil when the nation declared its independence from Portugal in 1822, it retained its largely peripheral status. "We have always been a place apart," declares a recent candidate for public office, "Brazilians who are still almost foreigners within Brazil."[6]

Like their Spanish counterparts, to whom the papal Treaty of Tordesillas had given the western half of South America, the first Portuguese settlers to arrive in Brazil were looking for gold and silver. Instead, they found a land whose dazzling fertility held out the promise of long-term riches. As a result, the wealthier and more enterprising colonists founded sugar, cotton,

3. Henry Walter Bates, *The Naturalist on the River Amazons,* p. 2.
4. The area officially designated as "legal Amazônia" includes the states of Pará, Amazonas, Amapá and Acre; the northern parts of Goiás and Mato Grosso and the northeastern corner of Maranhão; the former territories (now states) of Roraima and Rondônia; and the newly created state of Tocantins. For information on various aspects of the region see *Amazônia: Bibliografia, 1614–1962,* and the later *Amazônia: Bibliografia,* which covers studies published between 1963 and 1972. For a review of a number of more recent works that focus on development and deforestation see Kenneth Maxwell, "The Tragedy of the Amazon"; and the *Tropical Conservation and Development Newsletter,* published by the Center for Latin American Studies, University of Florida, Gainesville.
5. Composed of present-day Maranhão, Pará, Amazonas, and parts of Ceará and Piauí, "Maranhão e Grão Pará" was founded in 1654. The provinces of Grão Pará and Rio Negro (present-day Amazonas) were then detached from this larger entity in 1772.
6. The speaker is Marlene Prado, a professor of education at the Federal University of Manaus, and a candidate at the time for state office on the leftist *Partido dos Trabalhadores* ticket in 1990. Personal interview, Carauari, 8 July 1990.

tobacco, and, later, coffee plantations, all of which demanded not only an initial cash outlay, but an ongoing commitment to the land. Those individuals who pushed into Amazônia, in contrast, were most often adventurers seeking their fortune in the spices, woods, gums, drugs, animal skins, and dyes known collectively as "backlands commodities" or *drogas do sertão.* Once they had depleted these materials, they were eager to move on.[7]

Some forty years after Vicente Yañez Pinzón first entered the Amazon from the Atlantic, Francisco Orellana navigated the entire length of the river from its western headwaters. By the early part of the next century, Irish, English, Dutch, and French colonies were thriving on the river's lower reaches. Their presence worried the Portuguese, themselves unhappy subjects of the Spanish Crown between 1580 and 1640. Although the foreigners were routed, concerns about the region's borders continued long after Portugal regained its independence. The Crown's acute awareness of the limits of its control over a vast and still largely uncharted territory often led it to tolerate miscarriages of justice involving the native population.

Although the colonists did not encounter anywhere in Brazil an unmistakably complex social, economic, and political order comparable to that of the Aztecs, the Incas, or the Maya, they did find a variety of Indian tribes—Tupi, Gê, Arawak, and Carib speakers—scattered throughout different regions of the country.[8] Faced with a scarcity of eligible female compatriots, Portuguese male settlers regularly cohabited with, and sometimes married, Amerindian women and, later, African women. By the middle of the nineteenth century, the nation's authors were turning out a stream of poems and novels celebrating the native peoples of the Brazilian heartland. As epidemics, armed confrontations, and assimilation had caused the latter to disappear almost completely by this time, writers found them easier to mold to their own purposes than they did African slaves or the members of surviving forest tribes. Even the wickedly ironic Machado de Assis, one of Brazil's greatest writers, began his literary life as a sentimental Indianist poet, while romantic novelist José de Alencar makes his honey-lipped Iracema (the name, which became widely popular, is an anagram for America) the mother of the first Brazilian.[9]

To the extent that the Portuguese settlers in the Amazon embarked on an energetic despoilment of the landscape, colonization there resembled that in the rest of Brazil. The rivers that had "boiled with fish" and the

7. See John H. Hemming, *The Search for El Dorado.*
8. See William M. Denevan, "The Aboriginal Population of Amazônia." Contemporary archaeological research suggests previously unsuspected high levels of artistic sophistication, and thus, social organization, in the ancient Amazon.
9. José de Alencar, *Iracema, the Honey-Lips.*

skies bright with flocks of wild parrots quickly faded into a remote, idyllic past. At the same time that the colonists were laying waste to the land in the name of civilization, epidemics decimated an indigenous population which some writers believe included upward of five million persons.[10] The Indians—who often fought each other as well as the white settlers—were also the object of various military campaigns.

Given, however, the lack of a mixed-blood labor force in much of the region (black slaves would arrive somewhat later in eastern Amazônia), early settlers were generally much more interested in forcing the Indians to work for them than in killing them outright.[11] As a result, provincial "rescue" troops (*tropas de resgate*) joined professional slavers in selling whole tribes into bondage. Generally ignored, when not actually legally sanctioned, these kidnapings continued into the twentieth century, with whole tribes being pressed into the service of the rubber barons in some areas of the western Amazon.

Then too, the immensity and remoteness of much of the river basin permitted at least some Indian groups to avoid or minimize contact with whites. Until well into the nineteenth century, Amazônia remained a bilingual society in which Portuguese intermingled with a sort of Tupi-based Esperanto called *língua geral*. As late as 1970, some thirty Indian tribes were "pacified" as part of the Trans-Amazon Highway project.[12]

Although today, there are only about 220,000 native people in the Brazilian Amazon—and these in varying states of acculturation—their legacy remains obvious in the physical appearance of many of the region's inhabitants. It is equally visible in fishing and farming practices still in effect throughout much of the countryside; in the design of plaited straw houses, log canoes, and long woven tubes for squeezing the poison juices out of manioc; in the continued observance in many cases of dietary, hunting, and menstrual prescriptions; in curative beliefs and practices; and in place names and numerous loan words, as well as in narrative traditions of the

10. Estimates of the size of the current indigenous population vary widely. While most calculations are in the range of two to five million, Susanna Hecht and Alexander Cockburn argue that "with the growing body of information on indigenous agricultural productivities and land use technologies, and more archaeological effort in Amazônia, it is likely that precontact numbers will be pushed upward . . . to levels approaching 15 million" (*The Fate of the Forest,* p. 12).

11. See Colin M. MacLachlan, "The Indian Labor Structure in the Portuguese Amazon, 1700–1800."

12. For an overview of the effects of this and other development schemes on the indigenous population see Alcida R. Ramos, "Frontier Expansion and Indian Peoples in the Brazilian Amazon."

sort we will examine.[13] "You can't dig here without turning up something left here by the Indians," says one rubber tapper, fingering a piece of fossilized manioc bread long hidden in the earth beneath the intersection of two well-traveled paths. "These pieces of bread, they buried them here for one another, and today it is we who discover them, almost as if they had been left here for us as reminders that this land was theirs."[14]

When the Marquis de Pombal came to power in Portugal in 1750, he launched an intensive centralizing campaign in Amazônia that resulted in a shift from extractive industries to export-oriented agricultural development. It was Pombal who gave the powerful new General Commerce Company of Grão-Pará and Maranhão a monopoly over trade with the exterior, as well as the slave traffic. As a result of his incentives, increasing numbers of plantations and cattle ranches, dependent on African slave labor, began appearing on the lower reaches of the Amazon during the second half of the eighteenth century and early nineteenth century.[15]

The vast interior, however, remained relatively untouched. Even today, despite massive immigration, the Amazon accounts for less than ten percent of the Brazilian population of 154 million. Furthermore, the realities of life within the region remain relatively little known within Brazil, and thus, while there are indeed huge areas that remain largely uninhabited (some places are accessible only by airplane during certain seasons of the year), the growing urban population finds itself impatient with portrayals of themselves as solitary fishermen. "I can't stand it," says one banker in Parintins. "When they show the *Boi-Bumbá* on television, they always cut to shots of herons out there on some lagoon. Where do they find the herons, I would like to know? Probably in some zoo there in Rio de Janeiro. Because I haven't seen herons like they show on TV for twenty years. Why, the feathers they use in the *Boi* are all acrylic, from São Paulo."[16]

Among the historical events of the nineteenth and twentieth centuries most significant in shaping the Amazonian present are the *Cabanagem* revolt of the 1830s, the rubber boom that began in the 1840s and stretched on into the next century, and the federal government's purposeful opening of the Amazon to settlement and development over the last four decades.

13. See Eugene Parker, "Caboclization"; and Eric B. Ross, "The Evolution of the Amazon Peasantry."

14. Man, age 33, born interior of Carauari, lives Seringal Cupuaí (years not stated). Married, rubber tapper, no formal education.

15. See Colin M. MacLachlan, "African Slave Trade and Economic Development in Amazônia"; and Vicente Salles, *O Negro no Pará*.

16. Man, 37, born Belém, lives Parintins (9 years). Married, bank manager, university education.

The intertwining of golden dreams and intense exploitation, thwarted opportunities for increased regional autonomy, and an accompanying reaffirmation of Amazônia's peripheral status within the Brazilian state mark all three.

The Jesuits played a significant role in the Amazon throughout much of the colonial period, founding numerous mission communities for Indians.[17] Although the directors of these *aldeias* often forced indigenous peoples to adopt Christianity and various European customs, the order nonetheless was virtually alone in opposing the wilder abuses of the Portuguese slaveowners. Late seventeenth-century preacher António Vieira once turned his back on a hostile public in Maranhão, and went down to the sea to preach to the ostensibly more attentive and less greedy fishes.[18]

The lay population's sacking of the Jesuit college in Belém in 1661 attests to the fury that the missionaries' intervention—and perceived monopoly of indigenous labor—inspired. Forced out of Grão-Pará and Maranhão the next year, the order was soon readmitted. When, however, the fiercely anticlerical Pombal definitively expelled its members from all of Portuguese America almost a century later, the provincial elite rejoiced. Although Pombal outlawed the enslavement of Indians, the new secular directors of the *aldeias* largely ignored this injunction. Unbridled exploitation of not only indigenous laborers but also African slaves and the theoretically independent mixed-blood riverine population helped inspire the massive popular rebellion called the *Cabanagem,* which exploded in 1835.

The first so-called *cabanos* (the name comes from river dwellers' straw huts and, by extension, their inhabitants) were primarily small-scale agriculturists who opposed the wealthier, monarchist elite of Pará.[19] The beleaguered masses, however, soon entered the fray on the *cabanos'* side and violent uprisings spread upriver all the way into the headwaters of the Amazon. While some of those who took up arms were primarily interested in avenging past abuses, others dreamed of an Amazônia governed by and for people like themselves. Even today, residents often speak of the revolt as if it were yesterday. Any coin found in the earth—even a shiny Lincoln's head penny from the pocket of some distracted tourist—is quickly pronounced "buried treasure from the *Cabanagem.*"

17. These *aldeias* follow the model of others in the Missions region of Uruguay, Argentina, and the Brazilian South. According to Robin Furneaux (*The Amazon,* p. 74), in 1750, the Jesuit reductions in Paraguay contained 144,000 Indians, while those on the lower Amazon numbered about 30,000, and those on the upper Amazon about 25,000.

18. Dauril Alden describes this incident in "Black Robes versus White Settlers." For an introduction to the Jesuits in Brazil see Serafim Leite's *Suma histórica da Companhia de Jesús no Brasil.*

19. For a study of the rebellion see Pasquale Di Paolo, *Cabanagem.*

Internal dissension doomed the initially victorious rebels as much as did their lack of money. Although Félix Malcher succeeded in having himself proclaimed president under terms acceptable to the Brazilian Empire, his murder spurred protracted infighting that helped defeat what many present-day historians consider to be the most significant popular rebellion in postcolonial Brazil. By the time the last rebel surrendered in 1840, approximately thirty thousand people—a full fifth of the total population of Brazilian Amazônia—had died. The *cabanos'* failure cemented existing power relations in what would otherwise today be a separate and independent nation.

The stakes in Amazônia were to become progressively higher. In 1839, Charles Goodyear's discovery of a process for vulcanizing rubber created a world market for a product previously regarded as little more than a handy treatment for galoshes. Almost overnight, small-time traders, and then steamships, began plying the western tributaries, buying up balls of crude rubber from rubber plantation owners, or *seringalistas*.

From the beginning of the boom, local traders resold the raw material to larger river merchants associated with the giant export houses in Manaus and Belém. Content to pocket easily won and ever greater profits, the owners of these houses—often foreigners themselves—passed on the raw material to clients in Great Britain and the United States. Not only did they make no attempt to foster industrial development within Amazônia, but in addition, as rubber became increasingly important, the agricultural and cattle ranching enterprises that had prospered from Pombal's time until the *Cabanagem* fell into decline.

The single most striking monument to the rubber era is the Manaus Opera House. Constructed at enormous cost during the last decade of the nineteenth century, the rose-colored structure was intended as homage to Culture with a large and very ornate capital "C." The main theater, where today a live piano player practices behind a velvet curtain, is ringed by the busts of famous European artists and composers. It is not hard to imagine the often illiterate rubber barons squinting up at Goethe and Cervantes, or the women drenched in jewels and perspiration briskly fanning themselves beneath the crystal gas lamps. The upstairs sitting rooms and galleries are replete with portraits of quintessentially native subjects—graceful herons, noble Indians, peaceful streamlets with a lone canoe—all surrounded by painted borders of very pink, very European roses.

Conspicuous by their absence in the opera house are the *seringueiros*, or rubber tappers. It is tempting to imagine their present-day descendants, who continue to eke out an existence in decaying rubber settlements far from schools and hospitals, gazing admiringly at the rose-ringed portraits and intricately patterned hardwood floors. Nowhere in the opera house, however, does one find any hint of the unrelenting toil to which those in attendance owed the gilt boxes furnished with elegant cane chairs.

As a direct result of the rubber boom, the population of the Brazilian Amazon rose steadily from a quarter of a million in 1853 to nearly a million in 1910, more than doubling between 1870 and 1900. During the same period, rubber production almost tripled, and in 1903, Brazil succeeded in annexing rubber-rich Acre, formerly a Bolivian territory and, briefly, an independent state.[20]

Although newcomers to Amazônia—many of them impoverished laborers from the drought-ridden Northeast—often tried to enslave the native populations they encountered, they quickly adopted the latter's cultural practices in the interest of their own survival. "Poor thing," one woman says of her great-grandfather, who came to the Amazon as a rubber worker from the arid Northeast at the turn of the century. "He arrived without knowing anything about the forest. The first year he got here, the ants ate all he planted, and eight of his nine children came down with malaria. On top of everything, my great-grandfather had never caught a fish before. Why, he couldn't even row!"[21]

Furthermore, the same individuals who willingly exploited and often killed the Indians often lived as virtual slaves themselves. This ambiguous legacy is nowhere more obvious than in many present-day residents' at once sheepish and condescending reactions to the term *caboclo*. Although dictionary definitions include "a civilized Brazilian of pure blood," a "Brazilian half-breed (of white and Indian extraction)," "any copper-colored mulatto with straight hair," "a frontiersman," a "resident of the interior," and "a farmhand or agricultural laborer," in Amazônia, the term most often applies to mixed-blood residents of the interior who engage in a range of seasonally determined economic activities, including fishing and agriculture.[22] Significantly, *caboclo,* much like *negro* (black), is often a term of endearment when pronounced in conspicuously colloquial fashion. ("Vem cá, meu caboc[l]o," "Vem cá, minha neg[r]a," a person may say.) And yet, while they are celebrated on Saint John's Eve, when people may dress up like backwoodsmen, *caboclos* are customarily looked down on, and the term may also be an insult. Gullible, unsophisticated, and, thus, implicitly different from the speaker, *caboclos* always live down the road apiece.

The great majority of rubber tappers arrived in the Amazon already in

<hr>

20. See Leandro Tocantins, *Formação histórica do Acre.*

21. Woman, age 55, born interior of Juruá. Married, field and housework, no formal education.

22. See *Dicionário Novo Michaelis,* s.v. "caboclo." In some parts of the region—such as the Juruá River Valley—the term is used as a synonym for "Indian."

debt for their passage to the *seringalistas,* who filled palatial homes on often remote rivers with French armchairs, English silver, and grand pianos no one for miles around knew how to play. By charging exorbitant prices for tools, food, and rudimentary medical supplies, the wealthy retained their hold over the workers. But although the price of rubber continued to rise steadily for seven decades, competition from better-organized Asian plantations triggered a precipitous decline after 1910. As a result, new extractive industries, such as Brazil nuts, diamonds, and tin-ore mining, became increasingly important. Giant enterprises largely financed from abroad dominated these ventures.[23] (The jute colony of Vila Amazonas, a half hour from Parintins, where picnics now take place beside a crumbling pagoda, was established by the Japanese-run Nippon Planning Company.) Even today, two to three million of the region's people are extractivists who depend on forest products for a livelihood.[24]

Rubber's brief revival when the Axis cornered Asian supplies during World War II prompted a new wave of northeastern migration. Often, the so-called *soldados da borracha* (literally, "rubber soldiers") found themselves tricked into debt peonage by much the same sort of promises that had lured their great-grandfathers to the Amazon.[25] In this case, the government actively sought recruits by excusing rubber workers from military service when Brazil joined the Allies in 1942. An estimated forty thousand of these forest conscripts died of hunger and disease, and today, many are having trouble collecting even the tiny pension allotted them by the most recent Brazilian constitution. ("They want a piece of paper saying that I worked for so-and-so at such-and-such a time," explains one old man, who has lived in the same rubber settlement for almost half a century. "But I never had a 'document.' Who gave anyone a 'document' back in those days? Why, neither my *patrão* nor I could read!")[26]

The much-touted opening of the Amazon that began in the later 1950s under the civilian president, Juscelino Kubitschek, had roots in the Vargas years. In the tradition of Pombal some two centuries earlier, but responding

23. The most powerful of these were the Amazonian Exploration Company, the American and Brazilian Exploration Company, and the Canadian American Company, later joined by the Nippon Planning Company.

24. Because residents of the interior traditionally have relied on a portfolio of economic activities oriented to the shifting opportunities and constraints of the environment, they are often part-time or seasonal extractivists. Actual numbers are therefore difficult to calculate.

25. See Pedro Martinello, *A 'Batalha da Borracha' na Segunda Guerra Mundial e suas consequências para o Vale Amazônico,* as well as the extremely poignant interviews with the descendants of earlier northeastern settlers conducted in 1942–43 by Samuel Benchimol in his *Amazônia,* pp. 257–306.

26. Man, age 77, born Quixadá (Ceará), lives Carauari (12 years). Widower, retired, no formal education.

to decidedly contemporary political pressures, Vargas created in 1952 a federal administrative agency for the Amazon as well as a national institute for research on the Amazon.[27] The Kubitschek government, which began construction of Brasília in 1957 as part of its dramatic "fifty years in five" plan, initiated the first great highway into the Amazon, the Belém-Brasília, in 1960. At the time, this expansion—just one part of an ambitious industrialization program intended to transform Brazil into a modern country and world power—was widely seen as confirmation of a specifically Brazilian Manifest Destiny.

The military government that had staged a successful coup four years later and that went on to rule Brazil until 1984 intensified already existing development efforts. Chief among these were more new highways linking Amazônia to the rest of the country, an ambitious land redistribution scheme, economic policies calculated to attract foreign capital while easing demographic pressures, and the creation of new administrative and financial agencies charged with achieving these ends.[28]

The civilian regime that assumed power in 1984 continued the development projects of the 1970s and early 1980s. Among the most important of these were the Polamazônia and the Grande Carajás initiative (an immense iron-ore mining center and hydroelectric dam). Work on a military buffer zone called the *Calha Norte* (literally, "Northern Moat" or "Northern Trench") began in 1986. These ongoing development efforts triggered an increasing exodus to cities. It also saw ever more violent land conflicts and deforestation in the Araguaia-Tocantins area, a heavy influx of gold miners following the discovery of the Serra Pelada deposits in southern Pará in 1979, and exacerbated tensions between newcomers and indigenous groups.[29]

Today, development efforts continue with such projects as the Polonoroeste ("Northwest Hub"). To the extent that they combine massive injections

27. Article 199 of the Constitution of 1946 allowed for federal investments totaling three percent of the gross national product in Amazônia over the next two decades. The agencies Vargas founded were the SPVEA (Superintendência para o Plano de Valorização da Amazônia) and INPA (Instituto Nacional de Pesquisas de Amazônia).

28. The SUDAM (Sperintendência para o Desenvolvimento da Amazônia, or "Superintendency for the Development of Amazônia") replaced the now-defunct SPVEA. In 1970, the INCRA (Instituto Nacional da Colonização e Reforma Agrária, or "National Institute for Colonization and Agrarian Reform") was created, along with a regional bank.

29. For a list of critiques of the development efforts of the past few decades, see Hecht and Cockburn, pp. 237–53. Among the more important are Ronald Foresta, *Amazon Conservation in the Age of Development;* Anthony L. Hall, *Developing Amazonia;* John H. Hemming, *Change in the Amazon Basin;* Dennis Mahar, *Government Policies and Deforestation in Brazil's Amazon Region;* Lúcio Flávio Pinto, *Amazônia;* and Marianne Schmink and Charles H. Wood, *Contested Frontiers in Amazonia.*

of foreign capital with a steady stream of cheap labor from other parts of Brazil, these efforts recall the rubber era and virtually all other previous development cycles in Amazônia. Now, as in previous epochs, the emphasis is on export rather than on the creation of local and regional infrastructure, and economic initiatives dovetail defensive strategies.

This new boom, however, presents important contrasts to the past. First and foremost, it involves widespread and irreversible alteration of the physical landscape. In addition, it demands the existence of a regimented urban proletariat as opposed to a farflung network of rural extractive workers. Finally, the current rush into Amazônia did not simply happen, but was in large part planned and presided over by a modern nation state.

Much like the rubber boom, in which Brazilians provided labor while foreigners supplied the necessary capital and the markets for both raw materials and manufactured goods, the current development initiatives rely in large part on foreign money. Although most of today's investors are multinational corporations, often with southern Brazilian affiliates, they exercise much the same function as the single-nation commercial houses of the past. Drawn to the region by an array of subsidies, credits, and concessions, U.S., Japanese, and European capital has financed mile upon mile of factories in Manaus's duty-free zone, as well as large-scale agricultural and extractive schemes.[30]

Also, as in the past, many of the two to three million persons who have moved northward into Amazônia in the last few decades are subsistence farmers. Others are small-scale agriculturists from south and central Brazil (often, originally Northeasterners) pushed off small plots of land by the expansion of mechanized agriculture. The national agrarian reform plan of 1985, which aimed at the distribution of a hundred million acres to a million and a half Brazilian families, assigned a prominent role to Amazônia's most thinly populated forest states.[31]

Largely unsuccessful in terms of land distribution, the plan had the unhappy effect of intensifying already massive deforestation. In contrast to the rubber boom, which left the landscape largely untouched (no one was about to cut down the "weeping trees" on which continuing profits were dependent), contemporary development schemes have irrevocably altered the Amazonian landscape. Although assessments of the degree of environ-

30. One of the most spectacular examples of the latter is Daniel Ludwig's immense and unsuccessful Jari Plantation. In many ways a successor to Henry Ford's similarly doomed rubber plantations at Belterra and Fordlândia, Jari occupied three million acres in northern Pará. For a critique of both projects see Marianne Schmink, "Big Business in the Amazon."

31. Although 100 million acres is a significant amount of land, this figure represents the sum total for the entire country. Twenty-three of the largest twenty-eight landowners in Brazil hold estates in Amazônia totaling approximately sixty million acres.

mental impact vary, some experts warn that as much as a third of the forest may be gone in fifteen years.[32] Worse yet, once the land has been burned or flooded to a degree that it can no longer sustain the plants and animals on which still other species depend for survival, the circle of destruction widens exponentially.

Like the rubber boom and not unlike the Pombalian initiatives before it, contemporary development schemes are oriented toward extraregional markets. But while the United States and Great Britain dominated nineteenth-century trade, São Paulo and Rio de Janeiro are among today's most important consumers. Thus, the hardwoods of Amazonas and Acre, the iron and palm hearts of Pará, the manganese of Amapá, and the gold of Rondônia and Roraima move southward to be processed and, often, resold abroad. Likewise, most of the tape recorders, cameras, and computers produced in Manaus by SONY, Sharp, Royal, General Electric, and Mitsubishi find purchasers outside the Amazon.

And yet, if this outward orientation is hardly new, the nature of the work force has changed dramatically. We have seen that the rubber boom depended on a farflung network of *seringueiros* who sold their rubber to the *seringalistas* linked in turn to an ever-widening web of river merchants and urban trade house representatives. In practice, workers might be held thrall by debts impossible to pay (the company store system) or, less often, by outright physical coercion (eighty percent of the Indians on the Putumayo River are said to have died at the hands of slavers and plantation owners).[33] In theory, however, and at least sometimes in actuality, the individual rubber tapper could decide his hours, as well as the parameters of the territory worked.[34]

Today, as in the past, rubber tappers are apt to move from rubber settlement to settlement in search of marginally better work conditions. ("I've worked my way upriver from Acre to here looking for a good *patrão*," explains one rubber worker on the Juruá River. "I've never found a really good one, but some were a little better than the others, at least for a

32. In 1987, for instance, 31,000 square miles—an area equivalent to over a fifth of California—went up in smoke. Maxwell ("Tragedy," p. 26) notes that most experts concur that if the present rate of clearing continues, "15 percent of all plant life in the Latin American rain forest will become extinct by the end of the century."

33. See Roger Casement, *Correspondence Respecting the Treatment of British Colonial Subjects and Native Indians.* Michael Taussig's *Shamanism, Colonialism, and the Wild Man* analyzes the roots and lingering effects of this campaign of terror.

34. Barbara Weinstein ("The Amazon Rubber Trade," p. 60) stresses the *seringueiros'* isolation and notes that while some were, indeed, miserable debt-peons, "the vast majority of the rubber tappers as late as the 1870s were squatting on vacant lands and freely moving on to new areas as soon as the output of the rubber trees began to decline."

time.")[35] This freedom, while only relative, contrasts with the regimented life of a growing urban proletariat.

The last few decades have seen massive migration from the countryside into Amazônia's capital cities. Both Manaus and Belém are presently home to well over a million people, and even the smaller capitals are growing rapidly.[36] Hard-pressed to eke out a living as independent fishermen or farmers in the face of mechanization and growing competition for resources, the newcomers take up residence in squatters' settlements or satellite housing projects with such ironic names as Garden of Happiness 1, 2, 3, and 4. "In the countryside," one woman says, "I had to get up every morning at four and walk an hour to my first field. I'd come back at noon to make the lunch and wash the clothes and sweep the house. Then I'd set out for the second field and work there till sunset. When I came home, I'd have to go down to the river to get water. I'd take a bath [in the river], then I'd make the dinner and start sewing. Often I would go to sleep until the baby started crying. Now then, Manaus is different, but I think it's just as bad."[37] Her teenage son, a busdriver turned barber, has been held up three times at gunpoint. "The worst part," he says glumly, "is that the company made *me* pay back the fares those guys had robbed."[38]

Although payments on Brazil's $120 billion foreign debt and cutbacks bent on curbing spiraling inflation have resulted in widespread urban unemployment, approximately half the population of heavily forested Amazonas now lives in Manaus, where only a handful of trees brave the acrid air. "I hate the city," one man says. "No one can breathe here. If I could, I'd go back to the countryside tomorrow. There, at least, a man can get in his canoe and come back with a fish for dinner. Here, no, everything costs money, even the polluted water! But I can't go back because there is no school there for my children, no doctor for my wife."[39]

---

35. Man, age 54, born Boca do Acre, lives Seringal Pupunha (2 years). Married, rubber tapper, no formal education.

36. Although both Manaus and Belém have grown precipitously in the last two decades, Lúcio Flávio Pinto notes that while Manaus has accounted for an ever greater percentage of the population of Amazonas (32 percent in 1970, 44 percent in 1980, and 48 percent in 1990), Belém has gone from 30 percent of the population of Pará in 1970 to 25 percent in 1990 (Pinto, "O Amazonas é Manaus," p. 3). As for the smaller capitals, Macapá's 150,000 people represent well over half the entire population of the new state of Amapá. The Rondonian capital of Porto Velho has more than tripled in size over the last twenty years.

37. Woman, age 37, born Juruti Velho, lives Manaus (3 years). Separated, laundress, 1 year school.

38. Man, age 17, born interior of Parintins, lives Manaus (3 years). Single, bus driver, 4 years school.

39. Man, age 44, born interior of Tefé, lives Manaus (6 years). Married, night watchman, no formal education.

In part, last century's rubber boom was something that just happened. No one—including Goodyear—could have anticipated vulcanization. Both the Brazilian Empire and the republic that succeeded it in 1889 sought to shape events through specific economic and military incentives, such as the Madeira-Mamoré Railroad and the annexation of Acre, but Rio de Janeiro, like Lisbon before it, could only partially control events.

In contrast, although the development policies of the last three decades had numerous unforeseen consequences, they reflected a conscious desire to integrate Amazônia into an industrializing nation whose hopes and dreams the new capital, Brasília, symbolized.[40] Unlike their predecessors, the planners could rely on airplanes, computers, and telephone and television networks to publicize and implement their plans. Thus, the Trans-Amazon Highway began with one of the biggest and most sophisticated advertising campaigns in Brazilian history, and military, not commercial, airplanes often carried colonists into remote forest areas chosen for them by planners in Brasília.[41]

And yet, if now, as in the past, much of what happens in Amazônia is imposed top down from the outside, nascent grass-roots movements are emerging. Many of these are, or were initially, associated with the progressive wing of the Roman Catholic church, which began establishing a series of Christian base communities throughout the western Amazon in the early 1970s.[42] Religious-affiliated organizations influenced by liberation theology, such as the Human Rights' Commission (Commissão de Direitos Humanos) and Pastoral Land Commission (Commissão Pastoral da Terra) offer legal advice and moral support to peasants, indigenous populations, and factory workers in many parts of the region.

40. The planners' aim was not just the rapid accumulation of new wealth ("the Brazilian Miracle"), but also the defusing of potentially explosive demographic pressures, and the fortification of Brazil's borders against insurgents from both within and without. After the coup of 1964, the military sought to keep out foreign "agitators" and to isolate and destroy the remaining leftists within the country, including a guerrilla group that had taken refuge in the Amazonian Araguaia region. This experience—as well as fears of leftist infiltration from Colombia and Peru—prompted construction of the highway system and the *Calha Norte*.

41. I will never forget my own encounter with a group of Transamazon settlers from Piauí during an unexpected stopover in the airport in Teresina in 1973. The dazed-looking men and women and numerous screaming children, who had been waiting there for more than two days, appeared to have little idea of where they were headed, but assured me that they would be rich enough to return home in style in a year or two. All wore glossy name tags that read "Projeto Transamazônia: Para a Frente com o Brasil!" ("Transamazon Project: Onward with Brazil!").

42. This progressive wing encompasses quite different, often conflicting perspectives. Of Catholic clergy in the Amazon, 95 percent are foreigners. Of the 5 percent who are Brazilians, only .05 percent are from the region.

These and similar groups have often provided models and an informal or initial framework for various secular organizations, such as local branches of the Brazilian Workers' Party (PT), the politically efficacious Union of Indigenous Peoples, and the internationally known Rubber Tappers' Union.[43] The leader of the latter, Chico Mendes, became a virtual celebrity after his slaying in 1988 by ranchers eager to block the union's push for an extractive reserve.[44] Despite the often precarious position of fledgling associations within a political and economic structure dominated by local elites representing powerful outside interests, their mere existence is noteworthy. Owing in part to its size, Amazônia has always been extremely varied. Striking differences exist between the booming outskirts of Porto Velho and tiny, centuries-old Atlantic fishing villages, the violence-racked farmlands of southern Pará, and the sparsely inhabited hinterlands of Amazonas, where fish still glide undisturbed through waters strewn with gauzy seedpods, and a "nearby" village is two days, as opposed to two weeks, down the river. Life is not at all the same for the teenage girl who works the night shift in a factory in Manaus, the fourth-generation cowhand on Marajó Island, and the newcomer to Roraima's gold mines, with a knapsack full of movie magazines and threadbare T-shirts cradling a plaster saint. The teenage army conscript on the Colombian border may have little or nothing in common with the shamanic healer who works as a janitor in Óbidos during the week and returns to the interior to perform traditional cures on weekends, or the young father of twelve children desperately seeking "a job, any job" in Parintins. While some places come closer than others to satisfying regional stereotypes—Indians and rubber tappers locking arms against well-fed cattle farmers with shiny rifles and pockets full of matches—there are many Amazons. One of these is the small city of Parintins.

"Duller than the dullest small town in Texas," says the U.S. guidebook, "you can see it all in fifteen minutes." And indeed, at least at first glance, the book seems right. Early every afternoon, when the big boats headed for Manaus or Santarém pull into the sunstruck harbor of this island city, improbably labeled "the Switzerland of Amazônia" by at least one regional writer, passengers in transit complain about the lack of things to do.[45]

43. See Scott Mainwaring, *Grassroots Popular Movements, Identity, and Democratization in Brazil.*

44. Mendes's death has spurred a plethora of books, a number of which are reviewed in Kenneth Maxwell, "The Mystery of Chico Mendes."

45. Antonio Jobim, *Aspectos sócio-geográficos do Amazonas*, p. 245. The heavily perspiring outsider will be astounded by the author's references to the city's "adorable climate," the sweetness of its air, and the mildness of its temperature "even in the hottest months, from July to December."

Once the visitor has dutifully toured the cathedral and the big new stadium known as the *Bumbódromo,* and gazed out upon the river from the dusty Christ the Redeemer Plaza, few obvious points of interest remain. Usually, the heat that makes the sidewalks wave and shimmer leads all but the most intrepid would-be explorers to join residents in sleeping away the afternoon. Even the hands on the clock in the cathedral tower appear to move more slowly between two and four o'clock, when the boat finally drags itself out of the harbor and the town begins to stir.

Parintins, however, is a long way from Texas. A genuine cowtown in the sense that its economy depends on livestock (horse and cow vaccines vie with photocopies as the big sellers in the Agro-Verde Supply Shop), it, unlike its Texas counterparts, happens to be located on a large island in the middle of the Amazon. Although tiny in comparison to Rio de Janeiro or Manaus, it is nonetheless the second or third most populous city in Brazil's largest state. Hub of the region known as Médio Amazonas, Parintins boasts two commuter flights a day to the state capital.[46] It is *the* big city for numerous visitors from the interior who come to town to vote, collect their pensions, see a doctor, or visit married sons and daughters or younger children lodged with friends and relatives so they can attend school.[47] "Parintins is so exciting!" one older jute worker who has lived all of her life in the interior exclaims with an enthusiasm that would floor the guidebook writers. "There is so much to see, always so much to do."[48]

The city's history reflects, directly and indirectly, the major historical currents traced out above.[49] The name "Parintins" refers to one group of renowned warriors, finally subjugated in 1922 in the Madeira River Valley. The graveyard behind the cathedral, in which Jewish residents have their own corner, offers up a number of indigenous artifacts. Parintins' location directly on the Amazon made it obligatory passage for Orellana's expedition, as well as present-day riverboats connecting Manaus and Belém.

In Parintins, as throughout much of the Amazon, the religious orders played an important role in colonization. In 1660, two priests gave notice

46. "Amazonas" is the name for both the river and the state. Thus, when people refer to Parintins as "Baixo" or "Lower" Amazonas, they are referring to the state. When, however, they refer to it as "Médio" or "Middle" Amazonas, they are referring to the river.

47. The city offers grade school and three years of high school education, which consists of specialized instruction in, say, education or accounting. For further schooling, students must go elsewhere, usually Manaus.

48. Woman, age 61, interior of Parintins. Married, jute worker, no formal education.

49. Principal sources for the history of Parintins are Arcângelo Cerqua, *Clarões de fé no Médio Amazonas;* and Antonio Clemente Ribeiro Bittencourt, *Memórias de Parintins.* A broader historical context is provided by Arthur Cezar Ferreira Reis, *História do Amazonas.* For a sense of place see the stories and chronicles in Tonzinho Saunier, *Várzea e terra firme.*

of an "Indian settlement" where, nine years later, a third curate dedicated a chapel to Saint Michael. Although the town reported a population of just under five hundred Indians in 1730, smallpox and beriberi wiped it out a decade later, leaving José Pedro Cordovil, captain of the Portuguese Militias, to refound the community in 1796. Cordovil's following of slaves and hired laborers devoted themselves primarily to agriculture and fishing. Seven years later, a group of Carmelite friars arrived, and were soon accusing Cordovil of providing the local Indians with large quantities of sugar rum (cachaça) in order to exploit their labor. Cordovil, for his part, blamed the missionaries for encouraging the natives' "natural laziness" and fomenting insubordination. Not surprisingly, the Indians later supported the rebels during the Cabanagem.

Given the region's scanty supply of rubber trees, the rubber boom did not affect Parintins directly. Like other river ports, however, it prospered from the rubber trade. In 1852, the settlement then known as Vila Nova da Rainha became a municipal district or município with the far more important-sounding name of Vila Bela da Imperatriz ("The Empress's Fair City"), which became Parintins in 1880.

Although the growing cattle and agricultural center could not compare in wealth or size to Óbidos, with its strategic fort and extensive sugar plantations, by 1920 it boasted ten avenues, ten cross streets, five plazas, and more than fourteen thousand persons. Most of the older two-story houses that still face the river are remnants of this period. "My grandfather," the owner of one of these homes explains as we rock back and forth in caneback chairs beneath the tall trees on her front sidewalk, "was the child of Moroccan Jews. His parents were living in France at the time, but he happened to be born in the waters of Gibraltar, and thus became an English citizen. He came here as a young man and soon owned a great rubber plantation, living for years among the Indians. Finally, he came to Parintins and bought this house. He was really very rich. A week after he settled here, he got a toothache. They pulled out the tooth with rusty pliers because there were no dentists, and he died a few days later. So you can see what life was like then, even in the cities."[50]

Another older woman displays a sack of doughnut-shaped coins with peonies and Oriental characters, which her father bought from one of the directors of the Japanese jute-producing community in Vila Amazonas. "People from all over came here to get rich," she explains. "At that time, Parintins was little more than a clearing in the forest. But here was this Japanese man with his sack of coins with flowers no one here had ever

---

50. Woman, age 63, born Parintins. Single, 3 years high school.

seen. I think my father bought them for the flowers. The sun here is too strong, you see, for a proper garden."[51]

As during the rubber boom, the current expansion has had a largely indirect, though for this reason no less profound, effect on Parintins. At present, the *município* is home to some ninety thousand persons, approximately two-thirds of whom live within the city limits. Deforested long ago to make room for cattle, the area has not witnessed the massive burnings common in much of Amazônia today. Nor, for this reason, has it seen the barrage of newcomers seeking farmland or the sorts of violent land disputes that plague the new state of Tocantins and the south of Pará. Many families have at least one relative who works as a *garimpeiro,* or gold miner, but the mines themselves are fairly distant. And although the city is home to a branch of the controversial national Indian protection agency, the FUNAI, and a shelter called the Indian's House (*a Casa do Índio*) that provides lodging for indigenous visitors, the nearest reservation is several days by boat. Thus while Parintins did not escape the dramatic confrontations between colonists and native peoples still common in Amazônia, today's land disputes are far more likely to pit small-scale farmers against large landowners.

Like much of the Amazon, Parintins has seen steady and ongoing movement from countryside to city. But again, the movement here has not been as striking as in the former territories of Amapá and Rondônia, where trees fall and buildings rise at a breathless pace. Nonetheless, if growth in Parintins has been considerably slower and less spectacular than in a number of other Amazonian cities, it is no less real. The desire for better health and educational services finds compelling reinforcement in increasing competition for once-abundant natural resources. The growth of large-scale fishing in particular has led to hunger in the interior of Parintins. Unable to vie successfully with the *geladeiras,* big boats equipped with drift nets and refrigerated storage, small fishermen as well as farmers continue trickling into the city. "When my father arrived here in 1953," says one man in the interior of Parintins, "he was the only one for miles around. In Parintins itself, the fishermen gave away half their catch, there were so many fish. Today, there are hardly any fish, just people and more people. I think about moving, but then I ask myself, where would I go?"[52]

The single greatest source of migrants to Parintins is the rural community of Juruti Velho and its environs, just across the border in Pará. The newcomers are apt to make their homes in the city's poorest neighborhoods

51. Woman, age 69, born Parintins. Widowed, family income, 3 years high school.
52. Man, 33, born interior of Parintins (Zé Açu). Married, fisherman and farmer, no formal education.

such as Palmares, Santa Rita, and Dejard Vieira. Most of these districts began as squatter settlements and have since mushroomed. (Over half a dozen new neighborhoods, including a massive encampment known as Itaúna, sprang up between 1984 and 1992.) Palmares, for example—the name comes from a celebrated sixteenth-century *quilombo,* or runaway slave settlement—founded in 1971, is now home to over twenty-five thousand people, or about a quarter of the city's population. With their straw huts, wooden shacks, and backyards full of pigs and chickens, the frequently unpaved streets recall the interior. Although most homes have electric light and water, these services are often intermittent. Few people have built-in bathrooms; instead, most rely on latrines and bathe in the custom of the interior, fully clothed, beneath a spigot behind the house. Televisions are more common than toilets or refrigerators, their number having risen steadily ever since the city began receiving direct images in 1982.

Almost devoid of industry (an important jute plant closed several years ago, leaving the city with only three sawmills, two brickyards, and a meatpacking plant), Parintins suffers from chronically high unemployment that some estimates place at as high as seventy percent. Young people unable to find any sort of steady job regularly move on to Manaus, approximately a day's journey by boat. Some go still farther, abandoning the Amazon entirely for Brasília, São Paulo, or Rio de Janeiro. For many residents of Parintins, the symbol of wealth and well-being is not a car or even a motorcycle, but a bicycle with two good tires. "We live," one young man says, "in a rich land, and yet we have to import everything. There is no work; there is nothing here. In the past, there was no luxury, everything was more humble. Today, there is more luxury but the poor continue poorer than ever. For the person who owns a bicycle, everything is marvelous. But for the person who doesn't own one, life is very hard."[53]

At the same time that the lack of jobs in Parintins fuels movement toward the capital, it also encourages continued ties to the interior. Female migrants are fairly likely to find work within the city as laundresses, domestics, schoolteachers' assistants, and—sometimes—prostitutes, but their husbands are usually less successful. As a result, those men who do not head for Manaus often continue to work in the interior, passing weeks and even months apart from their families. Not infrequently, they abandon their wives and children entirely.

The newly prominent *Boi-Bumbá* festival that draws large numbers of tourists and television crews to Parintins for three days every June has

53. Man, age 16, born interior of Parintins, lives Parintins (12 years). Single, unemployed, high school education.

made the city Amazônia's "folklore capital."[54] It provides little, however, in the way of needed goods and services. In the past, the players, or *brincantes,* of the opposing teams dressed up in homemade costumes (the skirts of the "Indians" were always made of stitched-together banana leaves) and went parading through the city, stopping at the doorsteps of various homes to play out segments of the drama of a prize bull who is slain, only to magically revive. The homeowners would then invite the group inside to eat and drink, sometimes rewarding their performance with a coin or two. Not infrequently, overly enthusiastic players and their supporters became involved in skirmishes which prompted police intervention.

A far cry from its humble, if spirited, predecessor, today's *Boi-Bumbá* is a far larger, more opulent, and outward-oriented spectacle. Many months before the actual celebration, representatives of both sides begin planning a multitude of floats and accompanying dances. Although the themes are inevitably related to local and regional folk traditions, and may rework elements of the original drama, the narrative thread of the first *Bois* has long since disappeared. The emphasis on elaborate floats and luxurious costumes, financed in large part by the state government, has fostered comparisons between the festival and *Carnaval* in Rio de Janeiro. "In the past, everything was poor," says an elderly shamanic healer who has participated in the *Boi* since the age of seventeen. "Today there is more show, more animation. But I liked the past too—it was poorer, but more fun."[55]

Rehearsals begin in early May as loudspeakers blare out each side's theme song and the participants and their supporters engage in prefestival parties and parades. Then, during the last week of June, the population doubles and triples as visitors from all over Brazil and various foreign countries pour into town. The harbor is full of boats crammed with hammocks for sleeping, the city's three small hotels are overflowing, and virtually every family receives out-of-town guests. The *Boi* itself lasts three nights, beginning around nine in the evening and continuing almost till dawn in a stadium that sways with stamping, cheering people.

During the *Boi,* the island runs out of beer and soda. Crews film the spectacle for national television and politicians and foreign dignitaries jockey so that cameras catch their smiling faces. Vendors offer T-shirts, caps, and photos, and sidewalk bars do a nonstop business. On the Sunday morning following three long days of competition, the winner is announced with much fanfare. A victory parade ensues, then everyone goes home to sleep. Next day, a small army of women in wide-brimmed straw hats and

54. For an introduction to the *Boi-Bumbá* see Bruno Menezes, *Boi-Bumbá* (*Auto Popular*).
55. Man, age 69, born Parintins. Married, healer and barber, 3 years school.

T-shirts with the city logo sweeps away the acres of empty bottles, red flags and blue streamers, single rubber sandals, and stray feathers.

The festival's many supporters argue that the *Boi-Bumbá* provides a channel for popular creativity that brings welcome revenue and recognition to the city. "Before the *Boi,* no one had ever heard of Parintins, and now everybody knows it," one young woman says approvingly. Equally impassioned critics see today's *Boi* as a deturpation of regional traditions and the reduction of a way of life to hollow *folclore.* Arguing that the city's elite control who and what gets money, they point out that the festival is oriented toward an outside audience with little knowledge or appreciation of local realities. ("These people just come to party," one man grumbles. "They say they like our folklore, but they really like our beer and women.")[56] The critics also say that while the festival does bring considerable short-term profits to some merchants, the great majority of these are nonresidents, and that most goods that bear the name of Parintins are produced outside the city. In addition, they complain that the influx of tourists into the city has fostered a serious drug problem and the growth of street gangs called *galeras* among the largely jobless youth.

Once the last float has been dismantled, the last pennant sold at half price, Parintins goes back to being a small town on a big river. There are still few cars, and when the dilapidated city bus makes a rare appearance—usually late at night or very early Sunday morning—it is inevitably vacant. The great majority of people get about on motorcycles and brightly colored bicycles. It is not uncommon to find two and three individuals perched on a single bicycle. A small boy may sit on the handlebars, facing his older brother. Or a husband may pedal while his wife, seated on the back wheel, continues to nurse their baby, an umbrella in one hand warding off the rain of light. Peddlers saunter by with fish clumped through the gills like bananas on a stalk. The Dalila ("Delilah") Barber Shop, Cinderella Shoes, and Brasa ("Live Ember") Ice Cream all do a thriving business. Schoolchildren mill about the parks and plazas where vultures eye them from the tops of towering mango trees. A horse-drawn cart hauls an oversize refrigerator down the main street, while a sweet-faced grandmother, oblivious to the meaning of the "Give me hot love" emblazoned on her T-shirt, converses with friends beneath a canopy of glistening leaves.

From June through November, when sudden rains are less apt to thump and sizzle on the tin roofs, the sidewalk before the municipal market is crammed with vendors seated before plastic dishtubs full of onions and

---

56. Man, age 50, born Nhamundá, lives Parintins (19 years). Married, fishnet maker and vegetable vendor, 1 year school.

tomatoes and tin basins brimming with tiny river shrimp. Inside, the stalls are stacked high with medicinal leaves, straw baskets that double as bird cages, homemade fiber brooms, foul-smelling, honeylike *andiroba* oil to soothe the itching caused by minuscule insects called *mucuim*. One can also buy the teeth and left eye of dolphins, believed to aid in winning over the object of one's desire.

The streets are full of vendors selling paper cones full of shaved ice over which they pour a choice of neon-colored syrups. Others ladel out a pungent, gummy soup called *tacacá*. Men congregate beneath the trees in games of bottle-cap checkers and fruit-pit billiards. Women sweep their houses, nurse new babies, mend, scrub, yell at children, gossip, worry whether their husbands will come home on time. Teenage boys eye teenage girls while their younger brothers and sisters lurch about on tin can stilts, kick at a fragment of an ox skull baked into the mud, or suck on buriti palm popsicles. A young mother carefully pours water into the tin cups in which she has set the kitchen table in order to keep the ants from crawling up the legs. A child balances a cricket on the end of a broomstick. The new traffic guard struggles to get the attention of the motorcycles that cheerfully roar by him.

The river shines up into the sky as the town eases into evening. Older students congregate on benches on the central thoroughfares, waiting for the school's last session to begin. Scrawny dogs full of scabs slink by the vendors who sell roasted meat on skewers, hoping for an accident or a rare burst of charity. A light goes on in an elderly couple's front room, illuminating photos of pouty nudes above a large gold plastic crucifix. A parrot destined to be first prize in next Friday's parish bingo game looks up from a bowl of mashed bananas, and a spotted pig curls up in the middle of an unpaved street.

By midnight on weekdays, most of Parintins has gone to bed. Only a few young people sit at the rickety metal tables, talking and drinking beer in the sidewalk bars that look out upon the river. In the red light district, a few men survey the women in scanty skirts and enormous earrings as politicians' firecrackers pop briefly in the distance. Boats of various sizes move across the harbor's filthy, moon-striped water, their throbbing motors like a heartbeat in the stillness of the night. Sleepers toss in hammocks crisscrossed over one another as the mosquitoes feast. A dog barks at a shadow; a cock crows for no good reason; a dolphin arcs above the water, snorts, and disappears. A fisherman pauses briefly in the middle of the river to light a cigarette. The tiny light glows briefly as he slaps at a mosquito. The night, all of a sudden, is almost cool and very dark.

2

THE STORYTELLERS

Eu, eu não sei nada de história. Não conto nada. Não sei dizer nadinha do
Boto ou desse negócio de Cobra Grande. Só que uma vez . . .

(Me, I don't know any stories. Not one. I can't tell you a thing about the
Dolphin or this business of the *Cobra Grande*. Except that just one
time . . .)

—*Young rubber worker, Seringal Cupuaí (Juruá River)*

The people who tell stories about Dolphins include fishermen in tiny
hamlets who swear to have had steamy encounters with Dolphin-women
("She was blonde and she was beautiful!"), young computer technicians
in Manaus who can remember "tall tales" spun by a favorite uncle in the
countryside, high-school students in Parintins who may assert that the
encantados "are a part of our folklore." Although Amazonians themselves
tend to strongly associate the stories with persons of limited education (by
far the greater part of the regional population) and with the countryside,
they actually are told by a wide variety of individuals. Newcomers to the
region may be wholly unfamiliar with the Dolphin stories, and many persons dismiss the subject with a shrug or laugh. Nevertheless, the great
majority of people with whom I spoke in my travels had heard something,
somewhere. Even individuals who themselves could recount nothing were
often familiar on some level with the Dolphin. "I've seen the movie [*Ele,
o Boto,* a film about a Dolphin-lover]," "I've watched Jacques Cousteau on
television," or "My grandmother used to tell these stories when we'd go to
visit her in the interior," they might explain.[1]

The people who recount the narratives in the following chapters are

---

1. People often refer to Cousteau's *Amazon: Journey to a Thousand Rivers,* which was
widely shown on Brazilian as well as European and U.S. television. The documentary includes
a segment in which a fisherman speaks of a seductive dolphin.

from quite different parts of Amazônia. Ranging in age from five years to over a hundred, some are well-schooled and well-to-do; many others are illiterate or semiliterate and very poor. An interest in the Dolphin unites the otherwise extremely different grandson of the founder of a chain of department stores and a young widow in the interior of Parintins whose husband died of a snakebite when no serum could be found for him in the city hospital ("They had run out of it, I guess," she says matter-of-factly).

Although differences in birthplace, education, age, sex, and occupation are often reflected in the *encantado* stories, dissimilarities also may exist within the same community and even the same family. The rubber workers in the tiny settlement of Cupuaí, for instance, disagree as to whether or not the Dolphin appears at local dances. ("I don't believe a word of this," one man says. "It's absolutely true!" his best friend insists.) Likewise, the three young daughters of a subsistence farmer with whom I stayed in the city of Macapá recounted three notably different versions of a single story their father had told to them as children. ("My sisters tell this all wrong!" each of them complained to me.)

My particular focus on half a dozen storytellers introduced here and not six—or eight or sixteen—others was largely arbitrary; above all, I found them interesting as people and enjoyed their company. Although they reveal a variety of ideas and attitudes common among many storytellers, they are not intended to be representative in the Oscar Lewis, *Five Families,* sense.[2] Unavoidably, some elements of their stories stand out here while others have been consciously or unconsciously omitted. Moreover, although the resulting sketches underscore various aspects of life in Parintins and the Brazilian Amazon, they do not pretend to offer any sort of total picture.

The following sketches give particular attention to the place of the supernatural and, more specifically, the *encantados* in the storytellers' lives. They also provide a necessary backdrop for the narratives we will consider. All of the people in question told and retold numerous stories, and I asked all of them to comment on accounts I had heard from the others. (Although Parintins is relatively small, most of these individuals knew each other only by name or not at all.) Interested in their immediate reactions to particular tales, I prevailed on each to accompany me on visits to other storytellers of their acquaintance. In addition, I spent many hours with these particularly close friends in which they told no stories and I asked no questions—about Dolphins, anyway. They were kind enough to invite

2. Lewis presents five Mexican families as full-fledged representatives of a larger national culture in his *Five Families.*

me to share meals, to take trips into the interior, to go for strolls about town, to help me find someone who could wash a muddy hammock or mend an umbrella smashed by yet another cloudburst, produce a remedy for *mucuim* bites ("Now don't just go walking through the grass next time!"), and to sit around talking for hours while the rain poured down. Sometimes, I looked after children and deciphered written instructions or took dictation from a visiting relative with little schooling. I met their friends, their parents and grandparents, their spouses, their children, their sisters, brothers, aunts, uncles, and first, second, and third cousins. All of them knew that I was writing a book and all gave me permission to quote them and their stories, though I suspect that none believed I really would.[3]

Some of the remarks I cite here were inspired by my questions. ("What would you do if you were mayor of Parintins?" I might ask, or "Is life easier for men or women here?" or "What do you most want for your children?") However, much of the information that appears here emerged spontaneously in conversations to which I happened to be party. Moreover, although I was particularly interested in certain issues, I made every effort not to force the conversation or put words in people's mouths.

These individuals vary not only in their viewpoints on the supernatural, but also in their degrees of political consciousness and attitudes toward perceived injustice, and in their assessments of their own and Amazônia's past and future. Nonetheless, their opinions often recall those of other storytellers and their lives reveal a number of common themes. Although, for instance, these persons' economic situations vary, all at some point have endured hardships of a sort routine in Amazônia and all are well aware of the constraints the lack of money has placed on their own lives. Furthermore, although some long to travel, not a one has ever been outside the Amazon.

None of the individuals described here fails to remark on perceived flaws, if not outright injustices, in the political and economic system. Five of the six were born in the interior, and direct references to transformations in their own lives underscore an awareness of rapid social change. A strong consciousness—though not necessarily acceptance—of traditional gender roles also pervades their comments. All but one of the six describe them-

3. I have changed these individuals' names, and modified or omitted certain details in order to protect their privacy. Also, I have made no attempt to incorporate events occurring after 1990. There were, however, significant changes in the lives of three of these persons between 1990 and 1992. Maurício got married, found a new job in the city bureaucracy, passed the university entrance exam, and began a program in geography on a satellite campus in Parintins. Tô Pereira became extremely ill and lost so much weight I no longer recognized him; indeed, even his voice changed. And Gerineldo moved with his family to Santarém.

selves as Roman Catholics (the other is a Protestant Pentecostal) and four attend mass on a fairly regular basis.[4]

Then too, all six express ideas or engage in practices that suggest larger tensions between official church dogma and folk cosmology. (Alzira's husband Argemiro, for instance, is a member of both an extremely traditional religious brotherhood and a progressive, worker-oriented political party.) Although the individuals in question tend to dismiss these apparent contradictions ("Why should I be all one thing or another?" demands Tô Pereira), there are nonetheless occasions on which their multiple identities collide.

TÔ PEREIRA

Born in the interior, Tô Pereira has lived in Parintins now for well over half a century. Almost seventy years old, he is a strong, handsome man with dusky skin set off by a full head of white hair. His tiny, tin-roofed shoe repair shop—a veritable oven in the noon sun—sits in the middle of town. I first limped into Tô's shop when a strap on my only pair of sandals snapped. I liked him from the start, and because his shop was so centrally located, there were few days in which I did not stop to talk to him and his assistant, Gerineldo. ("So, where were you yesterday?" he would demand if I failed to check in.)

Tô's shoe shop is located right next to the house of his first wife, who died after some ten years of marriage. "She was of good family," he explains, "but still, it was me she wanted for a husband. Not that I married her for money!" Although he keeps up the residence for their son, who has moved to Manaus, he himself lives in another, sunny yellow house on the edge of sprawling, much poorer Palmares.

Tô sells the fruit from the towering mango tree in the backyard of the first house, as well as telephone tokens, in order to add a few more pennies to his income. Several times a month, he leaves the shop to thirteen-year-old Gerineldo, in order to go fishing in an old canoe. His two greatest pleasures are sitting out on the river waiting for a hefty *tambaqui* to bite, and strumming away the afternoon on a well-tuned guitar.

An outgoing man with a wide smile, Tô Pereira enjoys talking with the customers who arrive throughout the day to leave and pick up shoes. Proud of his reputation for honesty, he reacts angrily to any suggestion of distrust.

---

4. As such, they once again reflect a larger population. There are, to be sure, a number of persons in Parintins—and, even more, in the small communities of the interior, where a priest may visit only once or twice a year—who do not engage in any sort of formal religious practice. However, the majority of Parintins residents are at least nominally Catholic, and there is also a small number of Protestants (above all, Baptists) and Jews (most, the descendants of Moroccan Sephardim who came to try their fortunes during the rubber boom).

I once was present when the wife of a longtime customer pointedly questioned Tô's explanation of a past bill before leaving a pair of boots for repair. Taken aback at the woman's offensive tone, I later asked why he had not reacted. "Why say anything?" he asked me. "When she comes back for the boots, she'll find the price so high she'll never bother me again."

Tô has watched Parintins grow from a haphazard collection of straw huts and wooden shacks into a real city. "In my day," he says, "it was very hard to get an education. It's not like Gerineldo here, who can both work and study; by the time I turned ten, I already had a job, and so I had to drop out of school after just two years. My mother washed clothes and my father fished and I filled buckets full of [river] water to sell to shops and homes. There was no such thing as turning on a faucet in those days. Later, I worked in people's houses, scrubbing pots with sand and palm leaves because there were no scouring pads. Next, I became a carpenter's assistant, then I started fixing shoes. For a while, I was a peddler in the interior—buttons, pans, more buttons. Then, when I'd had my fill of traveling, I went back to shoes."

At one point, Tô was on the point of establishing a business of his own in Belém when the entire shipload of goods with which he planned to launch the enterprise sank to the bottom of the Amazon. "My life has always been this way," he observed matter-of-factly. "Everything starts out well, only to end up crumbling like a house of sand."

Tô claims his ill luck extends to women, a point on which the local gossips do not agree. He remarried soon after his first wife died, but the union was unhappy and his spouse now lives with their six children in Manaus. Although Tô soon acquired a third family, he, unlike many of the men in his situation, continues to send his second wife small amounts of money as well as fruit and fish. "I'm not one of these who chews the meat and leaves the bones," he says, only grinning when I make a face.

His bad luck, explains Tô, is the result of a hex or *feitiço* directed at him by an envious older man when he, Tô, was seventeen.[5] He explains that the shoemaker for whom he was working at the time was also an amateur musician who taught him to play the violin. During this period, the most sought-after musician in Parintins was a man named X. Once, when X was packing up his violin at a late-night gathering, a very drunk judge ordered him to resume playing. After X respectfully explained that

5. A number of dictionaries define the term *feitiço*, which comes from the past participle of the verb *fazer*, "to make," as "witchcraft" or "sorcery." However, it does not have the same rather exotic connotations as these terms presently do in English, and for many of the region's inhabitants, *feitiço* is a fact of life. "Do I believe in *feitiço*?" people often said in response to my question. "Oh no, I don't. But it exists." For various examples of popular beliefs regarding *feitiço* in the Parintins area see Antonio Cantanhede, *O Amazonas por dentro*.

he was too tired to go on ("Another day, of course, sir!"), the judge ordered the police to beat him. Humiliated by this injustice, X declared on the spot that he would never again perform in public. "It was wrong of them to beat him, but these *brancos* ["whites" or "powerful people"] are accustomed to getting their way," Tô explains when Gerineldo expresses shocked surprise.

As X proved adamant in his refusal to perform in future *festas*, various groups began asking Tô to play in his stead. Not long afterward, X asked the young musician if he wanted to buy his handsome violin. "We'll exchange instruments and you can pay me such-and-such a sum for the difference in their value, since mine is of better quality and will help you get more jobs," X told Tô.

Excited about this apparently generous offer, Tô hurried to X's house after work the next day. The older man received him warmly, repeatedly insisting that he drink the *cafezinho* traditionally offered guests. In a hurry to get home, Tô refused politely. Handing the man the money, they exchanged violins, and precisely at this moment, Tô experienced a jabbing pain. By the time he got home, he had a fever and a rash, and by next morning, he could not get out of bed. For many days afterward, he lay immobile in his hammock, unable to swallow so much as a spoonful of porridge.

When Tô showed no signs of improving, his father went to see the city's best-known *sacaca*. (The term denotes the most powerful sort of *pajé*, said to travel in body as well as spirit to the river bottom.)[6] "Let's go at once," said the man, who had been waiting for him on the doorstep. "Your son is very sick."

When they reached Tô's house, the *sacaca* blew smoke from a special *tauari* (couratari bark) cigar all over him to purify his body, making crosses as he did so, and murmuring special prayers. He then told Tô's father to be sure to catch a lot of fish that day because his son was going to wake up very hungry. When the father returned home that afternoon, Tô's fever had broken and his mother could not fry the fish fast enough for him to eat.

The next day, the *sacaca* explained what had happened. Still angry at the injustice visited upon him, X had taken out his resentment on Tô through a powerful *feitiço*. Had the young man drunk the coffee offered him, he would have been carried off immediately to the Enchanted City at

---

6. A *sacaca* is one category of *pajé* or *curador*. *Sacacas* claim to transform themselves physically into aquatic beings—most frequently, a dolphin or an anaconda—in order to journey to the river bottom. They are more powerful than other healers who must rely on spirits to respond to their summons because they can visit the Enchanted City at will.

the river's bottom, never to return. The *sacaca* then asked Tô if he wanted to avenge himself on X by "boomeranging" the *feitiço,* but Tô demurred. "Why didn't you? He made you suffer!" Gerineldo exclaims. "Because," Tô responds, "the man had eight children, the oldest just your age. For a minute I was tempted to teach him a lesson but then I thought, 'No, I am alive and well, and what's done is done.'"

Early the next morning, in accord with the *sacaca*'s directions, Tô went to the river to bathe. As he entered the water, he found himself surrounded by dolphins. "I had never seen so many dolphins in one place before," he says. His father, who was waiting for him on the riverbank, then poured a bucket with a special medicinal mixture over his son's head. As the water ran down Tô's body, it became a fishy-smelling, bluish gum "just like the surface of a dolphin's skin." Almost immediately after completing this ritual, Tô ran into X. "From that day on," he says, "X was always afraid of me. Because he knew *I* knew what he had done."

"Why were there so many dolphins when you went to bathe in the river?" Gerineldo wants to know. "Because X had used them in order to prepare that *feitiço,*" Tô replies. "Dolphins are often party to these sorts of black arts. The *pajé* told me that if I had drunk that coffee they [the dolphins] would have taken me with them to the bottom of the river. Well, they did not succeed but, all the same, I have always had a crooked star."

Has he ever seen the Enchanted City that people say lies deep beneath the water, Gerineldo inquires. Here, Tô only shrugs. "People say a lot of things," he says with a grin. "Now and then, the Dolphin does transform himself into a man, because when I was eight years old, my father and I saw a Dolphin go running toward the river from my aunt's house. He knocked over all the dishes in the kitchen as he went rushing out the door! But people also say the Dolphin goes to dance at *festas* and I don't believe it for a minute, not a minute!" Tô laughs and bangs a nail into a leather sole, then inspects the shoe from all sides. "You can be sure I wouldn't believe in this talk of *feitiço* either," he says, tapping the shoe against his hand for emphasis, "if it hadn't happened to me."

GERINELDO

Although Gerineldo listens carefully to Tô Pereira, he has his own ideas. A resident of Parintins for a little over a year now, he still misses life in the interior which his family left in search of schools for him and his eight sisters and brothers. "I like to hunt deer and wild boars," he says, "and there are none here. Some of the boys I go to school with have never even bagged so much as an armadillo."

Gerineldo's dream is one day to own a motorboat as well as a chain of supermarkets. "The supermarket will make me rich enough so I can take my boat all up and down the river anytime I want," he says. "I'll have one big house in the interior and another here in Parintins." Although he has mastered the skills Tô has shown him, he does not foresee a future full of other people's shoes. "Shoemakers earn very little, they have lots of headaches with their customers, and they have to use cheap material so that people will come back soon for a new pair of heels," he says. In his fifth year of school now, he plans to go on to study accounting. "Then I'll save my money and buy my first supermarket," he says. His more immediate goal is a secondhand bicycle that would put an end to the forced hikes from his home to the shoe shop in the relentless sun.

It is not hard to understand why Gerineldo should think a good deal about money. His family lives in a one-room shack without electricity and running water in a swampy section of Palmares. There is no place except a tiny, inconvenient outhouse for family members to change clothing and Gerineldo's sisters tease him as he squirms before us, under bedsheets, into his school uniform. The first time I came to visit, Gerineldo's mother scolded him for bringing a guest to the house. Although she was soon inviting me to visit ("Hardly anyone I know likes to listen as much as you do!"), she inevitably apologized for the poverty that made her own life an unceasing round of chores and small humiliations.

Crowding the edge of the river, the houses in Gerineldo's neighborhood are set on stilts to minimize the effects of the winter floods, and the street itself is regularly cut in two by an immense puddle. Skinny roosters poke about the garbage-studded mud. During the summer, great clouds of mosquitoes occasionally drive the family to eat dinner beneath the nets that make cocoons of the hammocks in which they sleep.

Gerineldo's father arrives in the city every Sunday. Previously a farmer ("beans, manioc, the usual"), he now ekes out a living as an independent river merchant (*regatão* in Portuguese).[7] As soon as he arrives in Parintins early Sunday morning, he starts selling produce and buying coffee, sugar, soap, and various manufactured items not readily available in the interior. He will devote the next day to standing on long lines in several banks to make small deposits and withdrawals, visiting customers who can pay him only on installment, and outfitting his boat so that he can set out again at dawn for the interior. "Being a merchant is, perhaps a little better than being a farmer," he says, thumping the day's dust out of his straw hat. "But I would not say that it is really all that good a life."

7. The *regatão* is technically the riverboat that traders use. By extension, the term applies to the boat owners who, like Gerineldo's father, customarily offer hard-to-obtain foodstuffs (coffee, sugar, margarine) and manufactured products (matches, lanterns, fishing hooks, combs, saints' portraits) in exchange for manioc flour and local produce.

Tall, wavy-haired, and darkly handsome like his father, Gerineldo is as self-conscious as most adolescents anywhere. Once, a pimple on the tip of his nose caused him to drop out of view for almost a week, leading Tô Pereira to visit his home in great concern. ("I told him that I had the flu," Gerineldo later confided to me somewhat sheepishly, "because I didn't want him to think me vain.") A member of the Pentecostal Church, like the rest of his family, Gerineldo, who does not go to parties, drink, or dance, expresses horror at the drugs that have begun to enter Parintins.[8] ("The pushers are all really stupid, but they think they're smart," he says. "And I ought to know, because two of them are in my class at school.")

Tô suspects that his young assistant has a girlfriend, but Gerineldo only grins and will say nothing other than that he wants his future wife to be a hard worker, a good mother, and "not silly like these girls who only giggle when you try to talk to them." Above all, he is looking for a partner who likes life in the interior "because the city's ugly, but life on the river's good."

Gerineldo's mother, Dona Maria, is a gifted storyteller. The daughter of a rubber worker from the state of Acre, she can go on for hours about awesome and mysterious forest and river beings. Her sister is a medium who advises gold miners in Santarém ("they come from miles around to see her") and Dona Maria thinks that a visionary propensity may run in the family. As evidence of her own familiarity with the supernatural, she cites an encounter she and her brother had as children with an unfamiliar woman on a deserted beach. When her brother ran after the stranger, demanding that she reveal her identity, she vanished on the spot. Then, when the two children returned to the beach the next day, they discovered the skeleton of a huge snake in the spot where the woman had disappeared. Dona Maria believes that the mysterious stranger was an *encantado* who might well have made off with both of them forever had her brother not taken the offensive. ("Was I scared?" she asks. "Of course!")

Gerineldo can repeat a number of accounts he has heard from numerous relatives in the interior, who appear from time to time in Parintins with a fresh supply of tales. He is, however, considerably more cautious than his mother in affirming their truth. Demonstrably sensitive to some of his new friends' lack of credence in the enchanted beings, he fidgets when she launches into stories in front of nonfamily members. The tales he likes best are almost always funny. Sometimes, to Dona Maria's dismay, he confuses incidents and begins laughing in the middle of an account that is supposed

---

8. Protestant Pentecostalism is on the rise not only in the Amazon, but throughout much of the nation. For an introduction to it and the other major religious movements within Brazil see Rowan Ireland, *Kingdoms Come.*

to be serious. "Good grief, Gerineldo," she admonishes, "these things can't be taken lightly" ("Estas coisas não se brinca[m]").

Although Gerineldo does not believe that man went to the moon ("I think it's just a trick they showed on television"), he is convinced of the potential truth of most of his mother's stories. "Here in Parintins," he says, "these things hardly ever happen. But there in the interior, they happen all the time." He also speaks enthusiastically of his aunt, the traditional curer ("she cures malaria, she cures cancer, she cures everything!"). "Once," he says, "she went to the *garimpo* [gold mine] and told the poorest miner where to dig for gold. He did as she said and today he is rich." In addition, Gerineldo's great-grandfather was a well-known *sacaca*. "People came to see him from miles around," he says with obvious pride.

Tô Pereira's story confirms Gerineldo's faith in the existence of *feitiço*. He believes that his own father has not done better as a river merchant because of the *olho grande* (literally, "big eye," or jealousy) of which a local healer warned the family several years ago. Brushing off any suggestion that Tô's sickness following his visit to the older musician could be a coincidence, he sees no reason to believe that the unease Tô almost certainly experienced at supplanting X in the wake of his unjust humiliation might have affected his later interpretation of the event.

Gerineldo is convinced there is a city at the river bottom. He himself has heard strange noises—dogs barking, cattle neighing, the muffled sounds of partygoers—at a bend in the river not far from where his family used to live. "Maybe it is not the Dolphins' city," he says as we throw stones into the river, waiting for his father's boat to dock, but there is something there beneath the water, of that you can be sure."

DONA MARINA

Although Gerineldo and Dona Marina have never met, they live no more than a few blocks apart. Now in her late fifties, Dona Marina came to Parintins from the interior almost a decade ago. Her street, unlike Gerineldo's, boasts both electricity and running water, and she regularly dozes off before an ancient television on sunny afternoons. Often, I would sit with her in the early evening while she watched a string of soap operas interspersed with news. Once, we spent a particularly sultry afternoon watching reruns of an ice skating pageant, after which Dona Marina, a midwife, hurried off to deliver a baby girl who was later baptized "Katarina" in honor of the winning female skater.

Dona Marina's house, like Gerineldo's, abuts the river and is subject to the winter floods. Although her husband likes the rainy season because he can moor his boat right at the house's back door, fish are hard to come by at this time and the family eats badly. In addition, Dona Marina hates sloshing through the water in the outhouse, and last year, the rains almost carried off the chicken coop. Worst of all, she had to kill half a dozen of the snakes that slithered up from the river into her kitchen. "I whacked the smallest with a frying pan," she says with a scowl as she offers me and several neighbors plastic teacups half full of sweet, grainy coffee.

Dark-complexioned and slightly plump, her hair tied back with a bit of knitting yarn, Dona Marina has a slow and radiant smile. Her neighbors are fond of her because she never charges for the chilled water those who do not own refrigerators are apt to request on particularly hot days. Born far from Parintins on the border of French Guiana, she was still very small when her widowed mother ran off with a man bound for the distant rubber region. As a result, she was raised by her grandmother, "one of these real northeastern women with whom no one would dare to fool." Not long after her mother's disappearance, Dona Marina moved with her relatives to a rural community not far from Parintins. Although she liked the wide green landscape, life was hard and often dull. "We had no idea what a school was and there were no priests or doctors," she says. "I guess you could say that we grew up like little animals. I never learned to read and my profession was the hoe."

When she was only seven, Dona Marina dreamt she visited the river bottom. There, she claims to have met a number of kindly beings in dolphin and anaconda clothing who promised to teach her how to cure the sick. When Dona Marina later told her family what had happened, her grandmother took her to a shamanic healer, who confirmed the truth of her account.

At least in retrospect, this experience was not wholly unexpected. Dona Marina claims that her mother often danced at parties with the Cobra Norato, a famous *encantado* whom some older storytellers claim as a personal acquaintance. "This Noratinho," she explains [the name is an affectionate diminutive], "was more or less short, with Indian hair, stiff hair—it wasn't soft. And he was crazy for my mother; he would dance with her all night. He would have given anything to marry her, but she wasn't interested."

While her mother was still pregnant with Dona Marina, Norato informed her that the child would be a girl and a *pajé*. True to this prediction, as Dona Marina grew older, she began going into trances during which the spirits of the deep instructed her in how to heal. "Of course," she says, "I was never conscious of what was happening. But there were always others who would tell me afterward."

Dona Marina makes a distinction between her activities as a midwife or *parteira* and the shamanic cures which she claims to no longer perform.

49

She explains that the work of a *pajé* is very tiring, particularly for a woman, who must take special care during menstruation, when her body is dangerously open. She also says she could take no more of the local priests referring to her as a sorceress or *macumbeira*. Once, to her great embarrassment, an *encantado* possessed her in the middle of a mass, causing her to fall to the floor amidst considerable commotion. ("I have been a catechist, a Daughter of the Virgin Mary, and the angel of Veronica," she says ruefully. "I have done almost everything within the church, but still, the spirits attacked me then and there.")[9]

At the age of sixteen, Dona Marina fell in love with a young man from a neighboring community. Her grandmother, however, disapproved and she did not have the courage to elope as he suggested. Some time later, she married another man more acceptable to her family, but for whom she did not feel the same passion. "I got married," she says, "like a person goes on a trip, wanting to see something new, without knowing anything about the place he is going or when or how he will arrive. The traveler reaches his destination and finds everything different from what he had imagined. But for me, at least, there was no going home."

In the beginning, when Dona Marina's husband would go hunting or fishing, she tended to the house, playing with the dolls her grandmother had forwarded along with the rest of her personal belongings. After she became pregnant with the first of her eight children, however, "there was only time for work." In between pregnancies, Dona Marina helped her husband in the jute fields, often standing all day long in water up to her waist, then coming home to cook and sew. "It's a bad life," she says, "because you catch cold and your bones hurt. Besides, you can work seven days a week and still end the month in debt. Because those bosses [*aqueles brancos*] are very wily [*muito espertos*]. They charge you for everything until you end up paying *them* for having worked."

Today, Dona Marina does not see much of her husband, who periodically arrives with fish from the interior. While his absence makes her lonely, she is not unhappy with her life. "I wanted more than anything else to have children and I had them," she says, waving proudly at the sun-bleached photos on the wall. "I wish I had been able to give them an education, but they are healthy and all good to me, and this matters more than money." Although her children are now grown, the house is full of their offspring as well as a small boy Dona Marina is raising as her own.

Dona Marina's one great sadness remains the disappearance of the

---

9. The Daughters of Mary (*Filhas de Maria*) is a lay women's organization within the Roman Catholic church. The angel of Veronica is a figure in a church pageant commemorating Christ's passage through the Via Dolorosa.

mother, who, in her memories, retains her youth and beauty. While acknowledging that it would be difficult to find her after so many years, Dona Marina has not abandoned hope for their reunion. "Who knows?" she says. "Stranger things have happened."

Like Gerineldo's mother, Dona Marina is a spirited storyteller. Often, when she relates a funny occurrence, she laughs so hard that she has to stop to catch her breath. ("Get ahold of yourself, Dona Marina," says an eager neighbor, "and tell us what happened next!") Some of her best stories concern the Dolphin's appearance at country dances she herself attended. She asserts, however, that the Dolphin and his fellows are presently retreating from the world of human beings. "They don't live in cities; the noise gives them headaches," she explains as a motorcycle roars by as if on cue. "Things change and the *encantados* have to change with them," she adds above the din.

ALZIRA

Unlike Dona Marina, Alzira did marry her childhood sweetheart. She was fourteen at the time; her husband had just turned twenty. "How could I not have married Argemiro?" she demands in mock exasperation. "He was so persistent! Everywhere I went, there he was, a step behind me."

Argemiro laughs and acknowledges that he was determined to win over Alzira. "She was the prettiest *cabocla* for miles around," he says. Still a handsome couple, they have been married now for over thirty years. Originally from the interior, the family has lived for some two decades in a brick house just down the road from the Big-Love Auto Body Shop and across from a grade school where successive waves of children chirp out their lessons in unison. Alzira's spur-of-the-moment inspirations were a source of delight to me. "Let's go see my friend, Maria!" she would exclaim, and we would go bouncing off together on a single bicycle. I liked to climb the *jambo* tree in Alzira's backyard, tossing down the fruit to her as she laughed at my awkward motions. "You're going to fall and end up in the chicken coop!" she would caution gaily.

One of four daughters in a family with no sons, Alzira quickly mastered the traditional sweep net called the *tarrafa*, and worked beside her father in the fields with a miniature machete. "After lunch," she recalls, "I would play with my doll. Then my father and I would march off down the road while my sisters swept the house and sewed."

The first years of their marriage were difficult for Alzira and Argemiro. Their house burned down twice, forcing the young couple to live with relatives. Alzira's second pregnancy resulted in twins, born without assistance in the middle of a stormy night. Later, as the babies grew, she would wait for Argemiro to return from fishing so that he could tend them while she made a fire to dry their scanty store of diapers. Numb with sleep, Argemiro would tie a string to his wrist so that he could keep on rocking the twins' hammock with one hand while he fried the day's catch with the other.

The harshness of life in the interior did not dissuade Alzira from giving birth to seven more children. "I think that God is great and powerful because he gave me not only ten children, but also the strength to raise them," she declares. Like Gerineldo's parents, she and Argemiro moved to Parintins primarily for the schools. "We left the interior because I didn't want my children to grow up illiterate like me," Argemiro says. "I wanted to free them from a life of fishing, of jute, of hoeing and digging, of all that backbreaking work that makes a person old by the age of forty."

The city had its own problems. When her unmarried daughter became pregnant—hardly a rare occurrence in either city or countryside, but still a blow to Alzira—she decided that she had been too strict. She therefore proceeded to adopt a more lenient, more "modern" approach with her second daughter, who also soon became a mother, leaving Alzira thoroughly confused. "The priests say it is the fault of the parents when these things happen," she asserts with obvious exasperation. "But what in the world, I ask you, is a mother supposed to do?"

Faced with the reality of a new grandchild, Alzira rose to the occasion. As her teenage daughter was bent on working in Manaus, Alzira informed the baby's father that she would raise the child as her own. He, however, was to pay "for the midwife, the milk, the baby's food and all twelve diapers, and he would pay that very day, in cash, and every penny!"

Four of Alzira's children now live in Manaus, where they work in bars and factories. A fifth has settled in burgeoning Porto Velho. Two of the remaining four children (one died as a baby) live next to Alzira's father on the outskirts of Parintins. The final two, a son and a daughter, are still at home. The girl is in high school; the boy assists Argemiro on carpentry and construction jobs. When father and son work together, they can earn a daily wage of about twelve dollars, "enough for all of us to eat, but not to pay the gas or fix the front step, which has been cracked now for a year."

Although Alzira would like to see her husband work full-time as a carpenter ("I think that it is safer than fishing"), Argemiro prefers to spend his days out upon the river. Usually, he leaves the house at three in the morning, then rows for several hours. "In the old days," he explains, "you could catch boatloads of fish right here in Parintins. But today you have to row for hours or else rent a motor for which they charge a half day's catch." "Still," he adds, "I like the fact that there is no one in my boat to give me orders. Besides, the days that I work as a carpenter, I come home all tired and sweaty and there's no fish in the cooking pot."

Like many fishermen, Argemiro is an accomplished storyteller. Alzira loves to listen to his accounts of ghosts, forest spirits, and, above all, *encantados,* but Argemiro complains that she always interrupts to ask him questions. "That's because there are things that I do not understand," she says. "How, for instance, can the *pajé's* soul just up and leave his body? And why do so few people come back from the *Encante?*" "And can it be true that those who were once *encantados* forget their former lives?"

Argemiro says that Alzira's questions have no answers. Furthermore, he says, there are more important matters to occupy one's time. A longtime member of the Marianos, a highly conservative Roman Catholic brotherhood, he is also active in the local branch of the leftist Workers' Party (*Partido dos Trabalhadores,* or PT), which finds support among more progressive members of the clergy.[10] "I am not an educated man," he says. "I have very little schooling. But I do understand that every human being has rights."

As a young man, Argemiro worked as the assistant to the local shamanic healer. "I poured glasses of *cachaça* for him, rolled his [*tauari*] cigars and took note of the prescriptions he dictated when he got into a trance," he explains. Although he and Alzira laugh about the man's liberal use of liquor in his healing activities ("He always seemed half-drunk!" exclaims Alzira), the intensity of the *pajé's* healing visions frightened Argemiro. When the man once offered to take him to a party at the river bottom, Argemiro first accepted the invitation, only to desist after smoking the fifth of seven cigars. "I all of a sudden got frightened that I would never return home. So then I said to him, 'You go, have a good time, and I'll just stay here, keeping an eye on things for you!'"

And yet, while Argemiro is by no means a *pajé,* he is nonetheless a *rezador,* or folk healer. He puts great stock in the prayers he hears in dreams, and when the local bishop warned a group of Marianos that no good Catholic would ever visit a shamanic healer, the normally deferential Argemiro informed the man that he intended to keep on healing. Although Alzira sometimes complains that people take advantage of her husband, she accompanies him on his visits to sick neighbors' homes. "He says he cannot take money for a gift God gave him and I understand that," she says. "It's just that this healing business takes an awful lot of time. Once, Argemiro went to pray over a woman who was all curled up like a snake and hissing, and it was almost dawn before we finally got to bed."

10. The candidate of the PT, Luís Inácio da Silva ("Lula"), narrowly lost out in the Brazilian presidential elections of 1989.

Aware that her younger children look with a somewhat jaundiced eye on both Argemiro's curative activities and his numerous stories of enchanted beings, Alzira finds their skepticism normal. Much like Dona Marina, she associates the *encantados* with the past. "Even in the interior today," she says, "hardly anybody talks about them."

And yet, if the enchanted beings are gradually abandoning their old haunts, Alzira herself still worries when her husband forgets to lock the door when he leaves on his predawn fishing expeditions. Not only could a thief enter the house, but who knows if a Dolphin in the form of Argemiro—or some other equally unwelcome alien—couldn't slip into the couple's bed? Alzira also confides that one of her daughters has been afflicted for some years now by a hostile spirit that may or may not be an *encantado*. Although she has consulted a wide array of doctors and traditional healers about the young woman's situation, the attacks continue. "And so you see," she says with a trace of sadness, "things go on changing. But sometimes they don't change as much as people think."

KÁTIA

In contrast to the other individuals we have met so far, twenty-six-year-old Kátia has never lived in the interior. Although her mother grew up in the countryside, she, like her father, was born and raised within the city. One of the first persons I met in Parintins, Kátia, at that time, was working as a manicurist. Because she had swallowed a fishbone the day before my arrival, she was in no mood to talk. The more questions I asked, as we sat hand in hand beneath the mango tree in her backyard, the more she eyed me glumly, occasionally forcing a wan smile. Later, we often laughed about our first encounter. "Why didn't you just tell me you had swallowed a bone?" I demanded. "I was embarrassed!" she exclaimed. "And besides, you were so earnest. All those questions! I thought you must be lonely."

Quick to anger, quick to laugh, Kátia is fond of rings and bracelets, paints her long nails scarlet and streaks her dark hair gold. A lifelong supporter of the blue team in the *Boi-Bumbá,* she loves the months-long preparations that fill the house with people, as much as the festival itself.

One of seventeen brothers and sisters, Kátia recalls the sacrifices her parents made to put them all through school. While her father worked first as a carpenter—Tô Pereira was for a time his assistant—then an advocate for various workers' associations, her mother took in laundry and peddled *munguzá,* a sweet corn porridge, in the streets. Today, her older sisters sell steaming cups of the thick golden mixture in a makeshift snack shop adjacent to the house.

Married at age sixteen, Kátia lives with her husband, Paulo, and their five-year-old son in a small but attractive cottage behind the family home. Usually, the three of them join her now-widowed mother for meals. Often, as many as twenty adults and children crowd around the lunch table. They may be joined by friends and relatives from the interior who have come to Parintins to see a doctor, cash a check, or collect a pension.

Paulo works with his father in a nearby trade shop. Although he does not make large amounts of money, the couple eats out with friends upon occasion and Kátia regularly sends the family's wash to a nearby laundress. ("I do the ironing myself, though," she observes.) From time to time, she buys her son a toy or a smart new jacket in the city's one and only department store. She purchases cosmetics and costume jewelry from door-to-door vendors who allow their customers to pay on the installment plan. Kátia supplements the household allowance Paulo gives her by working on costumes for the *Boi*, and by participation in frequent political campaigns.

As one of her relatives is a member of the city government, Kátia's entire family feverishly supports his party at election time. Although Kátia willingly joins in the activities, she has trouble asking favors of the candidates for whom she works. "All my friends say I am foolish," she confesses. "Here I am with the cheese in one hand and the knife in the other, and still, I do nothing. I suppose that they are right, and yet, the whole thing bothers me."

Decidedly ambivalent about the supernatural, Kátia is ultimately less skeptical than her ninety-two-year-old grandmother. "I lived in the interior for almost fifty years," says Dona Rosinha, "and I never saw anything extraordinary. Oh, I did come upon a thirty- or forty-foot snake once, but nothing *really* unusual." When one of her daughters claimed to hear a ghost outside the door on one occasion, Dona Rosinha went out into the darkness with a single candle. (" 'Lost soul, what do you want?' I asked. 'Prayers? Holy water? A rosary? Speak up, I can't hear you!' But I didn't hear a word.")

Kátia's Aunt Alda is, in contrast, a firm believer in the supernatural and has worked as a diviner now for some forty years. A devout Catholic, she uses a glass of water and a Saint Francis's cord to diagnose various ills. Aunt Alda's warnings that Paulo must pay more attention to his health worry Kátia. "Paulo likes to drink a little," she says. "All men in Parintins do. And I consider myself lucky, because he isn't one to get abusive or parade about with other women in the street. Nevertheless, I wish that he would listen to Aunt Alda. These spiritists are sometimes wrong, but other times, they're right."

Paulo's mother is also a medium, but of a very different sort. Long a practitioner of Umbanda, Dona Délia is presently constructing a new *terreiro,* or cult center, behind her home where she can consult more readily with the spirits when others come to ask her counsel.[11] In contrast to Kátia's aunt, who has relatively little to say about the *encantados,* her mother-in-law claims to have gone in dreams to the Enchanted City that lies at the river bottom.

Kátia expresses doubts about the *Encante.* "If it's really down there," she demands, "why has no one ever photographed it?" "In the end," she adds, "I think these things are all a matter of faith." To illustrate her point, she cites the stubborn fishbone that was tormenting her the day of our first encounter. When doctors at the local clinic told her the bone could not be extracted ("'Come back tomorrow,' they told me"), she began to despair. When, however, she threw herself upon her father's grave in the nearby churchyard, the bone dislodged of its own accord. "I don't really believe that my father was responsible," she says. "I think it was most probably coincidence and that that bone would have come free in any case. But I also think that people's faith is very powerful, and that what you believe with all your heart is apt to happen."

MAURÍCIO

Two years older than Kátia, and thus almost thirty, Maurício has lived in Parintins for close to twenty years now. He nonetheless retains strong affective ties to the countryside. Wiry and intense, with dark eyes and an engaging, slightly crooked smile, he is an aficionado of the dancelike African Brazilian martial arts form known as *capoeira,* a volunteer teacher of the handicapped, and a self-taught mechanic. He also became the friend on whom I could depend to return a borrowed umbrella when I knew I would be leaving town next morning, to slip Dona so-and-so a little money for her sick son, and to be there at the harbor when the ship came in.

When Maurício was a small boy, his father owned a fair amount of land in the interior. "We weren't rich," he says, "but we also weren't poor." One day, his father entrusted a boatload of jute to an associate who was to use the money from the sale to pay off a bank note. When the man instead absconded with the proceeds, Maurício's father had to sell a portion of his property in order to cover the debt. Angry and disgusted, he lost interest in the remainder and moved to Parintins.

Things only got worse when the family reached the city. With the death

---

11. Umbanda refers to a mixture of African Brazilian religion with a brand of spiritism closely associated with Allan Kardec in France. For an introduction see Ireland, *Kingdoms Come.* In the Amazon, African Brazilian religions have incorporated numerous indigenous features. For a detailed study of the *batuque* cult of Belém see Leacock and Leacock, *Spirits of the Deep.*

of Maurício's grandfather, his father began to spend increasing amounts of time away from home. "Like most men here in Amazônia," says Maurício, "he had always had other women. But when we moved to Parintins, he left my mother to take up with one of these."

His father's subsequent departure for Manaus placed the family in such a difficult financial position that ten-year-old Maurício became a street vendor. After returning home from school, he would go out on the street with his wares. First, he sold candied bananas; next, pitomba fruit; then, popsicles; and finally, a kind of meat dumpling. Later, he cut the grass for a priest for whom he also served as altar boy. He went on to work in a billiard parlor ("they paid more than the priest but the police said I was too young to work there"), and then the local telephone agency, transmitting messages to people who did not own telephones. Because, like Gerineldo today, he could not afford a bicycle, he had to sprint from one end of town to the other in order to deliver messages in the allotted time.

Finally, a relative got Maurício a janitorial job with the city government, and he proceeded to work his way up within the municipal bureaucracy over the next ten years. When, however, he began to speak his mind on various matters, his superiors froze his salary until he finally resigned. Most recently, he has been giving classes on the use of office machines in the local high school. "I know almost nothing about these machines and there are none, in any case, for me to use for demonstrations," says Maurício, "so I just talk about whatever enters my head. One day last week I told the students *they* were like the parts in a machine. Well, they didn't like it, but I can't say I'm sorry. Because that is exactly how things are in Amazônia today."

If Maurício were governor of the state of Amazonas, he would make immediate changes. For starters, he would imprison anyone found guilty of corruption ("in which case, of course, I'd have to build large numbers of new jails," he observes wryly). He also would reform the public school curriculum, open new health centers, encourage research on native forest remedies, and enact measures to support the native population. He also would improve access to the regional university.

Maurício's interest in this last point reflects his own narrow misses on Brazil's extremely competitive national university entrance exam on two occasions. Given a choice, he would study either agronomy or law ("but I would study almost anything"). At present, he attends an intensive philosophy and social science course in Manaus offered twice a year through a university in Rio de Janeiro. The course is sketchy and exhausting, but Maurício sees no other option for the moment.

Like many of his peers Maurício continues to live at home with his mother and unmarried siblings, reading borrowed books and balefully eyeing the bricks he bought a year ago to rebuild the house. Although he would like to start a family, it would be hard for him to do so on the approximately seventy dollars he earns a month.

Lack of money, however, is not the only thing that stops Maurício from marrying. His childhood experiences have given him an unusually critical perspective on male-female interactions, and he gets angry at his cousins' gleefully graphic descriptions of alleged conquests. Maurício cannot understand why women would become involved with men who do not respect them. "And yet, they do," he says glumly; "they really do—I swear it!"

The *encantados* remain a vivid part of Maurício's childhood. As a boy in the interior, he once came down with a high fever after watching a group of dolphins playing near the river's edge. His father then took him to see his uncle, a particularly powerful *sacaca,* who explained that a Dolphin had carried off the boy's *sombra.*[12] After praying and blowing *tauari* smoke over his nephew, the uncle proceeded to prescribe a series of herbal baths to facilitate the *sombra*'s return. "And so I believe that the Dolphin can do these things," asserts Maurício, "even though I cannot tell you exactly how or why."

In addition to stories rooted in his own experience, Maurício repeats a number of tales he learned from his grandmother, such as that of the blue fly of happiness who lives concealed beneath a vulture's wing. "And so you see," Maurício says at the tale's conclusion, "the unknown is always near us, ready to engulf us too."

For the moment, Maurício would like a bit less mystery in his own life. "Sometimes," he says, "I think I must have been born with my back toward the moon." Unlike Tô Pereira, however, who attributes life's disappointments to the ill effects of *feitiço* and an impersonal destiny over which individuals have little or no power, Maurício lays the blame less on crooked stars than on a particular political and economic system that has made Amazônia "the backyard of Brazil." "We are being robbed," he says, "of our possessions, of our culture. And the thieves don't realize that what they are stealing belongs to them as well."

---

12. The word *sombra* literally means "shadow." Maurício says that the *sombra* resembles, but is not exactly equivalent to, the soul. For an introduction to this belief, common throughout Latin America, see Luís da Câmara Cascudo, *Dicionário do folclore brasileiro,* pp. 718–19.

3

STORIES AND BELIEFS ABOUT DOLPHINS
AS SPECIAL FISH

O boto é um peixe todo especial.

(The dolphin is a really special kind of fish.)

—*Fruit seller (male), age 53, Parintins*

Much like their larger cousins, whales, who have long excited intense curiosity, fear, and speculation in those parts of the world to which they are native, Amazonian dolphins exhibit anomalous features that place them in a special relationship to human beings. Although I encountered growing outward skepticism about the *encantados,* the sheer volume of dolphin narratives I recorded attests to these animals' special place within the Amazonian imagination.

All of the assertions that appear here can be found in widely different corners of the Amazon. A number, not surprisingly, are more prevalent in some places than others, and many reveal considerable regional variation. Moreover, although the tales and assertions summarized here are particularly widespread, there are unquestionably countless others of a more local nature that I did not hear.[1]

1. Nineteenth-century British naturalist Henry Walter Bates, for instance, cites reports that blindness would result from the use of dolphin oil for illumination. Although this belief apparently is still common in some rural areas today, I never heard it, nor did anybody suggest to me that *botos* come to the aid of drowning women while *botas* rescue drowning men, or that penned-up dolphins sprout legs and walk away (see Ross Allen and Wilfred T. Neill, "White Whales of the Amazon," p. 327).

Other researchers have documented a small number of human-to-animal metamorphoses. In one narrative from Ecuador, an unfaithful wife and her lover turn themselves into dolphins after the woman's sorcerer-husband discovers her infidelity (see Juan Santos Ortiz de Villalba, *Sacha Pacha,* pp. 49–50). There is also an indigenous Colombian story of a village whose badly behaved inhabitants turn into dolphins in the wake of a great flood that sweeps them away during a great *festa* (Sarita Kendall, personal communication, 14 March 1992). Although I attempted to elicit these sorts of stories, I did not hear a single one.

From the outsider's viewpoint, all of the affirmations outlined here and in the next chapter address the by no means fixed relationship between nature and culture (both themselves, to be sure, social constructs), and define, even while challenging, a particular set of social institutions. For some individuals in some places—above all, shamanic healers in tightly knit and relatively isolated communities—the overarching vision which these beliefs suggest is still clear. Increasingly, however, individual story-tellers are apt to treat the affirmations discussed here not as aspects of a single, cohesive explanation of the universe and human beings' place within it, but rather, as largely unrelated items to be judged on the basis of personal experience. As a result, they often accept some assertions while re-jecting or claiming ignorance of others. Thus, while Tô Pereira sees dol-phins as agents of sorcery, he laughs off the suggestion that they take on the form of men and women in order to dance away the night at country gatherings.

This chapter and the next build on the distinction many storytellers make between the *boto* as an animal with decidedly extraordinary qualities and as an *encantado,* or superhuman entity who moves at will between animal and human form.[2] Although this distinction is common, it is by no means clear-cut, since for a number of people, the *boto* is *both* extraordinary animal and supernatural being.

The two sets of beliefs give rise to different sorts of stories. The great majority of narratives associated with the dolphin-as-fish are either bor-rowed testimony or first-person reminiscences. In contrast, although tales of the dolphin-as-*encantado* may take the form of personal experience nar-ratives, they also include a large number of frequently repeated third-person tales. Often, first-person stories of the Dolphin, as opposed to the dolphin with a small "d," draw directly on these very familiar accounts.

While the stories and beliefs concerning Dolphins often suggest widely common folk motifs, the material in both chapters reflects a complex inter-mingling of influences in which European, African Brazilian, and, above all, Amazonian Indian oral traditions play a central role.[3] Because present-day indigenous parallels to the *encantado* tradition generally have been over-looked or flatly denied by previous scholars, I will emphasize them here. In the end, however, the Dolphin stories form a distinctive, unmistakably

2. For a wider context see Gary Urton, ed., *Animal Myths and Metaphors in South America.* Also useful in terms of a broader theoretical perspective is Stanley J. Tambiah, "Animals Are Good to Think and Good to Prohibit."

3. When I refer to "motifs" here and throughout this discussion, I mean recurring folk narrative themes. The standard Indo-European folk motif index is Stith Thompson, *Motif-Index of Folk Literature.*

Amazonian and thoroughly contemporary corpus. "These accounts must be at least half invention," says a young man selling tape recorders on a street corner in the center of Manaus. "All the same, I like them; they are very much our own" ("De todo jeito, gosto; são um troço muito nosso.")[4]

The ambiguous, often contradictory, and markedly metaphoric nature of many of the propositions that appear here is readily apparent. Thus, while, for instance, the man who insists on the pleasures of dalliance with female Dolphins may well find the idea of sex with an actual *bota* at once intriguing and frightening, he does not necessarily act in any way upon his own claims. "A lot of this talk about dolphins is probably not true," says Gerineldo. "But there is a lot that *could* be true if you really think about it."

O boto vermelho malina da gente; faz a canoa virar e todo mundo morre afogado. Mas o boto tucuxi é o amigo do homem e até salva a gente. ("The *boto* consciously harms us; he capsizes the canoe and everybody drowns. But the *tucuxi* is a friend to people and even saves us [from drowning].")

Over and over, the persons I encountered in my travels insisted on the *boto*'s propensity to willfully inflict harm on human beings. Although the dictionary associates the verb *malinar* with "prankish" or "frolicsome" behavior, the word's darker connotations in popular usage are obvious in the above quotation. Especially in the interior, people complain about the *boto*'s tendency to follow their fishing boats. (Most often, these are small canoes, scooped out of tree trunks, that bear a distinct resemblance to oversize pistachio shells.) Residents of the region accuse these "bad" dolphins of purposely nudging the fragile craft until they capsize. "The *boto* is terrible," says one older woman in the interior of Parintins, as we and several neighbors savor large chunks of watermelon in a lean-to kitchen. "He follows our canoe and doesn't let us be. I knew a man who almost drowned, he and his three children. That big, red *boto* kept on nudging the bottom of that canoe, and by the time he finally vanished, all four of them were trembling like branches in a gale."[5]

The *boto*'s reputedly hostile behavior often finds a counter in the generosity of the *tucuxi,* who is said to guide shipwrecks to land, and who even may return a corpse to a grieving family so that it can receive proper burial. These supposedly beneficent creatures serve as a foil to their perverse red

---

4. Man, age 20, born interior of Manaus, lives Manaus (5 years). Single, sidewalk vendor, schooling unknown. The word *troço*, meaning "piece" or "thing," is urban slang.

5. Woman, age 47, born interior of Parintins (Tracajá), lives Parintins (11 years). Married, teacher's assistant, no formal education.

cousins, and comparisons between the two often preface denunciations of
the latter. The woman quoted below, one of Kátia's country cousins, contrasts the two dolphins by way of introduction to her own account of a
malicious *boto*.[6]

1. And so, you see, the *boto*
        is far worse than the *tucuxi*.

    Look, this happened in the time
        in which there were a lot of Brazil nuts on that island
            people here call *Faz-favor*
    [literally, "If You Please" or "By Your Will"].
    It is quite far from home,
        but I went anyway with my little boy
            —it takes a good five hours to get there.

    So then, we arrived
        and I spent the whole day gathering Brazil nuts
            —good grief, what an abundance!
    There were enough to fill the canoe,
        and then some, there were so many!

    So then, toward the end of the afternoon
        I decided to return home.
    And look, there in the middle of the trip
        that multitude of *botos* appeared.
    I smacked them with my paddle,
        tossed garlic over them,
            called on all the saints.
    So then, they went away, only one remained.

    But this one, ah, he was the very devil,
        he just kept following the canoe.
    My son cried and cried,
        and there I was, with that terrible fear.

---

6. I have divided this story, and those that follow, into lines and stanzas that emphasize
their spoken rhythm. As first pointed out to me by Dell Hymes, stories told by men tend to
fall into three- or five-line stanzas, while those told by women are more likely to form two-
or four-line stanzas. For the Portuguese originals, see Appendix 2. For reasons of space, I
often have chosen shorter stories or pieces of much longer narratives, many of which are
extremely detailed.

Finally, I threw overboard almost all of the Brazil nuts
   in order to row faster.
It really made me feel bad,
   even today it makes me mad!

Now then, the *tucuxi* is much better.
He doesn't torment people in this way.[7]

Because this story, like many others, suggests not only cultural realities but also physical differences between the two Amazonian river dolphins, it is worth commenting briefly on the latter here.[8] *Inia geoffrensis* (the *boto vermelho,* or "red dolphin") is quite different from *Sotalia fluviatilis,* a smaller, generally blue-gray dolphin known in Portuguese as the *boto tucuxi* or simply *tucuxi.*[9] While the latter belongs to the very common *Delphinidae* family also found in seas and oceans, the former is a member of the much rarer, exclusively freshwater, *Iniidae* genus.[10]

---

7. Woman, age 34, born Juruti Velho, lives Zé Açu (8 years). Married, housework and farming, schooling unknown.

8. Freshwater dolphins inhabit lakes and rivers in parts of Peru, Ecuador, Bolivia, Colombia, Venezuela, and the Guianas, as well as Brazil. Some researchers believe that *Inia* entered the Amazon basin from the Pacific before the rise of the Andes, while others suggest a more recent Atlantic origin (see Robin C. Best and Vera M. F. da Silva, "*Inia geoffrensis,*" p. 2). According to G. Pilleri (personal communication, 20 September 1991), the most recent taxonomy includes *Inia geoffrensis* (the Brazilian Amazon *boto*), *Inia geoffrensis humboldtiana* (the Orinoco and Guaviare river dolphin), and *Inia boliviensis* (the *bufeo* of the Beni basin of Bolivia) within the *Iniidae* family. However, not all specialists agree. I thank Dr. Pilleri for his written responses to a number of my questions regarding the possible physical bases for popular beliefs, and Mr. Fernando Rosas of the Instituto Nacional de Pesquisas Amazônicas (INPA), who provided useful information both in a personal interview and subsequent personal communications. I was also fortunate enough to speak at some length with Dr. Vera M. F. da Silva, also of INPA, just as this book was going to press.

9. The masculine form of the word is *boto(s),* the feminine *bota(s).* (*Boto* has been frequently mispelled as *bouto* or *boutu.* The animal is also referred to in Spanish America as the *bufeo* or *tonina.*) The masculine and feminine forms of *tucuxi* are the same, as are the singular and plural. For an introduction to these two types of dolphins see Richard Ellis, *Dolphins and Porpoises,* pp. 23–26 and pp. 55–57. A comprehensive summary of *Inia* with extensive bibliography appears in Best and da Silva, "*Inia geoffrensis.*" See also the numerous articles on *Inia* in the journal *Investigations on Cetacea*. Photographs of both *boto* and *tucuxi* against a regional backdrop appear in Allen and Neill, and in Earl S. Herald, "Bouto and Tookashee: Amazon Dolphins."

10. The *Iniidae,* found exclusively in the Amazon, Orinoco, Guaviare, and Beni rivers, belong in turn to the *Platanistoidea* super family, representatives of which may be found off the Atlantic coast of Uruguay; India's Ganges, Brahmaputra, and Indus rivers; and the Yangtze River in China. Increasingly menaced by human beings, the Amazonian dolphin population has been estimated at anywhere from thousands to tens of thousands.

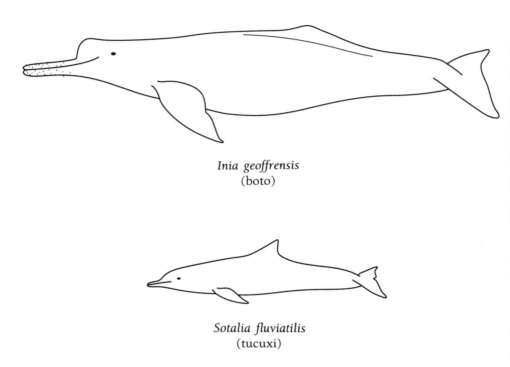

Inia geoffrensis
(boto)

Sotalia fluviatilis
(tucuxi)

The *boto* and the *tucuxi* share a number of features common to all dolphins: an elongated snout or beak, a blowhole for breathing, a dorsal fin or ridge, fins, flukes and a raised "melon" on the head that facilitates the transmission of various clicks, whistles, and barks. Although their olfactory and visual capabilities are minimal, they have excellent hearing and rely heavily on echolocation (a kind of cetacean sonar) to locate fish and crabs. Unable to survive long outside water, they nonetheless must surface regularly in order to exhale and take in a new supply of air. Like other dolphins, they are distinguished by their epimelectic (care-giving) behavior.[11] And yet, at the same time that *botos* and *tucuxi* share various traits

---

11. Dolphin mothers—often with the assistance of other female dolphins, known in Amazônia as "midwives" or *parteiras*—will push the newborn calf to the surface so that it can start breathing. Dolphins of both sexes have been reported to bite free one of their number trapped in a fishing net, to sever harpoon lines, and even to charge a ship. See Melba C. Caldwell and David K. Caldwell, "Epimelectic (Care-Giving) Behavior in Cetacea," for various examples.

common to all dolphins, they are strikingly different in appearance and interact with humans in quite separate ways.

Streamlined and smaller than most adult humans (the biggest animals are usually no more than four and a half feet long), the *tucuxi* resembles Flipper and his fellows.[12] They are thus very different from *botos,* who have long beaks, protruding melons, and broad, paddlelike flippers. (One pair of researchers describes the *boto* as "a beady-eyed, humpbacked, long-snouted, loose-skinned holdover from the past" whose "grapefruit-sized lump perched atop of the head adds nothing to its ridiculous appearance.")[13] In addition to and unlike other platanistids, *botos* have short bristles on their beaks, two types of teeth, and low, boat-keel-shaped dorsal fins.

In further contrast to *tucuxi, botos*—who are the largest of all river dolphins—may grow to an imposing seven or eight feet.[14] They also range in color from off-white or pinkish gray to striking hues of rose. (Exact coloration appears to vary in accord with a range of factors including age, sex, and the water type and temperature.) Although they can send a misty jet of water some eight feet into the air, these animals normally expose only a portion of their bodies when they surface and are given to less spectacular, near-horizontal dives that lead native observers to describe the *tucuxi* as *engraçado* ("amusing") and *brincalhão* ("playful").

The social behavior of *botos* and *tucuxi* also presents striking contrasts. Because, like most cetacea, the latter's vertebrae are partially fused, these animals have little ability to maneuver in shallow areas, and thus, customarily prefer the river's center to its margins. Extremely group-oriented, *tucuxi* regularly fish together in schools of eight to twenty. Although they participate in similar dolphin courtship displays, they, unlike *botos,* appear to go through periods of reproductive inactivity.[15]

12. Ellis (p. 56) notes that *tucuxi* are actually one of the smallest cetaceans, reaching a maximum of about five and a half feet and a weight of 100 pounds.

13. Melba C. Caldwell and David K. Caldwell, "The Ugly Dolphin," p. 309. The authors go on to refer to the *boto* as a "biological Model T."

14. This is almost double the length of an adult *tucuxi.* Allen and Neill report the presence of nine-foot *botos* (*bufeos*) near Leticia, Colombia.

15. These displays include successive stages of "high-speed chasing, crisscross swimming, demonstration of the ventral field, rubbing of different body regions of the partner with the snout and fins, leaping out of the water, head-butting, and copulation" (N. L. Krushinskaya, "The Behavior of Cetaceans," p. 154). Best and da Silva report that sexual foreplay "is apparently initiated by the male nibbling the female's flippers and flukes" ("*Inia geoffrensis,*" p. 4). According to Fernando Rosas (interview, 28 August 1990), courtship activities may also include a rhythmic slapping by the male with beak or tale against the female's vagina to facilitate ensuing penile penetration. For a comparison of *boto* and *tucuxi* reproductive behavior see Robin C. Best and Vera M. F. da Silva, "Preliminary Analysis of Reproductive Parame-

Because, unlike most other cetacea, the *boto*'s vertebrae are not fused, it can move its neck and head with ease and swim in shallow reaches where *tucuxi* rarely appear. Despite its weight and size, it is therefore extremely maneuverable. Particularly at dawn and toward dusk, *botos* frequent the river's margins and those rivulets and flooded woodlands where fish feed on seeds and fruit that fall from inundated trees.[16] Far more solitary than the gregarious *tucuxi, botos* tend to appear alone or with a single companion.[17] They are also more aggressively curious than their mild-mannered cousins and have been reported to toss objects and even animals—such as sea turtles—into the air in a playful, exploratory fashion.[18]

One can readily see how the *boto*'s unusual appearance might occasion suspicion and discomfort. Its peculiarly shaped head and often reddish hue ("the devil's color," points out Gerineldo's mother) lead people to attribute unsavory motives to them more readily than to their smaller, less obtrusive, and frankly cuter counterparts. Then too, *botos*' ability to navigate shallow waters makes them more apt to come in contact with human beings. Thus, nineteenth-century explorer Alexander von Humboldt reports how "a herd" of *botos* surprised him in a sunken meadow.[19]

Botos' curious nature, coupled with their size and penchant for physical contact, makes it easy to imagine they *could* tip over a fragile canoe. (They "often greet boats with a curious nudge, and may investigate swimmers

---

ters of the Boutu, *Inia geoffrensis,* and the Tucuxi, *Sotalia fluviatilis,* in the Amazon River System." See also the sections on dolphin sexual behavior in Karen Pryor and Kenneth S. Norris, eds., *Dolphin Societies.*

16. James N. Layne surmises that the *boto*'s apparent preference for these times may have something to do with water temperature ("Observations on the Freshwater Porpoises in the Upper Amazon," p. 17).

17. Well over half of the sightings of *botos* reported by Layne in the upper Amazon involve unaccompanied animals, and in no case did he encounter groups of more than a half-dozen ("Observations," p. 18).

18. Despite its ungainly, even primitive appearance, the *boto*'s high cephalization ratio—a calculation based on the relationship between body length and weight to body weight and brain weight—puts it in the company of the notably intelligent bottlenose dolphin and killer whale. (See M. Gihr and G. Pilleri, "Interspecific Body Length–Body Weight Ratio and Body Weight–Brain Weight Ratio in Cetacea.") Da Silva reports seeing dolphins toss up the sea turtles (personal communication, 5 June 1993).

19. When Humboldt's Indian guides began to cut down the branches blocking the boat's passage, the animals, who had been hiding under the branches of a silk cotton (kapok) tree, "went off through the forest squirting into the air the jets of water and compressed air which in all languages have earned them the name of blowfish." See G. Pilleri, "Alexander von Humboldt (1769–1859) and the *Inia* of the Rio Orinoco," p. 119. If the sight of these animals startled the adventurous Humboldt, one can appreciate the reaction of a lone fisherman to a dolphin who emerges from seemingly nowhere to "walk" across the mud.

from nearby.")[20] The competition between humans and *botos* for fish at the river's margins fuels doubts and suspicions about these odd-looking creatures.

That *tucuxi* seldom intrude on human fishing grounds, and that they are smaller, less aggressive, and less remarkable in terms of appearance, help explain why people find them less threatening than *botos*. Thus, although both sorts of Amazonian dolphin exhibit care-giving behavior, storytellers credit the *tucuxi* alone with this willingness to lend assistance.

In its propensity to aid those in trouble, the *tucuxi* resembles dolphins in many different times and places.[21] However, while other traditions may have enhanced and partially transformed certain attitudes toward dolphins, the belief in *botos*' malevolence and the firm division between them and *tucuxi* appear to be uniquely Amazonian.

One can appreciate how the occupants of fragile craft might be leery of an inquisitive *boto*. Nevertheless, these animals' supposed propensity to capsize canoes does not explain the degree of hostility, if not outright terror, they evoke. Although storytellers themselves often have no awareness of any indigenous heritage (and, indeed, may have no Amerindian blood), their reaction recalls notions of Aquatic Seducers still operative among various contemporary Amazonian (and, in some cases, Caribbean and eastern Andean) Indian groups.

Extremely powerful beings that link the skies and waters, Aquatic Seducers are embodiments of cosmic forces which possess a blatantly sexual dimension.[22] The quintessential Aquatic Seducer is the anaconda, who "rains upward" during mating season when the female slaps her tail upon the water as a summons to the male. The "nexus of several distinct properties: excessive sexual desire, unreasonable attraction, and shamanistic power, the mythic Anaconda is sexually ambivalent (the prototypical Fish Woman is at once the anaconda and the anaconda's daughter)."[23] As the mythical shaman and, often, primal human ancestor, the anaconda "repre-

20. Layne, "Observations," p. 17.

21. The Greeks had numerous stories in which dolphins save drowning people out of gratitude to the god Dionysus. A well-known Chinese legend tells of how one of these "wind worshipers" rescues a drowning princess; and in Christian lore, a dolphin transports the body of the martyr Lucian the Syrian. For a consideration of the dolphin in classical antiquity see Anthony Alpers, *Dolphins*, pp. 3–36. For Chinese legends see G. Pilleri, "The Chinese River Dolphin (*Lipotes vexillifer*) in Poetry, Literature, and Legend." The Saint Lucian story appears in E. Cobham Brewer, *A Dictionary of Miracles*, p. 31.

22. Peter G. Roe discusses Aquatic Seducers at length in *The Cosmic Zygote*. For examples of contemporary South American Indian stories in which these creatures impregnate human women see Aurelio Chumap Lucía and Manuel García-Rendueles, "*Duik múun . . .*," vol. 1, pp. 443–55; and Juan Santos Ortiz de Villalba, *Sacha Pacha*, pp. 46–48.

23. Santos Ortiz de Villalba, *Sacha Pacha*, p. 159.

sents the ultimate source of the powers used to manipulate human senti-
ments and physical well-being."[24]

Particularly likely to take the form of water serpents, Aquatic Seducers
also may appear as numerous other aquatic creatures, such as the caiman,
the piranha, the stingray—and the dolphin.[25] In one Aguaruna story of a
jealous wife who tries to kill the snake-woman who has come to occupy
her husband's affections, the snake-woman's mother retaliates by sending
to earth the "terrible animals who obey her orders: the boa constrictors,
lizards, and dolphins."[26] Among the Shipibo-Conibo, the dolphin is believed to cause sickness by commanding the parasitic fish that normally
affix themselves to his skin to move into the human bloodstream.[27]

It is not hard to see why river-dwelling people might be afraid of a
twenty-foot-long snake that gulps down chickens, dogs, and even cows.
The dolphin, however, inspires fear largely because of its anomalous qualities (a "fish" that gives live birth and is deemed inedible) and its everyday
association with the river, which both engenders and destroys. One writer
suggests that the dolphin's exhalation may have reminded some indigenous
peoples of the sorcerer who blows magical darts across great distances into
his victims' bodies.[28] And yet, even native groups who do not have this
practice—and who, indeed, may have no direct contact with dolphins—
often fear them.[29]

Not one of the storytellers I recorded identified the dolphin's father as
the anaconda. Nonetheless, the insistent presentation of these animals as
ostentatiously sexual beings recalls indigenous tradition. So does the often
contrastive, ultimately complementary relationship between *boto* and
tucuxi.

24. Michael F. Brown, *Tsewa's Gift*, p. 159.

25. Lévi-Strauss has noted that in Guiana and throughout most of the Amazon, Aquatic
Seducers, whether male or female, "often take the form of a cetacean, usually the *boto*, or
white Amazonian dolphin (*Inia geoffrensis*)" (Claude Lévi-Strauss, *From Honey to Ashes*, p.
200).

26. See "Tsunki, la sirena del Alto Marañón" in José Luís Jordana Laguna, *Mitos e historias
aguarunas*, p. 50. Another version of the story appears in Chumap Lucía and García-Rendueles,
"*Duik múun* . . . ," vol. 2, pp. 651–53.

27. Angelika Gebhart-Sayer, *Die Spitze des Bewuβtseins*, pp. 318–19. These little fish are
likely to induce pregnancy in women.

28. Rafael Karsten, *Studies in the Religion of the South American Indians East of the Andes*,
p. 58.

29. Although, for instance, the Aguaruna have had few first-hand encounters with dolphins (which are found only downstream in the larger Amazonian tributaries), they nonetheless insist that these animals tip canoes, particularly those in which there is a pregnant woman,
in order "to deliver the woman and the fetus to the dolphin's father, the anaconda" (Michael
F. Brown, *Tsewa's Gift*, p. 156).

Although a similar bi-partite impulse can be found in many different cultures, it finds its own particular expression in native South American concepts of the Magical Twins. Literally as different as night and day, these entities are identified as Sun and Moon in many indigenous cosmologies. And yet, despite their diametrically opposing temperaments, the two remain brothers "born of a single womb." Their resulting complementarity and ultimate unity make the dualistic principle they embody quite different from Christian ideas of God and Lucifer, who is not the Creator's complement or negative double, but rather, a fallen underling. That contemporary storytellers often alternate between notions of the *boto* as necessary complement to the *tucuxi* and as diabolic double suggests a meshing of traditions in which both are transformed.

O boto fica com raiva da mulher menstruada. Se tiver uma mulher menstruada dentro da canoa, ele sempre vai atrás. ("The *boto* is angered by a menstruating woman. If there is a menstruating woman in the boat, he inevitably pursues it.")

Men, as well as women, are apt to insist that *botos* (and, occasionally, *tucuxi* as well) are acutely sensitive to, and abhor the smell of, menstrual blood. "This problem of the menstrual period," Dona Marina explains, "was a very serious problem for women in the past. A [menstruating] woman didn't appear in the fields, the kitchen, the river's edge; she remained seated in one place, making a special lace called 'labyrinth,' for an entire week."

Alzira can remember how she herself used to remain at home for "eight long days," taking meager baths in a pail of water brought by others from the river and abstaining from a wide variety of foods. ("I hated every minute!" she declares.) Likewise, Kátia's mother recalls the terror she felt on those occasions in which she found herself obliged to go down to the riverbank during her period. "The dishes had to be washed, the clothes were dirty, and I was the only one at home to take care of them, but still I was afraid," she says. "I didn't raise my daughters in this manner, but it was the way my mother raised me and, even today, I don't like to be alone there by the river."

Though strongest in the interior and among illiterate or semiliterate people, the belief that dolphins with a small "d" are at once attracted to, and repelled by, the odor of menstrual blood appears as well among the residents of cities, some of whom have had considerable formal education. The very first time I went out on the Amazon, the boat in which I was traveling got stuck in the mud. The two men in the party—Maurício and his uncle—jumped overboard and tried to scrape a rope beneath the bottom in an attempt to dislodge the craft. When they were unsuccessful, they asked me and another woman, also in a bathing suit, for help. As all four of us fumbled about in the mud, the third woman, Maurício's sister, who had remained on board, motioned me over to her. "You aren't 'sick' are you?" she asked in a worried tone. In the moment, I did not fully understand the question, let alone the motives for her concern. Only later, when Maurício commented in a teasing manner on the presence of a large number of dolphins about the unmoving boat did I comprehend the source of her unease. ("Which one of you called all those *botos,* eh?" he asked the three women.) When I then expressed doubt about dolphins' ability to discern the presence of a menstruating woman, both he and the others gave numerous examples in support of his contention. ("It doesn't seem possible," his sister agreed with a nervous laugh, "and yet, there is no other explanation.")

Another incident that suggests the lingering force of the belief that dolphins actively pursue menstruating women occurred during a trip I took to Zé Açu, a small rural community about an hour by boat from Parintins. The occasion was a local folklore competition modeled on the *Boi-Bumbá* festival of Parintins. One side was clearly smaller than the other and thus at a disadvantage. "Why isn't your team bigger?" I asked a teenage girl. Because I was expecting to hear that her friends had discovered better, more modern ways to spend their time, her answer doubly surprised me. "Our team *was* bigger," she replied. "A lot of my girlfriends had made all the preparations. We'd worked really hard for weeks and were all set to win. But at the last minute, half of them got "sick" and couldn't come. We got bunches of chili pepper and made crosses of garlic to take with us to keep away the dolphins, but they still felt afraid and so only half of us are here."[30]

The belief that *botos* react violently to menstrual odors appears to have no basis whatsoever in fact. As already noted, dolphins in general have poorly developed olfactory abilities, and would thus be unlikely to perceive a menstruating woman's presence in the water, let alone in a boat. If, however, these insistences have no scientific basis, they again suggest native Amazonian parallels. Although menstrual taboos can be found in many cultures, present-day indigenous ideas of menstruation as a dangerous, liminal state recall Aquatic Seducers' propensity to impregnate those women who dare to pollute their watery domain. Among the Peruvian Shipibo, for instance, filth "is identified with females through menstruation" and a woman is particularly susceptible to the boto's sexual molestations during this "bad time of the moon."[31] For this reason, Shipibo and

30. Woman, age 16, born interior of Parintins. Single, helps parents in home and fields, 6 years school. 26 June 1989.
31. Roe, *The Cosmic Zygote,* p. 243.

other Panoan group women refuse to bathe in lakes or rivers when they are menstruating.[32]

Various South American Indian mythologies speak of a subterranean-subaquatic lunar phallus, whose presence is particularly inimical to women during their periods.[33] The Barasana in particular recount a number of stories in which menstruation is a punishment for various misdeeds by the Poison Anaconda's daughter.[34] And in the Yekuana story of Medatia, the water spirits called *mawadi* go crazy for menstrual blood.[35] Although I encountered no trace of these particular myths among the storytellers I recorded, their insistence on dolphins' horror of menstruation suggests the potential influence of non-European beliefs and taboos.

O boto não gosta de pimenta malagueta, de tabaco ou de farinha. Para afastar ele, a gente coloca uma cruz de alho na porta. Também pode botar uma faca na água e ele vai embora. ("*Botos* don't like chili pepper, tobacco, or manioc flour. To scare them off, a person places a cross of garlic on the door. One can also run a knife through the water and they will go away.")

Many people believe that certain substances will dissuade an intrusive dolphin. Chief among these are garlic and chili pepper, both of which are said to burn the dolphin's nostrils. Thus, in an account that Kátia's mother-in-law offers of her vanished brother's return from the *Encante,* her other brother tries to ward off the dolphins who accompany his visitor with garlic crosses. ("He put a cross on every door and every window," she explains, "nine crosses. And yet still those *botos* kept coming; they saw the cross but didn't stop.")

Tobacco smoke is thought to be similarly irritating to dolphins. ("That's why he [the Dolphin spirit] comes when the healer starts in with his *tauari*

---

32. By way of explanation for this behavior, the Shipibo recount how a woman crossing the river on the back of a giant water serpent begins menstruating, thereby soiling the snake-bridge, which recoils in anger (ibid., p. 120). In a personal communication (26 July 1990), Roe points out that "the boa (*Rohin ehua*) is angered by the menstrual blood *because he caused it.*" "Based on regional Panoan and Arawkan myths," he says, "one might argue that the Boa is the father of the Fish Woman, whose incest with her caused the first menstrual flow. He is also the Moon with an ambulatory, sub-aquatic phallus" so that the Boa "'homes in' on his daughter's menstrual blood."

33. Roe notes that the Shipibos' association between the moon and the anaconda is itself reminiscent of the Barasana people's contention that the sky-day anaconda lives in the roof of the moon's house, and the River Campa Indians' portrayal of an underwater lunar phallus.

34. See Stephen Hugh-Jones, *The Palm and the Pleiades,* pp. 127–28, 178–80, and 198–99; and Christine Hugh-Jones, *From the Milk River,* pp. 137–42.

35. Marc de Civrieux, "Medatia." F. Tagliavini and G. Pilleri report similar folk taboos in present-day Ecuador in "Occasional Observations," p. 68.

cigars," says Argemiro. "He smells the smoke and cannot rest.") People also may claim that raw tobacco effectively clogs the blowhole, threatening the dolphin's air supply. Some individuals are quick to dismiss these claims as nonsense. ("How could you get near enough a dolphin to stop up his blowhole?" asks Kátia's grandmother, Dona Rosinha. "Why, an animal like that is not going to just stand there while someone dumps a sack of flour on his head!") Gerineldo's mother, however, asserts that the *boto* will flee upon hearing a knife tip drawn along the bottom of a boat. His father says that it is better to trail the blade through the water. ("I have tried this and it works," he declares authoritatively.)

Botos' reported aversion to these prophylactics appears to have little or no basis in fact. Any cetacean almost certainly would attempt to escape the insertion of a foreign substance into its blowhole or the application of an irritating substance to its mucous membranes. Nevertheless, as Kátia's grandmother suggests, a person would have to get very close to one of these moving targets in order to effect any sort of direct hit. While a scraping noise might frighten an animal who had had prior encounters with fishermen, the knife's metallic gleam would be unlikely to scare off these notably nearsighted animals.

The use of sharp-smelling substances to repel supernatural entities recalls medieval Europe, where persons often employed garlic as protection against vampires. In addition, tobacco smoke occupies a central role in both indigenous and African Brazilian religious rituals where healers use it to "smoke out" and purify the body.[36] Thus, the *pajé* blows tobacco smoke over the body of Tô Pereira in order to undo the effects of a powerful *feitiço,* and Maurício's uncle employs both tobacco smoke and herbal baths to retrieve his *sombra* from the Dolphin. As chili peppers create a burning sensation, and tobacco actually burns when ignited, all three are associated with hot or cooked (that is, cultural), as opposed to raw (natural) entities.[37] Various native Amazonian peoples use chili peppers to ward off evil spirits because of their purifying and deodorizing properties, and the smell of pepper smoke is said to recall that of menstrual blood.

Manioc, for its part, is Amazônia's single most important food crop. Particularly in the interior, fish and manioc derivatives provide the basis for most people's daily diet. Poisonous in its natural state, the raw root

36. See Lévi-Strauss on the dialogue between honey and tobacco in *From Honey to Ashes,* pp. 51–68. Although in the stories under consideration, tobacco inevitably repels the *encantados* (or, in the case of shamanic healers, goads them into action), it has a long history of propitiatory use (see Johannes Wilbert, *Tobacco and Shamanism in South America*).

37. Here, I am following the logic of Claude Lévi-Strauss as set forth in his *The Raw and the Cooked.*

must go through an elaborate process that transforms it into a golden, grainy flour. Thus, while the reliance on manioc to ward off dolphins has a practical aspect (the flour conceivably could block the blowhole), it is above all a statement of humans' ability to modify their surroundings, and thus, an assertion of the power of culture over the dolphin's animal nature.

A similar logic almost certainly underlies the use of knives to scare off *botos*. Fashioned of steel, itself a manufactured product, these implements regularly serve to transform natural substances (above all, wood into harpoons and other fishing implements), as well as to kill and skin animals. Although knives are primarily associated with men, women also use them in transformative activities such as gardening and preparing fish for cooking. In a double insistence on the power of cultural institutions, people also may attempt to scare off dolphins by carving the sign of the cross into the air.

O boto sabe das coisas antes delas acontecer(em) muitas vezes. É difícil pegar ele, pois é muito esperto. ("*Botos* often know things before they happen. It is hard to catch them because they are very clever.")

"Just as *botos* possess a sixth finger, so they possess a sixth sense that lets them read people's thoughts," asserts Tô Pereira. (He and a number of other people insist that *botos,* much like particularly powerful shamans, possess six fingers.) This dolphin telepathy explains why these animals are so hard to catch with traditional fishing techniques. Although most residents of Amazônia consider dolphin meat to be fatty and foul-smelling, fishermen sometimes retaliate against those animals who tear their nets, and a man also may hunt down a particular dolphin whom he believes is persecuting either himself or a female family member. However, it takes skill and luck to catch one of these animals. "The *boto* foresees things," one old fisherman from the interior of Óbidos explains to me and a group of male companions as we await a boat's arrival. "He has an air of magic about him. I don't know how to explain it. I have passed the entire night, half dead with sleep, waiting for him to show up, and he never came."[38]

The seeming ability of dolphins to read minds, or, at least, to react very rapidly in order to evade harm or capture, definitely has some basis in fact. Research has documented their ability to store information and to learn by association, as well as to respond to potentially threatening human behaviors with appropriate defensive action. In addition, dolphins' special abilities have long been apparent to people in many cultures. The Greeks and Romans spoke admiringly of them, and in Hindu tradition they serve as

38. Man, age 72, born interior of Óbidos. Married, fisherman, no formal education.

73

steeds of the deity Kama.[39] The commonly used adjective *esperto,* however, has connotations of wiliness, trickiness, and even roguery conspicuously absent from these other traditions—recall Dona Marina's use of the term to describe the bosses who exploit jute workers. Thus, even though she and others express admiration and astonishment at the speed of these animals' reactions, her profound distrust of dolphins would have shocked those classical authors who revered them as reincarnations of the human soul. Dona Marina, for her part, was frankly scandalized by my assertion that the dolphin has frequently served as a symbol of Christ. "But not here!" she told me firmly. "Only in some other place!"[40]

The *boto*'s *esperteza* is often linked to other extraordinary qualities, above all, the ability to command human attention. "The *boto* has a kind of magnetism," explains Maurício. "One has to look at him, even if one doesn't want to." Alzira remembers how, as a child, she would sneak down to the riverbank to watch the dolphins despite her mother's prohibitions. ("I was scared," she says, "but they were so much fun to watch that I couldn't stay away.") Likewise, a teenage girl in Terra Santa finds dolphins both beautiful and frightening. "They know when we are paying attention to them and jump even higher," she says, smoothing out the bunched material in the exuberantly flowered skirt she is mending. *"It's as if they knew what we were thinking even before we do."*[41]

O boto é o dono das águas. ("*Botos* are the owners of the waters.")

Storytellers often claim that dolphins use their remarkable abilities to protect and preserve their less powerful fellows. On the Juruá River, for instance, many people affirm the *boto*'s special relationship to the manatee or sea cow, who has effectively vanished from the Parintins area, and much of Amazônia. Anecdotal evidence accompanies many of these assertions. "The *boto* protects and always accompanies the manatee," says one story-teller. "When the fisherman appears, the *boto* sounds the alarm."[42] He goes on to recall the time in which he was just about to harpoon a particularly plump manatee when a *boto* "whistled like a policeman," causing that day's lunch to flee.

39. Gertrude Jobes, *Dictionary of Mythology, Folklore, and Symbol,* vol. 1, p. 460.

40. Symbol of Apollo as well as of Christ, dolphins have been sacred to deities in various religious traditions. Early Christian artists used them to signify "diligence, love, and swiftness," and they later served as a heraldic emblem of "charity and kind affection toward children." (See ibid., p. 459.)

41. Woman, age 16, Terra Santa. Single, student, 5 years school.

42. Man, age 34, born interior of Eirunepe, lives Carauari (4 years). Married, fisherman, no formal education.

People's tendency to pair the dolphin with the manatee may reflect these animals' tendency to seek out food in similar places. While *botos* regularly fish in shallow waters and sunken woodlands, manatees feed on the grassy vegetation called *canarana* that fringes the flood plain, and both are likely to feed close to shore during the winter rains. Dolphins' speed and agility in relation to their decidedly somnolent fellow mammal encourage human observers to assign them a more active, tutelary role. Fishermen, who hunt the manatee for its much-prized meat, are particularly apt to link the two. "Look," says one, "the dolphin plays the devil with us. Because the fisherman does his best to harpoon the manatee and he [the dolphin] puts himself right in the middle. It seems he takes pleasure in making trouble for us, that he actually wants us to go hungry."[43]

Although probably the *boto*'s most commonly identified charge, the manatee is not alone in this role. People may insist that *botos* "take care of" the river and river beings, functioning much as an underwater watchman or *vigia*. This protective stance is not unusual for dolphins, whom classical mythology portrays as humans' friends and allies. Greek tradition is full of stories of dolphins who demonstrate a special affection for young boys, and a Chinese story tells of a pair of dolphins who carry the poet Li Tai-Pe up to heaven after he drowns.[44] And yet, while such tales reinforce the notion of the dolphin as a sort of aquatic guardian angel, they stand in contrast to contemporary Amazonian accounts which cast dolphins as the guardians of other animals pursued by human hunters.

The *boto*'s particular brand of stewardship recalls widespread, if often considerably more abstract native Amazonian notions of the Master of Animals (*Vai mahsë*).[45] The Portuguese word *dono* literally means "owner." (Thus, the respectful address, *dona*, for women, carries the idea that the person being addressed is the figurative, if not literal, owner of a home.) But when storytellers insist that "Tudo tem dono" ("Everything has an owner") or, synonymously, "Tudo tem mãe" ("Everything has a mother"),

43. Man, age 49, interior of Juruá, lives Carauari (5 years). Married, fisherman, no formal education. The man says that the dolphin "pinta o sete com a gente" or "paints the seven with us," seven being a number with diabolical associations.

44. See Herodotos for the story of how a dolphin saves the poet, Arion of Lesbos, when a group of Cretan sailors toss him overboard (*Histories* 1.23–24). In the Chinese story, the poet gets drunk and tries to embrace the moon's reflection (Pilleri, "The Chinese River Dolphin," pp. 343–44).

45. Gerardo Reichel-Dolmatoff finds "no similarities whatsoever between the *encantados* and *Vai mahsë*" because of the latter's fluid, nonpersonifiable nature. "He [the *Vai mahsë*] may appear in many guises," he states, "all of which are related to phallic concepts, but above all, *Vai mahsë* is an abstract concept. He is, in all essence, a Master of Game and a Master of Fish, as the case may be." (Personal communication, 10 October 90.)

they are referring less to the possession of material goods than to a position of responsibility in a cosmic chain of command. As such, the word carries a moral as well as a proprietary force.[46]

Not unlike the Animal Masters, the owner or the mother in the Dolphin stories is responsible for all living creatures inhabiting the area under its control. Fishermen and hunters are expected to ask permission of the forest's or the water's owner before they kill fish or game, and are prohibited from taking more than they and their families need.[47] ("Every time I hunted game to sell, I would come down with a fever the next day," a former rubber worker explains as we and his young wife watch a group of adolescent boys kick a soccer ball about the muddy street. "I needed the money, but the forest owner [*mãe da mata*] persecuted me until I finally stopped.")[48]

Even if a person does no more than gulp down a few swallows from a lake or river, he or she should first seek permission of its *dono*. "I always say, 'My mother, I am thirsty, please let me have a little of your water,' before I drink from a spring in the forest," a ten-year-old girl from the interior of Parintins explains shyly when I ask.[49]

Although *donos*, like Animal Masters, generally accede to properly deferential requests by humans, they resist unauthorized inroads on their domain. Thus, Argemiro's cousin describes the fevers and nightmares he suffers after he harpoons a female dolphin. Although he denies the *bota*'s supernatural identity and ignores his wife's urgings that he see a shamanic healer ("I, for one, just don't believe in these sorts of superstitions"), he admits to feeling very much afraid.

> 2. It's going on three years now
>   that I was there on that lake, Remanso Grande,
>   when this *bota* appeared before me.
> She wouldn't keep away from the canoe.
> So then, I got angry and harpooned her,
>   because she was bothering me, you see?

46. Significantly, although the noun *mãe* is always feminine in Portuguese, the mothers of animals and other natural entities (bodies of water or entire forests, for instance) may be either masculine or feminine. Thus, a storyteller can easily identify a male *encantado* as the mother of a particular location, and the literal translation of an assertion such as "Esse bicho, ele é a mãe daquele lago" would be "That creature, he is the mother of that lake."

47. The obvious ecological aspects of these beliefs are discussed in Gerardo Reichel-Dolmatoff, "Cosmology as Ecological Analysis."

48. Man, age 53, born interior of Rio Branco (Acre), lives Seringal Cupuaí (Amazonas, 6 years). Married, rubber tapper, no formal education.

49. Girl, age 10, born interior of Parintins (Zé Açu). Single, student, 3 years school.

Good grief, that night there were so many dolphins!
They kept on surfacing to breathe,
    it wasn't possible to sleep.
And when, finally, I dozed off, she appeared in my dream
    and said that she was never going to let me be.

I passed three nights like that,
    can you imagine?
My wife wanted me to see
    one of these types who smokes *tauari*.
But I didn't want to
    —I think it's superstition,
        because the *bota* is just an animal,
            don't you agree?

But I have to tell you,
    I was afraid,
        really afraid!
Finally, I took some tobacco and threw it,
    —like this—
        on the water [he demonstrates].
And she went away.
    She never showed up in these parts again,
        thank God![50]

A belief in powerful aquatic entities appears in many different cultures. The dolphin's role as guardian finds parallels, and probably partial roots, in European and African beliefs.[51] At the same time, however, the notion of the dolphin as *dono* of the manatee suggests a chain of ideas more specifically associated with native Amazonian notions of reciprocity.[52] Their identity as owners of the river not only reaffirms the difference

50. Man, age 44, Ilha das Onças. Married, fisherman, no formal education.
51. Although, for instance, the North African Iemanjá, Bantu Kianda of Loanda, and Kiximbi of Mbaka are not animals, but rather, water spirits who receive offerings of food from humans, they may exercise a similar protective function.
52. The Master of Animals sends his charges to be caught by human hunters, whose shamans must then propitiate his loss in order to assure an ongoing supply of game. Guss observes that the Venezuelan *encantados,* "even though their roles have been greatly altered, are still clearly designated as the masters of animals" and that older persons "continue to assert that if you wish to hunt a certain animal it is necessary to ask the encantados' permission, and that if you abuse the animals you will be punished" ("The Encantados," p. 243).

between *botos* and other animals, but also provides a ready motive for their perceived hostility toward humans.

Quem mata um boto, muitas vezes fica panema. Não mata mais nada, só fica bom na mão do curador. ("The person who kills a *boto* often becomes *panema*. He doesn't succeed in killing anything else [any more fish or game], and is only restored to health by a *curador*.")

Given the *boto*'s privileged identity as an aquatic steward, to kill or even wound one of these animals is to invite trouble. Although a fisherman may confront a *boto* with impunity on one occasion, the same action may have grave consequences on another. There is no way of gauging the outcome beforehand, or of effectively distinguishing a Dolphin from its dolphin look-alikes.

The Amazonian Indian term *panema,* often defined as "lack of luck" or "misfortune," indicates not simply occasional infelicity, but rather, "a temporary incapacity that afflicts the individual or object, a process whose causes and symptoms can be determined and are known."[53] A man may become *panema* in relation to women, and the term may also indicate a general condition. ("Fiquei panema da vida," "I became unlucky in life," a person may say.) Most often, however, the word applies specifically to a man's capacity to hunt or fish. (As women generally do not engage in these activities, they do not become *panema* and cannot partake of its happy opposite, *fama*.) Sometimes, an individual becomes *panema* in relation to a particular kind of fish or game. On other occasions, he becomes unable to kill game of any type.

A man can incur *panema* for many different reasons. An envious neighbor can devise a debilitating *feitiço,* or a menstruating or pregnant woman can contaminate his hunting or fishing implements. Improper disposal of animal remains will also trigger this condition. In addition, *panema* may be the result of hunting too much of one species or of killing an animal considered to be inedible—such as a *boto.*

Prohibitions against killing dolphins exist in various traditions, including the native Amazonian.[54] Contemporary groups such as the Tupi-Kagwahiv and Shipibo refrain from injuring these creatures out of fear of reprisal not just against themselves, but also the community at large. Thus, one writer describes a Shipibo curing session involving the infant brother

---

53. Eduardo Galvão, "Panema," p. 59. For a quite different approach to the phenomenon see Roberto da Matta, "Panema."

54. The Greeks treated offenders the same way as any assassin, and sailors in the Red Sea "believed that disaster would come to them if they wounded a dolphin" (Jobes, vol. 1, p. 459). At least one of the early emperors of India also forbade the killing of dolphins (G. Pilleri, "Indian River Dolphins").

of a young fisherman who had accidentally harpooned a dolphin.[55] Although the storytellers I recorded offered an array of reasons for not harming *botos,* virtually all concurred that killing one was to invite trouble.

O boto pode ajudar o pescador; arruma muito peixe para ele. ("*Botos* can help the fisherman; they round up lots of fish for him.")

In apparently direct contradiction to foregoing assertions about the *boto*'s dangerous, when not unabashedly malevolent, nature, some fishermen speak enthusiastically of specific dolphins' benefit to them and their fellows. "When it is summer and there are beaches everywhere, we go fishing with the *boto,*" explains one older man in Faro. "All we have to do is light the lantern and he comes to help us like a hunting dog. Yes, this big red dolphin, he brings in a lot of fish."[56]

Almost all those fishermen I encountered who consider dolphins as potential allies work with the implements traditionally employed by small-scale fishing boats along the river's margins, rather than with the giant drift or gill nets (*malhadeiras*) favored by larger commercial fishing boats. Unlike the bow and arrow, the harpoonlike *zagaia,* and the smaller, artisanal sweep net (the *tarrafa* Alzira learned to use while still a child), the drift nets are used in deep water, while these other implements are reserved for clear, shallow waters, and are most employed on rainless, moonlit nights.

Several of the men with whom I spoke said they summoned particular *botos* through the use of individualized whistles.[57] Not only did they insist on their ability to pick out "their" dolphins from others based on such factors as size, color, and markings on the dorsal ridge, but they also referred to these animals by proper names such as "Juvenal," "Margarida," or "Daniel." The men were quick to demonstrate their distinctive whistles ("two long tweets and then a trill, like this, you see?") and to describe their dolphins in considerable detail. They also reported that fishermen occasionally try to lure away each other's dolphins, and that such thefts trigger violent altercations. ("Better slash a net than steal a dolphin," several men asserted with considerable feeling.)

Statements regarding helpful *botos* find support in a wide variety of

55. Roe, *The Cosmic Zygote,* p. 168.

56. Man, age 63, Faro. Married, fisherman and farmer, no formal education. The speaker uses the lovely expression "quando está tudo praiado," which literally means "when everything is beached" [that is, become beach].

57. Dolphins themselves are known to have individual "signature whistles." I personally witnessed fishermen apparently summon two *botos* with whistles in the community of Igarapé Açu, interior of Parintins. To be sure, the animals also may have been responding to the disruption of the waters caused by the boat.

quarters.[58] Aelian and both Pliny the Elder and Pliny the Younger describe how dolphins fish in partnership with humans.[59] Dolphins in China, Burma, India, and Australia provide similar fishing assistance, and a much-cited report from the Amazonian Tapajós describes a fisherman summoning a *boto* by whistling and knocking on the side of the canoe.[60] The dolphin then drives back the fish that scatter before the approaching boat.

Although the dolphin is interested in fish, rather than in helping fishermen (the disruption of the waters results in a bigger catch), it is easy to see how some people might interpret a helpful motive from their actions. The *botos'* perceived willingness to form alliances with fishermen, however, is hardly of one piece with previous insistences on these animals' innate malevolence. This apparent discrepancy underscores a sense of dolphins as supremely ambiguous beings. Aggressive on some occasions, these owners of the waters can be persuaded on other occasions to share their bounty. It is in their power to help as well as harm humans; all depends on whether they can be cajoled and propitiated, if not by the blandishments of powerful shamanic healers, then by a familiar whistle and a generous stack of fish.

When I asked people how the same animal could exhibit such blatantly contradictory behavior, they responded that many human beings display similarly conflicting tendencies. ("Who is always good or always bad?" Tô Pereira demanded when I asked about the *boto*.) They also asserted that everything depends on the individual dolphin—again, like humans, some are altruistic, and some ill-intentioned. Other persons explained that while dolphins who are strictly animals (*boto mesmo*) may serve as human allies, those who are supernatural beings in dolphin form (*boto encantado*) are more likely to display a darker side. "Here in Amazonas, almost everybody is afraid of dolphins," a young copy shop employee says as he extracts a bit of crumpled paper from the machine. "I myself am scared of them. Yes, yes, they really scare me! And yet, I have gone fishing many times at night with them and so, despite my fear, you could say I almost like them."[61]

58. Alpers, pp. 145–72, offers a number of observations on dolphins' fishing prowess from varied sources.

59. Aelian's description of dolphin fishers occurs in his *On the Characteristics of Animals*. Pliny the Younger explains that "the reason wherefore the dolphins be so beloved of the fishers is because they drive the fish into their nets." See Ronald M. Lockley, *Whales, Dolphins, and Porpoises*, pp. 40–43, for this and a number of other quotations from classical authors.

60. F. Bruce Lamb, "The Fisherman's Porpoise." Although the reader familiar with Portuguese will sourly hope that the author's observations are more accurate than his spelling, the article offers one of the few documented instances of symbiotic interaction between humans and dolphins and is thus quoted time and again.

61. Man, age 33, born interior of Maués, lives Maués (14 years). Single, copy shop worker, high-school education.

O boto é igual a um homem e a bota é igual a uma mulher. ("Male *botos* are just like human males and female *botos* are just like human females.")

Assertions regarding dolphins' supposed anatomical similarity to human beings are extremely common throughout much of the Amazon. Such comparisons center on the sexual organs, secondary sexual characteristics, and various aspects of reproductive behavior. Many people claim that the genitalia in human beings and dolphins are virtually identical. "The *boto* is a perfect man and the *bota* is the spitting image of a woman" ("O boto é um homem perfeito e a bota é a mesma mulher") they may assert conspiratorially. Or "It's true dolphins don't have legs, but otherwise, they're just the same as people. That is, of course, in some respects. You know what I mean!"

These persons also may insist that female dolphins menstruate, that they possess breasts, as well as underarm hair, and that dolphin calves cry "just like a baby." Some go so far as to credit dolphins of both sexes with long, flowing hair. "Once," recalls the mother of twelve small children, who has recently moved to Carauari from an outlying rubber settlement, "I was washing clothes in the river when I saw an enormous dolphin. He had very curly hair to his shoulders, he was up to his waist in water—a well-known dolphin, he used to appear a lot in those parts. So then, I ran home. My children had to retrieve the clothes for me. For a week I didn't set foot on the river bank. I felt that curly-haired dolphin was always near me, watching. Even today, it scares me to remember."[62]

There is no scientific basis for the existence of long-haired dolphins, females of the species do not have underarm hair, and their mammary glands are located to either side of the vagina. Furthermore, although baby dolphins emit sounds, they do not cry "just like babies." Nevertheless, because dolphins are mammals, and thus give live birth and nurse their young, they are necessarily closer in some respects to humans than are crabs, fish, stingrays, snakes, or virtually any other river creatures, including the manatee. Furthermore, assertions about resemblances in the sexual organs of dolphins and human beings have at least some grounding in fact. Although the dolphin penis—which is retractable in order to facilitate the animal's passage through the water—is far thinner and proportionately longer than a man's, the vagina is roughly comparable to that of a human female.

Insistences on the physiological resemblances between human beings and dolphins once again find at least partial parallels in native Amazonian

62. Woman, age 44, born Acre, lives Carauari (6 years). Married, housework, no formal education.

(as well as, to a lesser extent, European and African) tradition. The contemporary Aguaruna, for instance, believe that the genitalia of the female dolphin are identical to those of human females.[63] Various indigenous groups also tell of men who try to copulate with dolphins. Because, however, the sexual mores that guide different segments of present-day Amazonian society are often very different, the implications of these supposed physical resemblances are by no means constant.

O boto tem muita cagila. Quem pega o olho dele, consegue a mulher que quiser. A mesma coisa com a bota. Não tem homem que resista. ("The *boto* has a lot of *cagila*. Whoever makes use of his eye, obtains the woman of his choice. The same thing with the *bota*. There's not a man who can resist her.")

Perceived resemblances between the sexual organs of dolphins and human beings, as well as more general notions about the *boto*'s ability to attract men and women against their will, help explain why the genitals of both male and female dolphins, as well as the animal's left eye, should be in such great demand as aphrodisiacs. Notions of the *boto*'s aggressive sexuality spring not only from ideas of them as latter-day Aquatic Seducers, but also from the fact that they, unlike *tucuxi*, do not go through periods of reproductive inactivity. ("Those *botos* are just like dogs," one teenage girl confided as we swayed back and forth in neighboring hammocks on a day-long boat trip. "Watch them and you'll see they're at it all the time; they never stop!"[64] When I objected that female dogs did indeed go into limited periods of heat, she shrugged her shoulders. "Yes, but the male dogs are always out there looking for a female," she responded, offering me an orange from a long mesh sack.)

While the dolphin's teeth and oil serve a number of curative purposes, the eyes and genitals are said to possess great *cagila,* or sexual magnetism, that can literally or figuratively rub off on individual men and women. Dried dolphin skin is said to serve as a fumigant for snakebite or ray sting; children wear the teeth around their necks as a cure for diarrhea; and a dolphin ear, worn around the wrist, will "guarantee a large and lasting erection."[65]

Particularly in evidence in Belém's huge, open-air Ver-o-Peso Market, these organs appear in fairs and markets throughout Amazônia. Because of the taboo on killing dolphins, the wares often come from already dead

63. Brown, *Tsewa's Gift,* p. 156.
64. Woman, age 15, born interior of Parintins (Zé Açu). Single, house and farm work, 4 years school.
65. Shoumatoff, *The Rivers Amazon,* p. 126. Charles Wagley alludes to these and numerous other folk beliefs about the *boto* in his *Amazon Town,* pp. 238–39.

animals. With the influx of newcomers from other cultural backgrounds into Amazônia, however, and with the growing use of drift nets, a rise in the number of dolphins killed expressly for their body parts seems possible. Because, however, the organs must be specially treated to conserve them, people without specialized knowledge would be unlikely to realize a profit. Left eyes (right eyes are considered less potent and are therefore cheaper) and genitals bring upward of thirty-five dollars in the Manaus municipal market, a high price when one considers that a whole string of fish may sell for no more than a few dollars. The vendors who sell these organs usually also offer a variety of herbal remedies, bath potions (*banhos*), and colognes (*cheiros*) employed heavily—though not exclusively—within Umbanda and various other African Brazilian cults. Kátia's mother-in-law, for instance, regularly prescribes baths with such enticing names as *Chama Emprego* ("Gets You a Job"), *Chore nos Meus Pés* ("Cry at My Feet"), *Dinheiro em Penca* ("Bunches of Money") and *Raios de Sol* ("Sunbeams").

All of these items, as well as many others, are readily available in Parintins. Dolphin organs can be found in the municipal market along with various medicinal herbs and other sought-after animal substances, such as alligator teeth and rattlesnake excrement ("very white, very nice, very cheap for you, ma'am!"). *Banhos* and *cheiros* are available in two Umbanda shops as well as two boutiques that also sell frilly underwear and imported jeans. Although, as one might expect, virtually all of the customers in the boutiques are women, persons of both sexes seek out these products in the first two locations.

Some individuals are fully convinced of these organs' power; others regard them a bit as persons elsewhere might regard a four-leaf clover or lucky penny. Although there are numerous jokes and anecdotes about people duped into buying counterfeit wares (Maurício tells a very funny story about a man who becomes a virtual lothario thanks to a forged dolphin eye), the brisk traffic in these items confirms their appeal.

Dolphin eyes are almost always sold whole, since, for maximum effect, the buyer should squint through the *boto's* left eye at the object of his or her desire. The sexual organs—often euphemistically referred to as *brinquedos,* or "play toys"—may be sold intact, casually packaged in a dampened newspaper to help retain their moisture, or, more often, as fragments suspended in alcohol or perfume. The latter alternative, though cheaper and definitely better smelling, is considerably less effective, according to the vendor who explained the various options to me with ill-contained enthusiasm ("You are the first American lady to ask!"). In the second instance, the buyer rubs a little of the liquid on his or her own genitals in order to attract the object of desire. The dolphin eyes and genitals can also be burnt, and later sifted through a coarse cloth, then mixed with a bit of sugar. According to Argemiro, who attributes these instructions to a *curadeira* of his acquaintance ("I don't say *I* ever did this!"), the resulting mixture is rubbed on the arms and head.

The use of animal parts, as well as various other organic substances, in love charms is by no means limited to Amazônia.

At the same time, however, that they can be found in many cultures— eighteenth-century Spain, for instance, or Elizabethan England—the more specifically Amazonian concept of *cagila* (and, indeed, the name itself) suggests at least partially indigenous roots.[66] The use of dolphin organs to attract the object of one's attention recalls the contemporary Aguaruna's use of a variety of vegetal, mineral, and animal substances—including dolphin teeth—to attract members of the opposite sex. These charms, called *puságki* or *puçangas* (*pusangas,* in Spanish) are said to render the affected person mad with desire.[67]

And yet, if there are obvious similarities between the *puságki* and these dolphin love charms, there are also various differences worth noting. While the Aguaruna, for instance, regard these objects as a potential source of incest, suicide, and social conflict, they rarely possess these more negative connotations for the people I met. This is probably because sexual passion—which is for many native Amazonian peoples an obsession and thus a potentially dangerous aberration—acquires explicit connotations of both pleasure and power over others in mainstream Brazilian culture. The redefinition of sexual passion in accord with the Western romantic love tradition helps explain why, while the *puságki* would appear to be employed almost exclusively by male Aguaruna, I encountered persons of both sexes who claimed to make use of dolphin parts.

66. Elizabethan plays reveal numerous examples of magical concoctions known to, and presumably used by, at least some of Shakespeare's contemporaries. In sixteenth-through-eighteenth-century Spain (and "even now in rural areas"), love magic involved various spells and potions, the more sensational of which might include menstrual blood, pubic hairs and semen, mixed in with a dash of wine or pepper and the brains of an ass. (M. Helena Sánchez Ortega, "Sorcery and Eroticism in Love Magic," p. 58.) Although the present-day purchasers of rabbits' feet key chains and rearview mirror ornaments usually regard these as mere decorations, their use almost certainly originated in a similar principle of contagious magic through which the animal's perceived qualities would be transferred to the human owner.

67. See Brown, *Tsewa's Gift,* for a discussion of *puságki,* which he describes as "agents of demented attraction" (pp. 153–61). Karsten notes that Shipibo males employ as part of their love magic a powder made from the dolphin's pulverized eye, fat, teeth, or penis (p. 198), and Norman E. Whitten, Jr., notes that the teeth serve a similar function among the Canelos-Quichua (*Sacha Runa,* p. 61). Marlene Dobkin de Rios documents the presence of the *pusanga* amidst the Peruvian mestizo population ("A Psi Approach to Love Magic, Witchcraft, and Psychedelics in the Peruvian Amazon," p. 93). See also Regina Harrison, *Signs, Songs, and Memory in the Andes,* pp. 144–45.

Dizem que a bota é melhor do que a própria mulher. Dizem que o homem que transa com ela morre de gozo. ("They say that female dolphins are even better than a woman. They say that the man who has sex with one [a dolphin] dies of pleasure.")

References to the *bota*'s specifically sexual attractions comprise a logical, if extreme, extension of beliefs in the dolphin's *cagila*. A number of story-tellers of both sexes assured me that intercourse with a female dolphin was memorable, to say the least.[68] And yet, while many people insisted that the man who had sex with a *bota* could literally die of pleasure, no one claimed first-hand knowledge in these matters. "Dizque" ("It's said"), "Vejo contar" (literally, "I see tell"), "O povo diz" ("People say"), they asserted over and over.

Probably because of my identity as both a foreigner and a woman, it was many months into my research before I began to hear these kinds of statements. The resolute ingenuousness on which I relied to fend off male strangers convinced that any female on her own must be fair game for their advances may have worked almost too well at times. ("How come you're not like the women on [U.S.-imported] TV shows?" one man once asked me with a trace of rueful indignation that made me burst out laughing and feel almost sorry for him.) In any case, although some storytellers may have dropped hints involving human-dolphin sexual encounters, it was an American male friend doing fieldwork among rubber tappers, most of whom are also fishermen, on the Juruá River, who first made me aware of such accounts.

Fascinated by the information but unsure about how people would react to questioning on my part, I gingerly began asking women about these reports ("You know, I've heard these stories and I was wondering . . ."). Although many shook their heads a little, the question did not seem to offend them. Some, indeed, eagerly affirmed the stories' truth. A number manifested clear disapproval, but although many concluded with the statement, "É muita perversidade" ("It's extremely perverse"), some did so almost formulaically. A few undercut this judgment with laughter or a knowing wink.

Cheered by women's willingness to talk about what I saw as a potentially delicate matter, I next began approaching men. "Look, is it true that there are people who use [*se servem de*] female dolphins? I've heard something

---

68. F. Tagliavini and G. Pilleri report hearing that "the local people [in the Napo River region of Ecuador] sometimes catch female dolphins to have sexual intercourse with them, after which they release them" ("Occasional Observations," p. 68). Joanna Overing (personal communication, 10 October 1992) reports hearing similar stories of desirable dolphins in Iquitos during summer 1991.

to the effect but I'm not sure what to think," I might say. As the verb *servir* ("to use") has several meanings in addition to the overtly sexual, the man had a ready out. Also, as my question indicated that I had already heard the stories, there was no need for him to feel that he was revealing confidential information or to worry about shocking or offending the wide-eyed foreign *professora*.

Here again, I quickly found that if I asked the question in a matter-of-fact, strictly informational manner, men, like women, were inclined to answer without any particular embarrassment. Some shook their heads and laughed, but others gave me numerous and vivid details. Not infrequently, a storyteller would provide the names of men who supposedly had engaged in sexual relations with female dolphins. "Look," says one fisherman, "one night we harpooned one [a dolphin] and brought her to the riverbank. So then, we looked her over, me and my brother-in-law. She was exactly like a woman. Now then, precisely for this reason, many people want to have sex with the *bota*. And so, it happens. I myself have seen it happen, I know people who have done the 'service'—João Arias there in Jacaré do Paraíso and Chico Chaves, who now lives in [the community of] Maranhão."[69]

According to the stories, the man who wishes to have relations with a *bota* (who can easily be as big as or bigger than he is) must first bring her to shore. Often he will drag her up in the net in which she has become entangled, or else he will harpoon her in the tail. Sometimes, the man is said to simply penetrate the animal, who, according to most persons, must be alive in order for the act to have any meaning. "A dead dolphin isn't good for anything" ("Não presta ela morta") or "Dead dolphins are no fun" ("Não tem graça a bota morta") some people say.[70] Other individuals assert that the man must first beat himself and/or the dolphin with a branch of *pião branco,* whose medicinal leaves frequently figure in shamanic cures. They also may claim that the man who has had intercourse with a dolphin must see a curer following the encounter.

When I asked why a man would want to have sex with a dolphin, some people insisted that the latter "is better than a woman." They also stressed the beneficial consequences to the man of this sort of ritual rape. "They grab her," explained one of Argemiro's fisherman cousins as the family and I gobbled down the mound of fish he had provided, "then they do the work [*o serviço*] with her, then they throw her back into the water. Still

69. Man, age 41, born interior of Parintins, lives Santo Antonio de Tracajá (8 years). Married ("actually, I've had three wives"), fisherman and farmer, no formal education.

70. There are people who claim that the dolphin is dead during the encounter, and Wagley notes that the fishermen of whom he heard reports had intercourse "with boto females which they killed on the beach" (p. 239).

alive? Oh yes, still alive. The guy becomes deliciously attractive, you see? I don't know how to tell you this in classic Portuguese, but when the guy goes with a woman, she can't get enough of him."[71] (Here Alzira rolled her eyes and everyone, including the children, laughed uproariously.) "But is what he said true?" I later asked her. "Oh yes," Alzira assured me. "At least, that's what they say."

Claims that a man can die of pleasure may be understood figuratively; some people, however, may insist that so-and-so literally expired upon the spot. Male storytellers, in particular, often joke about what a great death it must have been, but both men and women may see the man's untimely demise as retribution for a forbidden action. Sometimes, the man is reported to become trapped inside the dolphin.

From a purely physiological viewpoint, human penetration of a full-grown female dolphin appears difficult, but not impossible, as the vagina could conceivably accommodate a man. Not only does the rhythmic beating of the dolphin with the green branch recall fishermen's reports of the male dolphin's rhythmic slapping with beak or tail to facilitate penetration, but it is possible that a vagina dilated by this type of stimulation could abruptly contract.

More symbolic sorts of stories about the dolphin as a sexual being are fairly common. (The ancient Greeks and Romans, for instance, emphasized these animals' phallic shape and pronounced them sacred to Venus.) Nonetheless, although one may argue for the sexual undertones—or, in some cases, overt eroticism—of some boy-and-dolphin stories, explicit references to dolphin-human intercourse in classical mythology are rare.[72] At least some contemporary Amazonian Indian groups, in contrast, judge the genitalia of female dolphins "more desirable than those of human females," and men who have tried to copulate with dolphins are reported to have found the experience "so pleasurable they were unable to stop."[73] Moreover, stories of humans mating with water creatures (stingrays, caimans, various fish) comprise one subset of a much larger group of narratives concerning human/nonhuman relations, common among various indigenous groups.[74]

71. "Arpoam ela, fazem o serviço com ela, depois largam. O cara fica gostoso, né? Não sei como lhe dizer em português clássico, mas quando ele vai com a mulher, ela não tem condições de deixar o cara." Man, age 44, Ilha das Onças. Married, fisherman and farmer, 2 years school ("but I can read a bit").

72. See Aelian's "The Dolphin Rider," in which the dolphin and the boy are lovers.

73. Brown, *Tsewa's Gift*, p. 156. He is once again speaking of the Aguaruna.

74. For one Kalapalo example involving human intercourse with a caiman see Ellen B. Basso, *In Favor of Deceit*, pp. 185–92. Interestingly enough, I heard a few reports—the most detailed from Argemiro—of a group rape of one of these animals. They are far less common, however, than accounts involving dolphins.

And yet, while the tales in question clearly draw on this much broader indigenous tradition, their implications are often very different. Furthermore, although I heard sporadic reports of bestiality involving various domestic animals—dogs, pigs, cows, chickens—these are by no means invested with the ritual aura that attends some (thought not all) reports of intercourse with *botos*. ("No one," says a young friend of Gerineldo categorically, "goes to see a *pajé* after messing with a dog.")[75] Human-animal intercourse frequently possesses a profound metaphoric dimension in which "unspeakable desires" stand as a challenge to everyday social constraints.[76] "People say the *bota* is very delicious [*muito gostosa*] but I would just as soon eat a piranha," says a young fisherman from the interior of Parintins. His words have a double sense since the verb *comer* means both "to eat" and "to have sexual relations," and the piranha is not just a flesh-eating fish (that many residents of the Amazon do eat) but also a widely used slang term for a prostitute. Transgressions of human-animal boundaries thus provide commentary on a wide range of social relations, including, but by no means limited to, the sexual.

In sum, even as "just" an animal, the *boto* exists in a unique relationship to human beings. These creatures' perceived capacity for both good and evil, as well as their real or imagined physical resemblances to men and women, provide a unique bond between them and the latter. Thus, at the same time these creatures display frightening, distinctly asocial qualities, they also reveal human or quasi-human traits not characteristic of their fellow animals. Although the parameters suggested here will stretch yet further as the dolphin is transformed into an *encantado,* there is no doubt that *botos* are a really "special kind of fish."

75. Man, age 14, born interior of Parintins, lives Parintins (1 year). Single, student, 2 years school.

76. Ondina Fachel Leal makes this point very well in her study of bestiality among cowhands, or *gauchos,* in the Brazilian south. The section on bestiality and the meaning of sexual practices has particular relevance for Amazônia (see Leal, "The Gauchos," pp. 248–87).

4

STORIES AND BELIEFS ABOUT DOLPHINS
AS SUPERNATURAL BEINGS

O Boto vira gente e vai nas festas, como esta. Pois, quem sabe se não vai
aparecer aqui mais tarde?

(The *Boto* turns into a man and goes to *festas* just like this one. Why, who
knows if he won't show up here later on tonight?)

—*Fisherman, age 52, interior of Parintins, at a festival in Zé Açu*

In contrast to propositions that focus on dolphins as extraordinary fish,
those that appear here deal with them as supernatural entities that move
with ease between animal and human form. Often amplifications and
transformations of beliefs in the preceding chapter—the perverse *boto* who
knocks canoes off course, for instance, now spirits away people to an
Enchanted City—they tend to display an at once more strikingly composite
and original character. In addition, they are apt to be associated with frequently repeated, third-person stories employing widely familiar folk
motifs.

From the outset, it is worth reemphasizing that although most people
make a distinction between dolphin-as-fish and Dolphin people, a given
individual can believe in both. ("Not every dolphin," asserts Tô Pereira, "is
an *encantado,* but there are many *encantados* who appear to us in dolphin
form.") This overlapping helps him and others explain why not all *botos*
should reveal the characteristics outlined below.[1] As in the preceding chapter, storytellers may affirm the truth of only some beliefs, dismissing others
as doubtful, if not blatantly untrue. Moreover, these individuals may alternate assertions regarding Dolphins with others concerning their unen-

---

1. Although there appear to be regions of the Amazon where people credit both the *boto*
and the *tucuxi* with the sorts of superhuman powers described here, all of the assertions that
I heard specifically concerned the former. Thus, when I speak of Dolphins, I mean *Botos.*

chanted counterparts, thereby blurring the divisions they themselves propose.

O boto/a gera para homem/mulher e vai lá na festa dançar. ("Dolphins transform themselves into men/women and go to dance at parties.")

The most widely told Dolphin stories in the Parintins area, and quite possibly in the Amazon as a whole, concern the *Boto*'s ability to assume human form at will. Although Dolphin-men are considerably more likely than Dolphin-women to show up at country *festas,* some storytellers report encounters with pairs or small groups of these enchanted beings. The following man, a musician, recalls how a Dolphin couple once appeared in a country celebration where he was playing the *rabeca,* a sort of rustic violin. Although the two simply join the dance for a few hours, the inexplicable intrusion of the supernatural on the previously joyous gathering sobers and profoundly disorients the other guests:

3. In that time, my dear young lady,
   a lot used to happen.
   Look, once they asked me to play in a *festa*
   there in a rubber settlement near Boca de Acre.
   So then, I went.

   I was playing my fiddle—it was a good party, you see?—
   when two people arrived,
   a young woman and a young man.
   I had my wife go out to receive them.
   So then, they came up [the embankment from the river],
   entered the room, and joined the dance.

   There are people here who still recall what happened,
   who were there with us at the time.
   The young man in a white shirt, green trousers,
   and the woman in a pale green dress and a white coat.
   I played almost nonstop,
   people danced and danced,
   and they too danced a lot.

   So then, somewhere between eleven o'clock and midnight,
   they disappeared;
   we didn't see them anymore.

We all started shouting,
>> we looked everywhere for them
>>> —and nothing, nothing!
They were so good-looking,
>> but they weren't people at all.[2]

On occasion little more than declarations of the *encantados'* ability to assume human form, references to one or another Dolphin's appearance in the *festa* may prompt full-fledged narratives. ("These big red *botos,* they turn into people and go to parties. It's a fact because a man from Mamuru once told me the following story about a case that happened there . . .") Because Dolphins are known troublemakers, their hosts are rarely pleased to see them, and, indeed, do all they can to make them feel unwelcome. In the conclusion to one dancing Dolphin story, told to me by a barber as he clipped a wide-eyed child's hair, the men of the community chase a handsome stranger in a starched white suit down to the river when he refuses to remove his straw hat.

4. Ah, miss, we went right after him,
>> I, lantern in hand,
>>> and the others yelling,
>>>> "What do you want, you son-of-a-bitch?"
We almost caught him,
>> but he jumped off the bridge
>>> into the water.
He was a man on land,
>> but when he hit the water,
>>> he was a dolphin—we saw absolutely everything.

The man vanished in that instant
>> and there appeared that big dolphin
>>> exhaling in the distance—"Chahhhh!"
Because he had wanted to flirt with that girl,
>> he was hoping to become the brother-in-law
>>> of her three brothers, see?
[Here, the speaker laughs at his own pleasantry.]
But his plan came to nothing
>> —it seems they didn't go for the idea![3]

2. Man, age 82, born Acre, lives Carauari (21 years). Widowed, musician and retired rubber worker, no formal education.

3. Man, age 62, born interior of Parintins, lives Parintins (41 years). Married, *curador* and barber, no formal education.

Literally "parties" or "celebrations," the *festas* of the interior are often linked to saints' days. Regardless, however, of whether they are of a public or more private character, these gatherings generally feature dancing enlivened by ample quantities of drink. Given the continuing semi-isolation of many rural communities, *festas* in regional centers such as Parintins attract large numbers of people from both within and outside the city, many of whom linger on with friends or family for several days. ("I wouldn't miss the *festa* of Our Lady of Carmo for anything," says one of Kátia's teenage relatives from the interior, as one of her cousins helps her twist her hair into a festive braid. "I like the rock bands, I like the procession with the [little children dressed as] angels, I like the Snake Woman [a kind of carnival attraction], I like the excitement. My aunt lets me stay out every night till midnight, my cousins lend me clothes and let me use their make-up, and I get to dance and flirt a little here and there—it's great!")[4]

It is not hard to see how storytellers might project their own anticipation of these breaks in the routine of daily life onto a party-loving Dolphin. One also can well imagine how the arrival of strangers from many miles around might cause apprehension in a tightly knit community. *Festas* provide a prime occasion for *namoros* (flirting and, often, full-fledged lovemaking) in which residents may vie with outsiders for the favors of a historically small number of eligible women. Not coincidentally, even today, these celebrations frequently end in drunken brawls. Almost every rural community can recount at least one instance of bloodshed triggered by a real or imagined affront to a man's honor, and the residents often seem to take a certain doleful pride in the elevated number of victims. ("Thirty-seven people died in one *festa* in São Vicente eleven years ago this April!" one rubber tapper excitedly reports.)[5] Stories of the dancing Dolphin clearly represent an amplification of far more limited assertions of the anatomical similarities between *botos* and human beings. The *encantados* who show up at *festas* do not simply resemble their human counterparts; rather, they actually become men and women, at least for the night. Aside from the blowhole in their heads (and, occasionally, their backward-pointing feet), there is no way of distinguishing these supernatural entities from any other partygoer—unless, of course, the Dolphin decides to appear in a celebration in which all the other guests are dark-skinned. ("He was the only

4. Woman, age 16, born interior of Parintins. Single, helps family in house and fields, 2 years school.
5. Man, age 44, born interior of Carauari, lives Seringal Concôrdia (16 years). Married, rubber tapper, no formal education. The big news during my stay in the Carauari region was the murder of a man and woman at a country *festa*. When the boat which was to transport the supposed assassin back to the scene of the crime ran out of fuel, rumors circulated that a *feitiço* had drained the originally full tank.

white man in the crowd, and so we all knew it was he. Now then, he never caused us trouble, and so we just let him be," says one very old man who grew up in a community originally founded by runaway slaves.)[6]

The Dolphin's predilection for the dance has obvious sexual connotations and, as such, recalls beliefs about the unenchanted *boto*'s magnetic appeal or *cagila*. Strikingly attractive, these glamorous visitors twirl about the dance floor amidst admiring glances.[7] ("They mean trouble, but still, everybody always wants to dance with them," remarks Alzira.) Tales of party-crashing strangers also underscore more general notions of malicious intrusion that many storytellers associate with the dolphin-as-fish. Just as *botos* may pursue fishermen's canoes for no apparent reason, so Dolphins show up uninvited in the *festa*, where they actively work mischief. "People are afraid of what the *boto* might do," explains one of Gerineldo's uncles, who is busily unloading a sack of dappled green melons. "But what really scares them is the fact that this transformation business is impossible to understand."[8]

The belief that animals and humans share a common nature, and that the former can assume human form on visits to this world is, or was once, common in many different societies.[9] In much of Amazonian Indian mythology, animals are viewed as a kind of people who live in one of various other (often three or seven) worlds. As the boundaries between living beings are therefore extremely fluid, tales of their interaction do not place great stress on physical appearance. In some cases, animal visitors appear in animal form; in others, they assume human guise.

This fluidity of form—and of underlying essence—distinguishes contemporary Amazonian Indian narratives about shape-changers from the Dolphin stories. That the Dolphin is inevitably a man or woman on land, and a dolphin in the water both suggests influences from European and African traditions, and underscores a far sharper division between the animal and human world than that evident in native Amazonian Aquatic Seducer stories.

6. Man, age 92, born interior of Óbidos, lives Oriximiná (27 years). Married, retired, no formal education. Slavery was definitively abolished in Brazil in 1888.

7. In the stories I recorded, the Dolphin is always physically attractive. In the work of erudite authors, however, he may be transformed into an ugly, as well as sinister, stranger. See, for instance, "O Baile do Judeu" in Inglês de Souza, *Contos Amazônicos.*

8. Man, age 37, born Pará, lives interior of Parintins (18 years). Married, fisherman and farmer, no formal education.

9. For a collection of oral and written texts from a range of cultures that reflect this belief see David M. Guss, *The Language of the Birds.* Robert Pogue Anderson offers an eloquent summary of ancient Near Eastern and European conceptions of an all-encompassing natural universe in his *Forests,* pp. 3–60.

Dolphins not only show up at *festas* fully clothed; their clothing has definite class connotations. Dolphin-men show up in starched white linen suits while Dolphin-women appear in the long white dresses once favored by the wealthy. As if to emphasize their own connection to a mercantilist, often foreign-born elite, Dolphins occasionally sport a sailor suit like those worn by the captains of the ocean-going steamships which plied the Amazon during the height of the rubber trade.[10]

O Boto, ele é muito safado. Pode gerar para homem e transar com a mulher que quiser. A gente vê muito filho de Boto por essas bandas. ("Botos are very shameless. They [the males] can turn into men and have sex with women. One sees many children of the Boto in these parts.")

A second widely held belief regarding Dolphins with a capital "D" concerns their not just fun-loving, but downright lascivious nature. Not only do they dance all night with the prettiest woman at the party, but once the lights and music fade, they show up in her bed. Dona Marina recalls how a handsome man "white as a tapioca" (a pancakelike manioc confection) seduces a young woman despite her father's attempts to shield her from the stranger's advances.

5. So then, when the party ended,
    there around three in the morning,
      everyone saw that handsome man
        standing there in the moonlight
          beneath the banana tree
           —white as a tapioca, he!
So then, he [the Dolphin] went down toward the river.

The girl's father remained there waiting,
    he didn't see anyone pass by.
Because he [the Dolphin] had already gone
    to the man's house!
"That creature is going to end up in my daughter's hammock!"
    the father said when he realized what had happened.
So then, he grabbed his harpoon
    and ran home.

10. Luís da Câmara Cascudo observes that accounts of party-going Dolphins do not appear before the early nineteenth century (*Dicionário do folclore brasileiro*, p. 143). Angelika Gebhart-Sayer notes that among the Shipibo-Conibo, the Dolphin is the captain or wheelman of the *Acuronin* ship, one of the manifestations of the cosmic Anaconda. Like a policeman, the Dolphin wears a club which is really a *cuni* fish, his head is a stingray, and his watch is a crayfish (*Die Spitze des Bewußtseins*, pp. 318–19).

But when he arrived on the doorstep,
    the Dolphin was already leaving through the window.
There was nothing he could do.

Nine months went by
    and the girl went into labor.
The baby was the image,
    the spitting image of a dolphin!
        —I saw that little dolphin-child with my own eyes.

Although Dolphins have a rakish reputation, the women who become involved with them in these stories rarely suspect their true identity while they are making love. Only in the morning, when the handsome stranger's shoes turn into stingrays or hard-shelled *bodó* fish, and the hat he has left behind becomes a tortoise that goes ambling off in the direction of the river, do they become aware that something very strange is going on. Occasionally, in the heat of passion, the Dolphin reveals his true identity to the woman, urging her to accompany him to his kingdom beneath the river. ("Can you imagine?" giggles Kátia. "I think I would die of fright.")

Some Dolphins may appear to the object of their affections not as attractive strangers, but rather, as husbands or lovers.[11] Unlike the partygoers given to one-night stands, these Dolphin impersonators are apt to make repeat appearances in the woman's bed. Usually, the couple realizes that something is amiss when the woman refers to amorous activities in which the man has not engaged. ("Again, Zezinho? But you just left here less than an hour ago! Don't you ever get enough?") The man will then look disconcerted, mumbling something on the order of "But Raimunda, dear, I've been off fishing for three whole days now and I just walked in the door.")

The many stories in which the Dolphin cheerfully dupes the woman and her partner reveal a transformation of the *esperteza* or cunning of the dolphin-as-fish into a more specific form of roguishness that storytellers themselves often identify as *safadeza*. Although the term is sometimes translated as "rascality" or "shamelessness" (the verb *safar* literally means "to slip away" or "escape"), the Dolphin's *safadeza* resides both in his specifically sexual appetites and in his fondness for deception. Other storytellers may describe the Dolphin as *sacana*, a stronger term with a decided sexual connotation, that invariably implies the forbidden and perverse.[12]

11. Thompson, *Motif-Index of Folk Literature,* D.658.2, "transformation to husband's (lover's) form to seduce woman."

12. For a discussion of *sacanagem* see Roberto da Matta, *Carnivals, Rogues, and Heroes,* pp. 198–238.

Quite often, the woman herself does not actually see the Dolphin. He arrives when she is already sleeping, or else "hypnotizes" or "magnetizes" her so that she later has no recollection of the encounter. Although the other household members may remark slyly on the hammock's particularly energetic swaying or the woman's drawn-out moans of pleasure, they generally do not suspect what is transpiring. (That is, they do not realize *who* is making the hammock creak.) Often, the Dolphin leaves behind a gift for the object of his affections, most often a ring or necklace, or a silvery pile of fish.

Recurrent visits inevitably have a negative effect upon the still unsuspecting woman, who grows thinner, paler, and more listless with each passing day.[13] ("The woman becomes thin as a fishing pole and yellow, very yellow," Tô Pereira asserts.) Often, her skin will develop a peculiar, soapy texture, and a pronounced fishy smell, and she will display an inexplicable desire to go down to the riverbank at all hours of the day and night. Sometimes, she begins to sing hauntingly lovely songs whose words no one can understand, develops a persistent fever, and reveals incipient signs of madness.[14] If her symptoms are not promptly treated, she either disappears or dies.

Only two hopes exist for the woman who is sleeping with a Dolphin. The first is for a shamanic healer to drive away her tenacious suitor either by direct contact with the offending *encantado* or more indirectly through a strict regimen of ritual baths and defumations. ("The person smells like a walking chili pepper for weeks afterward, but sometimes this is the only hope," Tô Pereira says, pinching his nose.) The only other solution is for one of the woman's family to kill the unwelcome visitor. Sometimes, the woman's husband or lover lies in wait for the Dolphin and harpoons him. On other occasions, the man attacks what he thinks is a human rival, only later to discover his knife embedded in a dolphin. In the following conclusion to Argemiro's detailed account of one such jealous boyfriend, the

13. From the viewpoint of a medical anthropologist, this "Dolphin sickness" constitutes a culture-bound syndrome. For a definition see Ronald C. Simons and Charles C. Hughes, eds., *The Culture Bound Syndromes;* and David Landy, ed., *Culture, Disease, and Healing,* especially pp. 465–518. The physical symptoms of Dolphin possession suggest hepatitis, which is common, and often deadly, in the Amazon. They also may be present in cases of severe anemia and various nervous afflictions, as well as malaria, whose periodic fevers may bring on an obsessive urge to bathe.

14. "It's absolutely true," says one young schoolteacher from the Juruá River as we watch her students run about a makeshift play yard. "I knew such a woman. Every day at six o'clock she would go down to the water and start singing. Finally, she disappeared. I don't know what happened to her. But I still remember those strange songs." Charles Wagley relates a case involving seduction by a *Boto* in which the affected woman begins to sing "a strange, unintelligible song" (*Amazon Town,* pp. 240–41).

switching between past and present tenses underscores the drama of the event.

6. So then, he went home,
  and when he arrived there,
    he called his mother and said,
      "Ah, *mamãe,* I am a murderer."
  "My son, what are you telling me?"
  "Yes, Mother, I murdered Antonio."

  "But why?"
  "He was betraying me with my girlfriend."
    (It was the fellow's fiancée, you see?)

  "My son, are you sure?"
  "I am.
    He entered the house at sunset,
      and only left now.
I stabbed him and he fell into the water."

So then, the mother starts crying all over the place, you see?
Finally, he said,
  "I'm going to turn myself in."
And so, he waited for the sun to come up a little more
  and he set out.

When he arrives where the canoes are moored
  he sees one of these really big red dolphins,
    dead there on the shore,
      with his own dagger sunk into its back.
So then, he pulled out the dagger.
[Here Argemiro laughs delightedly at the man's astonishment.]
It's true,
  this really happened.
[More laughter.]

Transformations of either animals or supernatural entities into human form for the express purpose of seducing men or women occur in many narrative traditions.[15] Snake paramours are particularly common in Asia and Africa.[16] Dolphin seducers, however, are considerably less common.[17] Their actions in the *encantado* stories often reveal a cosmological dimension that recalls tales of the *boto* as *mãe* or protector of the waters. Just as ordinary dolphins are said to pursue canoes carrying menstruating women, so their enchanted counterparts may force themselves upon a woman who ignores these sorts of taboos.

Then too, much like their various counterparts in native Amazonian tradition, offended Dolphins may vent their displeasure on not just the woman in question, but also, the community at large. Thus, a young woman explains that her own recurring problems with the Dolphin began at the age of seven when she was swimming in the river where a menstruating woman had just bathed. And one of Kátia's sisters-in-law recalls how her own mother sternly prohibited her and her sisters from going to the riverbank during their periods "because of the bad things that might happen *to the children there* where we used to live" (my emphasis).[18]

Beliefs about the dolphin's exceptional sexual attraction or *cagila* reinforce notions of his enchanted cousin's prowess as a conquistador. Not only is there no resisting these sweet-smelling strangers who make love in their straw hats (male Dolphins are acutely self-conscious about their

15. Demon lovers include the Greek Ephialtes and satyrs, the Celtic dusii, the Hindu bhuts, the Arabic jinn, and the Samoan hotua poro. The ballad of the Great Selchie of Sule Skerry from the Orkney Islands, which tells of a sea lion who makes love in human form to a woman, recalls numerous other European ballads of shape-changers and mortals who traffic with the folk of the other world. (See Bernard Harris Bronson, *The Traditional Tunes of the Child Ballads,* vol. 2, pp. 564–65.) For other examples of aquatic beings who woo mortals see Thompson, F420.6.1.1.

16. For an account of ongoing changes in the Japanese tradition see Carmen Blacker, "The Snake Woman in Japanese Myth and Legend." A number of African versions of the "Beauty and the Beast" story feature a giant water snake (tale type 425C in Antti Aarne and Stith Thompson, *The Types of the Folktale*). See, for instance, the two accounts of the Aquatic Seducer Monyohe in Minnie Postma, *Tales from the Basotho,* pp. 58–77; and the section on aquatic snakes who take human wives in Luc de Heusch, *The Drunken King; or, The Origin of the State,* pp. 39–48.

17. In Talmudic-Midrashic legends regarding the creation of the world, the dolphins are said to be "half man and half fish; they even have sexual intercourse with human beings; therefore they are also called 'sons of the sea,' for in a sense they represent the human kind in the waters" (Louis Ginzberg, *The Legends of the Jews,* vol. 1, p. 35). However, in a subsequent note, Ginzberg comments that "in the Talmud nothing is said about a union of the sirens and men, and it is uncertain whether this statement . . . is based on a different text . . . or whether, influenced by the belief in fays and naiads, prevalent in the Middle Ages, all through Europe" (vol. 1, p. 54).

18. Woman, age 29, born interior of Parintins, lives Parintins (9 years). Married, housework, 4 years school.

blowholes, which some storytellers compare to a vagina), but they would appear to have an astonishingly high fertility quotient. Time and again in these stories, women become pregnant after a single encounter. ("With these really shameless types [esses caras mais descarados]," grumbles Dona Marina's daughter as she pounds soap into a massive tub of laundry, "that is always the way it is.")[19] And yet, although some people insist that there are many Dolphin children, and boys and girls may refer to each other teasingly as sons and daughters of the Boto, no one with whom I spoke ever identified a single, living example.[20] It is easy to see how the Dolphin could serve as an excellent cover for an illicit, if strictly human, sexual encounter. Nonetheless, "real, live Dolphin babies" are almost always malformed children who die (or are ostensibly carried off by the enchanted father) shortly after birth.[21]

The idea that botos engage in intercourse with women appears in various indigenous Amazonian traditions. In one Shipibo story, for instance, a dolphin regularly has sexual relations with an unsuspecting woman. Here, as in many of the tales I collected, the victim's languor causes her relatives—in this case, two nephews—to become suspicious. ("A dolphin is probably entering the vagina of our dear Aunt with his penis. That is why she sleeps all the time," one says to the other.)[22] The Shipibo tale, however, is different from the stories I recorded in that the dolphin retains its animal form during intercourse. Despite his appearance in an iscohina (a sort of ceremonial poncho), there is no suggestion that the dolphin actually metamorphoses into a man.

The transformed Dolphin's distinctly human quality is apparent in the

19. Woman, age 33, born Juruti Velho (Pará), lives Parintins (4 years). Single, unemployed, no formal education.

20. People did mention various cases in which so-and-so was said to be the Dolphin's child as a cover-up for sexual activity on the part of a man who did not wish to assume paternity. They did not, however, recount instances, such as that cited by Melba C. Caldwell and David K. Caldwell, in which "the father of the [illegitimate] child is dutifully recorded on birth certificates in some districts as bouto" ("More about the Ugly Dolphin," p. 311). Janet Chernela notes findings similar to mine in northwest Amazônia (Chernela, personal communication, 11 January 1992). It is possible that people were ashamed to tell me about "filhos do boto," but I doubt this because of the great number of other intimate details they readily revealed. Most recorded cases in which a woman names the Boto as her child's father involve reports to authorities. Lisa Swanson (personal communication, 9 April 1993) says that a relative of hers who works as a doctor in the Ecuadorian Amazon frequently hears such attributions from his female patients.

21. It appears that these children are often allowed to die. On occasion, they are placed in the river in response to a summons by the encantado father.

22. Peter G. Roe, "Anciently, there was a Woman who was always being molested by a Dolphin" (The Cosmic Zygote, pp. 51–52).

safadeza alien to Amerindian oral traditions. Although Aquatic Seducers are often sinister and terrifying in the way that Dolphins can be, they are rarely, if ever, merrily outrageous. That *Botos* regularly display emotions such as jealousy and sadness underscores not only their culturally hybrid identity, but also their more specifically human one.

Cuidado com a Bota, rapaz. Pois ela persegue o homem que mexe com ela. ("Be careful with the female Dolphin, fellow. Because she relentlessly pursues the man who provokes her.")

Although the majority of Dolphin stories told to me by persons of both sexes feature males, a significant minority feature females. While the latter simply may take a liking to one or another human being, their persecution of a man is often a direct response to inappropriate behavior on his part. Just as male Dolphins are particularly apt to pursue women who ignore menstrual taboos, so their female counterparts may vent their wrath on men foolhardy enough to flirt with the unknown.

Warnings not to "mess" or *mexer* with dolphins underscore the explicitly sexual nature of these perceived affronts. To *mexer* with a stack of books is to get them out of order, but to *mexer* with a woman is usually to have physical contact with her. Even such relatively unremarkable pleasantries as "Oh *minha filha* ["my dear" or, literally, "my daughter"], it's too bad you're not a woman!" or "Oh little dolphin, if you were a woman I'd surely invite you into my hammock tonight!" may have dire results. Inevitably in these stories, the Dolphin takes up the speaker on his dare, appearing in his bed in the form of a seductive blonde.

Although the man's actual experience with the Dolphin is said to be intensely pleasurable, her appetites soon prove insatiable. Like the woman who receives a Dolphin-lover, the man in question grows pale, thin, and feverish, often displaying signs of incipient madness. Once again, the only hope is shamanic intervention or the death of his pursuer. In the following segment of Maurício's description of his twenty-four-year-old cousin's recent encounter with a Dolphin, recounted to several family members and me one night at the dinner table, the man cannot escape his enchanted pursuer.

7. He was there in the interior with the others,
          transporting cattle,
                    and when they stopped beside the river,
                              a dolphin surfaced near him, you see?
     So, he said, "Woman, come sleep with me!"
               because he'd been there more than a month,
                    without a woman, you know?

He spoke in a joking manner;
>> he had heard various stories [about female dolphins],
>>> and so, he spoke in that playful way.

Well, as he tells it, when night came,
>> he was asleep on the boat when he awoke
>>> and saw a woman approach his hammock.
So, he tried to pretend [that he was still asleep], right?
>> but the woman kept coming closer.
He didn't dare to close his eyes.

So then, as soon as dawn came,
>> he left there in desperation.
He set out for the city, for Manaus,
>> remaining there over a month.
But when he finally got up the courage to return,
>> that same woman was right there
>>> wanting to lie with him in the hammock.
So then, he knew it had to be that dolphin
>> whom he had invited to sleep with him.
Who else could it be?

These "taunt stories" recall beliefs in the *boto* as guardian of the waters. At first glance reinforcements of highly conservative sexual mores, the real problem in these stories is not incorrect sexual behavior, but rather, the man's confusion of eligible female peers or daughters ("Oh, minha *filha*," says the fisherman) with supernatural owners or mothers. As the *mãe*, unlike a prospective sexual partner, must be treated with respect and caution, it is by no means surprising that an inappropriate gesture should trigger an obsessive, recriminatory pursuit. Thus, although the stories focus on what looks like sexual behavior, they are ultimately about the need for deference and caution in the face of powerful natural and supernatural forces.

The parallels between Dolphin-women and a number of other female river beings are fairly obvious. Like the primordial native Amazonian Fish-Woman, Dolphin-women are irresistible to men. But unlike this prototype for human woman, who is also a full-fledged, highly aggressive, and ultimately androgynous Aquatic Seducer, Dolphin-women are stereotypically female.[23] Thus, while the Fish-Woman actively pursues unwary humans, her more retiring Dolphin counterpart is more apt to respond to provocation.

23. Michael F. Brown, *Tsewa's Gift*, p. 52.

Although the stories I recorded make no mention of the Fish-Woman, some storytellers do speak of European-style mermaids (*sereias*) and African Brazilian *mães d'água* or "mothers of the waters."[24] Certain individuals may equate or conflate the Dolphin-woman with the latter, as well as with various other water-dwelling deities who figure in most Amazonian versions of the African Brazilian pantheon. Others, however, underscore the differences between these figures.

Sometimes storytellers insist that mermaids are a special class of *encantados,* going so far as to use the terms *Bota* and *sereia* interchangeably.[25] Others identify the African Brazilian *orixá,* Iemanjá, as either a mermaid or a Dolphin-woman—or sometimes as both. (Quite appropriately, the Yoruba word *Yemonja* means "mother of the fish.")[26] People may pose similar correspondences between the Dolphin-women, *sereias,* and the lesser African Brazilian deity, or *cabocla,* Mariana, who is frequently represented as not only a beautiful young woman, but also the parrotlike *arara,* and the *pirarara* fish. Because Iemanjá is herself often equated with the Virgin Mary in her guise as Our Lady of the Immaculate Conception, her identification with these other figures suggests a many-layered syncretic process.

Those storytellers who insist on the differences between Dolphin-women and these other river entities often stress that a mermaid remains half fish and half woman, while the Dolphin alternates between animal and human form. This distinction underscores the more enigmatic nature of these enchanted beings, who are often not what they appear. ("Mermaids are always mermaids," Tô Pereira explains, "but the *encantado* often looks like something else.") The Dolphin's shifting identity also holds out hope for those enchanted beings who aspire to permanently human status.

24. Geoffrey Parrinder notes that in Africa, "wells, springs, rivers, lakes and the sea are believed to have spirits dwelling in them, like mermaids, and in some places great cults are made of these naiads" (*African Traditional Religion,* p. 50). For an introduction to the *mãe d'água* (sometimes referred to as the *iara* or *uiara*) in both African and indigenous traditions, see Luís da Câmara Cascudo, *Geografia dos mitos brasileiros,* pp. 122–42; and Osvaldo Orico, *Mitos ameríndios e crendices amazônicos,* pp. 68–73. A survey of aquatic seductresses in various European traditions appears in Géza Róheim, *The Gates of the Dream,* pp. 314–54.

25. Gebhart-Sayer notes that among the Shipibo-Conibo people, female dolphins called *sirenas* seduce human men (p. 318). The use of the Spanish term *sirena* clearly suggests some degree of cultural intermingling. The same sort of cross-identification between serpent-tailed, river-dwelling women and the mother of the waters is documented in Jaime Regan, *Hacia la tierra sin mal,* pp. 178–79.

26. For Brazilian folk narratives regarding Iemanjá see Zora A. O. Seljam, *Iemanjá e suas lendas.* Pierre Verger argues that "Iemanjá" comes from the Yoruba *Yeye omo ejá,* or *Yemonja,* meaning "mother of the fish" (Verger, *Orixás,* p. 190).

"The mermaid is a kind of fish," says Gerineldo as he shaves the excess rubber from a new heel, "but the *encantados* are more like people in fish's clothes."

Then too, although the *encantados* have been largely incorporated into many Amazonian Umbanda cults, some individuals pose a sharp division between *pajelança,* or shamanic-based healing traditions, and what they derogatively refer to as *macumba* or *feitiçaria* (black arts, sorcery). Rejecting any and all association between the enchanted beings and potential African Brazilian counterparts, they may observe that Iemanjá "is a woman who lives in the water, but she does *not* become a fish."

In a similar vein, storytellers may observe that while European-style *sereias* inevitably lure men to the river bottom, Dolphin-women are less likely to do so without provocation. "Besides," notes Alzira, "I never heard anybody say that Dolphin-women sing." People often regard the *encantados* as more familiar, even local entities, while mermaids and figures such as Iemanjá are thought of as more remote. "I think that the mermaid must live in the ocean," Gerineldo remarks, applying a dab of black polish to the heel. "At least, I never heard of one who lived here in Amazonas." "These mermaids," his uncle adds later that evening as we try to dodge the smoke from the kitchen lantern, "they only show up on soap operas, but I myself know people who have made love to a Dolphin."[27]

Quem mata um Boto é sempre castigado. ("The person who kills a Dolphin is always punished.")

We have seen that killing a *boto* often results in *panema.* If the victim, however, turns out to be an *encantado,* the consequences are apt to be both more serious and more enduring. Here, we are not talking about retaliation for a Dolphin's incursion into human space—the husband who kills the handsome stranger who has just bounded out of his own wife's hammock—but rather, an unprovoked attack upon a supernatural being in animal form. As there is no sure way of distinguishing enchanted Dolphins from their more run-of-the-mill cousins until it is too late, human aggressors are taking a tremendous gamble.

Mysterious visitors often appear to the man who harms a Dolphin. Sometimes, they simply warn him never to repeat his actions. On other occasions, their appearance triggers bouts of illness and insanity. In the following story, told to me by a rubber tapper as he carefully singed off the loose ends of his net with a candle, the man who kills a *boto* that turns

27. Man, age 37, born Pará, lives interior of Parintins (18 years). Married, fisherman and farmer, no formal education.

103

out to be enchanted finds himself surrounded by a blinding light. Although the local *pajé* is able to alleviate his condition, the eerie brilliance plagues him one month of every year.

8. This fisherman, he harpooned an old Dolphin,
    all wrinkled,
        just like a very old person, you see?

So then, it seems the other Dolphins began pursuing him
    so persistently he was obliged
        to kill another nine.
They crowded in around him
    and wouldn't let him leave.
Because he had killed their granddad, see?
    —and so, they were very angry at him.

Well, after that day,
    there was no way he could sleep at night.
He would set up his mosquito net in the dark
    but the minute he lay down in the hammock,
        he says it would be bright,
            bright as day,
            bright as an electric light, around him.
And if he finally dozed off,
    they would shake the hammock
        so he couldn't sleep.

So then, he went to his father's house,
    because his father understood about prayers.
And his father called a person to help cure him
    —a kind of *sacaca,* you see?
And this man told him,
    "Look, whenever this month arrives"
        —I don't know if it was November or December—
        "every time this month arrives
            you won't sleep right."

And sure enough, whenever that month arrives
    in which he killed the Dolphins,
        he doesn't sleep a wink.
To this day!

But once the month is over,
    that's that,
        he returns to his old self.[28]

In one cautionary tale involving a wounded Dolphin, also found in contemporary indigenous oral tradition, a group of soldiers arrest a fisherman for wounding a *Boto* who turns out to be a colonel (or, sometimes, a general named Napoleon) in the Dolphin army.[29] After taking the man to the infirmary of the Enchanted City, the man's captors inform him that they will allow him to return home only once the wound has healed.[30] The following example is unusual in that the fisherman himself does not cure the Dolphin, but instead relies on counselors who turn out to be good dolphins, who are black like the storyteller.

9. Well then, he didn't know how to work this cure.
   And so, time went on and on until one day
      he came upon four or five little black boys
         playing ball in the woods of the *Encante*.
   And he asked their help
      because that wound wasn't healing.

So then, they taught him the cure
      —he was to carefully scrape the scales from an *acara-açu* fish
         and add various things to the mixture.
I forget now how it was,
      but they explained everything to him very clearly.
Well, those little black boys were *tucuxi*,
      don't you know?

So then, he did as they had taught him
      and the colonel recovered right away.
Then they gave him a boat full of fish
      to take home with him.
To this day, he eats well, that man.[31]

28. Man, age 34, birthplace unknown, lives Seringal Cupuaí. Married, rubber tapper, no formal education.

29. See "Wiyu and the Man Who Liked to Shoot Dolphins," translated by David M. Guss, for a Yekuana example. For a Portuguese-language version of this story see José Carvalho, *O matuto cearense e o caboclo do Pará*, pp. 22–24.

30. See Thompson, *Motif-Index of Folk Literature*, D2161.4.10.2, "wound healed by inflicter."

31. Man, age 64, Silêncio do Matá (Pará). Married, fisherman and farmer, no formal education.

Although the theme of supernatural retribution for ills inflicted on an animal that turns out to have human characteristics can be found throughout much of the world, these stories affirm a specifically Amazonian brand of reciprocity. That provocation directed at a dolphin or Dolphin is always a threat to the fragile equilibrium between the human and the natural world sets apart these stories from Indo-European narratives in which the protagonist enters into a more strictly personal, if ultimately emblematic, relationship with one or more extraordinary animals.

Storytellers may use humor to bring home the seriousness of the relationships underlying many Dolphin narratives. Maurício, for instance, recounts a version of the hospital story that concludes with a sea tortoise guiding the man back up to the riverbank after his successful surgery on the Dolphin colonel. When they arrive on land, the man says he wants to thank the tortoise and holds out his hand. When the tortoise takes it, the man yells, "Off to the kettle with you!" and the tortoise, albeit enchanted, ends up as turtle soup. His account suggests that while the *encantados* control the river and its creatures, they lose much of their power once outside their watery domain. This power, however, is not for this reason any less real. ("You can laugh," says a suddenly serious Maurício, "but the *encantados*, they exist.")

Os botos levam a gente para a cidade encantada para ficar com eles lá no fundo do mar. ("Dolphins take people to the Enchanted City to live there with them at the bottom of the river-sea.")

The assertion that Dolphins spirit away people to the river bottom actually contains two separate, if related, propositions. The first concerns the existence of an Enchanted City or *Encante* somewhere beneath the water. The second involves Dolphins' power to carry off and transform human beings into new *encantados*.

As in various narrative traditions, including the native Amazonian, the *Encante* resembles earthly cities. ("They say it is just like Parintins, only much richer," Kátia observes as her small son waves down at her from a branch of the backyard mango tree.) Most storytellers suggest that the Enchanted City lies somewhere beneath the riverbed, beyond the reach of scuba divers and submarines; and Gerineldo, for his part, insists that it must be located in a part of the river "where there are caves full of oxygen because how else could the people who live there breathe?"

This underwater city is sometimes conflated or confused with an enchanted island said to appear and disappear without warning.[32] Storytellers

32. Thompson, F944.3, "island sinks into sea."

often identify the latter as a rural community that sinks to the bottom of the river during a particularly animated *festa*. Even today—ten, twenty, or a hundred years after the fact—people may hear the partygoers laughing amidst the joyous wailing of the violin. Unlike the Enchanted City, however, which remains fixed beneath the surface, this mysterious island resurfaces in diverse locations. Tô Pereira tells the story of a friend who once fell asleep upon the island, only to be awakened by revelers who quickly faded into the morning mist. ("He *swears* it happened," Tô says with a noncommittal shrug.)

Most storytellers suggest that the island's residents have been enchanted. In the conclusion to one particularly lovely version of this narrative told to a handful of visiting rubber tappers and me late one night by a young health worker, the island's disappearance follows the slaying of a rare white manatee. A mysterious old woman who later appears at the site to collect the remains mumbles ominously about a wave that will sweep away its inhabitants to the river bottom.

10. Well then, the day after the party,
        a little old woman appeared,
            collecting the manatee's bones
                and placing them in a small sack.
    She seemed to be a relative of his, see?
    She said those people there were going to regret
        what they had done.

    So then, everyone thought she was crazy.
    Only one fisherman perked up his ears.
    This one, yes,
        he grabbed his family
            and left that place at once.

    The others, no,
        they decided to have another party.
    So then, when night came,
        everyone was having a good time,
            everyone was singing and eating when,
                in that instant,
                    the earth began to move.
    There was an awful noise,
        and the earth started sinking and sinking,
            until only a sort of sunken island remained.

Even today, whoever passes by this spot
    hears that noise of people talking and singing.
You don't see anything, but you can hear roosters crow,
                    dogs bark,
                    children cry.
There's music at all hours of the day.

Have I heard that music?
I have,
    yes,
        I have.[33]

The sort of en masse enchantment this young man describes is not the rule, but the exception, and the great majority of Dolphin abductions involve a single human. Attracted to adults of the opposite sex, these enchanted beings also may become enamored of particular children. In the following account, the Dolphin does not simply whisk away the boy, but instead, tricks his mother into surrendering him by assuming the form of the boy's father. The speaker is a cook who tells the following story as we watch her young daughter chase a muscular black chicken around the palm-fringed backyard.

11. Well then, this aunt of mine
        had given birth a few days earlier.
And so, she went down to the river
      with some other people
         —she was there with the baby in her arms
           when a really big wave arrived.

In that moment, her husband asked for the child
      and she handed him over.
So then, she went home to see to dinner [literally, the cooking
                                        pot];
      it was he who remained there with the child.
But when later on she returned for him,
      her husband didn't know the slightest thing,
        can you imagine?
Because he hadn't even been there in that hour.

33. Man, age 22, born Tefé, lives Carauari (1 year). Single, health worker, high-school education.

Afterward, the child kept on appearing in her dreams.
So then, the *curador* told her to have him baptized
    with blood and holy water before he turned eighteen
        before he sprouted gills, you see?
But after that, he stopped appearing to her;
    she never again saw him.
And so, there was absolutely nothing she could do,
    poor thing![34]

Once the Dolphin or other enchanted being carries off a nonhealer of whatever age, one of two things happens.[35] In a minority of instances, the Dolphin who has seized the person allows him or her to return to dry land. Most often, these individuals remain in the Enchanted City where they gradually take on the identity of *encantados*.

The unexplained disappearance of a son or daughter occasions readily comprehensible feelings of grief and guilt in the child's parents. In the absence of a corpse, belief in the *Encante* undoubtedly makes such losses easier to bear. Because enchanted children are not really dead, family members need not worry about their inability to provide a proper burial or blame themselves unduly for their inability to watch over numerous offspring. How could the mother in the preceding story, for instance, possibly have known that she was entrusting her infant son to a Dolphin and not the boy's father? Then too, there is always a slim chance that the abducted will one day reappear. "My brother was carried off by a Dolphin when he was seven years old and the *pajé* said he would return to see us when he was sixteen. Six years have gone by and so it won't be long before we see him. I am looking forward to that day," says one young man in a faded Harvard sweatshirt.[36]

And yet, if the belief in enchantment, like that in the Dolphin's ability to father children whose paternity otherwise might raise awkward questions, has obvious practical implications, it would be shortsighted to reduce it to mere need. While the healer's claims that a particular child has been enchanted may give the parents some relief, they also reaffirm for the entire community the profoundly perilous interdependence between the natural and human worlds.

34. Woman, age 26, born interior of Nhamundá (Amazonas), lives Parintins (1 year). Single, cook, 2 years grade school.

35. Shamanic healers and healers-to-be constitute a separate case. As in Amazonian Indian tradition, healers continue to move back and forth between the river bottom and dry land. Those nonhealers who succeed in returning to their homes rarely, if ever, make repeat visits to the *Encante*.

36. Man, age 16, born Itacoatiara, lives interior of Parintins (Paraná dos Ramos). Single, fishing and farm work "but soon I'm off to the gold mines," 4 years school.

This sense of uneasy equilibrium once again helps distinguish stories of the *Encante* from other tales of submerged cities found in a wide array of folk traditions.[37] The parallels between the *Encante* and the lost kingdom of Atlantis—to which some Amazonian storytellers specifically refer—are obvious. In addition, African oral tradition is particularly rich in tales of water spirits who live in houses beneath the water and who may spirit off unsuspecting humans.[38]

The idea of an underwater city, sometimes known as "Temendauí," is also firmly present in various South American Indian traditions, which tend to see the residents as either the ancestral Anaconda and her people, or else fair-haired immortals who "stage celebrations in the manner of the white man."[39] These beings may kidnap and transform their human captives. (In various Yekuana narratives, for instance, the stolen women assume a new identity as the water people's mothers and daughters.)[40]

O sacaca é aquele que vai lá na cidade encantada, se transforma em boto ou outra coisa qualquer e viaja pelo fundo do mar. ("The *sacaca* is he who goes to the Enchanted City, who transforms himself into a dolphin or any other creature and travels along the river bottom.")

In order to rescue a person believed kidnaped by a Dolphin, family members customarily turn to a shamanic healer. We have seen that the *sacaca* is the most powerful representative of a much larger class of traditional curers known by the general terms of *pajé, curador, cura(n)deiro/a,* or less frequently, *cirugião* (this last word literally means "surgeon"). All of these individuals—who may be either male or female—regularly enter into communication with the spirits of the deep. In addition, there are

37. See Thompson, motif F725.1, "submarine cities." For two early references to the *Encante* see Francisco Bernardino de Sousa, *Lembranças e curiosidades do Valle do Amazonas,* p. 261; and Frederico José de Santa-Anna Néry, *Folk-lore brésilien,* p. 181. Various present-day Andean stories of submerged cities appear in Efraín Morote Best, *Aldeas sumergidas,* pp. 241–82; and Anne Marie Hocquengheim and Max Inga, *Los encantos de La Encantada,* pp. 47–51.

38. See Thompson, F420.5.2.1.5, "water-spirit drags children into river"; and F420.5.2.2, "water-spirit kidnaps mortals, keeps them underwater." Among the best-known African water spirits are the aforementioned Iemanjá, who occupies an important place in the African Brazilian pantheon; the river god Tano, known to peoples in Ghana and the Ivory Coast; and the Bantu entity Kianda, also called Kiximbi. For more on the latter see Heli Chatelain, *Folk-tales of Angola,* pp. 114–17 and 283–84. The owner of the sea, Ol-Okum, is thought by the Yoruba and Benin peoples of Nigeria to live in an underwater palace with a great retinue that includes both human and fishlike attendants.

39. For the first interpretation see Marc de Civrieux, "Medatia." The quotation is from Curt Nimuendaju, *The Tükuna,* p. 138.

40. De Civrieux, "Medatia," p. 69. Only the culture hero Medatia can bring the women to remember their human identities.

rezadores (sometimes called *benzedores*), such as Argemiro.[41] Although the latter do not summon spirits, they may exorcise a variety of ills through the recitation of Roman Catholic prayers mixed with songs and incantations heard in dreams or learned from shamanic healers.

Both *pajé* and *sacaca* are indigenous terms which suggest a larger, non-European curative tradition. These Portuguese-speaking healers' reliance on tobacco wrapped in *tauari* bark in divining an illness's supernatural agents and their use of curing practices including herbal baths, the sucking out of foreign bodies, and the censing of the sick person's body link them to indigenous shamans. Born with special gifts that allow them to link otherwise disparate worlds, both shamans and *curadores* develop their healing potential in successive voyages to the river bottom, or other normally off-limits spaces.[42]

And yet, although some *pajés* closely resemble native shamans, virtually all have incorporated elements of official and/or folk Catholicism—and, often, African Brazilian religion—into their repertoires. In some cases, these borrowings appear largely nominal (making crosses over the body during censing or beginning a spiritist session with ritual salutations to the *orixás* or a few Hail Mary's). In other instances, however, the presence of these other traditions is notable and deep.

Conversely, even healers who would not consider themselves *pajés* or *sacacas* often reveal debts to a larger, indigenous cultural legacy. Both Kátia's aunt and mother-in-law are excellent cases in point. While the former's reliance on a Saint Francis's cord and a glass of drinking water to diagnose and divine recalls European folk tradition, her exhaustive knowledge of local herbs and herbal medicines suggests native Amazonian influence. Likewise, within the framework of an African Brazilian trance religion, Kátia's mother-in-law regularly summons a host of *encantados*, who may take her to the river bottom.[43]

Shamanic healers are professionals with trade secrets which they do not share easily with noninitiates. Although I found some of these individuals more forthcoming than others, all were extremely sensitive to potential incursions by fellow curers ("Who sent you here?" "What other healers do you know? What did they tell you about me?" they inevitably demanded). They also were often bitter about both the church's general hostility toward

41. *Rezadores* (female, *rezadeiras*) are literally those who pray over, while *benzedores* (female, *benzedeiras*) are those who bless, the sick.

42. For an introduction to the vast literature on South American Indian shamanism see Lawrence E. Sullivan, *Icanchu's Drum*, pp. 386–467.

43. The *encantados* frequently enter the African Brazilian pantheon in Amazônia, taking their place beside the *caboclos* ("old Indians"), *pomba-giras*, and other lesser deities. The *orixás*, or principal deities, are themselves syncretized with Roman Catholic saints.

them, and derisive equations between themselves and African Brazilian curers on the part of a more general public. "It's really hard to be a *sacaca* today," one man in Maués complained to me as he chopped up various healing herbs with a large fish knife. "People think you are a fake and then when you show your power, they get angry. Once I summoned up an Anaconda spirit to cure a woman. Well, I had to do it, she was really sick. But then when the Anaconda arrived and started crawling up my body, damned if she didn't nearly die of fright. Still, today, her brothers want to fight me. So I hardly ever cure now. I mean, what's the use?"[44]

Unlike other healers, who travel in spirit to the Enchanted City during trances, *sacacas* claim to make the trip in body. "The *sacaca*'s flesh is the same as his spirit" ("O sacaca, a matéria dele é mesmo o espírito dele"), explains Dona Marina. They are said to assume the shape of a dolphin, great fish, or anaconda much as another person might pull on a coat and boots. Able to travel at will to the Enchanted City, they have privileged access to its powerful inhabitants, and eventually take up permanent residence at the river bottom. "The person who is a *sacaca*," Dona Marina explains, "lives more in the *Encante* than in our world. Oh, I knew a *sacaca* who would remain for a week at a time in serpent form. At the end of his life, he went and stood there in the middle of the river and said, 'My time has come to leave you.' Right there in the middle of the river, he let everybody know. And then he disappeared, laughing and laughing. It was wonderful to see."

Both *sacacas*' privileged knowledge and their ability to journey at will to the Enchanted City leads nonhealers to regard them with marked ambivalence. At once admiring and deeply suspicious of their powers, they tell numerous stories of how one or another healer chides people for stealing bananas from a faraway location or secretly courting so-and-so's youngest daughter. ("He'd had his eye on her himself, I think!" they may exclaim.) Stories, such as the following, in which the storyteller undercuts his own initially merry picture of the rumguzzling healer and his Dolphin buddy, prompt nervous laughter.

12. There was a Dolphin who kept following a child.
    So then, the father sought out this Antonio Sacaca.
    This man was a real *sacaca*
        —he would travel to the river bottom with a lighted
                                                        cigarette
            and then return with the cigarette still lit, see?

44. Man, age 61, born interior of Maués, lives Maués (2 years). Single, curer, no formal education.

So then, he [the *sacaca*] went down to the riverbank,
    and called the Dolphin with rum and special songs,
      and so, he showed up right away.
The two remained talking by the river a long time
    —it seems that both got really drunk
      from so much *cachaça*.
All I know is that the dolphin
    never again popped up beside that child.

Because this Antonio Sacaca, he was a very good *pajé*.
It's just that when he turned himself into a snake,
    no one could stand to look at him.
Holy Mary, what an ugly sight![45]

Because *sacacas* do not die, they may continue to communicate with particular human beings after their disappearance. Thus, while one state malaria
official in the town of Carauari repeatedly poked fun at his own wide
detours about the bend in the river where a missing healer was last seen,
he refused to take me there. ("Anywhere else you'd like to go, miss, I'd be
glad to take you, but not that place, just not that place, you see? That
fellow used to like to talk with me a lot. Who knows if he isn't going to
want to play a trick on me, ha, ha? And if he did, I assure you, you
wouldn't like to be along!")[46]

*A pessoa que o Boto leva fica encantada. Mas nem por isso ela deixa de
querer se desencantar.* ("The person whom the Dolphin carries off becomes
enchanted. But this does not stop him or her from wanting to become
disenchanted.")

Shamanic healers occasionally succeed in retrieving persons. By the time
the family gets around to consulting the healer, however, the kidnaped
party usually has already eaten or drunk something at the river bottom,
thereby initiating metamorphosis into an enchanted being. "Do new *encantados* suffer?" asks Dona Marina with a trace of sadness that may well
reflect her own nostalgia for her vanished mother. "No, why should they?
They have everything they want. The ones who suffer are those who remain
here, remembering. Enchanted people, no, they lead an enchanted life."

And yet, while at least some persons are said to adjust well to their new
existence beneath the river, others never give up trying to regain their
human state. (Although, theoretically, a full-fledged *encantado* may experi-

45. Man, age 44, Mazagão Velho (Amapá). Married, farmer, 3 years grade school.
46. Man, age 35, born interior of Carauari, lives Carauari (13 years). Married, state health
official, 6 years school.

ence the urge to become human, the malcontents in the stories I recorded are invariably people carried off as children or else Dolphins or Anacondas with one human parent.) These disenchantment-minded enchanted beings may appear to healers with messages for their families, including detailed instructions for obtaining their release.

Customarily, the abductee announces that he or she will reappear at midnight on a certain day and place in the form of an enormous snake. Someone must then anoint the monster with one or more designated substances (the milk of a black cow is the most common, but lemon juice and eggs are also possibilities) before proceeding to shoot it in the eye or forehead.[47] More often than not, the terrifying prospect of confronting a giant snake on a moonless beach, armed with nothing more than a ladleful of cow's milk, leads the person to forget an essential part of the instructions.

The best-known instance of disenchantment concerns the Cobra Norato, who supposedly danced with Dona Marina's mother.[48] Although, as the name suggests, the Cobra Norato is an Anaconda, he acts far more like a Dolphin. Often, in fact, storytellers will start out by identifying Norato or Noratinho as a dolphin, then get confused in midstream when they remember that he was, indeed, a snake. ("Oh Maria, come here!" one man calls to his wife, who is off in the corner cleaning an enormous stack of fish. "This Norato, was he a *Boto* or was he a *Cobra Grande*?")[49]

The following version of the Norato story, recorded in the small city of Maués, recalls native Amazonian Magical Twin stories in its insistence on Norato's goodness as opposed to his twin sister's evil nature. While, however, Norato and his sister are often the children of an *encantado* and a human mother, here they are fully human siblings who are carried off to the river bottom when their boat capsizes. Here too, it is the sister, instead of the soldier who goes on to disenchant him, who blinds Norato in one eye.

13. So then, when they fell out of the canoe,
    a great snake carried them off to the *Encante*.

47. See Thompson, motifs D712.6, "disenchantment by wounding"; and D712.7, "disenchantment by shooting." These remedies—and, indeed, the whole idea of the return of the disenchanted—suggest European influence. The fertility symbols of milk and eggs suggest a rebirth, while the blackness of the cow hints at witchcraft. The lemon cleanses and purifies. Often, the human assistant is asked to shoot the monster in the forehead, so that it may die to its previous existence.

48. For an introduction to the Norato or "Honorato" story see Cascudo, *Geografia*, pp. 254–58.

49. Man, age 54, born interior of Maués, lives Maués (12 years). Married, carpenter, schooling unknown.

And they were transformed into two snakes, you know?
    one male, and the other, female.
And the male was this Norato.

So then, the woman,
    she was very evil-hearted.
Wherever she would come on a canoe
    or boat that was passing by,
        she would sink it without a second thought.
And the young man, the boy-snake,
    he didn't like his sister doing this.
So that, once, they got into a fight
    in the middle of the river
        and he blinded her.
What's more, she blinded him as well.

Afterward, this Norato, he went to a *festa,*
    and talked with a fellow there.
He asked the fellow
    if he had the courage to disenchant him,
        because all he had to do
            was shoot the great snake in the forehead
            and wait for him to emerge in the form of a
                man.
And whatever was in his hand would be a present for him.

So then, the fellow went there to the riverbank
    at the appointed hour.
He shot that huge snake right smack in the forehead
    and sure enough, ten minutes later,
        a man emerges from the snake's skin
        with a diamond in his hand.
And the fellow grabbed the diamond and took off,
    and to this day, no one knows
        what happened to him.

Now then, this Norato, he still lives someplace
    here in the interior of Parintins.[50]

50. Man, age 25, born interior of Parintins (Jacu). Married, fisherman and farmer, 2 years grade school.

The idea that people can fall under a spell that causes them temporarily to adopt another shape appears in many folk traditions. So does the related notion that victims can be restored to their former states. The *Encante,* however, reveals peculiarities which make it unmistakably Amazonian.

O Boto pode fazer tanto o bem quanto o mal. ("The Dolphin can just as soon do good as evil.")

Much like the perverse dolphins who may function as a friend to fishermen, the often nefarious Dolphin also may come to the aid of human beings. Usually, when I responded to accounts of these creature's dire misdeeds with the question "And so Dolphins only do bad things?" the teller looked surprised. "There are thieving Dolphins, rum-drinking and woman-chaser Dolphins," Dona Marina once assured me, "but there are also well-mannered Dolphins, who are everybody's friend."

Unlike ordinary *botos,* who generally restrict their aid to fishing ventures, their enchanted counterparts exhibit a much broader range of actions. One Dolphin, for instance, endears himself to the community by diving down to the river bottom to retrieve lost oars. Other Dolphins watch over fishing boats during bad storms, bailing out the water that otherwise would sink them. Still others provide much-needed transportation over vast expanses—such as the Dolphin who speeds home a tardy fisherman to his daughter's wedding. Although the storyteller in the last instance clearly intends for the listeners perched beside him on a beached canoe to laugh at the tale's formulaic conclusion ("Why, just yesterday, I passed by there and they were still eating"), he insists that the Dolphin "really can help people; I myself know many cases."[51]

Supernatural beings in many different narrative traditions possess the power to help, as well as hurt, human beings. They may present them with protective talismans or aid them in accomplishing otherwise impossible missions: transforming straw to gold, for instance, or divining the answer to an otherwise impossible conundrum. Dolphins, in contrast, are most apt to cure bodily afflictions. Unlike in many Indo-European narratives which portray a direct relationship, or actual friendship, between human protagonists and supernatural beings, the *encantados'* assistance is almost always mediated through human healers, be these *pajés* and *curadores* or African Brazilian *pais-de-santo.* Furthermore, the enchanted beings' ability to cure as well as cause sickness provides a cosmological dimension often lacking in superficially comparable tales of supernatural assistance.

51. Man, age 39, born interior of Parintins, lives Zé Açu (21 years). Married, owns passenger boat and small trading post, MOBRAL literacy program.

The very particular sort of humanization of the *boto* we have seen here is unusual. Although human beings may turn into dolphins in other traditions (witness the Greek and Chinese examples cited in the last chapter), reverse, ongoing metamorphoses from dolphin to human form are hard to find outside the Amazon. Conversely, we have noted the relative dearth of Amazonian stories in which people become ordinary dolphins.[52]

In the end, it is impossible to pinpoint the origins of the Dolphin stories. A fluid and ongoing mix of Amerindian, European, and African elements, they are a record of the present as much as a myriad of pasts.

52. Speaking primarily of the European and Asian traditions, Pilleri notes that although various peoples have credited dolphins with human characteristics, dolphins "*have apparently never been shown with human features* but have always been regarded as having something in common with, and being the equal of man" (G. Brenner and G. Pilleri, "The Dolphin in Ancient Art and Literature," p. 295).

5

QUESTIONS OF PERFORMANCE

Negócio de Boto todo mundo conta. Agora, todo mundo conta dum jeito diferente.

(This business of the Dolphin, everybody tells the story. Now then, everybody tells it in a different way.)

—*Carpenter, age 19, Parintins*

f the Dolphin stories reflect individual differences in age, sex, and place of residence, they also suggest peculiarities in the storytelling context. The following description of three sessions that occur in socially distinct, but geographically proximate, settings underscores the importance of this larger social setting.[1] The first exchange takes place within Parintins, the second in a fishing and farming community less than an hour from the city, and the third in a hamlet about three hours south. Although the sessions reveal undeniable dissimilarities, in all three instances the overriding theme is metamorphosis, the storytellers move constantly from one sort of tale to another, and the larger context is a society in frank transition.

On a number of occasions during my travels in Amazônia, I was able to tape stories that arose as a part of conversation. This was particularly easy in the interior, where people often congregate in one or another neighbor's house at early evening (*a boca da noite*) in order to chat, or *palestrar,* before going to bed.[2] Then too, I once fell asleep on the dock in Óbidos

1. By "performance" I mean the storytelling session as a whole, including the nonverbal behavior and asides of both storytellers and their listeners. For an introduction to performance as a concept in folklore studies see Dan Ben-Amos and Kenneth Goldstein, *Folklore.*

2. Most communities have at least one accomplished storyteller, whose prowess prompts expressions of admiration. "So-and-so is a real pro at this" ("Fulano tirou carteira disso") the person's neighbors may assert. This jocular suggestion of professionalism notwithstanding, there is no formal role within the community for gifted storytellers comparable to that reserved for talented musicians or shamanic healers. (Many *pajés,* by the way, happen to be excellent

waiting for a boat that only arrived toward dawn, and I started to dream that I was listening to a long and complicated *encantado* story. When I opened my eyes, I found that the people huddled next to me were indeed talking about a woman rumored to have been hauled off by a Dolphin to the river bottom, so I clicked on my tape recorder before going back to sleep. The next morning, I was sure that I had imagined the whole thing, but the hushed, excited voices on the tape confirmed that the story was no dream.

In almost every case, my presence clearly had an effect upon the story-tellers. People did not appear in any way uncomfortable about my being there (I was a known quantity in the first case, a friend of friends in the others), but they did incorporate me into their midst in different ways. Although some folklorists would argue that I should have awaited, and then neutrally observed, spontaneous performances, I believe I would have affected the course of the sessions described here far more dramatically by feigning invisibility than by responding in a natural manner when people asked me questions or shot glances in my direction. The very few stories I taped without people's knowledge—the tale recorded on the Óbidos dock, for instance—do not strike me as any more authentic than the ones in which my presence was openly acknowledged.

A number of the Dolphin narratives represent a parenthesis in an ongo-ing conversation. Often, these accounts take the form of news, gossip, or personal recollections. ("But what story? We were just talking," one older woman exclaimed when I asked if I could tape her account of how a Dolphinlike stranger had showed up last night in a neighbor's bed.) In the instances described here, however, the tales are part of relatively lengthy exchanges involving multiple storytellers, not all of whom were present for the entire period.

No storytelling session is fully representative. Although, for instance, men dominate two of the interchanges described below, I was present at numerous others in which all or most of the tellers were women. Two of my examples involve persons of widely different ages, while the storytellers in the third case are all in their late teens or twenties. However, I just as easily could have selected sessions limited to children, old people, or per-sons of middle age. Then too, while I have focused on Parintins and its environs, I could have chosen widely distant locations, or three separate performances within the city proper.

And yet, despite the necessarily partial character of these--and all—

---

storytellers, but not all good storytellers are by any means *pajés*.) Unlike musicians and healers, who are paid in cash or kind for their services, the storyteller usually does not receive—and would not expect—more than appreciative attention.

examples, the performances described here reveal much about storytelling as a whole. Spirited exchanges, in which people regularly interrupt, contradict, and corroborate each other ("That's absolutely right, Dona Maria!" or "No, no, you've got it all wrong, João!"), they suggest the *encantados'* ongoing role in daily life.

PARINTINS

The first session to be considered takes place in a sidewalk bar in Parintins over a period of some four and a half hours on a rainless Friday night. Located in the city's central square, in front of the municipal market, the so-called bar is actually no more than a collection of rickety metal tables where younger people customarily gather over beer and soft drinks while a loudspeaker sputters American and Brazilian popular music. The participants were Maurício and four unmarried male friends, ranging from sixteen to twenty-eight years old. Three of the young men, including Maurício, were born in the interior of Parintins, but all five have lived most of their lives within the city, where they have completed, or are attending, high school. On this occasion, Maurício has invited me to hear one of his friends, Paulo, retell a treasure tale that has particularly impressed him. Upon arrival, we find Paulo accompanied by another friend, Mané. Somewhat later, two other longtime acquaintances, Zeca and Eduardo, join the group.

Although the fast-moving, very animated conversation is primarily among the five friends, they occasionally address me directly ("You've heard of Saint Cipriano, haven't you?" or "You mean to say, you don't have ghosts in California?"), looking a bit warily in my direction when the stories become off-color. And yet, although I worried about inhibiting them, they appear to be reacting to me more as a foreign, and for this reason, slightly exotic, female for whose attention, from time to time, they vie directly, than as a researcher bent on judging their narrative capabilities. Initially self-conscious about my tape recorder ("Hey, hey, I want to make sure that everyone can hear me there in America!" exclaimed Paulo) the young men quickly become caught up in the ongoing discussion, and do not appear to notice when I fumble in the darkness with the batteries or pause to click in a new cassette. When I later ask Maurício if long sessions like this one are usual, he replies that he and his friends often exchange similar stories, but that extended conversations of the type described here are most common "when we go on trips to the interior and there is really nothing else to do but talk."

The conversation starts with a bottle of beer and dark-eyed, self-consciously handsome Paulo's detailed account of how one of his father's workers discovers an ancient coin which brings him numerous misfortunes until he has it "baptized" by a traditional healer. This talk of unearned wealth triggers a lengthy interchange among Paulo, Mané, and Maurício about greedy politicians and the negative effects of current economic policies in Amazônia. "Today, the politicians trip over themselves trying to sell what doesn't belong to them," Paulo observes with a bang on the table that almost topples the foam-crowned glasses. Maurício then offers various concrete examples of graft within the state and local government, while Paulo himself goes on to denounce the adverse living conditions for factory workers lured by false campaign promises to Manaus. ("You should see how those people live there!" he says to me with a dramatic scowl.)

After a pause, Mané, a wiry, somewhat shy young man, who has been carefully constructing a small tower of bottle caps, topples his creation with one finger. He then suggests that avarice leads to an unquiet afterlife "because the money that was buried remains as a link between the material world and *mundo astral* [the astral plane or spirit world]." Paulo goes on to describe the sensational sufferings visited on people who attempt to dig up hidden treasure. At this point, Maurício takes a long swallow of beer and launches into a long account of how many persons buried their valuables during the *Cabanagem* rebellion. The waiter, who has arrived with a new bottle, chimes in that a group of foreigners ("Germans, maybe, or maybe they were Italians") have just discovered a chest of "pure gold" coins.

Returning to the treasure theme, Mané proceeds to recount a dream his mother once had in which a tall, dark man directed her to dig beneath a tree at a fork in the road. ("Did she ever do it?" Maurício inquires. "No, she didn't," Mané tells him. "I mean, who wants to go scrounging around in the dark, right?") Paulo grins appreciatively and launches into an account of how a female relative was making "piles of money" in the unofficial lottery called the *jogo do bicho* until a particularly terrifying nightmare persuaded her to stop playing.[3]

Maurício interjects a comment about São Cipriano, who went on to become a saint after abjuring the black arts, and Mané observes that various African Brazilian cult practitioners are involved with magic of the sort the saint renounced ("There's a *macumbeira* in Palmares who will slap a *feitiço* on anyone if you pay her enough money"). When I ask where the woman lives, the friends cannot agree on the location, and, in fact, name several

3. For the origins of the *jogo de bicho,* in which people bet on symbols of twenty-five animals, usually based on dreams they have had of these, see Luís da Câmara Cascudo, *Dicionário do folclore brasileiro,* pp. 411–12.

different parts of town. "She must move around a lot!" I say. "No, no, she clones herself just like in the movies!" Mané assures me, and the others laugh.

Paulo then describes how a cousin of his once etched into a candle the name of a former girlfriend who came hurrying back to him just as the flame consumed the last drop of wax. This leads to a long aside about the cousin's more flamboyant successes with women. When he remarks that the cousin was equally skilled at taming wild animals, I can no longer restrain myself and make a wry comment that causes all three storytellers to laugh. Mané next tells a funny story about a man who cockily attempts to seduce a dozen women with a dolphin eye that everybody but he knows was really taken from a stingray. "These things are all psychology," Maurício assures Mané with a deprecatory wave of the hand.

After a short pause, Paulo recounts the evening's first Dolphin story. Although he joins Maurício and myself in laughing at the smooth-talking stranger whom a fast-thinking woman leaves stranded on the dance floor ("See, the women here are very clever!"), he concludes by insisting that "these things really happen." Mané, who has just pulled up his chair again, offers a series of self-described *casos acontecidos* ("true stories"), followed by an account of how a group of *encantados* surrounded his hammock the evening after he killed an enormous water snake.[4] "You may not believe this," he tells his friends solemnly, "and I might not believe it either if I had not been there."

At this point, tall, curly-haired Eduardo and his prankish cousin, Zeca, appear, and the waiter brings them glasses on a metal tray. Toinho, a native of Parintins now living in Manaus, also greets us before joining another table. ("So long, guys, this stuff spooks me!" he says with an exaggerated wink in my direction.) Having heard the end of Mané's story, Eduardo launches into an account of a Dolphin child born on a stormy night. "I don't know if this story is true," concludes Eduardo, picking at the label on the quickly emptied bottle. "I only know that the people there in Paraná dos Ramos all swear he has caused a lot of problems."

Eduardo's story leads Paulo to recount a version of the Cobra Norato tale that ends with the protagonist's successful disenchantment in a foreign country. In response to Maurício's insistence that it was a local soldier who aided Norato ("You want the *gringos* to have everything, man, even the

---

4. Storytellers divide accounts of supernatural entities into categories including the *caso acontecido* (true story), *romance* (adventure tale), *piada* (joke or funny story), and *boato* (rumor). They may also refer to their own or others' stories as *notícias* (news stories), *trancosos* (folktales or well-known, fictive accounts), or *coisas dos antigos* (tales handed down by an older generation).

power to disenchant our *encantados!*"), Paulo observes that he is simply repeating what he has heard from his grandfather. Maurício signals the waiter to bring us yet another bottle ("cold, make it super-cold, hear?") before offering a blatantly fictional account of a fisherman who goes flying out of an anaconda's mouth after starting a fire for that night's dinner in its belly. This tale, which he concludes with a feigned belch meant to recall the anaconda's action, prompts a series of jokes, one scatological (Mané), and three mildly pornographic (Paulo, Eduardo, Paulo), the last involving an enchanted tree. (The Portuguese word *pau,* which they use for "tree," has the same sort of double meaning as "rod" or "pole" in English.) When I laugh at the conclusion, the five friends also begin laughing.

Although consciously lighthearted, the tale of the tree initiates a very serious discussion of the *encantados.* When Eduardo expresses doubts about their existence, Paulo responds that "these things could—I say they *could*—be true." While refusing to take a firm stand in relation to the *encantados,* Zeca pointes out that Amazônia is "richer, far richer than anyone can imagine. If we could only see beneath the surface of the river, we would go crazy, truly crazy at the sight of so much unsuspected wealth."

This last remark sets the stage for Mané's story of an enchanted Sea Horse, a single hair of whose golden mane brings fabulous wealth to its possessor. Gently swirling about the beer remaining in his glass, Paulo then tells an apparently unrelated story of a mysterious woman whom he identifies as a ghost. ("She looked like an *encantado* but she was someone who lived here in Parintins and died a long time ago.") He also passes on a rumor or *boato* (told to him by the same person to whom he attributes the ghost story) about a man said to turn into a horse on Friday evenings, which leads Zeca to paw and snort.

Clearly somewhat offended, Paulo insists on the reliable character of the original narrator ("I know him and he wouldn't lie"). "Besides," he adds with a restraining tap on Zeca's shoulder, "I'm not saying that the story's true, I'm just repeating what he told me." Unconvinced, Zeca sneezes and counters with an "absolutely true tale" involving a cousin of his and the forest spirit called the *Neguinho do Campo Grande.*[5] He and Maurício then exchange childhood recollections of the formerly bucolic outskirts of Parintins.

Hearing a dolphin exhale (the central square is very near the river and by this time the music has faded to an intermittent whimper), Eduardo offers me the beer remaining in the bottle, draining the final drops into

5. The literal translation is "little black boy of Campo Grande." For an introduction to the *Neguinho* in various parts of Brazil see Cascudo, *Geografia dos mitos brasileiros,* pp. 285–91.

his own glass when I decline. He then goes on to tell of a fisherman who taunts a female Dolphin who later reappears as a fair-haired woman. When Paulo laughs, Mané frowns at him and tells another story reinforcing Eduardo's account. ("Some things you cannot joke about. They are like a fourth dimension.") At this juncture, Zeca yawns loudly. Paulo looks at his watch, Maurício expresses amazement at the hour ("Have we really been talking that long?"), I snap off the tape recorder, and everyone goes home.

ZÉ AÇU

The second storytelling session takes place in the community of Zé Açu amidst ongoing preparations for that miniature, distinctly homespun version of the *Boi-Bumbá* of Parintins from which the teenage girl's companions desisted because of fears of being accosted by a Dolphin during the river journey. The community has a total population of approximately fifteen hundred persons spread out over several clusters known as *centros* ("centers"). More likely to be constructed of wood or straw than stucco, the houses do not have the running water, electricity, or television found in most, though not all, dwellings in Parintins. Because, however, at least one passenger boat makes the hour-long trip back and forth to the city each day, the residents of Zé Açu are far less isolated than the inhabitants of many smaller and more remote locations.

Dominated by the chapel, which doubles as a grade school, the unpaved central plaza is used for soccer games and *festas*. On the afternoon of the so-called mini-Boi, people mill about the square, with an air of anticipation, as some of the men set up the loudspeakers that have just arrived by boat from Parintins. A number of those present sit or stand about a rough-hewn table and benches which overlook the river.

The approximately two dozen people who become involved in telling stories are of both sexes and range in age from ten to eighty-seven years. Unlike Maurício and his friends, whose parents moved to Parintins in part out of concern for their children's education, few of these individuals have more than several years of grade school, and a good number are illiterate. Also in contrast to the young men, who either study or work at a variety of mostly white-collar jobs within the city (only Paulo sometimes helps his father in the interior), the male residents of Zé Açu are overwhelmingly fishermen, hunters, and farmers, while the women keep house and work beside their husbands in manioc and vegetable gardens.[6]

My own place in the proceedings was somewhat different than in the

---

6. *Ribeirinhos* (riverbank dwellers) customarily engage in fishing and hunting in addition to farming. Even rubber tappers and Brazil nut gatherers usually hunt and fish as well.

1. Milkman, Parintins. The milk in the metal cannister is ladled out into various receptacles provided by clients, who await his morning visit.

2. Boys with the morning catch in Silêncio do Matá, a rural community founded by runaway slaves in the early nineteenth century.

3. Child in homemade *Boi-Bumbá* costume, Parintins.

4. *Boi-Bumbá* organizer and African Brazilian cult leader, Seu Setenta, in his home in Belém.

5. Umbanda practitioner, Parintins. The "Solomon's Star" around her neck is a mystic, not specifically Jewish, symbol.

6. Crossing the Amazon, Santárem. This passenger boat, operated by a small agricultural community for members with business in the city, is heading toward the "encounter of the waters" in which the lighter waters of the Tapajós River run alongside the darker, more sediment-laden waters of the Amazon.

7. Rubber tapper and granddaughter, interior of Carauari. The forest and the man's machete are in the background.

8. Vendor and customer, Embers Ice Cream.

9. Banana seller, Porto Velho.

10. Old woman, Parintins.

11. Gold miner, Agua Branca gold field, interior of Itaituba. The man, who goes by the nickname "Ratão Branco" ("White Rat"), wears a plastic rosary around his neck and holds the key to the makeshift bar in the front room of his house, where miners go to drink sugar rum *(cachaça)*. Originally from the Northeast, he has worked in several dozen different mines over the past eighteen years.

12. Girl and younger sister, São Joaquim, Amapá.

13. The great-granddaughter of a runaway slave lowers the plaited window of her straw house in Silêncio do Matá.

14. Gerineldo's mother and one of his younger brothers in the open-air kitchen of their home in Palmares, Parintins.

15. Fisherman and farmer, interior of Parintins. The man is one of Kátia's relatives by marriage.

16. Girl with pet toucan, in Parintins.

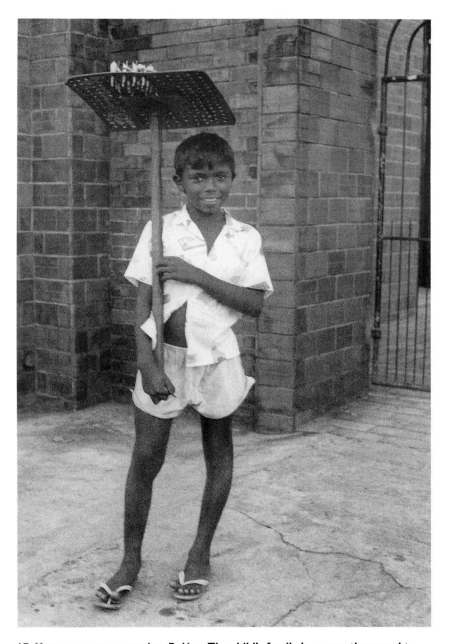

17. Young sugarcane vendor, Belém. The child's family has recently moved to the city from the interior.

18. Man grinding sugarcane in a press originally purchased from Japanese settlers in the once prosperous jute colony of nearby Vila Amazonas.

19. Young gold miners, Rondônia. Note the barge in the background.

20. Children on a sunlit *igarapé*, interior of Amapá.

21.Woman, Maués.

22. Man and woman beneath shade trees, Parintins. The pot in the foreground holds the pungent, gummy soup called *tacacá*.

23. Woman and child outside the market in Óbidos.

24. Children, Parintins. The painted gourds in the background are used for *tacacá*.

25. The author.

first instance, where I was a friend of a key participant and the only female. Here, in contrast, I was just one of a number of relative outsiders of both sexes, who descended on Zé Açu for the festival along with the sound crew from Parintins. (I say "relative" outsiders because many of the visitors were already familiar to the residents either from past association or through common friends and kin.) As I went to Zé Açu in the company of the sister of the community's schoolteacher, I was readily accepted. Although people were aware I was taping, and most perceived that I was a foreigner ("You aren't from around here," they would say expectantly), they did not appear to find my presence off-putting or even unusual. "Came here all the way from California to see the *festa,* did you?" one man in a bright green baseball cap asked, patting my shoulder. "Well, I made the trip here myself from Caburi and I sure hope it will be good!"

What would extend into an afternoon-long storytelling session begins innocuously when a middle-aged woman with a single long gray braid responds to her visiting sister's inquiry about a young neighbor rumored to have been the victim of a *feitiço.* ("What happened?" demands another visitor, who has come in on the end of the story, leading the speaker to repeat her entire account to the growing group of onlookers.) This initial narrative prompts a long string of tales punctuated by the arrival of new storytellers and the departure of others. Throughout the course of the session, people engage in unrelated conversations on the sidelines, comfort or scold children, yawn, poke each other playfully, stretch, sigh, and drum their knuckles on the table while staring out at the now blue, now pewter-colored river. Although they speak primarily to one another, they sometimes look at me to see how I am reacting, and from time to time provide information they think I might be lacking. ("Paraná das Ilhas is three hours up the river" or "Seu Manuel was a *pajé* who used to live here.")

The initial account of the *feitiço,* whose perpetrator is said to transform himself into a birdlike entity called a *Matinta-perera* or *Matins* every Thursday evening, sparks a series of stories by three men of different ages about people who turn into various sorts of animals at will.[7] Their assertions prompt heated debate among a dozen or so listeners of both sexes about

---

7. For an introduction to the *Matinta-perera* see Cascudo, *Geografia,* pp. 103–5 and 279–82. People often argue that there are actually two types of *Matinta:* one, a birdlike creature; the other, a somewhat nebulous entity into which human beings transform themselves with the help of diabolic incantations. Both are said to emit a high-pitched chirping sound that induces headaches, fever, and, sometimes, madness. If one encounters a *Matinta* of the second type, one should invite the creature to coffee the next morning. The person who then shows up on the doorstep is the shape-changer. Reminiscent of the *Saci-pereré,* found in the south of Brazil, the *Matinta* is also present in indigenous traditions, where it appears as a terrifying spirit of the dead.

whether, and in precisely what circumstances, these sorts of metamorphoses occur. Despite the general consensus that such transformations were far more common in the past ("today one hardly sees these things any more," remarks the oldest of the three men), some people are clearly more inclined to believe these accounts than others. "What do you think?" one young man in bright blue rubber sandals asks me, appealing to my outsider's status as a supposedly impartial judge. "Nobody who's been to school believes these things!" interjects one of his friends—a thin young man with chipped front teeth—before I can answer. "I didn't ask what *you* thought," the first young man retorts with a flip of the hand that makes several people laugh.

The youngest of the three men—a teenager from a nearby hamlet—next describes the enormous tunnel supposedly created by the giant Anaconda called the *Cobra Grande* on a beach near the fishing community where he used to live. ("I saw the tunnel but I didn't see what made it," he admits in response to a question by a clearly dubious visitor from Parintins.) The woman with the long gray braid goes on to relate a number of similar incidents, then recalls how her own father came upon the *Cobra Grande* in the guise of an enormous, brightly illumined riverboat one stormy night. "He only recovered in the *sacaca*'s care" ("Só ficou bom na mão do sacaca"), she concludes, going on to relate several more of this curer's feats. Her account prompts a jesting rejoinder on the part of an athletic-looking middle-aged male neighbor in a mesh shirt and cutoff bermudas. "Alas, today, there are no more *sacacas* here, Dona Joana, only *homens sacanas* ("shameless men") who go swimming in the river, then come out on land, and remain here sunning themselves on the beach, getting the ladies all excited."

Although the man's remarks produce generalized laughter (even the older woman giggles reluctantly), they lead a green-eyed, soft-spoken teenage girl from a neighboring community to insist that her father once had an encounter with the *Cobra Grande*. ("He'll be here tonight and you can ask him for yourself," she informs the obviously skeptical man.) An old fisherman in a ragged World Cup T-shirt then recounts his own experience with this enchanted being. ("I found it [the *Cobra Grande*] so lovely. It vanished and I went after it. I wanted to get nearer—I wasn't a bit scared.")

A very thin young woman from Zé Açu next recounts the story of the Cobra Noratins. ("This was in that time when people were not baptized and there were hardly any priests," she says.) In describing how Norato turns back into a snake at midnight, she compares him to Cinderella, a story she heard not long ago on a radio program aimed at children, but highly popular among rural adults as well. Her neighbor, a woman of roughly the same age with a heart-shaped face and tawny hair in a small bun, then describes her own encounter with a Dolphin one moonlit night. "He was coming toward me, closer, closer, but I called on all the saints to help me, and he disappeared into the river without a sound," she explains with a dramatic shudder.[8]

The first young woman declares it a mistake to believe everything one hears, since "even though there is a lot of truth in these stories, there is also a lot of invention." As an illustration, she recounts how a renowned *sacaca* insisted that a father cut down a magnificent old mango tree in order to facilitate the disenchantment of his son. Once the tree had toppled, the boy would supposedly reappear, but nothing happened. "So now he has no shade, no fruit, no son!" the storyteller concludes, prompting titters mixed with mutterings about some healers' chicanery. ("Still," adds a man with one clouded eye, who has been present since the beginning of the session, "there are *sacacas* who are very, very good.")

The sun is beginning to disappear into a suddenly rosy river when an older man in a straw hat who has just joined the group recounts an amusing story of a giant snake whose glowing eyes turn out to be very ordinary lanterns. Then, perceptibly serious, the storyteller proceeds to tell how a boat in which he was traveling suddenly anchored in a coconut grove. There, the passengers encountered a tall stranger all in white who suddenly vanished into the water with the dolphin's telltale "Chahhhh!" "So then," the speaker says so firmly that the people chatting on the margins suddenly grow silent, "I believe that the man was enchanted, because everybody knows that Dolphins have the power to turn into human beings."

After another lull in the conversation, the teenage boy tells a self-proclaimed *trancoso* of the man who harpooned what he thought was a dolphin, only to discover he had wounded the general-in-chief of the Dolphin army. "And I know that man," an older man interjects with a chuckle. "Every morning there is a big pile of fish stacked before his door. He really eats well!" The man then launches into a similarly jocular story which he introduces as "a fib a fisherman once told me."

The old man who told the story of the mysterious stranger now suggests that the enchanted beings are a holdover from a time in which "religion did not exist" and "strange things" routinely happened. He is about to recount another story when his grandson comes to tell him that a newly arrived boat has brought long-awaited farm supplies. "Excuse me," the man says as he leaves amidst respectful nods.

The exchange, which continues for some time in the growing darkness, includes various ghost stories told by a woman with a chubby baby on her

---

8. Saint Francis of Canindé is a northeastern version of Saint Francis of Assisi particularly popular among migrants.

shoulder, two tall tales by the teenage boy, an old man's graphic description of his encounter with a mountain lion, and a report of a UFO in the small community of Valéria by the schoolteacher's sister. This last story prompts a largely humorous description of a fearsome Big Foot–like creature called the *Mapinguari,* as well as more serious accounts of wild beasts and the club-wielding forest giant known as the *Juma.*[9] When a small child who has been listening intently suddenly begins weeping in fear, his mother soothes him. "There, there, Mama won't let the *Juma* get you!" she exclaims, stroking his hair as he hides his head between her knees.

A man from outside Zé Açu, new to the conversation, then retells the hospital story in a very serious manner. Although a few persons roll their eyes when he claims to have met the fisherman in question (here, the woman with the braid waves her finger at me as if to say, "Don't you believe a word of this!"), most listen with interest to his version of the tale. The man launches into another account of a Dolphin-abductor, but the festival organizers begin testing the loudspeaker, causing everyone to hurry home to change into costumes or party clothes.

TERRA PRETA

The third narrative exchange takes place in Terra Preta, a tiny fishing and farming community on a steep cliff above the very beautiful Uaicurapá River, about three hours by boat from Parintins. The approximately two hundred residents live in plaited straw huts without electricity or running water, arranged about a small church, which again serves as a school. Although they regularly travel to Parintins to sell produce, collect pension money, or see a doctor, they are more isolated than their counterparts in Zé Açu.

As I am making the trip to Terra Preta with several parish workers and the priest from Parintins who visits the community twice a year, people receive me warmly, laughing when the priest says I have come all the way from America to hear them tell *piadas* about the Dolphin and his friends. "I'll bet you know a few yourself, Father!" one older woman teases the Amazonian-born young cleric, who only grins.

The portion of the extremely animated session that I am recording lasts just over two and a half hours on a Sunday morning. Although it attracts numerous bystanders of both sexes, some of whom contribute to the con-

9. For an introduction to the *Mapinguari,* a fetid forest creature with a mouth in its stomach, see Cascudo, *Geografia,* p. 189–92. The *Juma* is a nine-foot-high Indian who walks through the woods with an enormous rosewood club, employing his large feet as an umbrella when it rains (Tonzinho Saunier, *O magnífico folclore de Parintins,* p. 16).

versation, the chief participants are three men named Raimundo, Seu João, and Carmelindo, ages thirty-seven, seventy-three, and twenty-eight. (*Seu,* a colloquial form of *Senhor,* is a title of respect.)

The extremely talkative Raimundo has never been to school but still can read and write a little, while younger and much shyer Carmelindo has completed several years of grade school. Like most older members of the community, Seu João has studied "just the sky, the river, and the woods." Although Carmelindo worked a year in Manaus as a hotel night watchman and a short-order cook, he, like the others, was born in Terra Preta, where all three make a living as fishermen, hunters, and subsistence farmers. The young men have wives and children; Seu João is a widower with at least one great-grandson, who is part of the group.

The session begins as a handful of community members sit on a log beneath a canopy of leaves, chatting, slapping sandflies, and cooing at drowsy babies as they wait for the mass to start. I am watching the river shift color in the sunlight and wondering if there will be time to tape a few stories during lunch when I suddenly realize that Seu João is talking about the *Curupira.* I am not sure what prompted his account—quite possibly a child's question, since he initially seems to be speaking to his great-grandson—but soon everyone is listening intently. "A true story told to my father by my grandfather," Seu João observes and the listeners nod appreciatively.

Warming to the occasion, Seu João goes on to describe a man from a neighboring community who had a disconcerting habit of turning into a *Matinta-perera.* "People changed shape in that time," he observes by way of conclusion. "Today it is more difficult, but in that time, they changed into horses, pigs, pacas, absolutely everything."[10] Swatting at a stubborn fly that keeps landing on his chin, he goes on to describe how a man's friend discovered his temporarily headless body in his hammock one dark night ("Now that one was a real *Matinta!*"). Although Seu João joins the group in laughing at the friend's astonished indignation ("Good grief, man, why didn't you tell me you had a habit of running off without your body?"), he observes that the story was "one hundred percent true."

An older woman then relates a similar instance in which a man transforms himself into a horse. When I ask why anyone would want to be a horse, she grins suggestively and said the man must have liked the mares. "It also could have been a penance," Seu João observes solemnly, with a nod in my direction.

Following Seu João's cue, Carmelindo notes that the supernatural is

10. "Se gerava naquele tempo," Seu João says. "Hoje está difícil, mas naquela epoca se gerava para cavalo, para porco, para paca, tudo, tudo."

serious business. He then offers a detailed account of how he remained *panema* for many months after a creature he suspects was the *Curupira* frightened him one night while he was hunting deer.[11] "Do people turn into *Curupiras?*" a very small child asks his mother. "No, no," she assures him. "The *Curupira* is the mother of the forest; no one becomes a *Curupira.*"

Carmelindo concludes his story by explaining how he had to see three different healers before he could successfully hunt again. ("It's not easy to find a cure for these things," Seu João declares knowingly.) Seu João then recalls how, when he was still a child, a group of men chased a stranger in white to the riverbank. Suddenly dropping to his heels (up to this point, he had been standing), Carmelindo notes that a young woman he met in Manaus started dreaming every night of the Dolphin until the latter finally carried her off, "body and soul." "Sometimes," Seu João interjects with a new swat at the fly, "people catch these *encantados*, but only out of the water, in human form. Those men I was telling you about, they would have caught the Dolphin if he hadn't jumped into the water in the nick of time."

At this point, a parish worker appears to say that mass will soon begin (the chapel bells have been ringing vigorously for some time now) and most of the women and children, as well as some of the men, disappear. I rise to accompany them, but Seu João, Raimundo, and Carmelindo are by now thoroughly caught up in telling stories and do not budge. Although I worry for a moment about whether the priest will perceive me as distracting people from religious obligations, it seems clear that the three men are about to go on swapping tales no matter what I do. I therefore sit down once again and Seu João begins a story in which a love-smitten Dolphin tries to win over a young woman with gifts of fish and flowers. ("What kind of flowers?" one of the older children who has remained behind with us wants to know. "Big white flowers that don't grow anywhere except the river bottom," Seu João responds without hesitation.)

Although the tale ends with the young woman's disappearance, Seu João's otherwise very funny portrait of the seductive Dolphin prompts Raimundo to tell a similarly amusing story involving buried treasure. "Money like that has to be baptized," interjects one of the men who stayed on to listen, pushing away a scrawny dog who is nosing at his big toe. "If

11. The *Curupira* is a forest spirit who most often takes the form of a small, dark-skinned child. Belief in the *Korupira* or *Kaapara* was common among the Tupinambá of eastern Brazil and can be found among various modern Tupian peoples. For a series of nineteenth-century Amazonian texts in indigenous tongues with literal Portuguese translations see Manuel Barbosa Rodrigues, "Poranduba amazonense."

it isn't baptized, it turns into something else." This man—a second cousin of Carmelindo's from a nearby community—then tells the story of a friend who repeatedly dreams of an Indian who instructs him where to dig for gold. But because the friend disobeys the Indian's warning not to share this information, the bright coins turn to charcoal as soon as he unearths them. "Hmmmm!" Seu João says disapprovingly, with a swat at his neck now, "One has to know when to be silent."

At this point, Raimundo's plump and pretty teenage daughter arrives to tell her father it is almost lunchtime, and asks Seu João if he knows the story of the *encantado* who once appeared to a neighbor, Seu Luís. Seu João nods knowingly ("Seu Luís, Casimira's father, right?" he asks). Instead, however, of recounting the tale, he begins to speak of a local water spirit said to frequent a nearby beach. "He [the spirit] used to live there," Seu João says, "but I don't know if he has become civilized or disappeared or died." Raimundo's daughter notes eagerly that she has two girlfriends who once saw a man in white walking on the beach at night while they were looking for turtle eggs. "It must have been a Dolphin," Carmelindo tells her with a baleful expression. "You tell those friends of yours that they had better be careful because the Dolphin is no toy."

Raimundo's daughter now asks Seu João whether he has known the Cobra Norato. He replies that while he himself hasn't "had that pleasure," his parents used to reminisce about the former *encantado*. "There are many old and lovely stories that are a reality, they are true, they occurred," he declares. Carmelindo then offers an account in which a soldier bent on disenchanting Norato blinds him in both eyes. Raimundo quickly objects that the former *encantado* was only blind in one eye "and that, just for a time." They then appeal to the older man ("What do *you* say, Seu João?"), who refrains from taking sides, launching instead into another story about a *sacaca* named Munju who had an Anaconda son.[12]

Carmelindo opines that Munju was not really a *sacaca,* but instead, a practitioner of the black arts. When I inquire about the difference, he describes in sensational detail an African Brazilian cult session he once attended in Manaus. Raimundo's daughter adds that a *feiticeira* in Parintins caused a man's arm to swell up overnight when he refused to marry the mother of his child. "They say his arm was this big," she informs the group, making a dramatic circle with both hands.

By this time, the mass is over and Raimundo's wife appears to collect her husband and daughter. ("You've been telling fibs for hours now!" she

---

12. In this widely told story, Munju (or Moju), who is occasionally identified as the father of the Cobra Norato, has two snake-children.

131

jokingly scolds with a polite nod in my direction.) When, however, the daughter excitedly asks her about the woman who gave birth to a Dolphin, the mother recounts how a distant relative became pregnant with a *botinho* or baby dolphin. She is about to offer yet another example when she suddenly remembers lunch and shoos home her husband and daughter. ("Excuse me, Seu João, but my family has to eat some time this afternoon!")

Despite Raimundo's disappearance and the increasingly late hour, Carmelindo and Seu João show no signs of budging. After the men trade various tales in which Saint Peter functions as a trickster figure, Seu João tells of a man who pretends to take a trip to heaven in order to steal his neighbor's chicken.[13] The chicken reminds him of a series of other birds, including the ill-omened *acauã*, or laughing falcon, said to metamorphose into a human being.[14] "Now then, in those old days, any and every creature changed shape, see?" ("Agora, naqueles tempos antigos, qualquer bichinho se gerava, né?") he asserts, returning to the theme that initiated the whole exchange.

At this juncture, a small child arrives to say that the priest and his team are expecting me at lunch and I leave Seu João and Carmelindo, still telling stories. "They'll be there till sunset," our hosts say with a laugh when I explain, with many apologies for the delay, where I have been. "But Seu João is very serious," the man quickly adds. "A person can learn a lot from him. Here, Father, have some more fish. There's plenty here for everyone."

QUESTIONS OF PERFORMANCE: COMPARISON AND OVERVIEW

The three sessions described here reflect differences in social and geographic context as well as personal identity. And yet, despite a number of obvious, and not so obvious, divergences, they are united by the participants' awareness of their own involvement in a social interchange. Their marked concern for the veracity—or nonveracity—of the events in question reflects a hyper-awareness of shifting attitudes toward the *encantados* and the regional and local culture they in many ways embody.

In the first instance, five longtime friends sit around trading stories on a Friday night in a small city that offers very few forms of organized diversion. The clink of bottles and insistent background music reinforce

13. For examples of these stories, common throughout Brazil and much of Latin America, see Osvaldo Elias Xidieh, *Narrativas pias populares.*
14. The *acauã*, like the *Matinta*, hummingbird, and *bacacu* bird, is often associated with the spirits of the dead in Amazonian Indian tradition.

QUESTIONS OF PERFORMANCE

the casual atmosphere of an extended conversation, or *bate-papo,* in which outsiders (such as the waiter) may momentarily join.[15]

In the second case, the residents of a good-sized rural settlement recount stories on a festive occasion that brings numerous outsiders into their midst. Here, far more so than in the first case, the exchange has a pronounced communal character. Storytelling provides those congregated in the plaza not only a way of passing time until the onset of the *Boi,* but also a framework for communication with persons whom they may know only slightly or not at all. It also permits, and even encourages, a certain amount of repartee among men and women (witness the *sacaca/sacana* episode.) Although many of the stories are familiar in their general outlines to all present, the details are often new. When I returned soon afterward to Zé Açu, I found that several resident storytellers had incorporated the visitor's account of the stranger in the coconut grove into their own repertoires. Two of the people attributed the story, which they told with various minor alterations, to the visitor; the third had already forgotten where he had heard it, but assured me it was a *caso acontecido* from the distant past.

Members of a small and tightly knit community, the third group of storytellers swap tales whose appeal lies in their familiarity. Once again, the exchange begins as a way of killing time before an organized activity— in this case, the Sunday mass. The participants, however, become so caught up in their own narratives that they forget about all else. In this last case, unlike the first two, there is definitely a dominant storyteller. Seu João in large part shapes the session, both through the sorts of stories he elects to tell, and through his answers—or failure to respond—to others' queries.

One would expect hunters and fishermen to recount stories different from those of persons who depend far less directly on the forests and the rivers for survival, and various narratives from both Zé Açu and Terra Preta reveal a telluric cast largely foreign to the Parintins tales. The storytellers speak, for instance, of a giant Anaconda who leaves huge fissures in the earth, as well as of local *encantados* believed to be the owners of streams and rivers. They also offer accounts of mountain lions and forest guardians which the Parintins group does not mention, and describe bouts of *panema,* as well as the dire consequences of flouting menstrual taboos. A number of persons recount the feats of powerful *sacacas.* (Although one of the Parintins storytellers does mention a local *macumbeira,* neither he nor his fellows make any reference to the traditional healers who appear in tales from Terra Preta and Zé Açu.)

15. *Bate-papo,* a slang term that literally means "chin-flapping," always refers to a casual conversation.

133

Also, not surprisingly, given their relatively greater isolation from a range of secularizing influences, rural storytellers tend to devote more attention to traditional Catholic holy figures. Thus, a woman in Zé Açu calls on the saints for protection in her own encounter with a Dolphin, and the men in Terra Preta exchange amusing stories of a roguish, down-to-earth Saint Peter. Although Maurício and his friends do speak of diabolic intervention and allude in passing to Saint Cipriano, they express considerably more interest in current social ills.

New Age–sounding explanations of events as "all psychology" and references to the "astral plane" and "fourth dimension," as well as joking references to the "cloning" of a particular *macumbeira* are conspicuously absent in Zé Açu and Terra Preta. Furthermore, despite the flashes of humor present in all three cases, Maurício and his friends are outwardly more skeptical than a good number of their rural counterparts. While it is by no means certain that Paulo ultimately rejects the existence of the *encantados*, his tale of the woman who stands up the Dolphin on the dance floor is unquestionably more lighthearted than the majority of accounts from Zé Açu and Terra Preta. Then too, whereas storytellers in these two locations present a number of personal experience stories involving supernatural entities, the only comparable tale from Parintins includes a distancing disclaimer ("You may not believe this . . .").

The markedly communal, in-group nature of the sessions in Zé Açu and Terra Preta recall countless other extended conversations in which various friends, relatives, and neighbors gather at nightfall to exchange news, gossip, and stories on a range of themes. Often, the owner of the house where they have congregated offers the guests strong, sweet coffee—*cafezinho*—or sometimes sugar rum, rinsing out a small store of glasses after each use so that a new guest may drink. As night falls, the owner lights the makeshift lanterns called *porongas,* or cements the first of multiple candles onto the center of the rough wooden dinner table with a bit of wax.

Seu João is not only a gifted storyteller; he is also the community's unofficial historian. For this reason, Raimundo's daughter repeatedly defers to him, even though, in at least one instance, she seems to know more than he. An accomplished orchestrator, the older man is also an experienced arbiter to whom the others take disputes about stories that are, in many cases, shared memories. ("What do *you* say, Seu João?" Raimundo asks when he and Carmelindo disagree.)

And yet, if the three sessions reveal obvious differences, each constitutes a momentary constellation of much broader possibilities. Although, for instance, Maurício does not tell a single *trancoso* in the exchange described above, he possesses a great store of these, into which he gleefully dips on other occasions. ("Why didn't I tell that story of the princess in the orange?"

he repeated with a shrug when I later asked him. "I don't know, I had no desire to tell it at the time.") Likewise, when I later returned to Zé Açu for several days, I recorded a large number of frankly supernatural narratives of a sort I did not hear during my first visit, as well as ample quantities of slightly off-color *piadas*. And when Carmelindo showed up one day in Parintins, he told a very funny story of the Dolphin that contrasts with the grimly moralistic accounts he offers here. Maurício's assertion that he and his friends are more apt to engage in extended storytelling in the country-side (*not* that rural inhabitants tell more stories) underscores the importance of context as much as that of personal identity.

Also, though one can speak in very broad terms of old versus young, male versus female, or rural versus urban, such divisions are relative at best. Older people, for instance, are often more respectful of tradition than their younger counterparts, but it is the teenage girl in Zé Açu who defends the *encantados*. One could similarly argue that twenty-eight-year-old Car-melindo appears to be as conservative in outlook as Seu João, who is almost a half century his senior. (He, and not the older man, harps upon the dangers posed by the Dolphin, warning Raimundo's daughter to keep a safe distance from the riverbank.)

Likewise, although men and women often disagree in their presentations of the *encantados,* individuals of the same sex—such as the two men in Zé Açu who offer such different versions of the hospital story—do not neces-sarily concur. Then too, while educated persons are generally less likely to speak of the *Encante* than are their illiterate counterparts, Maurício, a part-time university student, is an avid storyteller. Moreover, despite a surface skepticism, he and his friends are ultimately more credulous in many ways than are a number of rural inhabitants who reject the supernat-ural—or, at least, the *encantados*—out of hand.

The complexity of all three storytelling situations is further intensified by the participants' awareness that they are involved in a public exchange. Although Paulo, for instance, laughs off my wry comment about his cousin's romantic exploits, his ensuing description of a spirited female who outsmarts the Dolphin is meant to prove to me and all present that he is not like the cousin. Visibly offended when Zeca mocks his account of the man who transforms himself into a horse, he counters by placing the responsibility for the tale's accuracy on the original narrator. ("I'm not saying that the story's true; I'm just repeating what he told me.")

In like fashion, the storytellers in Zé Açu are well aware of the presence of outsiders, and to some extent, the exchange of narratives foreshadows the formal competition that is about to occur. In this context, the old fisherman's insistence on his lack of fear in the face of the *Cobra Grande* constitutes an effective us-them challenge. ("Now top that if you can!" his conclusion seems to say.) Here, yet more than usual, a storyteller's ability to make others laugh or, in one case, to create an unmistakable hush in the conversation, constitutes a show of power.

Little of this verbal sparring is apparent in Terra Preta, partly because Seu João is so clearly in charge. His judicious refusal to take sides in the debate between Carmelindo and Raimundo and his unwillingness to admit his unfamiliarity with any subject are intended to safeguard his reputation as a very serious storyteller. In addition, while his glosses on others' stories provide information, they serve above all to reaffirm his authority.

Storytellers in each instance clearly draw on a common body of narrative material. All three sessions include accounts of *encantados, Curupiras,* and *Matinta-pereras,* tales of buried treasure, people who change shape of their own volition, and the exploits of various *feiticeiros.* These similarities in content, however, are no less striking or important than the storytellers' shared concern for questions of truth. Although the Parintins group is seemingly more casual about the supernatural than its counterparts in Zé Açu and Terra Preta, belief, in every case, is decidedly selective. Not only do people debate the truth of particular stories, but the same individual may take varying positions on outwardly similar accounts.

Challenges to the veracity of a specific narrative ("How can anyone believe this sort of thing?") may occasion either a retreat from the material or a defiant affirmation of its figurative or literal truth. Individual tales often take the form of questions, and all three sessions reveal a tentative, sometimes frankly interrogatory quality that defies the stereotype of rural believer versus urban skeptic. Just as Zeca and Maurício recall how the increasingly developed outskirts of Parintins were once home to now-departed forest spirits, so the storytellers in Zé Açu agree that transformations of people into animals were far more common in the past ("Today one hardly sees these things any more," one younger woman asserts).

Seu João likewise utilizes the past tense in references to the events in question. ("There are many old and lovely stories that are a reality, that are true, they *occurred.*") Although he presents as fact events related to him by his parents and grandparents, he makes no claim for their contemporaneity. ("People changed shape in that time," he says; "*today it is difficult,* but in that time, they changed into horses, pigs, pacas, absolutely everything.") Similarly, he notes that while one *encantado* used to frequent a particular local, "now, I don't know if he has become civilized or disappeared or died."

The awareness of far broader changes in the human and physical landscape unites otherwise quite disparate narrative exchanges, reinforcing the central theme of metamorphosis. The active, almost obsessive skipping among themes and genres, and the larger backdrop of rapid social and environmental change can be found in other times and places; however the particularly forceful melding of form and content within the Dolphin stories takes on a unique significance in contemporary Amazônia. In the spirit of the Dolphin, who may change from malevolent abductor to disappointed suitor in the twinkling of an enchanted eye, contemporary storytellers bring to these tales of change their own sense of ongoing transformation.

6

THE DOLPHIN AS *ENCANTADO*

Acho que o Encante é como outro planeta. Pois o santo tem milagre mas o encantado tem mistério.

(I think the *Encante* is like another planet. Because the saint works miracles but the *encantado* has a mysterious force.)

—*Man, age 57, interior of Parintins*

Storytellers, much like those in the last chapter, rarely confine themselves to accounts of Dolphins or *encantados,* but rather, intermingle these with descriptions of other extraordinary creatures, including ghosts, extraterrestrial visitors, shape-changers, and a host of forest beings. In addition, both within and outside the framework of individual stories, people may compare or contrast the enchanted beings with the Christian saints. Although some use *encantado* and *Encante* very loosely to indicate virtually any sort of supernatural presence ("The *encantado* is any of these beings that suddenly appears," asserts one woman),[1] the majority have far more specific definitions for these terms.

On the surface, the *encantados* are most closely related to a myriad of forest guardians sometimes known collectively as *encantes da mata* or *encantados* of the woods. A number of the storytellers in the last chapter mentioned the *Matinta-perera,* or *Matins,* the *Juma,* and the Big Foot–like *Mapinguari.*

Yet more powerful than these is the *Curupira,* to whom storytellers also may refer as the *Caboquinho* or *Mãe da Mata* (Mother or Owner of the Woods). Prone to appear in the guise of a deceptively harmless-looking, dark-skinned urchin with backward-pointing feet, the *Curupira,* like the Dolphin, can be downright malevolent, delighting in the havoc its wiles create among unsuspecting humans. Also like the *encantado* (and unlike

---

1. "O encantado é qualquer coisa que surge de repente." Woman, age 32, São Joaquim (Amapá). Married, house and farm work, no formal education.

most other forest beings), it possesses the ability to change shape at will.

Whereas, however, the Dolphin invariably moves from animal to human guise, peeling off its aquatic shell or *capa* much as a diver sheds a scuba suit, the *Curupira* assumes the identity of various animals under its tutelage. It may appear, for instance, as a docile-looking agouti who suddenly becomes a fire-eyed monster off whom bullets ricochet. Or it may metamorphose into a deer who, instead of running from the hunter, rears up on its hind legs to advance against him. These terrifying visions bring on the fevers and madness that mark human interactions with supernatural beings in *caboclo* as well as indigenous tradition.

In further contrast to the *encantados*, the *Curupira*, even while its metamorphoses are the stuff of nightmare, may display another, more prankish, even goofy, side. According to Dona Marina, it likes "to piss in people's water pots," as well as to laugh uproariously in the unsuspecting hunter's ear. Once a person discerns the *Curupira's* presence, however, he or she need only construct the simplest of straw puzzles over which it will muse for hours, thereby permitting a safe retreat. A good cigar, a bottle of sugar rum, or a mirror (into which it will gaze for hours) provide its victims a similar opportunity.

In short, the *Curupira* is wild and treacherous, yet hopelessly ingenuous. The embodiment of forest forces, it is powerless before the trappings of civilization and easily manipulated by trinkets. Not only does the *Curupira* get drunk at the drop of a straw hat, but it has virtually no sense of a social self, as witnessed by its fascination with the mirror. In many ways a stereotype of native peoples (*Caboquinho* means "little Indian" and people often refer to the *Curupira* as an *índiozinho*), it stands in opposition to the *encantado*, who is frequently associated with the white man.

Both the *Curupira's* terrifying transformations and its apparently childish antics are responses to human disrespect for the natural world. The victims are often hunters who kill large numbers of a particular animal, thereby endangering what not only outsiders, but a growing number of television-wise insiders, would refer to as the forest's ecological balance. The *Curupira* also severely punishes those individuals who fail to honor contracts (*pautas*) designed to assure success in killing a particular animal.[2] Even its apparently random attacks on people can be understood as a logical outgrowth of its role as forest guardian. "Look," explains Argemiro, "you don't like anyone to enter your house without your permission, right? Well, God gave the woods to the animals and they don't like it when the

---

2. These contracts usually stipulate that the person may kill only a given species of animal, and often obligate the hunter to spare a certain number of animals before he begins to shoot.

hunter or the fisherman goes there to kill, to mess around, to destroy the forest."

Although the *encantados* are also *mães,* virtually no one reaches an agreement of this sort with a Dolphin or Anaconda. ("They don't make bargains. Besides, you could not trust them if they did!" Alzira declares.) Furthermore, the enchanted beings' malevolence does not always have a clear-cut cause. Although they, like the *Curupira,* often respond to invasions of their territory, they also may pursue one or another individual for no apparent reason. Gregarious beings whose home is not the forest, but a wondrous subaquatic city off-limits to most mortals, they stand apart from the solitary *Curupira* who, like the *Juma* and *Mapinguari,* rarely, if ever, intrudes upon the world of civilization. (No one ever claims that *Curupiras* like to dance.)

While the forest guardians may cause people to lose their senses, they do not physically transform them. In further opposition to the *encantados,* who are sexually attracted, and attractive, to human beings, they do not display the slightest amorous impulse. Unlike Dolphins, who are stereotypically male or female, the forest entities are sexually indeterminate. Thus, even though storytellers most often describe the *Curupira* as a *curumim,* or small boy, they may use either the masculine or feminine article before the noun (*o Curupira* or *a Curupira*). Most important, all *Curupiras* are basically the same. Not only do they lack individual personalities, but their responses to human beings are uniformly negative. It is unthinkable that a *Curupira* (or a *Juma, Matins,* or *Mapinguari*) be attracted to a given individual, let alone that one of these beings should come to a human's aid. Furthermore, although the *pajés* claim to speak with the *encantados,* I never heard of one who conversed with a *Juma* or *Mapinguari.*[3]

Storytellers' responses to questions about whether the *encantados* or the *Curupiras* (*Juma, Mapinguari, Matinta-perera*) pose a greater danger to human beings reinforce perceptions of the former's more elusive nature. "The *Juma* is worse because it eats people and the *encantado* only takes them to the river bottom," says one young woman as she attempts to replait a straw broom.[4]

"The Dolphin is worse than the *Curupira* because once it has been attracted to a particular woman there is nothing anyone can do," explains

3. Some shamanic healers do appear to speak with the *Curupira.* The elderly musician who claims to have played for the Dolphin couple reports that a *pajé* in one of the rubber communities in which he lived regularly talked with this forest spirit, who would direct specific persons to hunt a particular animal ("Joãozinho, it's deer for you this week, remember?"), chiding other community members who had recently killed too many of one or another species ("No more wild boar for you until I say so, Mané!").

4. Woman, age 16, interior of Parintins (Aruã). Widowed, agriculture, no formal education.

a middle-aged fisherman as he carefully inspects his net for tears. "The *Curupira,* no, it can be dangerous if you do not keep your wits about you, but you can deceive it with no more than a wisp of straw."[5]

"The *Mapinguari* is much worse because there isn't a single good one and there are gentle *encantados* [*encantados mansos*], like the Cobra Norato, who do no one harm," Gerineldo's country cousin informs him. "The problem is that no one knows which are the good *encantados* and which are the bad ones until it is too late."[6]

"The *encantados* are invisible," affirms one young woman from Terra Santa, whose baby sister is believed to have been carried off to the river bottom. "One only sees them when they assume the form of people. But they can be here among us without us even knowing. So they are more dangerous than the *Curupira,* because often a person doesn't even realize they are there."[7]

Along with these and other creatures of the forest, storytellers often couple or contrast the *encantados* with human beings believed to transform themselves into animals. We have seen various examples of men and women said to turn into *Matinta-pereras,* as well as horses, mountain lions, and pigs. As in the European narratives from which these stories are probably in part descended, the animals with which they are most commonly associated possess satanic associations.[8] Whereas in European tradition, however, most shape-changers are female, these persons may be either men or women in the Amazonian case. This significant discrepancy almost certainly reflects the existence of parallel African and, especially, indigenous, traditions in which shamans or sorcerers (the majority of whom are male) assume animal form.[9]

People may profess bewilderment as to why an individual should elect

5. Man, age 54, born Faro. Married, fisherman, no formal education.

6. Man, age 27, born interior of Parintins (Mocambo). Single, farmer and fisherman, 2 years school.

7. Woman, age 19, born Terra Santa. Single, student and manicurist, 5 years school.

8. The most common animals are horses, goats, snakes and (always black) pigs. In Amazônia—though, significantly, not in the Brazilian Northeast, where other such tales are extremely popular—people frequently turn into jaguars as well. This particular type of metamorphosis recalls transformations into jaguars on the part of Amerindian shamans, as well as African sorcerers' ability to turn into lions. Gerardo Reichel-Dolmatoff notes that "in Desana, the payé is called *ye'e,* a word that also means jaguar and, in effect, the payé is said to be able to change himself into this feline" (*Amazonian Cosmos,* p. 129).

9. Johannes Wilbert, coeditor of the forthcoming *Motif Index of South American Open Lowland Folk Literature,* notes that of the 4,216 South American motifs that do not appear in Stith Thompson's heavily Indo-European *Motif-Index of Folk Literature,* just under two-thirds have to do with transformation. Many, though not all, of the stories involved have to do with human-to-animal metamorphoses. (Wilbert, personal communication, 10 January 1992.)

to change shape. "I've never understood why someone would want to become a pig," Dona Marina confides. "Do they especially like pigs? Do they think being a pig is pretty?" Other persons express doubts about the ultimate meaning of such transformations. "It's a very delicate case," says Argemiro, "because God creates these examples to demonstrate the power of Christ. But I think that for some of these persons Christ does not exist because they go on turning into animals their whole life long."

Some storytellers refer to these sorts of metamorphoses as if they were a contagious, if chronic, disease. One young woman, for instance, notes that her uncle began to turn into a *Matinta-perera* soon after confronting a person in the act of transformation. "Look," she explains, "I had an uncle who changed shape. Yes, yes, he hit a man who was in the process of turning into a *Matins,* and, not long afterward, he came down with the same thing. He went to the *curador* but there was no remedy, and that was that, you see?"[10]

Other persons, such as Seu João of Terra Preta, view the transformation as an obligatory penance for past misdeeds. Often, the "bestial" behavior for which these individuals are atoning is of an explicitly sexual nature. "It's the father who sleeps with his daughter or who nurses at her breast; it's the *compadre* who sleeps with his *comadre,*" explains Gerineldo's mother.[11] Likewise, the woman rumored to have purposefully aborted is believed to turn into an enormous mother pig surrounded by numerous squealing piglets, while the priest's sweetheart becomes a headless mule (presumably, the priest himself may break his vows with impunity).[12]

Still other storytellers assert that shape-changers are simply people who take perverse pleasure in becoming animals (recall one woman's suggestion that the man who became a horse had a fondness for the mares). "The person who turns himself into a horse," says a friend of Gerineldo's father, "does it in order to rob or scare others. Or, who knows, maybe he just likes the taste of hay!"[13] Some storytellers claim that anyone can voluntarily effect such transformations through the recitation of special prayers associated with Cipriano, the saint who mastered, before abjuring, the black arts. Others suggest that persons who want to transform themselves need only

10. Woman, age 22, born Nhamundá, lives Parintins (1 year). Single, cook, "a little" grade school.

11. *Compadres* and *comadres* (literally, cofathers and comothers) are often the godparents of each other's children and especially close friends.

12. For a description of the headless mule see Luís da Câmara Cascudo, *Geografia dos mitos brasileiros,* pp. 162–66.

13. Man, age 61, born Belém, lives Parintins (19 years). Married, dry-goods store owner, grade-school education.

roll about either in the muddy water where animals have bathed or in the ashes of the Saint John's bonfire three years in a row.[14]

And yet, although storytellers may disagree on various details, these transformations are in every case the end result of fully comprehensible—if often, diabolic—processes. The overwhelming majority of accounts reveal a blatant moralism that contrasts with the far more enigmatic quality of many *encantado* tales. Moreover, in contrast to the Dolphin stories, which are sometimes funny but never ludicrous, the human shape-changer often invites laughter. Indeed, a number of these stories possess an almost slapstick quality that underscores the sense of such behavior as an aberration if not an actual disease. The following accounts of a shape-changer who literally takes a beating, and then of a Dolphin who merrily prances off into the waves before a furious fisherman, illustrate these differences. Both stories were told by the same man during a lunch for the visiting parish team (myself included) in a small community in the interior of Parintins. Whereas in the first case, the listeners laugh at the old woman who becomes a *Matinta,* in the second, the fisherman foolish enough to try to catch a dolphin is the target of their mirth.

14. This story occurred in Parintins,
near the corner of General Osório Street,
where there is now a guard.
In that time,
the men still wore suit coats,
and straw hats on their heads,
and carried canes.
Well then, exactly in the moment
this one man goes passing by the church,
someone yelled out like this
—"Matinta-perera!"

So then, he took his cane
and PAH!
right on the creature's head, you see?
So then, the *Matins* goes running off
and he [the man] goes home
and has a good night's sleep.
He doesn't give the matter a second thought.

14. Saint John's Eve coincides with the summer solstice. The bonfires are used to frighten away evil spirits, who roam the earth on this, the longest, most wide-open day of the year.

But when next morning comes,
    the police chief has him called in.
Because it seems that he had walloped an old lady,
    yes, it was the old lady
        who used to turn into a *Matins.*
So then, she was full of aches and pains
    —why, she couldn't even walk!
[Here, both storyteller and listeners laugh uproariously.]

15. There was in these parts a dolphin
    who would mess around with a fisherman's net.
So then, the fellow got angry,
    and said he was going to give that so-and-so a beating
        if he went on this way.
So then, he returned one day
    to find the dolphin inside the net,
        eating all his fish.

He grabbed a stick;
    he was going to beat him to a pulp.
But just at that very moment,
    the dolphin looks up at him
        and goes shooting out of the net.
"I'm leaving—
    I won't be back!" he says
        and dives down to the river bottom.

So then, the guy just stood there,
    at a loss.
That is to say, he was going to thrash the dolphin,
    but the dolphin managed to get away.
He had filled his belly
    and so, it was "So long!"
[Here, as in the first case, everybody laughs.][15]

In contrast to Dolphins, who regularly metamorphose into men and women, humans never turn into dolphins in these stories. Although the persons whom the Dolphin carries off to the Enchanted City eventually become *encantados,* it is not they who either choose or effect this transformation. Furthermore, while people who metamorphose into a particular

15. Man, age 35, born interior of Parintins (Cajual). Married, fisherman and farmer, no formal education.

animal regularly revert to human form (the transformation is almost always a temporary, Thursday or Friday night diversion), those who become enchanted beings regain their human status only at great cost.[16]

The ghosts and extraterrestrial beings who often appear in storytelling sessions stand apart from the *encantados* in their fully comprehensible—if, for this reason, no less frightening—behavior. Although ghosts or *almas penadas,* for instance, may interact in different ways with human beings, they invariably are either expiating past misdeeds or venting their anger at previous sufferings on the living. Thus while many storytellers express terror at reports of these unquiet souls' appearance in sites rumored to hold buried treasure, they have no trouble explaining the motives for their presence. "These *almas* are always people who failed to take advantage of their wealth during their lifetime," asserts Tô Pereira, who has just shown me a paper-thin gold coin he once unearthed within the forest. "They cannot leave this world until someone takes their money." Other storytellers explain that such apparitions are a creation of the devil. "He tries to scare off the person who might find that money," explains Kátia, "because he wants to keep its owner's soul imprisoned here on earth. Now then, don't count on me to free the *alma;* I'd rather get a good night's sleep!"

Extraterrestrial visitors, the most common of which are the *chupa-chupas,* or bloodsuckers, exhibit similarly frightening, but equally logical, behavior. Sometimes from outer space—usually Mars or "the country of the Moon" ("o país da lua")—they also may be foreigners in spaceshiplike airplanes, bent on siphoning off Brazilian blood.[17] ("Because look, we who live here are very poor," says one of Kátia's relatives who lives in the interior of Parintins. "We eat almost nothing—weak coffee and a handful of manioc flour—and still we manage to work hard from sunup to sundown. And so, the *chupa-chupa* envies us our strength and comes looking for our blood.") Regardless, however, of their perceived provenance, these unlikely visitors reveal a definite motive—greed—for their incursions. Thus, while they resemble the *encantados* in their extraordinary powers, they, like the other beings described here, are far easier to fathom.

SAINTS AND ENCANTADOS

The intensely enigmatic nature of at least some enchanted beings is nowhere more obvious than in comparisons between them and the Roman Catholic saints. In contrast to the saints, who are said to wield *poder,* or

16. The Thursday or Friday night transformation is also true for werewolves (*lobishomens,* or, colloquially, *labisônios*). See Cascudo, *Geografia,* p. 158.

17. If these bloodsucking beings clearly recall European vampires, they also bring to mind native Amazonian forest ogres who crave human fat.

power, the *encantados* possess *mistério* (literally, "mystery" or mysterious force). Likewise, storytellers speak of the saints' *lei* ("law" or "moral logic"), but are more apt to refer to the *encantados' ritmo* ("rhythm" or corporeal, intuitive direction). Not surprisingly, contrasts between the two are often part of more detailed cosmologies which, while couched within an ostensibly Christian framework, often present a series of more or less striking departures from official dogma. Thus again, while at first glance, people's comments on the *encantados* appear to confirm the victory of an imported, Christian worldview, closer examination reveals a far more complex, often reverse, situation in which borrowed elements cloak and ultimately bolster an older, non-European vision of the world.

Amazonian folk Catholicism, like that of Brazil in general, builds on the official vision of the saints as individuals whose exemplary behavior during their own lifetime allows them after death to serve as ongoing intercessors for other humans. Although the saints' aid is sometimes spontaneous, men and women may actively seek their assistance through prayer and *promessas,* two-way contracts whose terms are carefully spelled out by the human partner. If (and only if) the holy figure performs a certain action, then the supplicant will express his or her gratitude in a specified way. Like the pacts that some people make with the forest spirits, these contracts are binding. Unlike the *pauta,* however, which is usually the reward for an individual's successful struggle with a supernatural being, the saint's participation is wholly voluntary. Also, while *pautas* usually cover an extended time period (three to five years is the most common), the *promessa* tends to seek a conclusive remedy for an existing problem.[18]

Even when saints interact with individuals, they remain part of a communal order, and the *promessa* almost always involves some sort of publicly visible ritual. The successful supplicant, for instance, may express appreciation for Saint Anthony's healing of a severely fractured arm by sweeping the steps of his chapel every Friday for six months. A previously childless woman may lay a photograph, wax image, or wooden carving of her new son or daughter on a local Virgin's shrine. The fisherman whom Saint Benedict has aided in acquiring a much-needed motor for his canoe may organize a riverine procession in honor of the saint. Should, however, the bid for help go unanswered, the petitioner is under no obligation, and may propose the same or different terms to another holy figure.

Theoretically models of such fundamental Christian virtues as humility,

18. Native Amazonian ideas about agreements with supernatural forces have merged with Christian notions of the diabolic pact (*pauta* is a colloquial form of the Portuguese *pacto,* or "pact"). Although diabolic pacts involve a sale of the individual's soul, *pautas* with the *Curupira* and other embodiments of natural forces are usually the result of a person's successful confrontation with these beings.

charity, and forbearance, the saints may in (folk) practice prove temperamental and persnickety. Easily offended, they are apt to punish severely persons who fail to honor obligations such as the upkeep of an image or chapel, or the celebration of a feast day or traditional procession. Usually, however, the genuinely contrite offender can assuage their anger by making suitable (again, inevitably public) amends for infractions of moral agreements and momentary shows of disrespect. Patrons of the communities to whom they give their names (São Benedito, Santo Antonio, Santa Rita), they are unifying symbols as well as personal friends.

In the end, the saints serve as extensions of a very busy, if just and loving God. They too, of course, may find themselves overextended. "The saint doesn't always hear you," says Argemiro ruefully. "Now, the *bicho* [*encantado*] always does. Just yell, 'Come here, my pretty!' to a female Dolphin and she'll be there in a twinkling; you won't be able to get rid of her. But ask a saint for something and you may wait for years." And yet, despite the delays and disappointment, one does not have to worry about the saints working mischief in the manner of an enchanted being. Although physically removed from the human world, they remain committed to the welfare of its inhabitants.

The *encantados,* for their part, exist on the margins of human society. Their abode is not the distant heavens, but rather the waters and, less frequently, the shadowy forests into which men and women regularly venture. While the saints are equally at home in isolated hamlets and crowded urban settings, the hustle and bustle of the city is anathema to these embodiments of natural forces. "In the past," explains a *Boi-Bumbá* organizer in Belém who is also an African Brazilian cult leader, "the *encantados* used to come out of the river and walk about at night. I myself used to see them in the streets. But, as time went by, the lights and traffic began to drive them crazy. Yes indeed, now that I think about it, it has been at least ten years now since I last saw an *encantado* in Belém."[19]

In striking contrast to the saints, whose concern is for the human soul, the enchanted beings are motivated by carnal desires. Although sometimes helpful to individual humans, they rarely, if ever, promote the public good. As a result, despite the fact that they wield tremendous powers, no one seeks their protection and only the shamanic healer dares invoke their name. "Just imagine a community called 'Boto Ivo' instead of 'Santo Antonio'—no one would want to live there!" Gerineldo says.

Both the source and nature of the *encantados'* power is very different from that of the saints, whom Tô Pereira compares to "the moon that

19. Man, age 67, born Paraíba, lives Belém (53 years). Married, *pai-de-santo* and municipal functionary, 4 years school.

reflects God's sun." The origin of the enchanted beings' *mistério*, however, is considerably less obvious, and the question of who controls them excites considerable debate. Many storytellers admit that they do not understand the *encantados*. "Who controls them? Just so, no one can know" ("Quem manda neles? Pois é, ninguém pode saber"), they may assert.

"The *encantados* are another type of being," says one man known for his skill in curing snakebites. "The *sacaca* says they are people from another planet or, who knows, from this one, but who live in a world different from ours."[20]

"The *encantados* are not born and do not die," states Dona Marina as we slap at mosquitoes in the growing darkness of her kitchen. "They emerge from nothingness and for this reason, we who emerge from our mother's womb will never understand them."

Frequently, people suggest that questions about the *encantados* demand specialized, even classified, knowledge. ("How would I know who gives the *encantados* their power?" demands Kátia's mother. "After all, I've never journeyed to the river bottom.") Much like native Amazonian shamans, whose aquatic lineage makes them privy to the river's secrets, shamanic healers know far more than most people about the enchanted beings. Even they, however, may fail to fully comprehend them. Furthermore, although skilled healers exert a degree of influence and, sometimes, direct control over these spirits of the deep, they are by no means their creators, and there are various instances in which the enchanted beings inexplicably turn upon a former ally. Thus, people often tell the story of a healer named Munju who is devoured for no apparent motive by the twin serpents he raises as his own children. ("Why did they eat him?" repeats Dona Maria in surprise when I ask her at the tale's conclusion. "There wasn't any reason. Snakes are just a thing of nature—their nature made them do it.")

We have seen that some storytellers associate the enchanted beings with the devil.[21] "Is it the devil who commands the *encantados*?" asks a friend of Kátia's mother, shaking the water from her freshly washed hands. "Well, it certainly isn't God!"[22] According to these individuals, it is Satan who

20. Man, age 37, born Bailique (Amapá), lives São Joaquim (17 years). Married, fisherman and farmer, no formal education.

21. The Peruvian water people, or Yacuruna, are frequently cast as devils in the stories in Jaime Regan, *Hacia la tierra sin mal*, pp. 176–85. The heavily Christianized elements of a number of these narratives probably reflect in part the fact that the collectors were pastoral workers. For an interesting Greek comparison, in which the nymphlike beings known as the *exotiká* are unquestionably part of an Orthodox Christian cosmology, see Charles Stewart, *Demons and the Devil*.

22. Woman, age 57, born interior of Parintins (Mocambo). Single, house and farm work, no formal education.

gives Dolphins the special powers that allow them to kidnap human beings. "Haven't you read that Our Lord kicked out Lucifer from Heaven?" demands a carpenter in Faro. "Him and all the other angels who wanted Lucifer as chief. And where did they all end up? Why, they ended up right here in the river. Those Dolphins who transform themselves into a man so as to give women a big belly, they are nothing other than the fallen angels. God won't let them back in Heaven and so they stay here, causing trouble."[23] A young Seventh Day Adventist from the small community of Valéria notes that the *encantados* are in the service of the devil, himself a "very bad employee" whom God finally had to fire.[24]

Still other storytellers vehemently deny the *encantados*' diabolic affiliation. For them, these beings are not evil, but rather, amoral or morally ambiguous. "The Dolphin doesn't know God from the devil," says a young man in Oriximiná. "He is a creature of the depths; he follows his own law."[25] Dona Marina argues that the enchanted being is pure potential, a living mirror of the human beings with whom it interacts. "The *encantado*," she says, "only succeeds in frightening the fearful person. Because everything depends on the person [that is, the healer] who interacts with them. Look, the *encantado* has a generous nature but he can be malevolent with the person who treats him badly. The person who does not know how to control him, he abuses, he begins to womanize, to rob, to drink, in short, to do whatever he pleases." "Is the *encantado* good or evil?" one man says in response to my question. "*Maninha*, he is neither; the *encantado* just exists."[26]

The majority of people with whom I spoke about the *encantados* asserted that their power comes from nature. But while some see the natural world as a creation and extension of God, others view it as a largely autonomous locus of forces which, at times, appears to puzzle even its original creator. Occasionally, people assert that the enchanted beings are as old as—or, occasionally, even older than—God himself. "But if God made the world, then how could the *encantados* be older than God?" I demanded of one young woman born in the countryside, but now a student and domestic worker in the city. "In the beginning," she responded, "there was chaos,

23. Man, age 31, Faro. Married, carpenter and fisherman, 2 years school. For a Venezuelan parallel see David M. Guss, "The Encantados," p. 239. Guss goes on to suggest that the Amerindian dualism between Father Sky/Mother Water permitted Christianity to occupy the masculine sky, "leaving the feminine water as a reserve for native concepts."

24. Man, age 22, born interior of Parintins (Valéria). Married, fisherman and farmer, 4 years school.

25. "O boto não sabe quem é Deus e quem é o diabo. É bicho do fundo, segue sua própria lei." Man, age 18, Oriximiná. Single, part-time janitor, 4 years school.

26. Man, age 57, born Juriti Velho, lives Parintins (7 years). Married, unemployed, no formal education.

right? Well then, I think the *encantados* are like chaos. They were here long before God came and gave the world its shape."[27]

Explanations of the *encantados* are often part of intricate folk cosmologies in which the earth comprises only one of various (most often three or seven) layers or separate worlds. "We are in the third world," says a pharmacist in Carauari as he carefully counts out my purchase of two round and eleven oblong Band-Aids. "The first world is the sky, the second is the waters, and we are here, in the third. We are one type of people; they there in the depths are people too, but different from us. When it is night on earth, the sun is shining on the *encantados*. Because the *Encante* is another sort of dwelling place, another sphere" ("Que o Encante é outra moradia, outro ambiente").[28]

This other world remains subject to God in this first view. "There below," a basket seller who grew up in the Northeast explains, "it's like a city and here above it's like the second story of a building. So then, one has to be careful. Because the *Cobra Grande* exists, ma'am. In the sight of the *Cobra Grande,* we are just like a bird. The bird lives above us in the sky, but in a given moment we can grab it. So then, the *Cobra Grande* remains below us, eyeing us and waiting. But God is more powerful than the *Cobra Grande,* and doesn't let it eat us. Otherwise, you can be sure, we would all be in its belly."[29]

Those who claim that God exerts direct rule over the *encantados* see the latter's ambiguous nature as part of a divine plan that includes its share of irritations. ("The power of the *encantado* can only come from God, right?" says an eighty-four-year-old woman, widowed now for half a century. "Because he made everything in the world—the tick, the mosquito, the *encantado,* too.")[30] Some see the *Encante* as a lingering vestige of the cosmic tangle from which Christ's coming liberated humankind, and a sort of

27. Woman, age 16, born São Joaquim (Amapá), lives Macapá. Single, student and housekeeper, 5 years school. For this speaker, the *encantados* are nothing less than the formlessness and the void, the dark face of the waters over which the spirit of God moves in the opening lines of the book of Genesis. Her comments recall Roe's reference to Shipibo Forest Ogres and Aquatic Seducers as "leftovers from primordial time" (Peter G. Roe, "The Josho Nahuanbo Are All Wet and Undercooked," p. 119).

28. Man, age 62, born interior of Oriximiná, lives Pará (21 years). Married, pharmacist's assistant, no formal education "but my mother taught me how to read and write, and so I can defend myself, thank goodness." The idea of a multilayered universe is found in various traditions. It recalls native Amazonian notions of a seven-tiered heaven as well as of the seven houses in which all living beings are said to dwell.

29. Man, age 55, born Sobral (Paraíba), lives Parintins (35 years). Married, basket seller, "hardly any" formal education.

30. Woman, age 84, interior of Zé Açu. Widowed, farmer, no formal education.

magnificent beneath-the-river retirement home for representatives of a pre-Christian cosmic order. "In the old days," one woman says, looking up from the already patched sock she is mending, "there were kings like King Sebastian. Then Our Lord arrived to rule the world and the apostles took them all to the *Encante* where they remain today. You don't mean to tell me that you haven't heard this story!"[31] An elderly fisherman from Faro lays down his *tarrafa* and explains that Noah included a pair of *encantados* among the other creatures in his ark. "They come from the beginning of the world," he notes. "It says so in the Bible."[32]

Other storytellers propose a far less direct relationship between God and nature. Sometimes, the two are actually antithetical. "I think that the power of the *encantado* can only come from nature," says a woman who has just returned from a long day in the fields. "It doesn't come from God, no. Because God never harms anyone. But nature can be either good or bad."[33] In this second, far less Christianized vision, the enchanted beings may baffle God himself. Although it is "He who gave the *encantados* the breath of life, He who first invented them" ("Ele quem deu os encantados o sopro de vida, Ele quem inventou eles"), these beings enjoy a high degree of autonomy and may be wholly ignorant of their creator.[34] "The *encantados*," Dona Marina explains, "are from the beginning of time. They never received baptism. They have no church. It isn't God who commands them. Their ruler is *ciência* (very roughly, "wisdom," "science"); this God business does not exist for them, you see? Their spirit doesn't rise to heaven. It remains on earth forever."

The initial order (or disorder) represented by the *encantados* is not necessarily negative, or even particularly remote in time. Some individuals present it as one necessary step in a continuing evolution. "The butterfly, for example, emerges from the caterpillar," Tô Pereira says somewhat more cautiously as we sit in his small living room on a radiant Sunday morning. "And there is a type of little fish that becomes a frog. So then, perhaps, in

31. Woman, age 34, Faro. Married, house and farm work, no formal education. When the young Portuguese king, Sebastian, disappeared in the battle of Alcácer-Quibir in 1578, his grief-stricken subjects insisted that he had not perished, but would return one day. Bolstered by an existing Amerindian messianic tradition, Sebastianism became firmly entrenched within many parts of Brazil.

32. Man, age 77, born interior of Nhamundá (Amazonas), lives Faro (31 years). Widowed, fisherman, no formal education.

33. Woman, age 41, interior of Parintins (Tracajá). Married, house and farm work, no formal education.

34. Woman, age 33, born interior of Parintins (Parananema), lives Parintins (10 years). Single, 2 years school, cook.

this manner, people once turned into other things, but then they forgot how."

"My deceased grandmother, even my mother, said that in earlier times even birds turned into people," Alzira's father tells us. "There is a little red bird whom people call *ticuã;* so then, in the past they say he turned into a man. Today he is only a little bird and he will die a little bird too, but back in my grandparents' time, he still became enchanted."

"A long time ago," Gerineldo observes, running a comb through his wet hair before hurrying off to school, "Amazônia was all forest and the people were all pagans. How long ago? Oh, I don't know, but I would say at least twenty years."

According to many storytellers, the rite of baptism that identifies the Christian throughout his or her life also gives a fixed identity to animals and inanimate objects. Thus, even today, persons who unearth buried treasure are supposed to sprinkle holy water over their discovery. Although this ritual serves in part to ward off evil spirits, its primary purpose, according to Tô Pereira, is to keep the precious metal from vanishing before one's very eyes "*or turning into something else*" (my emphasis).

And yet, although the saints may be seen as representatives of a triumphant, stabilizing Christian order that permanently arrests flux, there nonetheless are things they cannot or will not do. Just as doctors (*médicos de butique*) and shamanic healers are generally recognized to have different spheres of curative action ("There are the doctor's sick people and the sick people who belong to those who smoke *tauari*," explains Dona Marina), so the saints and *encantados* participate in a sort of cosmic division of labor in which the two are good for different things.

The saints, for their part, cure ills resulting from bodily weakness and direct diabolic intervention. They, however, have little power over *feitiço* and diseases brought on by various woods and water spirits.[35] Furthermore, although theoretically more powerful than the enchanted beings because of their greater proximity to God and resulting freedom from natural laws, they rarely interfere with the Dolphin and his fellows. "The saints control the skies and the *encantados* control the waters; they are like the presidents of two separate countries," Gerineldo explains. "The saints don't go down to the *Encante*," one older man says. "They stay up there in heaven with the angels. That's the way it's always been."[36] "The priest calls up the saints and the *pajé* calls the *encantados*," asserts a young woman as we scoop

35. For a detailed analysis of these different categories of illness see Raymundo Heraldo Maués, *A ilha encantada.*
36. Man, age 60, born Acre, lives Seringal Cupuaí (Amazonas, 6 years). Married, rubber tapper, no formal education.

fine-as-sawdust manioc flour into a burlap sack. "They each have their own law and they never mix."[37]

This division, if not full-fledged cosmic standoff, helps explain why storytellers—who may credit at least some *encantados* with positive qualities—are astonished at the place of the dolphin in Christian iconography. "The dolphins there in these other places *must* be different," Maurício's grandmother says firmly. "Because the dolphins here, even the good ones, have *absolutely nothing* to do with Our Lord." When I explained to Gerineldo that the ancient Greeks believed that their deities had honored the dolphin with a constellation, he laughed and said that *Botos* might well do less mischief from afar. "Those gods, they probably stuck the *encantados* up there in the sky to keep an eye on them," he said, clearly pleased with his own joke.

On occasion, a person manages to distance the enchanted beings by invoking a particular holy figure. (Recall the woman from Zé Açu who calls out to "all the saints" for help in fending off an intrusive Dolphin.) In like manner, a teenager in Carauari recalls how her father managed to shoo away a pair of white-as-cotton dolphins with a Saint Francis's cord. However, as it is extremely rare for a saint actually to confront the enchanted beings, the following account of an old woman whom Santo Antonio (Saint Anthony) restores to her family in response to a *promessa* constitutes an interesting exception to the rule. As in the case of virtually all of the dozen or so stories I recorded in which Christian holy figures successfully square off against an enchanted being, the storyteller is a resident of a community originally founded by runaway slaves.[38]

16. It was my father who made a *promessa* with Saint Anthony
       to rescue my grandmother from the *Encante*.
Because she was looking for a remedy
      by the name of *paracuri* [a kind of mint]
         down by the riverbank
            when she saw two small boys who lived there.
But the boys who appeared to her that day weren't those two,
      —they were *encantados*
         in the form of boys.

37. Woman, age 22, interior of Parintins (Maranhão). Married, house and farm work, 3 years school. For an interesting contrast to this oppositional conception of saints and *encantados* see John M. Watanabe's comparison of Mayan saints and the spirit owners called *witz* (*Maya Saints and Souls in a Changing World*, pp. 61–80).

38. Saints Anthony, Benedict, and Thomas are the focus of many devotions by blacks in Brazil. The present-day residents of ex-*quilombos*, or runaway slave communities, sometimes introduce these figures into tales of *encantados*, an unusual practice in terms of the corpus

"Dona Claudina, what are you looking for?" [they asked her.]
       She said, "I'm looking for *paracuri*."
           "I know where there is a lot," one told her.
And so, they went deeper,
       ever deeper into the woods.
Then, they left her imprisoned
       in the hollow trunk of a big tree
           and there she passed the night.

We looked all over for her,
       but even though she heard our shouts,
           she couldn't answer.
She spent the whole night there,
       a night of heavy rain.
And when she finally managed to get out of there
       the next morning, she was dry,
                       completely dry.

So then, she showed everyone that big tree trunk
       in which she had spent the night.
She had not gone to the river bottom,
       but still, it was a thing of the *Encante*.
The boys were from the *Encante*,
       the *Encante* of the river bottom.

Well, after that,
       she remained a bit touched in the head
           —it wasn't long before she died.
But if my father had not made
       that *promessa* with the saint,
           she never would have returned.
Ah no, they would have carried her off
       right then and there.[39]

For every story in which the saint and Christianity emerge victorious, there is another in which the *encantados* reassert their powers. Thus, in one version of the tale of the island that suddenly sinks to the river bottom, even the community's patron saint does not escape enchantment. ("I think he must be there still in the depths, poor thing!" one older woman says

---

as a whole. For more on these narratives see Candace Slater, "Transformation Stories from a Changing Amazon."

39. Man, age 68, Silêncio do Matá. Widowed, farmer, no formal education.

with a solicitous click of the tongue.)[40] Argemiro expresses doubt that the saint can ever vanquish the *encantado*. "No one except God tells them what to do, and I think they give even him a lot of trouble!" he says, half jokingly. ("Ninguém manda neles, a não ser Deus, e mesmo para ele, acho que dão muito trabalho!")

In short, the cosmic scheme which emerges in discussions of the saints and *encantados* is by no means uniform. While some storytellers insert the latter into a formal religious context in which they become "yet another mystery of Christ, an astounding thing" ("mais um mistério de Cristo, uma coisa incrível"), others do the exact opposite, converting Christ from king of kings and prince of heaven into *sacaca* of *sacacas* and *dono* of the *Encante* beneath a close-at-hand, if unrevealing river. ("Catholic priests don't like this," one female curer remarks, "but God was a prophet, God was a healer. Didn't he cure the sick and lame? Why, he even raised the dead!")[41] Still others reiterate that the saints and enchanted beings enjoy separate but equal status. "I think that the *encantado* is a different model," says a young schoolteacher in the interior of Amapá, "something set apart, a wholly different way of being."[42]

Even when most firmly ensconced within a Christian framework, the enchanted beings retain an essential, troubling volatility. Their very alienness is a rebuke and implicit protest; their mere existence, a declaration of resistance to formal religious hierarchies. "The Dolphin is not a Christian," Dona Marina says resolutely. "He is something else, I don't know what, but certainly not a Christian."

Furthermore, although Christian ideas and institutions would appear victorious in many tales and commentaries, this victory is provisory. Storytellers in the Parintins area, for example, frequently conclude the Cobra Norato tale with the observation that Norato's sister does not die, but instead, remains trapped beneath the altar of the Óbidos cathedral. ("He tied her up there and put a big stone on her head, and there she remains until today," a friend of Kátia's sister, just back from a vacation in Manaus, explains.)[43] Thus, while her force is effectively contained, it is by no means definitively eliminated.

In a number of spirited postscripts to the story, all hell breaks loose when the city's bishop, dismissing accounts of the malevolent serpent as

40. Woman, age 53, born interior of Óbidos (Silêncio do Matá). Married, schoolteacher, grade-school education.
41. Woman, age 42, born Barbalha (Ceará), lives Parintins (31 years). Married, curer, schooling unknown.
42. Woman, age 19, born interior of Amapá (São Joaquim). Single, schoolteacher, high-school education.
43. Woman, age 15, born Parintins. Single, student, 6 years school.

nothing more than old wives' tales, decides to move the altar. "They say you can still see a big crack in the floor of the cathedral left over from that time," a young seamstress in Oriximiná observes enthusiastically, as she mends an umbrella shattered in a heavy rain.[44] "Maria Caninana came up from the water and nearly drowned the city," asserts Gerineldo. "If they hadn't put the stone back, Óbidos would have sunk to the bottom of the river. As it was, they say the bishop was almost washed away."

In short then, the tension between human and natural worlds embodied in the Dolphin is also very much a tension between institutional form and self-affirming movement. While official Christianity would appear to provide the dominant vision in some cases, in many others, the battle against its fixed, dualistic logic rages on beneath the surface of the tales. This continuing struggle is evident in Dona Marina's genuine loyalty and equally genuine anger toward the ecclesiastical institutions that would relegate the shamanic tradition she grew up in to the realm of witchcraft or hocus-pocus. "Noratinho is still alive somewhere, I'm sure of it," Argemiro declares.

THE DOLPHIN IN RELATION TO OTHER ENCANTADOS

Despite occasional references to forest or airborne *Encantes,* most storytellers specifically associate the enchanted beings with the rivers, lakes, and *igarapés* that cover such a vast percentage of Amazônia. Furthermore, while *encantados* may be sea horses, tortoises, fish, toads, or occasionally crabs or aquatic spiders, the great majority are either Dolphins or Anacondas.

The *encantados* are, by definition, supremely liminal beings. People often refer to them as *bichos,* but while this word is roughly equivalent to the English "animal," a more exact translation might be "creature" or "less-than-human." (Interestingly enough, the diminutive, *bichinho,* is often used as a term of endearment.) While a person referred to in English as an "animal" is usually simply brutish, the individual who is a *bicho* is often peculiar, repulsive, and, above all, unsociable—that is, a human being who does not act fully human. (His or her peers, for instance, may label an abnormally timid person a *bicho esquisito*—an "odd creature" or, more colloquially, "strange bird.") That storytellers often refer to the enchanted beings collectively as "the people of the depths" (*o povo do fundo*) further emphasizes their nonanimal—though not necessarily human--nature. On one hand, these enchanted beings are the owners or guardians of the waters, who oversee relations between the animals entrusted to their care and their earthbound predators; on the other, they *are* the river that shifts and rises with a seeming will and direction of its own.

Within the confines of the Enchanted City, the *encantados* are immortal. ("They can die of a harpoon wound here on earth," explains Alzira's father, "but they *don't* die of old age.") A concrete, geographic location, their Enchanted City or *Encante* is also a set of powers, a sort of magnetic field or energizing presence, and a state of mind. Thus, although giant water snakes who are not *encantados* also may work equally prodigious feats, they exist in a far different relation to human beings. "There is the snake that's just a snake [*a cobra-cobra*] and the other snake that is enchanted [*a cobra-encantado*]. Both are dangerous, but the *cobra-cobra* eats people while the *cobra-encantado* carries them off to the river bottom and transforms them into something else," Gerineldo says.

And yet, if Dolphins display the qualities of liminality, immortality, and moral ambiguity common to all enchanted beings, they also reveal a number of more idiosyncratic traits. Unquestionably more anthropomorphized than their fellow *encantados,* many Dolphins reveal uncharacteristically individual identities. Some, for instance, are shy and easily flustered; others are roguish, merry, even madcap. In further contrast to other *encantados,* who indiscriminately seek intercourse with human beings, Dolphins focus their attentions on particular men and women with whom they may even fall in love. Immortal like their fellows, they—unlike the overwhelming majority of enchanted beings—nonetheless experience the itch for mortality.

In striking confirmation of their individuality, all Dolphins possess proper names. Unlike the *boto* allies whom fishermen may dub "Daniel" or "Margarida," these *encantados* in dolphin form have personal identities which they may or may not choose to share with human beings. (Some reveal their names only to the persons to whom they make love.) A number of communities in the interior of Parintins boast resident Dolphins with names such as "Ivo," "Danielzinho," "Delfinita," or "Dona Júlia." Still others are called "Mariana," "Janaína," and "Rei Sebastião" ("King Sebastian"), all names that underscore the African Brazilian influence upon the *encantado* tradition.[45] The pair of white-as-cotton dolphins who dart away from the Saint Francis's cord brandished by an earlier storyteller's father are known to local residents as "Angelina" and "Estelita."

45. Mariana is a lesser African Brazilian deity; Janaína is another name for the powerful *orixá,* Iemanjá; and King Sebastian—perhaps because of claims that he was enchanted—has entered the African Brazilian hierarchy as an *encantado.* Although the historical Sebastian waged war against the Moors, his *caboclo* counterpart is also sometimes known as the *Rei Mouro* or *Rei Turco* (the "Moorish King" or "Turkish King").

When storytellers first began making statements to me such as "Dona Delfinita is a Dolphin who lives in my community," I thought they were referring to people who intermittently turned into dolphins, much as others are believed to metamorphose into dogs or snakes or pigs. With time, however, I came to perceive these Dolphin-people as full-fledged *encantados* who may appear in various public spaces as well as in individuals' dreams. "The Dolphin Ivo, yes, he used to show up in all the *festas* here," explains a fisherman in Faro. "But this was in the past, when there was less activity. So then, he frequented [the *festas*], he and many other Dolphins. Even now when the light goes off at midnight, so that the generator can recharge, they remain there on the street corners and stroll about with the women. There are a lot of them right here among us; it's just that we don't recognize them."[46]

These *encantados*-in-residence often contact shamanic healers with messages for individual members of the community. On occasion, various individuals will begin dreaming simultaneously of a particular Dolphin. While such dream epidemics may linger, they are more apt to come and go, like spurts of flu. The *encantado* may inform the dreamer or the person with whom they happen to strike up a conversation at one or another *festa* that they are really the Dolphin so-and-so. Often, they follow up this revelation with either an invitation to visit the river bottom, or a plea for help in their quest for disenchantment. Other Dolphins call attention to themselves in a more dramatic manner by shouting out their names when they surface to exhale. ("'Zé de Souza!' that one Dolphin where I live always shouts when he jumps out of the water, 'Zé de Souza!'" one man from the interior of Parintins says. "I have seen him many times, this Zé. He is very large and very red.")[47]

Some residents of the interior claim to have observed Dolphins with sashes bearing their names in gold letters. Not everyone takes these claims seriously, however. Thus, when I asked Alzira if she had ever heard of a Dolphin sporting a lettered sash, she first eyed me in astonishment, then laughed so hard she got the hiccoughs. Moreover, she made me repeat the question to a number of other persons, who appeared equally amused. Chastened, I returned to Kátia's mother, whose friend from the interior had given me this information during a conversation involving myself, both women, and Kátia. Had the woman been trying to pull my leg, I asked? "No, no!" Kátia's mother replied energetically. She then explained that while she herself had never encountered Zé de Souza during her own

46. Man, age 47, born Faro. Married, fisherman and carpenter, no formal schooling.
47. Man, interior of Parintins (Valéria). Married, fisherman and farmer, no formal education.

years in the interior, her friend was a trustworthy person who would not spread idle rumors. "If she said so, it must be so," Kátia interjected, albeit with a shrug.

A number of these self-promoting Dolphins are proud of their more nefarious exploits and may brag about impregnating a particular woman or abducting a particular child. "There where we live there is an old woman who is an *encantado*. She herself says so," explains one woman from the community of Marajó. "Her name is Dona Júlia and she speaks their language. She already has carried off many children to the river bottom."[48] A young man from Faro explains that the Dolphin Franciso Alves "is very bad, drives people crazy. In dolphin form, he is eight feet long, but as a man, he is of average height. They say he has enchanted many people. He got a young woman pregnant there in Tracajá. Besides this Chico Alves, there is Antonio Alves, who is every bit as bad!"[49]

In contrast to these confirmed troublemakers, other resident Dolphins may be playful and exuberant, such as the one who surfaces every afternoon at exactly five o'clock to whistle at a pretty woman, or his friend who puts on human form and eagerly scrambles up the hillside with a fish bigger than himself. Some, in turn, are bashful, such as the party-going Dolphin, who loves to dance but is self-conscious of his *Curupira*-like, backward-pointing feet, or his companion, who hides behind a mango tree in order to change clothes. ("I guess he doesn't like the ladies to see him naked," Alzira's youngest daughter giggles.) "There was a Dolphin where I lived by the name of Zé Patrício," says a fisherman near Maués. "He went to all our parties—everybody liked him; he did no one any harm."[50] Not unlike those dolphins in Greek mythology who trail after lyre-playing poets, some Dolphins go to *festas* primarily for the music. Gerineldo's mother, for instance, describes a Dolphin that used to play the saxophone in festive gatherings near her home. "People only knew he was a Dolphin because he had to leave at midnight," she asserts. "He tooted on that sax so well that people would come for miles to hear him. Why, I myself once heard him when I was still a little girl."

A world of difference exists between Dolphins on the order of this mild-mannered music lover and other, less individualized and certainly far less endearing Anacondas. With the important exceptions of the Cobra Norato, whom storytellers regularly confuse with a Dolphin precisely be-

48. Woman, age 41, born interior of Parintins (Ilha das Onças), lives Mocambo. Married, house and farm work, 1 year school.

49. Man, age 25, Faro. Married, fisherman and farmer ("also, I can fix refrigerators"), schooling unknown.

50. Man, age 30, born interior of Maués. Married, fisherman, no formal education ("but I'm still going to learn one day").

cause of his uncharacteristically human features, and Norato's misan-
thropic sister (variously identified as "Maria Caninana," "Floripes," "Floris-
bina," etc.), serpent *encantados* are unlikely to have proper names, let alone
diminutives, such as "Zé ("Joey") or "Danielzinho" ("Danny"). When they
do have names, they are almost always geographic designations that underscore their more telluric nature. Thus, in contrast to the Dolphin Ivo (who
may happen to reside in Faro or Terra Santa or Aguas Pretas) one finds
the *Cobra Grande* of Óbidos as opposed to the *Cobra Grande* of the Boca
do Limão in Parintins.

Because Anacondas in *caboclo* tradition, as in indigenous tradition,
rarely take the form of people, their lack of proper names is wholly under-
standable. Although shamanic healers who exhibit a particular facility with
serpents may later reappear in the form of an Anaconda—the widely
known Dom Anselmo, in the city of Maués, is an excellent example—it is
nonetheless extremely rare for an Anaconda to take on human guise. Instead, in striking contrast to Dolphins, these serpent *encantados* almost
always appear as an immense and eerie blue flame that plays upon the
waters or a big, brightly lit riverboat that suggests an updated version of
the native Amazonian Spirit Canoe.[51] Sometimes, the boat is empty; on
other occasions, it is packed with people in white clothing who gaze out
toward shore. "It is an enormous ship that looks just like a city," says
Argemiro, who claims to have seen it gleaming in the summer moonlight.
"It approaches full of lights and people, dogs barking, children crying, then
sails on without stopping. This happens every year, always around the
same time."

Unlike the Dolphins who may pass unperceived in city streets or rural
festas, the presence of the *Cobra Grande* is remarkable in every way. Moreover, while individual Dolphins prompt a wide gamut of reactions ranging
from anger and revulsion to affectionate amusement, the *Cobra Grande*
inevitably inspires intense fear and wonder. Although most persons' first
impulse is to turn and run from the terrible brilliance that surrounds the
Anaconda-boat, we have seen that others are inexplicably drawn toward
its mysterious presence. Regardless, however, of whether the encounter
with the *Cobra Grande* triggers unmitigated horror or awe mixed with
fascination, encounters with this *encantado* are always memorable. "So
then," recalls one younger man, the grandson of a well-known *sacaca,* "that

---

51. The boat, as most storytellers describe it, resembles a present-day *motor* or riverboat
of the type that carries vast numbers of passengers along the Amazon. The Shipibo also
refer to a giant Anaconda-boat called the *Acoro,* modeled on the black steel *garretas,* or
nineteenth-century steamships that plied the Ucayali (Peter G. Roe, personal communication,
26 June 1990).

deep blue fire drew nearer and nearer the middle of the river, and I shook the hammock; I called out to my companion. Because I had never seen such a thing before this time. I'm thirty-three years old and I'd never seen this business, understand? Everybody talks about it, but I'd never seen it, this was my first time. Good grief, how incredible! *I'd never felt such deep emotion*" (my emphasis).[52]

The other *encantados* about whom people occasionally tell stories tend to be even less anthropomorphized than the *Cobra Grande.* The *Cavalo Marinho,* or Sea Horse, for instance, undergoes no transformations but inevitably appears as a dazzling white steed with a golden mane.[53] Significantly, in one woman's recapitulation of her tale of how a *sacaca* successfully retrieves a child from the *Encante,* the Dolphins appear as men and women while the *Cavalo* remains very much a horse.

17. And so, the creature [the Dolphin] had taken on
        her father's shape, you see?
    So then, he took the girl to the river bottom.
    But she suspected something
        because everything there was very rich.
    Those people who said they were her parents
        even had a car and took her for rides.

    Now then, her [real] parents almost went crazy.
    They sought out the *sacaca* there,
        and he sent the *Cavalo Marinho* to bring back the girl.

    So then, when he arrived,
        she was having a good time.
    She was afraid to climb up on his back;
        she wanted to stay.
    But finally,
        he carried her home again.
    Because her parents were missing her a lot.[54]

52. Man, age 33, born Parintins. Married, parish worker, some grade school.

53. There is an island called Ilha do Cavalo Marinho near Parintins, to which there is early reference by Francisco Bernardino de Sousa (*Lembranças e curiosidades do Valle do Amazonas,* p. 93). Sousa notes the existence of native Amazonian beliefs about the *Cavalo,* which themselves must have absorbed elements from other, European-based stories, if only because the horse is not native to the Americas. According to him, the *Cavalo* is actually an enormous fish that has the ability to assume equine form. Peter G. Roe points out that both the white man and the horse (*Jënë Caballo*) are associated with the water and, thus, Aquatic Seducers in contemporary Shipibo tradition (personal communication, 9 January 1992).

54. Woman, age 57, born Remanso, lives Parintins (10 years). Separated, seamstress, no formal education.

Although other *encantados* regularly abduct human beings, only *Botos* actively select the persons they whisk away to their watery realm. In this sense, the Dolphin is very unlike the Anaconda, who may carry off whole boatloads of men, women, and children, or the equally indiscriminating Sea Horse, who simply thunders off with whomever happens to clamber up its back.

Then, too, while Anacondas impregnate women, they certainly do not court them. ("What an idea!" snorts Kátia's sister as we put the final touches on a birthday cake for one of her many nephews. "Look, Dadá, they're *snakes,* not people, understand?") In fact, as in a number of native Amazonian narratives, sexual relations usually take place without these *encantados* assuming human form. Some storytellers even describe a sort of intercourse by association in which the *Cobra Grande* inseminates the clothes a woman has left to dry on the riverbank. The case of the Dolphin is far more complicated. First of all, while the *Cobra Grande,* like the *Cavalo Marinho,* is an overwhelmingly male presence, we have seen that Dolphins may be of either sex. Not only are they attracted to specific men and women, but—in striking contrast to their fellow *encantados*—they actually may fall in love. "Se apaixona" ("He/she becomes impassioned"), "Se enamora" ("He/she falls in love"), "Fica gostando daquela pessoa" ("He/she comes to like that person"), storytellers often explain. "Is it bad to go to the *Encante*?" asks one older woman as her granddaughter waters several dozen plants in coffee cans. "No, no, there's nothing bad about it. Because when the Dolphin loves, he loves with all his heart."[55]

As this last comment suggests, for Dolphins, love is total, even obsessive. And although some storytellers stress the negative consequences for the object of the *encantado's* affection ("The Dolphin is very jealous; if he can't obtain a person's love, he kills that person," explains one man), others suggest that Dolphins themselves are prisoners of passion.[56] "They cannot help themselves; it is their nature to act the way they do," they often say. "The *encantado* has no malice; it's that he becomes impassioned," explains Dona Marina as she tugs a needle through a stiff cloth. "He starts to like the person and does everything he can for [him or] her. So then, the person who loses a daughter finds this very bad. But he [the *encantado*] didn't kill that daughter. She goes with him to the *Encante* where no one ever dies."

"The *encantado* takes a liking to the person and does everything in order not to lose that person," explained a man in Maués when I expressed

55. Woman, age 70, born Maués. Widowed, retired, no formal education.
56. Man, age 34, born interior of Carauari, lives Carauari (7 years). Separated, mechanic, no formal education.

surprise at what seemed to me a strange way of expressing love. "Sometimes he [the person] becomes so afraid that he or she goes crazy. But it's not that the *encantado* wants to harm that person; he acts the way he does because he *likes* him or her."[57]

If the loved one, or, more precisely, the loved one's family, invariably suffers, the Dolphin suffers too. "They [Dolphins] fall in love and they cannot live without that person," one young woman says as she prepares the garnish for her employers' evening meal. "It's like one of those loves you see on television where the man can't make the woman love him, and so, he finally shoots her."[58]

"Dolphins," explains Gerineldo's mother, "have a lot of knowledge, a lot of wealth, but they are sad and lonely. So they try to carry off people who will keep them company, and they are not happy until they succeed."

Their overwhelming physical attraction to specific men and women both illustrates and partially explains certain Dolphins' profound dissatisfaction with their own enchanted state. Occasionally, an Anaconda with one human parent will follow the Cobra Norato's lead in seeking to escape the *Encante*. The overwhelming majority of *encantado* malcontents, however, are Dolphins. ("They get fed up with being half human and half animal," one young basket vendor in Parintins explains. "So they do everything they can to escape that life.")[59] Although most of these enchanted beings fail in the quest for liberation, their lack of success does not appear to discourage others. While abducted humans—sometimes known as *marinheiros,* or sailors—are generally motivated by nostalgia for their families and their former lives, *encantados* with one human parent yearn for the independence they discern in mortals. "The *encantado*'s life is worse than ours here," declares Dona Marina. "Because the ruler of the *encantados* is the *Encante.* They are prisoners there in the depths; they don't enjoy the freedom we do, and so they envy us despite their riches."

In short then, although Dolphins display characteristics common to all enchanted beings, they nonetheless reveal human or quasi-human tendencies that set apart at least some of their number from the far less clearly anthropomorphized *Cobra Grande* or *Cavalo Marinho.* Part of the natural landscape, all enchanted beings exist outside time in that they do not die. And yet, although all regularly impinge on human space, Dolphins, unlike

57. Man, age 33, born interior of Itacoatiara, lives Maués (11 years). Single, works in photocopy store, 3 years high school.

58. Woman, age 27, born interior of Acre, lives Porto Velho (6 years). Single, domestic, 3 years school (ongoing).

59. Man, age 19, born interior of Parintins (Valéria), lives Parintins (6 months). Single, basket vendor ("and sometimes I make them too"), "not much" grade school.

their fellow *encantados,* do not simply sally forth into the world of human beings. Instead, this world already exists within them in the form of their desire for disenchantment.

Then, too, in contrast to the Anaconda, in whom the waters' grandeur and destructive force find apt expression, the Dolphin is first and foremost a subversive presence. If the former recalls the winter rains that uproot trees and swallow beaches, the latter is more reminiscent of the river's surface, which is always shifting color but whose surface remains opaque. While one is majestic in its alien might, the other is a duplicitous intruder who inspires a nagging surety that things are not what they appear. What looks like your best friend, your spouse, your brother-in-law, your lover, may well be a Dolphin. There is no way of knowing until it is too late.

The shamanic healer, to some extent, is the mirror image of the Dolphin. Just as Dolphins regularly appear as men and women, so *sacacas* put aside at will their human form to become creatures of the depths. ("I knew a *sacaca,*" says Dona Marina. "Even when he was married, he lived more in the *Encante* than here on earth. Finally, he left his wife. But even when he was still with her, he was not like other men, because he could turn whenever he wanted into a monstrous snake.") Furthermore, much as some Dolphins succeed in becoming disenchanted, and thus forfeit their immortal status, so the *sacaca* does not die, but permanently takes up residence in the Enchanted City. Although they may continue to fulfill familial obligations, dutifully leaving piles of fish each morning for a spouse or aged mother, they effectively renounce their status as social beings. Thus, while virtually all shamanic healers claim to work exclusively for the good of their fellow humans and people may concur that "when the *sacaca* is good, he is God here on earth" ("O sacaca quando ele é bom, é Deus na terra"), they often regard him as a kind of *encantado.* ("These *sacacas,* they spend so much time at the river bottom that they become just like the people there," declares Alzira.)

While the *Cobra Grande* or *Cavalo Marinho* often makes a sudden, unexplained appearance, it is only Dolphins who regularly go to *festas,* only they who flirt all night beneath a full white moon. While the idea of the Dolphin playing a saxophone at a rural gathering is amusing, even endearing, the image of a sax-playing Anaconda or Sea Horse is patently absurd. The difference lies not just in the Dolphin's greater propensity to mingle among humans in the form of a man or woman, but even more, in the display of sensibilities rarely, if ever, associated with other enchanted beings.

Although anacondas lurk beneath the waters' surface in much of the Amazon, people rarely enter into direct contact with these creatures. Most often, they become aware of the proximity of one of these great snakes when a pig or chicken goes missing during the winter rains that bring the river to their doors. The dolphin, however, is a far more familiar presence. Readily audible as well as visible from the shoreline of most rural communities and smaller cities, *botos* are a decided part of everyday existence. While anacondas evoke excited comment, dolphins elicit casual comment.

The widely held belief that at least some dolphins are enchanted suggests the potentially alien quality of the familiar and close-at-hand. Because there is no way of knowing which of these animals is really an *encantado,* all are suspect, all mysterious by association. Furthermore, if human beings are dependent on the natural world and all natural entities possess a supernatural potential, then individual men and women have no choice but to interact on a regular basis with forces beyond their understanding. That some people may be blissfully unaware of the extraordinary character of their surroundings does not make their dealings with these forces any less momentous. Even ghosts in Amazonian oral tradition are rarely invisible or diaphanous "the way they are in movies." Although they may vanish unexpectedly, they are almost always vivid, three-dimensional entities who leave footprints in the sand. The overwhelmingly physical presence of the *encantados* is therefore not surprising. The Dolphin's attraction to specific individuals reflects a desire not just momentarily to enter, but fully to possess, a foreign space. Yet, at the same time that they aspire to fill the human world with their presence, they exude the danger and allure of the unknown. This aura of the forbidden explains why even those Dolphins who restrict themselves to polkas in the middle of a well-lit dance floor represent an intolerable threat to the community. For if the supernatural regularly manifests itself in sexual behavior, then the sexual necessarily possesses a potentially supernatural dimension. As a result, the most apparently casual flirtation can have unexpected consequences, of which a baby Dolphin is, perhaps, the least mysterious and frightening.

While the Dolphin's cosmic dimension is far more notable in some stories than others, it is absolutely fundamental to the corpus as a whole. Now human, now animal, these creatures are ultimately both and neither. Truly "another planet" in the sense that the natural world is always alien, the Dolphin remains disconcertingly human and all too close at hand. "The *encantado* doesn't have a fish tail," a young bicycle repairman in Parintins remarks as he greases a stubborn kickstand. "This business of the mermaid is pure invention; it's just silly. But the Dolphin is a fact. I myself don't understand the *encantados* but I *do* know they exist."[60]

60. Man, age 16, born interior of Pará, lives Parintins (6 years). Single, bicycle repairman, 1 year high school.

7

THE DOLPHIN AS LOVER

O Encante, dona, é perigoso e bonito.

(The *Encante*, ma'am, is perilous and beautiful.)

—*Man, age 46, Jacu (interior of Parintins)*

Just as *Inia geoffrensis* is not found beyond the Amazon basin, so the Dolphin's actions acquire meaning in a very particular social arena in which men and women play out dramatically contrasting roles.[1] In presenting the Dolphin as lover, I am well aware of the strong personal reactions I had to some of the male-female interactions I witnessed. Although physical and verbal violence against women can be found in many other parts of the world—including, to be sure, the United States—it is particularly widespread and overt in Amazônia. I was caught off guard by occurrences such as one man's furious beating of the angry wife who showed up in the open-air bar where he was drinking with his mistress. (In fact, I thought the blows and curses were directed at a dog until Maurício and his sister explained what was happening.) Likewise, it would be hard to forget a fellow passenger on a riverboat who spent several hours telling me how her husband had seduced her younger sister after the girl came to live with them in order to attend the local high school. ("Do you think God hates me?" she demanded by way of conclusion.)

And yet, if it was difficult to accept some men's treatment of women (and some women's acceptance of brutal behavior), I also experienced a deep suspicion that many of the events I was witnessing were far more complex than they appeared. Despite all the rhetoric, for instance, about helpless females, women run a large percentage of Amazonian households and, not infrequently, refuse to marry the fathers of their children ("What

---

1. For a fuller perspective on gender definitions as cultural constructs see Sherry B. Ortner and Harriet Whitehead, eds., *Sexual Meanings*.

for? So he can order me around?" more than one woman said to me). Furthermore, I soon discovered that, in Amazônia as elsewhere, what people said was not necessarily what they did. Despite what looked to me like contradictory words and actions, I found a number of the men I encountered attractive as both males and human beings. In Parintins and elsewhere, I had close friends of both sexes who seemed eager to discuss male-female interactions. ("Everybody knows you're leaving," one man explained with a self-conscious laugh when I expressed surprise at the rather intimate information he was revealing. "Besides, I myself don't understand the half of what I'm saying!")

MALE-FEMALE RELATIONSHIPS IN AMAZÔNIA

Male-female relationships within Amazônia represent a special variant on the Mediterranean honor code, aspects of which are known more widely and less positively as *machismo*.[2] Within the Amazon, as other locations, the particular playing out of this cultural complex is unquestionably affected by personal as well as social and historical differences.

At its very simplest, this code—which necessarily has absorbed influences from the various other cultures that found a home in Brazil over the centuries—divides the world into active men and passive women.[3] And yet, if women do not act, they can be acted on, with serious consequences for the reputation of their spouses. As a result, great emphasis is placed on female chastity or "shame" as a necessary complement to masculine honor. Thus, while men are not just permitted, but fully expected, to attempt the seduction of women, the latter exert power through their denial of sexual favors. To the extent that the demands a woman places on a man tempt or oblige him to relinquish the active role prescribed for him, she threatens his masculinity. The wife who vociferously protested her husband's presence in the bar was thus not only denying a masculine prerogative (that of a man to pursue multiple women), but also affronting his honor by her public self-assertion. "Look," said Tô Pereira when I told him

2. While this code, which focuses on female shame and male honor, was once regarded as more or less monolithic (see J. G. Péristiany, ed., *Honour and Shame*), recent scholarship on the order of David D. Gilmore, ed., *Honor and Shame and the Unity of the Mediterranean*, has focused on regional and local differences. Richard G. Parker offers a specifically Brazilian interpretation in his *Bodies, Pleasures, and Passions*, pp. 30–66.

3. Brazilian culture reveals echoes of the Mediterranean and Semitic cultures which mingled in the Iberian Peninsula, as well as indigenous and African slave cultures. It also bears the traces of multiple immigrations from Germany, Japan, North Africa, and the Middle East. Indebted to French and British cultural models in the nineteenth and early twentieth centuries, the nation now reveals heavy U.S. influence.

what had happened, "I don't say that what he did was right; it wasn't. But what good did it do to have it out with him in front of everybody?"

Not surprisingly under these circumstances, much of women's social standing and emotional fulfillment comes from their role as mothers and, above all, mothers of sons. Throughout the course of my various stays in Amazônia, I was struck both by the tremendous affection mothers lavished on their male offspring, and by the great devotion of grown sons to their mothers. The expression "mãe é mãe" ("mother is mother") underscores the sense of permanence in the bond between mothers and their children.

While the honor code is by no means limited to Roman Catholic countries, the image of woman as ideal mother as well as potentially treacherous seductress has found reinforcement over the centuries in religious doctrine and iconography. The growth throughout Latin America of liberation theology, with its at least theoretical emphasis on the dignity and equal worth of women, represents a potential departure from the old virgin/whore dichotomy. This dichotomy lives on, however, in many men's highly deferential attitudes toward their mothers and their alternating aggressive pursuit and deep suspicion of potential sexual partners. While men are often viewed as taking or eating, women give or are eaten (*comer* versus *ser comida*).[4]

In Amazônia, as throughout Brazil, individuals of both sexes may undercut the explicit model of active male and passive female through subtle signals that temper and transform interactions between individual men and women (as well as persons of the same sex).[5] However, the active/passive division is not just hollow convention or consciously manipulable façade. The growing shift to an indirect, cash economy from an older system based on reciprocity and face-to-face personal exchanges has made always complex gender relations a veritable morass of conflicting responsibilities and interpretations. "How do I know what I think?" Kátia responded with exasperated laughter when I told her about the man who lashed out against

4. As Ondina Leal points out, individual women may be feared, but not ostracized, for exercising an active sexuality (Leal, "The Gauchos," p. 261). In practice, while both men and women can *dar encima* (literally, "give on top" or "come on to" a member of the opposite sex), in theory, only women or passive homosexuals (*bichas*) can *dar mole* (literally, "give soft" or "put out"). The word *mole*, one might add, also means "weak" or "spineless" and is everything a man is not supposed to be.

5. A number of these cues may be lost on outsiders from cultures which emphasize direct communication of feelings and equate indirectness with deviousness and a lack of respect. Brazilians of all social classes may go to great lengths to avoid direct confrontation. (The term *dar confusão*, literally "to create confusion," is itself a euphemism for the violence that such head-on encounters invariably occasion.) For an introduction to some of these everyday cultural patterns see Phyllis A. Harrison, *Behaving Brazilian*.

his wife in the bar. "Sometimes I think one thing, and sometimes I think another. And often, I think a lot of different things, all at the same time."

In Amazônia, a number of historical and cultural factors have intensified the emphasis on male dominance and female subordination. We already have seen how the limited number of settlers who chose to brave the region's harsh living conditions tended to be adventurers whose dangerous and solitary life encouraged acts and expressions of defiant self-reliance. Those newcomers to the Amazon who had wives and children tended not to bring them, and most constituted first or second families with native or mestizo women. Marriage, to be sure, was, and still is, largely a matter of economic and reproductive necessity for both sexes. "My grandfather died of gangrene," one older woman in Parintins explains, "so then, my mother became an orphan. She married at age fifteen, not for love, but rather, necessity. But afterward she came to like her husband; she, for one, was lucky."[6]

The variety of present-day Amazonian Indian societies and the relative lack of early historical records make it difficult to speak in any definitive manner about relationships between the sexes in indigenous cultures now, let alone in pre-Columbian times.[7] Various native peoples recount a myth in which women once held power, symbolized by the possession of special ceremonial flutes, which they later lost to men.[8] Early explorers' much-debated reports of a society of female warriors, whom Europeans dubbed the Amazons in accord with Greek mythology, raise the possibility of the existence at some time of a native matriarchy. And yet, while a number of present-day Indian societies are either matri- or uxorilocal, others reveal a pattern of male dominance and female subordination that, at first glance, would appear to reinforce the Mediterranean tradition.[9]

If sexual behavior reflects a variety of broader social and economic factors, it is at the same time shaped by these. In the interior, as in the poorer sections of most Amazonian cities, whole families often sleep side by

6. Woman, age 62, born Parintins. Single, family income, 3 years high school.

7. The question of gender definitions and relationships in indigenous societies is extremely complex. Werner Wilbert recounts how, among the Warao Indians of Venezuela, men appear to make the decisions about who may and may not enter a village, but that it is really the apparently retiring women who render the judgments which the head (male) shaman then communicates (personal communication, 8 January 1992). Some Amazonian Indian societies have both male and female shamans.

8. The Juruparí or Yurupary flute myth is summarized in a larger study of male-female relations in Yolanda Murphy and Robert Murphy, *Women of the Forest*. See also Sílvia Maria S. de Carvalho, *Jurupari*.

9. See Thomas Gregor, *Anxious Pleasures*, for a discussion of contemporary Amerindian sexual relations. See also the section on Kalapalo fantasies of erotic aggression in Ellen B. Basso, *A Musical View of the Universe*, pp. 141–41.

side in hammocks grouped beneath a single mosquito net of sewn-together bedsheets. The ensuing lack of privacy, coupled with the exhaustion brought on by malnutrition and a grueling workday, means that sexual contact is often perfunctory. Not surprisingly, given these close quarters, intercourse is widely regarded as natural, largely unmysterious behavior. Although promiscuity is generally frowned on, extramarital relations are common. A young woman's first child is often born out of wedlock, and marriage is not necessarily either lasting or formal. ("People say that the first baby is for the grandmother," explains Dona Marina.)

Even today, as the Amazon is increasingly drawn into a capitalist framework, the notion of romantic, or "television" love remains largely foreign, if not downright exotic, to a large percentage of the population. "I never knew what love was with my husband," one older woman from the countryside says a little wistfully to a group of friends who have gathered along with me in her straw home high above the river following the Sunday mass. "I hear people say, 'I love you,' these things, on the soap operas. Well then, I liked my husband but I was raised in that old system where no one said, 'I love you.' So, it is still hard for me to imagine how these things must be."[10]

Exposure to a larger, often contradictory world tends to foster a greater variety of sexual attitudes and practices, particularly within cities. Although sexual activity is not necessarily more frequent in an urban setting, it is unquestionably more visible (couples necking on park benches, dancing cheek to cheek in discotheques, etc.). Then too, city dwellers are far more apt to offer self-conscious, often highly critical commentary on specific male-female interactions.

One of the more interesting conversations to which I found myself party involved Kátia's seventeen-year-old sister and two of her friends. Although the young women varied considerably in their judgments of the supernatural, they were uniformly negative about the local men. "How can anybody trust them?" one of the young women demanded as she surveyed a sun-bleached fashion magazine. "All they want is to get you into bed!"[11] After recounting a long list of infidelities among persons of her acquaintance, Kátia's sister made a gesture of exasperation. "I'm never getting married!" she declared.[12] When the girls' mother, born and raised in the countryside, interjected that some men were certainly better than others, one of her

10. Woman, age 59, born interior of Pará, lives Parintins (10 years). Married, seamstress, no formal education. The woman says "Eu vejo falar," which literally means "I see speak."
11. Woman, age 19, born interior of Parintins, lives Parintins (6 years). Single, student and seamstress, 6 years school.
12. Less than a year later, she had dropped out of school to live with a man with whom she has since had a child. Kátia reports that he treats her and the baby badly.

daughters countered, "But not here, Mother, not in Parintins!" "Besides," added the other daughter once the mother was out of earshot, "how would she know? She was raised in that old regime where parents always told their children what to do."[13]

And yet, while it would be a mistake to underestimate the range and complexity of individual sexual behaviors in either countryside or city, men as well as women in both places are quick to affirm the continued existence of a double standard. Among its more obvious expressions are violent confrontations among men stemming from real or imagined affronts to their masculinity, the policing and not infrequent physical abuse of women, and men's insistence on their own (but not women's) sexual liberty. "Respect" in this context often means consideration for the physical needs of a man's family, rather than the feelings of his wife or children. For at least some men, the broad-minded husband would appear to be the one who does not kill an errant spouse. "It's not right for a man to take away from his family in order to support another woman, no," one man asserts, slapping his straw hat at the tiny gnats that whirl about us in the dawn light. "But if he respects his family, well then, I think he has a right to do whatever he wants. Now then, his wife won't like it but she has to accept what he does. What if my wife were having an affair with another man? Oh, I wouldn't kill her. I'd throw her out that instant, but I certainly wouldn't kill her."[14]

"I wanted to go to *festas* and my father didn't let me," explains one older woman who lives in the interior, but who has come to Parintins to visit a married daughter. "So then, I got married. But I left one prison for another; good Lord, how I regretted it! Because once I got married, my husband didn't want anything more to do with *festas*. Also, he was one of these men who goes chasing after women. I was six months pregnant with my eldest child when he left me. He stayed away six years and eight months, before he finally returned. Well then, I got pregnant with my other children . . . Why did I take him back? Love? No, no, not love. Stupidity, I guess!"[15]

Although the double standard takes different forms in different places, it is often obvious on a very public level. In the 1990 election for governor of the state of Amazonas, for instance, the opposition seized on reports of rightist candidate Gilberto Mestrinho's various illegitimate children with the ironic slogan, "Vote for Gilberto; he may well be your father!" The

13. Woman, age 20, born interior of Parintins, lives Parintins (6 years). Single, student, 2 years high school.

14. Man, age 37, born interior of Parintins, lives Parintins (6 years). Married, farmer, no formal education.

15. Woman, age 61, born interior of Parintins. Widowed, house and farm work, no formal education.

candidate's supporters, however, simply chuckled at this confirmation of their man's virility. "So what if he had ten children with four women?" a taxicab driver in Manaus demanded as we zoomed through yet one more red light. "Men are men, and besides, the kids all get enough to eat."[16]

My point here is not that all Amazonian men treat women badly (this is not true), but rather that the gender models this society imposes on both sexes—and which both regularly manipulate to their own ends—are particularly narrow. Furthermore, the marginalization of women fits much larger patterns of domination directly related to social class. "It's worse to be a poor man than a rich woman," Alzira says as we pore over a catalog of costume jewelry. "Because the person who has money always has more freedom than the one who has to go asking a neighbor for the oil to fry that evening's fish." She goes on to point out that Amazônia exists on the margins of an itself dependent nation. "Brazil is poor and we are poor within Brazil," she notes with an emphatic thump upon the table that causes her teenage daughter to look up in surprise.

Men, as well as women, may express dissatisfaction with a larger social system that pits one sex against the other, while imposing extreme economic hardships upon both. "Men do everything they can to deceive women, then they say they don't merit trust. Does this make any sense?" Tô Pereira demands.

"I like being a man, but I also like treating everybody well," declares Gerineldo, as if the two conditions were all but impossible to reconcile.

"When I get married," Maurício assures me as we sit on a cement bench in front of the now tightly locked cathedral. "I'm going to trust my wife. I'm going to treat her as if she were my best friend. People here all think I'm crazy, but that's the way it's going to be."

CLOSE ENCOUNTERS WITH THE DOLPHIN

The male-female differences obvious in Dolphin stories correspond in large part to the gender roles outlined above. And yet, if male Dolphins' generally aggressive courtship behavior and total lack of scruples in seducing unwary females find support in a social code in which—theoretically—men act and women react, closer examination reveals a number of discrepancies that suggest chinks in the active/passive division. Not only are men not

16. Another native of Amazonas, former Minister of Justice José Bernardo Cabral, supplanted Mestrinho in notoriety after the details of his affair with former Minister of Finance Zélia Cardoso de Mello became public in 1991. Asked to comment on the case, which caused a national scandal, Mestrinho remarked that "the Indians, after all, were traditionally polygamous, and Cabral's affairs only prove that the Portuguese settlers assimilated well the practice" ("E pro Bernardo tudo," in *Isto É Senhor*, November 1991, p. 37, my translation).

always so firmly in control as would seem at first glance, but women are not so helpless as might initially appear.

To the extent that desire is always "an appetite of the imagination," the Dolphin's lust (and persons of both sexes' unspoken longings for the Dolphin) can never be a simple extension of everyday behavior.[17] Instead, if "the real and the imaginary are co-present heterogeneous spaces" and desire "borders on reality anamorphically in that it is present at the edge of reality as different from it without being eliminated," then the Dolphin is less reflection than ever-shifting shadow that frequently appears to take on a life of its own.[18]

Although specific narratives suggest real and unquestionably important psychodynamic aspects, I will focus on the private-public interplay obvious in the Dolphin tales. Many stories suggest such classic Freudian mechanisms as repression, projection, sublimation, and denial, as well as Jungian notions of the shadow figure. And yet, while these and other academic categories of analysis—Lacanian desire, Girardian desire-cum-violence, or Kristeva's linking of desire and delirium, for instance—are useful up to a point, we are not dealing with individual deviations or delusions, or with Western literary representations of these.[19] Admittedly unusual, face-to-face encounters with Dolphins are, nonetheless, in no way abnormal. Part of a readily recognizable and socially permissible complex of behaviors, they constitute what medical anthropologists generally refer to as "culture-bound syndromes."[20] Dependent on "essentially privately held experiences of social processes for their deepest significance," they nonetheless possess an eminently public dimension.[21]

17. Leo Bersani, *A Future for Astyanax*, p. 10. Although Bersani is speaking of European literary texts, a number of his insights have wider application.

18. Jean-François Lyotard, *Discours, figure*, pp. 284–85.

19. Lacan sees desire as essentially narcissistic, arguing that the symbolic is the imaginary construction of the other ("To love is to want to be loved," he says in *Les quatres concepts*, p. 177). For Girard, desire is inevitably shadowed by violence, since the person who desires necessarily another actually desires nothing less than "*being*, something he himself lacks and which some other person seems to possess" (*Violence and the Sacred*, p. 146). Kristeva sees repressed desire as leading to a displacement and deformation that eventually climaxes in madness ("Psychoanalysis and the Polis," p. 308). While these observations can be fruitfully applied to aspects of the Dolphin stories, the writers are speaking from a very different cultural perspective.

20. See Ronald C. Simons and Charles C. Hughes, eds., *The Culture Bound Syndromes;* and David Landy, ed., *Culture, Disease, and Healing*.

21. Basso, *A Musical View*, p. 240. "In Kalapalo fantasy," she asserts, "the openly expressed feelings of men and women toward their own sexuality and their hidden fears about the very persons of the opposite sex to whom they are drawn by passion are all blended into complex mythological images that create a sense of the ambiguity of gender classification and the artifice in the cultural construction of sexuality."

We have seen that many people consider human-Dolphin interactions possible, and that some describe these in great detail. Even though the great majority of such accounts are told in the third person, a small but significant minority are first-hand recollections in which a more general ambivalence toward the Dolphin's amorous exploits is especially obvious.[22] Although I collected only twenty-one such stories over the course of more than a year of fieldwork, their importance far transcends their number.[23] As myths are never set in the present and legends, by definition, are always accounts of events that happened to somebody else, the existence of these stories in which people say "I did" or "I saw" underscores the complexity of the *encantado* corpus and prohibits rigid genre categorizations.

Eyewitness descriptions of the *Cobra Grande*—of which I recorded many dozens—invariably focus on the fear and wonder these beings inspire. Although the storytellers focus on their own reactions, the great majority of such tales deal with a collective experience. Thus while Argemiro recalls shouting out in fear at the approach of the mysterious blue fire that shoots across the formerly placid water, he presents himself as just one of various members of a panic-stricken group.

18. Month of June,
    the river very high.
We were transporting straw
    to higher land.
So then, around eleven o'clock at night,
    we saw that fire.

It drew nearer and nearer,
    it was the *Cobra Grande*.
It lit up everything,
    it was just like an electric light,
        but very blue.
We tried to flee,
    but that big wave broke.

22. For an introduction to the personal experience story as a folk narrative form see Sandra K. D. Stahl, "The Oral Personal Narrative in Its Generic Context."

23. This number does not include another dozen or so persons who admit to, or are said by others to have had, encounters with Dolphins, but who did not want to discuss them. ("The whole thing still makes me very nervous," one young woman said to me apologetically.) Although my status as a foreigner may have inhibited some people, it almost certainly encouraged others to confide in me. Although I took care to tell them I was writing a book about the Dolphin stories, in which their accounts might appear, the prospect did not seem to bother them. ("I hope you choose *my* story!" several exclaimed.)

Everybody screamed
    and I screamed too.

So then, the canoe tipped over
    and we had to grab
        the long grass of the embankment.
The owner of the straw
    —his name was Severo
        —was the only one who drowned.
That is, he didn't really drown;
    the *Cobra Grande* took him to the river bottom.
Because later he appeared to the *curador* there
    and told him all about it.

Stories involving Dolphins, in contrast, are far more apt to focus on solitary encounters whose unmistakably sexual overtones make them doubly private. Almost all of the people who shared these tales with me were either friends, or friends and relatives of friends. Moreover, in four of these cases, the individual claimed to be describing the event for the first time. The hesitation with which these people spoke underscores the Dolphin's power to evoke strong, often conflicting emotions. It also suggests the existence of a store of other personal experience tales far more numerous than those I actually recorded.

The great majority of first-person Dolphin narratives are told by individuals who, at the time of the alleged encounter, were experiencing considerable emotional stress. Unlike stories of the *Cobra Grande,* which feature people of all ages, most of the Dolphin tales focus on adolescents in the process of discovering their own sexuality. The protagonists are also often new mothers or individuals facing specific, usually temporary problems involving a spouse or lover. And yet, although experiences involving *encantados* tend to coincide with moments of personal crisis, the individuals in question are usually distinguished more by their particular sensitivity and intelligence than any sort of neurotic or pathological proclivities.

STORIES TOLD BY MEN

Men's accounts of male Dolphins almost always stress the latter's virility and gleefully devious behavior, and many reveal a strong cautionary undertone. Although the Dolphin need not demonstrate any particular motive for his shameless actions, men are far more likely than women to see his persecution of one or another (usually female) community member as retribution for inappropriate behavior. Men often use such tales as explicit

CHAPTER SEVEN

warnings to young women. ("You tell those friends of yours that they had better be careful because the Dolphin is not to be toyed with," Carmelindo of Terra Preta informs Raimundo's teenage daughter.) And yet, at the same time that men insist that Dolphins are a bad lot, they may take ill-concealed delight in describing how one seduces a particular woman. Not surprisingly, they show more ambivalence in cases where the Dolphin hoodwinks a husband or lover.

Men's stories about female Dolphins also reinforce prevailing gender definitions. Less gregarious than their male counterparts, Dolphin-women not only favor private, face-to-face encounters, but some are definitely marriage-minded. Then too, although Dolphins of both sexes may seek human aid in their quest for disenchantment, males are more apt to make general appeals to other males, while females seek the assistance of a particular man.[24] ("I have loved you since I saw you on the riverbank when you were eight years old, and now that you are grown, I want you to disenchant me," the Dolphin-woman may announce to a thoroughly surprised young man.) The storytellers often claim that such appeals cannot be trusted. ("She says she wants his help, but then she goes and drags him off to the *Encante*.") And yet, while they may dismiss Dolphin-women as *mulheres fogosas* ("hot" or sexually aggressive women), these appeals for male assistance are fully in keeping with the idea of women as passive, needy beings.

Men's stories also reinforce prevailing notions of female passivity by portraying Dolphin-women as responding to a male overture. Regardless of whether the man in question physically assaults a Dolphin, or simply yells, "Hey Baby, what about it?" the first move is usually his. Male storytellers imply, when they do not state directly, that nothing would have happened had the man not seized the initiative. Nonetheless, while the majority of taunt stories cast the man as the initiator, he may still go on to suffer a dramatic loss of control. Even if he succeeds in eluding his pursuer, her influence lingers on well after the shamanic healer has pronounced him cured.

In striking contrast to the numerous third-person stories in which one or another man makes overtures to a female Dolphin, fully nine of the twelve personal experience accounts told to me by men cast the *encantado* as initiator. All of the speakers stressed their fear and fascination, coupled with an overwhelming sense of isolation. In two particularly compelling instances that now-grown men related in my presence, *encantados* begin appearing without warning in their dreams.

24. *Encantados* who are the offspring of a human mother may ask assistance of her, particularly as their identity becomes fixed during adolescence. Abducted children may also seek their mothers' help. Full-grown men, however, never rely on women.

Those instances involving very young protagonists (boys of twelve years or under), may revolve about a Dolphin of either sex. (After the onset of adolescence, the enchanted visitor is always female.) In the first case, the Dolphin often functions as a kind of supernatural playmate who spirits off the sleeping boy to the Enchanted City on a wonderful white horse. "He [the playmate] appeared in my dreams," one now-middle-aged man says, "sort of like an electric shock; I don't know how he did it. When I wanted him to come I would go to sleep and he would suddenly be there. I told many people about it, but he appeared only to me. I don't know how to explain it, I just know that boy would arrive on a white horse and take me to the river bottom."[25]

These excursions to the *Encante* continue until the playmate divulges his identity as a Dolphin. Fearful at the revelation, the boy tells his mother everything, causing the enchanted child to vanish in a huff. "The next day he appeared and told me that I had been an ungrateful friend to him, and that was the end of it," the man explains. "Today I think that I should have said nothing, but I was young and very scared, you see?"

The sense of having been singled out for supernatural attention is equally apparent in an account by one of Maurício's cousins, a thirty-two-year-old man presently studying in a Roman Catholic seminary in Manaus.[26] The man tells of a much-loved aunt who claimed to have sexual relations with a Dolphin by the name of Zé Caetano and who became pregnant with his child. "She became very frightened at the idea of having a Dolphin baby," he explains, "and when her time came, she died all alone in childbirth, she was so afraid. At least, that's what they say. Now, that she died in labor, without help, this much is certain. The whole thing was very sad."

After the aunt's death, a number of people—among them her then adolescent nephew—begin receiving nocturnal visits from Zé Caetano. But while these dreams pass like a fever in most cases, they continue to plague the speaker for months and years.

Freudian analysts might see the young man's unconscious sexual attraction to his aunt as impelling him to punish himself for her unhappy death. They also might suggest that he continues to possess her through his own possession by her Dolphin lover. The community, however, views these Dolphin dreams as a more or less normal, if regrettable, turn of events. The speaker himself realizes that his obsession with Zé Caetano is

---

25. Man, age 44, born interior of Óbidos, lives Óbidos (18 years). Separated, municipal employee, 2 years formal education.

26. "But I'm not going to be a priest," the man says, "I just want an education and the university is hard to enter and very expensive."

impeding his participation in the sorts of adolescent activities—above all initiatory sexual experiences—on which his peers have long since embarked. Finally, in desperation, he appeals to his father, who takes him to a shamanic healer in Parintins:

19. I would be there in the water
        and, suddenly, I'd want to get out,
                but couldn't.
    People would begin approaching me,
        people who weren't part of my world,
                wanting to carry me off with them.

    Often, I ran,
        I ran and fell,
                diving into the water.
    It became so
        I was afraid to go
                down to the river.

    I think these things did me a lot of harm.
    Because I was one of three cousins
        and the others went on growing
                while I lagged behind.
    There they would be with their girlfriends, see?
        and there I'd be, over to one side,
                still very much a little boy,
        sitting there, all skinny,
                just wanting my own little bit of loving.

    Look,
        it was that atmosphere
                —I lived it.
    Everyone believed in the *encantados,*
        and so, I too
                started believing.[27]

A similar sense of powerlessness and alienation—sensations customarily reserved for women in third-person narratives—finds more explicitly sexual expression in the first-hand experiences of men slightly older than the first two storytellers at the time of the encounter. In these instances, a

27. Man, age 32, born interior of Parintins (Mocambo), lives Manaus (3 years). Single, seminary student.

distinctly female Dolphin once again impinges on the young man's previously unremarkable existence. Here, however, unlike our first two examples, the *Encante* is associated not just with marvelous, if frightening, sights
and sounds, but also with distinctly sensual pleasures.

Although the following storyteller describes a group of *encantados* on
the riverbank, a single female Dolphin attempts to lure him into the water.
Now a grade-school teacher in Carauari, the young man explains that the
experience occurred in his early teens, shortly after his family's move to a
rubber settlement from the city. The story's atypical features—the Dolphin-
woman's copper skin, naked body, and unabashedly voluptuous behavior—suggest the speaker's then-limited association with the *encantado* tradition. (Had he grown up in the countryside, one suspects, the
Dolphin-woman would almost certainly have been a fair-skinned blonde
in a white dress.) All the same, his account is a particularly eloquent
expression of the nascent sexual feelings that often surface in these stories,
as well as the overwhelming sense of strangeness prompted by the move
to the interior. Although we had talked at length over the course of almost
a month, the storyteller recounted this experience only minutes before my
departure from Carauari.

20. Something happened to me once
        about which I never told anyone, you know?
    [Here the speaker laughs self-consciously.]
    Even today,
        I find it somewhat strange.
    I would go down to the riverbank, you see?
        and there would be a whole band of people
            coming up out of the water.

    So then, there was among them a woman with very long hair;
        always, but always, when I'd go there to bathe,
            she'd approach me.
    She wore almost no clothes,
        in fact, she wore nothing,
            one could see every little bit
                of that woman's very perfect body, you know?
    They were a people with copper skin,
        more or less my color,
            all very attractive.

    But it was she who would call me,
        she who'd give me her hand.

And it was only I who saw her,
>no one else.
I asked my brother
>to go with me to the river once,
>>but he didn't see a thing.

So then, I got really scared,
>but even so, I still wanted to go
>>with them—that is, with her.[28]

The Dolphin-woman's allure is particularly notable in those cases in which she urges the man in question to rescue her from the *Encante*. The specific instance with which I became most familiar involves one of Kátia's relatives by marriage. Not only the young man, but his father, sister, brother-in-law, as well as Kátia and her mother spoke at length about the event, which had occurred three years earlier when he was sixteen.

In the version of the story coaxed out of the young man by a persistent Kátia, the mysterious woman's initial appearance in a dream, her account of her abduction by an *encantado* at the age of seven, and proclaimed fondness for the young man since his childhood are decidedly conventional. Her ideal, European physical features, her stated desire to marry her potential rescuer, and the detailed instructions she gives for obtaining her disenchantment are similarly predictable.

21. She was a very pretty blonde
>who always wore a white dress.
She talked a lot;
>she told me all about her life.
Always, but always, she'd appear in my dreams;
>later, I met her on the beach.
She said she'd been enchanted
>at the age of seven
>>and was now wanting to return to earth,
>>>that she would appear as a monstrous serpent,
>>>>and I was to shoot her in the head.
Then she would become disenchanted,
>and marry me,
>>and give me lots of money.

28. Man, age 24, born Rio Branco (Acre), lives Carauari (4 years). Married, grade-school teacher, 2 years high school.

Look, I found her very pretty.
I wanted to marry her, I did
    —it's just that later I got scared.
I began to have my doubts, you see?
Because I'd never known anyone who'd been
    to the river bottom.
Even today, I don't know what to think.[29]

Less common and considerably more interesting from the standpoint of analysis are the speaker's still-conflicting thoughts about his own reactions to the woman in white. Unlike the great majority of men's third-person stories, which present the enchanted visitor as blatantly untrustworthy, her true character in this case remains perplexingly unclear.

The young man's relatives are similarly divided in their assessments of the situation. His father, for instance, thinks he should have taken the Dolphin-woman at her word. ("Look," he observed to Kátia and her mother during one of his frequent visits to Parintins from the interior, "we are very poor; we don't have the means for anything. But if he had disenchanted her, he would have become very rich. He would have had a far better life than mine.")[30]

The young man's brother-in-law, in contrast, dismisses the *encantado*'s plea for help as a potentially fatal ploy ("He would have disappeared forever if he had done what she said!"), and his older sister expresses fear and horror at the whole affair ("I don't like to think about it").[31] While the storyteller himself regrets not helping the mysterious blonde ("Who knows whether she wouldn't be here with us today if I had done what she asked me?"), he is not sure whether he would respond any differently today.

Although Dolphin-women tend to play a more stereotypically passive role in third-person tales, a significant minority of these reveal a similar ambiguity. Not only do a number of apparently conventional taunt stories devote more attention to the Dolphin than the man, but there are actually tales—told by men—in which the initially cocky instigator is thoroughly humiliated. "So then," says Alzira's son:

29. Man, age 19, born interior of Parintins. Single, fisherman and farmer, 2 years school.
30. Man, age 51, born interior of Parintins. Married, fisherman and farmer, no formal education.
31. Man, age 33, born Parintins. Married, city bureaucracy, 3 years high school. Woman, age 27, born interior of Parintins, lives Parintins (7 years). Married, housework, 3 years grade school. Although the brother-in-law told me that he believes an *encantado* attacked the young man, he continues to feign disbelief in his presence "because I don't want him to take it too seriously."

22. After the guy called the dolphin,
        she appeared in the form of a woman,
              so pretty, so sweet-smelling
                      he just wanted to hold her tight.
Then she insisted
        he do something with her
               but he couldn't manage.
Nothing!
Can you imagine?
So then, she told him
        he should never
               bother her again.

Only afterward did he return to normal.
For days he kept on smelling the perfume of a flower
        he had never smelled before;
               he didn't know what flower it could be.
That smell lingered on and on,
        it almost drove him mad.

Only the *pajé* could help him.[32]

The out-of-control aspect discernible in various third-person narratives intensifies in personal experience accounts. The teller of the following story, a farmer who regularly travels between Parintins and the interior, insists he brought the incident upon himself by allowing the Dolphin to catch him off guard. ("If I hadn't gotten scared by what happened with the *tarrafa,* nothing would have happened, you see?") And yet, even if one accepts his self-portrayal as instigator, the events that follow possess a force and logic of their own. "Everything," he explains, as we sit with his wife and several neighbors in an urban backyard full of corn rows and chickens:

23. Absolutely everything,
        began with a fishing trip.
I threw the *tarrafa,*
        she grabbed it
               and pulled me toward the river bottom, you see?
So then, I got scared.

---

32. Man, age 21, born Parintins. Single, carpenter's assistant and odd jobs, 6 years school.

If I
    hadn't gotten scared
        by the *tarrafa*,
           nothing would have happened, see?
But precisely in that moment of shock
    I felt my head begin to ache,
        that splitting sort of ache, you know?
When I got back from the river, I already had a chill.

So then,
    I got a shirt;
        I got a sheet.
I lay down in my hammock,
    but I was really shivering.
I was so very cold![33]

After the initial shock, the man's condition worsens, and soon the Dolphin is appearing in his bed every night. Although the man compares his enchanted visitor to a white plastic doll of the sort sold in the city market, it is she who seizes the initiative in their sexual encounters. "So then," he says, "after two days, I began to sense something going on; that Dolphin had begun appearing to me. Every night she came to lie with me, you see? She played the very devil with me. When she was with me, I felt pleasure. Such a pretty girl, white as a doll, white as plastic! So then, she lay down with me in the hammock. *She did with me whatever she wanted*" (my emphasis).

A father for the first time at the age of fourteen ("My cousin began putting out," he says by way of explanation), he claims that women were created to put up with men's whims.[34]

The striking contrast between the man's assertions of his own masculinity and his complete loss of control with the Dolphin-woman offers a striking illustration of what a Freudian analyst might characterize as sublimation and compensation, and suggests the degree to which the Dolphin tales may provide an outlet for fantasies not easily indulged or even expressed in daily life. Significantly, his experience follows an earlier attack by a male Dolphin on his then-teenage adopted daughter, an event that

---

33. Man, age 37, born interior of Parintins, lives Parintins and Zé Açu (8 years). Married, fisherman and farmer, no formal education.

34. The cousin *deu sopa*, or literally "gave soup." There are, after all, few foods that offer less resistance.

must have left the man feeling powerless and angry, as well as, perhaps, a bit jealous.

The speaker's intense pleasure with the Dolphin is matched by an overwhelming sadness every time she leaves. "My heart seemed to constrict" ("Parecia que me apertava o coração"), he says with a worried smile. Frightened by the unaccustomed force of his own emotions (and not, significantly, the prospect of being hauled off to the river bottom), the man seeks out a shamanic healer. "Look," he recalls:

24. She'd make me doze off
>   but I wasn't really sleeping.
> So then,
>   I wanted to cry out
>   but I had lost my voice.
> And so,
>   she played with me all those hours,
>   she would only leave at dawn.
>
> When it was six o'clock in the evening,
>   I would make coffee
>   and a great sadness would come over me.
> So then,
>   I would remain there,
>   just watching the river's reflection.
> And that sadness would fill me,
>   bringing me to tears.
>
> So finally,
>   I couldn't stand it any longer,
>   I sought out the *curador*.
> Because I liked that woman,
>   she made me almost die of pleasure.
> But I couldn't stand the sadness that would come over me,
>   without my knowing from where.

Because men, in contrast to women, remain conscious during their amorous encounters with enchanted beings, they are more likely to seek out shamanic help in time. Men also may take matters into their own hands by killing the enamored *Bota*. In the conclusion to a story told by one of Maurício's relatives by marriage, the man stabs his Dolphin lover with the harpoon she herself has offered him as a token of her devotion. Although the victim follows shamanic counsel in mounting this at once practical and highly figurative act of counteraggression (the harpoon has obvious phallic associations), it is he and not the *pajé* who actually confronts the offending Dolphin. "So then," the man explains, "the curer told him to kill the Dolphin with the same harpoon she had given him. Well then, he [the man] became very frightened but he went after her, and, finally, killed her. Afterward, he went completely crazy; ten men couldn't hold him down. So then, the woman [here, the healer appears to change sex in midstream] prayed over him and he recovered. *But if he hadn't had the courage to kill her,* she would have carried him off, body and soul, you see?" (my emphasis).[35]

And yet, although men are far more likely than women to escape a love-struck Dolphin, the cure is not always so swift or total as some storytellers imply. Not infrequently, the man may endure recurring bouts of near madness, running down to the river at all hours, or consuming great heaps of raw fish. A howling wind periodically may fill his ears, a haunting fragrance linger in his nostrils, or a strange light shine about his hammock when he tries to sleep. Gerineldo's uncle tells the story of a man who dances with a Dolphin-woman at a party. Pressed by her to perform on the *rabeca,* he is amazed to find himself playing without the slightest hesitation despite his total lack of prior musical experience. Although he goes on to become a celebrated musician whose talents bring both fame and fortune, his memory of the encounter still troubles him profoundly. ("Even today," he says, "people come from far away to hear him. In his house, there is always plenty of everything. Now then, you can be sure he doesn't like it when people ask him how he learned to play so well.")[36]

The very indelibility of the experience, even in supposedly complete cures, belies the Dolphin's continuing hold. Not only are most recollections emotionally charged and unusually detailed, but men are often loathe to speak of these interactions many years after the fact. ("Here it is, almost forty years later, and I still don't understand what happened to me," the man who spurned his Dolphin playmate confides with a sheepish grin.) Kátia's relative says that although he has not had a face-to-face encounter with the woman in white for several years now, she still invades his dreams from time to time. "The dreams are always nice," he says, "and yet, I wake up scared."

35. Man, age 25, born Juruti Velho, lives Parintins (8 years.) Married, municipal employee, 3 years high school.
36. Man, age 37, born Acre, lives interior of Parintins (12 years). Married, fisherman and farmer, no formal education. For an interesting parallel in which Venezuelan water spirits teach a woman to read and write, then make her a famous painter, see David M. Guss, "The Encantados," p. 256.

STORIES TOLD BY WOMEN

Just as the dominant role of men in the Dolphin tales appears less clear-cut upon examination, so does the apparently passive behavior of women invite a closer look. Unlike men, whose accounts feature *encantados* of both sexes, women are more apt to focus on Dolphin-men. They are also far more likely to tell stories in which there is no readily apparent motive for the Dolphin's pursuit of a given individual. Even those stories that portray female protagonists as victims of their own temerity may undercut their apparent moral in a variety of ways.

Although female storytellers may point to the Dolphin's all-consuming passion for individual women as proof of his innate perversity, his obsessive interest confirms their desirability. If Dolphins' propensity to carry on with, if not carry off, particular members of their sex for "no good reason" is a source of unease and, sometimes, outright terror, it is also an affirmation of female power, since at least some of these *encantados* are reputed to fall very much in love.

Time and again, storytellers of both sexes insist that the enchanted pursuer hypnotizes or magnetizes the object of his affection, rendering her oblivious to his advances. Male storytellers in particular are apt to stress the threatening aspects of this loss of consciousness. "The person is as if dreaming, and does not notice a thing. And this is what is terrible," Tô Pereira says. And yet, at the same time that male Dolphins' ability to ravish the woman of their choice confirms the latter's vulnerability, it also frees the apparent victims from any responsibility for their actions. It is certainly not the woman's fault if her pursuer should cause her—against her will, without her knowledge—to moan all night with pleasure. Nor can she be blamed for her sudden indifference to household duties, friends, or family members. A victim demanding sympathy, she is also a suddenly desirable, even exotic, female. If the Dolphin wants her, she must be attractive, and his wild pursuit invests even the least likely candidate with new allure.

The unfulfilled or half-imagined desires experienced by storytellers thus find expression in an indefatigably seductive Dolphin. Despite numerous suggestions to the contrary, these enchanted visitors do not always render women oblivious to their surroundings, and a number describe the Dolphin's sexual exploits in graphic detail. Moreover, even when he is ostensibly a threat or obstacle, his actions may have beneficial consequences for the apparent victim.

If nothing else, an attack by a Dolphin is a good way to get a distracted husband to sit up and pay attention. Should jealousy and wounded pride not provide a sufficient spur to action, the added duties suddenly heaped on him are certain to elicit a response. The woman whom the Dolphin is pursuing cannot go to the riverbank—and thus cannot wash clothes or dishes, or draw the multiple buckets of water needed for drinking, preparing food, and cleaning house. If the attack is particularly severe, the husband also may find himself coping with the children, the cooking, and the dishes, along with his wife's share of the agricultural work. As both spouses normally must produce at full capacity for the family to survive as an economic unit, a man whose partner is plagued by a Dolphin will do virtually anything to obtain a cure. One man describes ferrying about his afflicted, postpartum wife, their new baby, and four other tiny children for days looking for a shamanic healer. "I have never been so frightened in my whole life," he confesses, "and this was thirty years ago."[37]

Although it would be a mistake to view the *encantados* from a purely functionalist perspective, encounters with them satisfy a variety of needs. In the following case, for instance, a handsome stranger appears to a woman with two small children, who has just left an unabashedly unfaithful husband. Although the Dolphin importunes her to accompany him to the river bottom, he does not insist when she rejects his offer in the name of her children. Instead, he sings her a tender love song whose words the woman is still able to repeat in a quavering voice today, half a century later. The encounter thus affirms the speaker's attractiveness as a woman at a time when she must have felt publicly humiliated and very much alone. The Dolphin's blandishments offer consolation while permitting her to voice her commitment to her children in a moment of intense personal crisis. Since "mother" is as specifically a female role as "wife," her declaration is itself an affirmation of female identity. Although the Dolphin is the initiator in this instance, the storyteller's response to his overtures determines the encounter's outcome. She recounts the incident to me and several of her adult children, mechanically brushing the crumbs off the table where we have just eaten lunch.

25. So then, there appeared there by the river,
    a very handsome young man.
  It was a Dolphin, you see?
    but in the form of a man,
      that very handsome man.

  So then, he wanted me to go with him
    to the river bottom.

37. The symptoms he describes in his wife sound to the outsider like a nervous breakdown triggered by a severe case of postpartum depression. The shamanic healer he finally located was indeed able to provide a cure. Although the man believes that his wife has no recollection of the event, my own conversations with her make clear that she does.

He wanted me to be his wife,
    he said he'd give me lots of money,
        lots of nice things.
Because he lived in a really lovely house, you see?
He was a sort of count;
    do you know what a count is, Dona Cândida?

So then, he was a count,
    and I wanted to go with him,
        I really did.
It's just that my children were still little
    and so, there was no way I could go.
Then, he began to sing that song
    I've already sung for you, remember?
[Here she tremulously intones a love song.]
Good grief, even today I still think about that man![38]

The Dolphin also may provide a safe, entirely guilt-free haven for new mothers overwhelmed by the physical, as well as psychic, demands of a new baby. Often, he affords them both a literal and figurative breathing space (many shamanic cures involve a period of relative isolation) without appearing to shirk traditionally female responsibilities. One good example is a nineteen-year-old woman born and raised in Parintins who moves to an isolated community in the interior with her country-born schoolteacher husband. The Dolphin attacks that begin almost immediately after the move intensify after the birth of the couple's first child. Finally, they become so severe as to force the new mother to seek treatment in Parintins. Although the woman in question dutifully repeats the shamanic healer's diagnosis of her as an *espírito fraco* or "weak spirit," she nonetheless has succeeded in surrounding herself with family members who can ease her sense of isolation and help care for her small son. While there is no reason to believe that she is consciously manipulating the situation, the Dolphin's intervention has effectively extricated her from an alien environment without occasioning any sort of confrontation between her and her husband. Note that this case involves not one, but rather, several Dolphins, who appear in animal, rather than their more customary human, form.

26. Look, each time I went down to the river,
    those Dolphins would show up
        wanting to talk to me.

---

38. Woman, age 75, born interior of Pará, lives Parintins (18 years). Married, housework, no formal education.

I thought the whole thing strange,
 they really scared me.
They would invite me to enter the water,
 to visit their city at the river bottom.
Right afterward, my head would ache,
 I couldn't eat,
  I couldn't sleep at all.

It got so I no longer paid attention to the baby
 —I wasn't even aware I had a child.
My husband had to do everything,
   everything,
 because I have no family in that place,
  there was no one to help me.

So then, he took me to the *curador* there
 who prescribed many herbal baths
  and said a lot of prayers,
But it did no good,
 those *Botos* just kept on coming.

Finally,
 he took me to a *pajé* here.
He [the *pajé*] explained to him
 that I had a weak spirit.
If I remained there,
 the *Boto* would carry me off
  to the river bottom
   and I would never return.
So that's why I'm still here in Parintins.

It's bad in part because my husband
 is back there in the interior.
But the cure takes a long time
 —you have to do it bit by bit
  for it to really work, you see?[39]

Women are more likely than men to form continuing relationships with
Dolphins which may serve distinctly practical, as well as more diffuse,
symbolic ends. One thirty-four-year-old resident of Parintins, for instance,

39. Woman, age 19, born Parintins. Married, housework, grade school education.

has had recurring dreams of a Dolphin by the name of Gerson since early adolescence. (Significantly, the woman's mother is a shamanic healer, whom this same Gerson occasionally assists in cures.) Although the younger woman complains about the Dolphin's stereotypically male jealousy, his presence nonetheless provides a useful, and in no way unflattering, explanation for her currently single status and the apparent failure of various past relationships with men. ("No man is going to mess with you, because you already have a husband. I'm going to keep on praying for you," the Dolphin says with a decidedly uncharacteristic show of piety.)

Despite the young woman's claims to have had no physical contact with her enchanted suitor, he is clearly the primary sexual presence in her life.[40] Introduced to me by Alzira, who sometimes visits her *curadeira* mother, she offered the following account one late afternoon that slowly turned to evening as we sat on the curb outside her home.

27. He comes in my dreams,
         but I'm not sleeping.
     He comes in a straw hat,
         he comes with yellow flowers.
     He tells me to take the flowers,
         but I never do.

     So then, he says,
         "I'm keeping you all for myself,
             I protect you.
     I am not one of those types
         who goes chasing after
             anything in skirts.
     I respect you,
         I will never leave you.
     But I want you just for me.

---

40. Given Dolphins' generally very physical nature, one may wonder exactly what transpires between her and Gerson in the woods. The speaker, however, insists on both his notably un-Dolphinlike restraint (twenty years of such encounters and still nary so much as a peck on the cheek) and the exemplary constancy that makes him unusual not only among his fellow *encantados,* but—in her view—males in general. When I encountered the same woman two years after she had recounted the story that appears here, her life had dramatically changed. She had found a better job, lost weight, and acquired a boyfriend. When I asked about Gerson, she said that she had undertaken a cure ("lots of baths, lots of prayers") to force him to depart. She also confided that she had often had sexual relations with him— usually beneath a veiled table in the forest—but that she had been frightened and embarrassed to admit this in the past ("He was the very devil, he really had no shame").

No man is going to mess with you
    because you already have a husband.
I'm going to keep on praying for you."

Look, he brings me the prettiest ferns
    from the river bottom.
Later, he takes me to the woods.
He says he was my first boyfriend,
    but I don't really like him.
If I really liked him,
    he would carry me off for sure.
Or he would use me
    and then leave me, you see?
Because that's the way men are.

And so, everybody respects me,
    everybody likes me.
But I'm not looking for a man, no,
    I get along with everyone.[41]

In this case, the Dolphin both frightens the object of his desire and imbues her with unusual abilities (here, the capacity to maintain satisfying nonsexual relationships with men). This empowering aspect of the Dolphin is equally obvious in a host of third-person stories in which the woman he is courting starts to sing mysterious songs that summon multitudes of river creatures, or else exhibits an astounding physical force. Almost certainly not by coincidence, the narrator of this tale of a woman whom no man can hold down is an older resident of Parintins whose reasonably well-to-do father dismissed her numerous requests to study. Now a widow forced to take in laundry for a living, she muses out loud that she could have done "something better with my life."

28. That woman lived in Parananema
    and we lived there too.
So then, she took sick.
She took very, very sick
    and finally,
        she went a little mad.
It took three men to hold her back
    when she'd try to run down to the river.

41. Woman, age 34, born interior of Parintins (Tracajá), lives Parintins (10 years). Unmarried, laundress, no formal education.

Well, one day, she had one of those attacks
    and she said to an aunt of mine and me,
        "Ah, I'm leaving, he has come for me"
—the Dolphin, you see?
"He's come to get me in a really pretty boat."
That's what she told us.

Now then, there were just the two of us to hold her,
    and so, there was nothing we could do.
She jumped out the window
    and by the time we caught up with her,
        she was already in the middle of the river.

Now then, I don't know how
    she managed to walk on that water
        —can it be that he was holding her up?
Because it's very deep there, right?
    it's very deep.

So then,
    one of my cousins came to retrieve her.
But look, she jumped about so,
    he couldn't do a thing.
So then,
    at least eight men arrived to subdue her.
But she just kept jumping about
    in the middle of the river,
        laughing and laughing.

Finally,
    they had to stop
        —and at this point, she vanished.
That is, she didn't really vanish
    —the Dolphin carried her away.[42]

If the Dolphin's ability to spirit off a given woman affirms a stereotypically female lack of power, it represents a resounding victory over men as well. For this reason, the apparent victim's defiantly aggressive, when not overtly mocking actions—as well as the *encantado*'s ability to befuddle and elude the husbands, fathers, and brothers who normally control women's behav-

42. Woman, age 62, born Parintins. Widowed, laundress, no formal education.

ior—may be a source not just of terror, but of half-conscious glee. "The Dolphin took her and there was nothing, absolutely *nothing*, he [the woman's husband] could do about it," storytellers may say with a baleful shake of the head. Furthermore, not all of their tales portray passive females. Just as the Dolphin may be unexpectedly shy or tender, so the protagonist herself may exhibit a courage that defies convention. In at least some stories, the intended victim handily outsmarts her would-be abductor. In addition, spirited women may shoo away or even pursue the startled Dolphin.

As one might expect, female storytellers are far more likely than their male counterparts to describe plucky women. Although the following tale is also told by a man—Maurício—it was told to him by his grandmother. Moreover, the first of the two versions that appear below was recorded in her presence and the transcription duly notes her frequent interjections. The second is another version of the same story that Maurício told to me, a slightly younger female cousin, and her new husband one lazy afternoon. Although each version begins in a similar manner, the second ends on a rakish, decidedly suggestive note.

29. A woman lived in the interior
    and her husband traveled a lot.
He left her alone
    for large amounts of time.
["Poor thing!" his grandmother exclaims with a click of the tongue.]

So then, one fine day
    he went off on a fishing trip for several weeks.
["That's just the way it is, because in the interior we women spend a lot of time alone," his grandmother says.]
Well then, toward the end of every afternoon,
    a bird called the *macucau* would sing.
And every time it sang, she would say,
    "*Macucau,* come get me,
    macucau, come get me,"
        just like this.

So then, when one day when she was making
    porridge for her children,
        banana porridge,
            a man arrived at her house,
                she didn't know from where.

[Here Maurício's grandmother interjects, "Just like a Dolphin, you see?" and he repeats, "Just like a Dolphin."]
So then, she became suspicious;
    she sent her children to the river to fetch water.
Only she told them
    to wait for her in the canoe
        because she didn't trust that man.
["He was an animal, you see?" says his grandmother. "He wasn't a man at all."]

Then, when the children started to delay,
    she excused herself
        and went after them.
When she got to the river,
    she jumped into the canoe with them
        and went paddling off down the river.
And when she looked back,
    that man was on the riverbank.

So then, he shouted to her,
    "Go on, go on, if you hadn't slipped away
you can be sure I would have taken you today!"
[Maurício's grandmother nods approvingly.]

30. [conclusion]
    So then, when the woman arrives there on the riverbank,
        she jumps into the canoe, you see?
    And the man remains behind.
    So then, he begins to flap his arms like this,
        yelling, "Hubba, hubba, hubba!"
    [Maurício demonstrates with gusto.]
    "Look, my girl," he told her,
        "Get out of here this minute!
    Because if you don't leave right away,
        I'm going to show you everything I have here
            in this sack of mine."
    [Here Maurício leers in an exaggerated manner and laughs uproariously.]

In contrast to the initial account, which emphasizes the wife's feelings of loneliness in her husband's absence, the second uses humor to emphasize more cautionary aspects of the tale. Maurício flaps his arms and yells gleefully when the *encantados* invites the woman to peek into his bag of tricks. Not only have his grandmother's amendments disappeared, but he also utilizes various expressions, such as the diminutive *agorinha* ("right now") and the familiar *minha filha* ("my dear" or literally, "my daughter"), that create a chatty, irreverent, and sexually suggestive tone quite foreign to the first account.

Other stories challenge the notion of the passive woman by portraying the intended victim as firmly in control. "'I don't want you; I don't like you; scram!' I told him!" says one woman with a triumphant grin.[43] One eighty-two-year-old woman, widowed now for over half a century, tells of catching a Dolphin in her melon patch. After giving the intruder a good whack with her broom handle, she runs him off her property. "I hear [literally, "see tell"] he later got a woman there in São Lourenço pregnant, but he never bothered me again," she says. "How do I know he was a Dolphin? By his clothes, of course—white hat, white suit, white shoes, all gleaming in the moon. Moreover, he is one of these well-known Dolphins—a real woman-chaser by the name of Barás."[44]

A woman also may turn the tables on a Dolphin by becoming the pursuer. "A handsome man like that, right?" says one young woman in Zé Açu half-jokingly. "Look, it's plenty hard to find a good man around here. So why let him get away?"[45] One woman tells the story of how her aunt jumps into the water in pursuit of an astonished Dolphin. "So then," she concludes, "when it was three o'clock in the morning he said to her, 'I have to go now'—like the Princess Cinderella, you see? So then, she said, 'I'm going with you!' And when he said he couldn't take her with him, she went chasing after him. He ran and she ran and when they reached the river, both of them dove in!"[46]

On other occasions, the Dolphin's supposed victim creates such problems for him that he voluntarily sends her packing. "I know a girl who went to the river bottom," confides one of Alzira's daughters as she, Alzira, and I perch on the bed in her straw house at the end of a rainy afternoon. "But she caused so many headaches there they finally let her leave. She didn't want to eat, she did nothing he told her. Finally, the Dolphin just gave up and said that she could go."[47] Both she and her mother laugh at

43. Woman, age 30, interior of Parintins, lives Manaus (7 years). Separated, radio station cleaning woman, 2 years school.
44. Woman, age 82, born interior of Parintins. Widowed, farmer, no formal education.
45. Woman, age 22, born interior of Manaus, lives Maués (14 years). Single, clerk in bakery, 5 years school.
46. Woman, age 33, Zé Açu. Married, housework and farming, MOBRAL literacy program.
47. Woman, age 27, born Ilha das Onças, lives Parintins (13 years). Married, housework, 4 years school.

this uncharacteristically insouciant conclusion. "I think I'd do the same if it were me!" Alzira says, reaching for her newest, suddenly cranky, grand-child.

Subsequent interpretations of a story often undermine its apparent message. Thus, one young seamstress in Parintins dismisses as "sheer foolishness" her great-aunt Artemísia's refusal to marry a Dolphin who proposes to her "like a proper gentleman."[48] Unlike the father of the young man who hesitates to disenchant a marriage-minded Dolphin, she does not so much lament the money as she does the aunt's subsequent unhappy marriage. "If it had been me," she says, "I would have gone with him to the Enchanted City. They say it's very pretty, very rich. But no, she married one of these men who can only think of rum and women—I say the Dolphin would be better than that no-good José Enrique!"[49]

Women also may take issue with men over the meaning of a particular story. In the following exchange, conducted at a lunch table laden with the fruits of a good day's catch, Alzira and Argemiro debate the motives of the female Dolphin who pursues a fisherman of Argemiro's acquaintance. Although their disagreement focuses on a specific narrative, it suggests broader, gender-based differences in outlook.[50] Argemiro is convinced that the Dolphin only wants to harm the man, but despite his insistence on having the last word, Alzira is by no means won over to his position. (Their son, for his part, shrugs and heaps more fish upon his plate when I ask his opinion.)

The story in question concerns a man who is regularly sleeping with a Dolphin. Unlike his colleagues, who often return home empty-handed, he always catches heaps of fish. Jealous of his good fortune, his friends surreptitiously follow his boat and catch him and a Dolphin-woman making love in the middle of the river. When the friends start shouting, the Dolphin vanishes and the man comes down with a terrible fever that forces him to consult a shamanic healer.

Argemiro: So then, if these guys hadn't startled them, she would have carried him off to the river bottom.

Alzira: I don't think the Dolphin wanted to carry him off, it's just that his friends frightened her. So then, she went away and he was left without her protection.

48. Woman, age 22, born Belém, lives Parintins (11 years). Separated, seamstress, 1 year high school.
49. Woman, age 47, born interior of Óbidos, lives Óbidos (15 years). Married, laundress in bishop's palace, no formal education.
50. James M. Taggart, *Enchanted Maidens;* and Daisy Hilse Dwyer, *Images and Self-Images,* provide useful models for comparing stories told by male and female Amazonian storytellers.

Argemiro: No, no, dear. It's that these Dolphin-women only want to carry off people.

Alzira: But if she had wanted to carry him off, why didn't she carry him off right away? Why did she keep on getting fish for him every day?

Argemiro: I don't know, but that's the way the Dolphin is. She always carries off the person.

Alzira: Well, it seems to me she really liked him.

Argemiro (now impatient): She wanted to harm him, dear. That's the only thing she wanted.

The existence of a whole group of narratives dealing with female *sacacas* further undercuts the customary male/female dichotomy, as the woman who can control a Dolphin clearly exerts considerable power over men.[51] Certainly the most amusing assertion of the female *sacaca's* power I recorded is the following story of the woman who prevails upon her husband to carry her suitcase on her regular trips to the Enchanted City. Although men as well as women are apt to laugh at the long-suffering valet in the following story, his supporting role constitutes an affront to the patriarchal order. Behind the laughter is the recognition that curers of both sexes enjoy powers that transcend customary social definitions, including those of gender.

31. My brother's father-in-law,
    he's a *sacaca*.
His mother traveled beneath the water
    —she was a *sacaca* too.
Every Thursday, she'd set out
    and would only return the next week.
She always wanted her husband to go with her
    —she'd say, "Let's go, José,
        you carry my bag."

So then, he would carry her bag for her.

---

51. A female curer can all too easily forfeit her privileged access to the supernatural through an ill-starred sexual alliance. Thus, Dona Marina describes how one of her daughters loses her considerable shamanic potential upon marrying a man who does not respect her gift. "This daughter of mine," she says, "was born after only seven months and at the age of seven months she was walking, talking, everything. But when she married, very young, she lost the gift of foresight. It wasn't for her to have married so young, in this way, it was for her to have waited. But she got married and that was that. The man didn't want to hear of her [spirit] masters; he became [venomous like] a snake with her at home, Holy Mary! All he wanted was to run after girlfriends, then he left her. And she never again traveled to the river bottom. No, no, she lost it all."

So then, he would carry her bag for her.
When they reached the river bottom she would say,
　"Pretty Dolphin, come and get him,
　Pretty Dolphin, come and get him."
Just like this, three times, you see?
So then, the Dolphin would come and leave him by the river,
　it was she who'd stay down there with the fishies, see?

So then, the Dolphin would leave him there,
　he'd wave goodbye
　　　and the poor guy would have to wait
　　　　　for his wife's return.
Heck, that lady cured everyone!
There wasn't anyone she couldn't cure.[52]

The great majority of men married to *sacacas* or other sorts of curers manifest a marked lack of enthusiasm for their wives' activities. Although most appreciate the material rewards of healing and are reluctant to anger potentially vengeful spirits, only one of the husbands I met—perhaps, by no coincidence, the youngest—voiced anything resembling support. Others, such as Kátia's father-in-law, would clearly prefer to see their spouses otherwise employed. Called away from work on a greasy car in order to corroborate the truth of a story involving an encounter between the two of them and an enchanted being, he rubs his hands on a rag before responding, "Yes, yes, it was an *encantado*—or perhaps something else."[53]

In short then, while on the surface, Dolphin stories would appear to reinforce broader notions of male dominance and female subordination, storytellers of both sexes subvert this dichotomy in numerous ways. The compensatory dynamic that informs many tales is much the same as that which underlies assertions that some fishermen have intercourse with dolphins.

We have seen that although some individuals may identify persons believed to have forced themselves on dolphins, virtually no one claims to have been party to such an action. If, however "perversions are as much pathologies of gender role as they are pathologies of sexuality," the significance of such behavior—real or imagined—cannot be underestimated.[54]

52. Woman, age 41, born Mazagão Velho (Amapá), lives Mazagão Novo (18 years). Married, housework, no formal education.
53. Man, age 52, born interior of Pará, lives Parintins (15 years). Married, auto bodyshop owner, schooling unknown.
54. Louise J. Kaplan, *Female Perversions*, p. 14. "Whatever else they are about," notes Kaplan, "perversions are certainly about the social constraints placed on human desire" (p. 18).

It is tempting to see men's reports of intercourse between fishermen and dolphins as retaliation for male Dolphins' seduction of their wives and daughters, as well as a defiant reseizure of initiative. Such claims also reinforce perceptions of women's inferior, if not unabashedly animal, nature. Conversely, female storytellers tend to see the same events as proof of men's bestial proclivities (and thus, by extension, the greater humanity of women).

The sexual exploits that some storytellers attribute to Dolphins give meaning to what the outsider might otherwise dismiss as strange, if not brutish, actions on the part of some men. By becoming the aggressor, a man asserts his lack of fear. Not only is he fully prepared to seek out the dolphin (who may, so far as he knows, actually be an enchanted being), but he has no qualms about his own reaction in the heat of intercourse. "Only a real man messes with a dolphin" ("Para mexer com bota, só cabra macho mesmo"), says Gerineldo's uncle. The man's ability to confront successfully and then withdraw from the dolphin on the most literal of levels suggests that no Dolphin—and certainly no mere woman—can hold him figuratively. By proving himself "man enough" to confront a doubly alien female other, he can control forces normally beyond his influence.[55]

This defiantly transcendent urge helps explain the reported ritual beating of the self or the dolphin (or, in some cases, both) with the branch of *pião branco* preceding intercourse as an act of purification that allows the man to emerge from the encounter in every sense unscathed. Likewise, one can comprehend the need to consult a shamanic healer "so that the mystery does not stick."

From many men's viewpoint, penetration of the dolphin is not simply a gratuitous violation, but rather, on some level, a form of preventive rape. By making the first move against one or another *bota,* the man in question may keep her enchanted counterpart from seducing him or carrying off his wife or sister. Above all, the choice of a dolphin as a sexual partner is a defiant response to women, and by extension, to anything and everything that would deny a man what he perceives as his rightful superiority. Thus, one man displayed visible irritation at my laughter when he informed me that dolphins outshine women as lovers. Although I was responding to the

---

55. In this sense, bestiality does not involve the animalization of the human being so much as the defiant transcendence of specific social boundaries. "The transgression from one domain to another, from culture to nature, to attain (and obtain) the wild and, at a symbolic level, to become *uncontrollable,*" Ondina Leal asserts, "is done through emotions. Desire is a fundamental component of any social imaginary and in this case (*and probably in other similar situations of profound social inequality*) it is the only element capable of operating this passage, since the desire allows an actual form of control, sexual possession" (my emphasis in the second case); Leal, p. 28.

sudden, absurdly graphic image of a man whispering sweet nothings to several hundred pounds of panic-stricken dolphin rather than to him as an individual, he clearly had expected me to be shocked and dismayed. "It's absolutely true," he grumbled to his fellow rubber tappers squatting on the floor beside him. "*They* can pretend it's funny, but it's absolutely true" (my emphasis).[56]

In short, a man's ability to dominate a dolphin is a declaration of his power over women and of the particular constellation of wild, natural forces that women represent in Amazônia.[57] From this standpoint, it is a reassertion not only of traditional gender roles, but again, of human willingness to confront that powerful, capricious nature which the Dolphin as *encantado* embodies.

THE DOLPHIN AS LOVER

If the prospect of a Dolphin falling in love with one is admittedly disquieting, the idea of one's becoming enamored of a Dolphin is more disturbing still. While male storytellers insist on their ability to elude the Dolphin's clutches and females plead total unawareness of his presence, at least some individuals become deeply involved with their pursuers. "The Dolphin liked her and she liked the Dolphin," says one man of a former next-door neighbor rumored to have followed her enchanted suitor to the river bottom.[58] "Do I like Gerson?" asks the woman who claims to have known one Dolphin for over two decades. "Oh no, no, I don't like him. At least, I don't like him *much*." Comments of this sort suggest that much of the *encantado* stories' dramatic force lies in the more universal power of human sexuality. Emblems of raw and ultimately impersonal desire. Dolphins are at once sinister and wondrous. Not only do they emerge from the depths without the slightest warning, but their tremendous physical attraction estranges the individual from a once-familiar world. Time and again, storytellers insist that the *encantados'* victims become beside (literally outside or beyond) themselves ("A pessoa fica fora de si," Tô Pereira observes.) Listless, without appetite, imbued with strange desires and stranger powers, they forget all about their former obligations and, even, former loves.

In the end, nothing remains but for the Dolphin to carry off these persons. "She was already very much under his power" ("Já estava muito

56. Man, age 37, born Boca do Acre, lives interior of Carauari (6 years). Married, rubber tapper, no formal education.

57. Clearly, the association of women and wildness is not limited to the Amazon. See Sherry B. Ortner, "Is Female to Male as Nature Is to Culture?"

58. Man, age 34, born Parintins. Married, mechanic and other odd jobs; schooling unknown.

alcançada"), storytellers often say. (The verb *alcançar* customarily means "to attain," as in to attain a goal.) In this context, it is wholly fitting that those abducted should take on a new physical appearance. Totally divorced from their previous selves, why should they not be literally transformed as well? Although a minority of these individuals remain nostalgic for the world they left behind them, the majority do not think about who and what they have abandoned. Then too, although some people may evade the Dolphin's clutches, the experience remains with them for the rest of their lives. Even limited access to that world beneath the water confers special gifts and privileged knowledge—be this an ability to cure others, or simply to pick out tunes on a previously mysterious violin. The person who returns from the *Encante* always returns richer. The catch, of course, is that not everyone returns.

The *encantado* stories highlight nuances and contradictions in the active male/passive female dichotomy that provides partial models for much of what people say and, sometimes, do. As such, they "are less about sexual ecstasy than the forms of life in a particular culture."[59] While female storytellers, in particular, are apt to find a surreptitious ally in the Dolphin, both men and women may encounter an escape from the strictures of everyday gender roles. By allowing people to flout roles they themselves often push to an absurd extreme, the *encantados* once again provide a channel for resistance to hierarchies and conventions that would freeze a world in constant motion. ("Dolphins," says Alzira, "almost *have* to dance.")

59. Regina Harrison, *Signs, Songs, and Memory in the Andes*, p. 170. Harrison's analysis of the metaphysics of sex in Quichua lowland women's love songs (pp. 144–71) suggests various parallels to the Dolphin tales.

8

THE DOLPHIN AS WHITE MAN

O Boto não é bicho; é uma gente diferente—alta, loira, rica—outra quali-
dade de gringo.

(Dolphins aren't animals; they are a different kind of people—tall, blond,
rich—another sort of *gringo.*)

—*Woman, age 44, Parintins*

The Dolphin's whiteness finds a partial explanation in the distinctive
coloring of *Inia geoffrensis,* whose skin ranges from a pinkish or grayish
white to a deep, shrimplike red. *Botos'* considerable size and weight also
facilitate their association with fair-skinned persons, whom many residents
of the region perceive as being uniformly tall and robust. This whiteness,
however, is far more than a physical attribute. Despite the frequent overlapping of racial, ethnic, and class categories in Amazônia, as in Brazil as a
whole, "white" or *branco* refers above all to economic and, by extension,
political and social standing.[1] (Recall Dona Marina's use of the term as a
synonym for *patrão,* or "boss.")

People of light skin do not necessarily define themselves as *brancos,* but
may instead reserve this term for darker-skinned persons of higher status.
Regardless of its residents' identity, a nice house is always a *casa de branco*
or "white person's house"; a *dia de branco,* a workday. "Let the whites work
it out among themselves" (*os brancos que se entendam*), a person may de-
clare sardonically in relegating a given problem to a group of politicians,
none of whom may have a particularly fair complexion. "It was wrong of
them to beat him," Tô Pereira says of the judge who orders his men to
pummel the musician reluctant to play for him at three o'clock in the
morning, "but these *brancos* are accustomed to getting their own way."

---

1. For a comparative introduction to race relations in Brazil and the United States that
helps explain the class connotations of the term *branco,* see Carl Degler, *Neither Black nor
White.*

Dolphins' pale color therefore reinforces their privileged socioeconomic position and corresponding ability to exercise control over those less powerful than they.[2]

The prime symbol of the *encantados'* wealth and power is the Enchanted City, which resembles, while outshining, its earthly equivalents. Although specific details vary, the *Encante* is invariably beautiful and—above all—very rich. "It's like Rio or Brasília," says Gerineldo, "except that everything is bigger, better, like a movie." "Even the divider curtains [which take the place of interior doors in poorer Amazonian houses] are made of gold!" a shoemaker exclaims.[3]

Descriptions of the Enchanted City often include elements suggestive of a larger Indo-European folk- and fairy-tale tradition. The underwater palaces, the sea creatures tooting saxophones in a sort of Amazonian fantasia, the chairs that are actually coiled serpents, recall a number of other enchanted realms. And yet, if images of the *Encante* possess a more universal and out-of-time aspect, they also draw in part on contemporary television soap operas as well as the reports of migrants to urban centers, many of whom find work in private homes as cooks, laundresses, night watchmen, and gardeners. On the one hand a flight from the material world, the Enchanted City is on the other a portrait—and sometimes parody—of upper-class Brazilian life. Because many storytellers feel (or think they would feel) more at home in a rural setting, the Enchanted City is an image less of how they themselves would live if they suddenly had the means to choose than of how they think that people with a great deal of money go about their daily lives.

While descriptions of forest beings such as the Indianlike *Curupira* are invariably evocations of the landscape with which many storytellers' own lives are, or were once, intertwined, the Dolphin city is distinguished by its artifice. The streets are often paved with gold or precious stones, while the glass or porcelain houses recall not only diamonds or imported glass, but also the shamanic healer's brilliant, magic crystals. Even the few natural attractions are invariably cultivated. The long expanses of peach-palm trees or sweet-smelling flowers, for instance, do not spring up in spontaneous, forestlike fashion, but instead, are arranged in gardens or carefully tended groves.

Most accounts of the Enchanted City stress its imposing habitations.

---

2. The Dolphin is equated with a white man, or *gringo*, in the Peruvian Amazon as well as in Brazil. For some storytellers, the *tucuxi* is the *cholo bueno*, or good mestizo, while the *boto* or *bufeo* is a *gringo malo* (Jaime Regan, *Hacia la tierra sin mal*, p. 180).

3. Man, age 54, born interior of Pará, lives Parintins (23 years). Married, shoemaker, "a little" formal schooling.

Time and again, storytellers describe carefully appointed two-story *sobrados,* when not palaces or buildings that bear a distinct resemblance to Brazilian governors' mansions or the Manaus Opera House. The *encantados'* homes boast air conditioning, telephones, vacuum cleaners, washing machines, and even Jacuzzis, which storytellers—who may have access to neither running water nor electricity—tend to describe in enthusiastic, if often garbled, detail. Nowhere in the Enchanted City does one find straw huts or plywood lean-tos. "There they don't have shacks like mine here," Dona Marina says with a sweep of the hand and an apologetic laugh. "There everything is luxury, you see? There you only find houses with tile in the kitchen and lots of pretty pictures in gold frames on the wall."

The Dolphins' sumptuous life-style matches their surroundings. Urbane as well as urban, the *encantados* do not roam the woods on deerback like the *Curupira,* but instead amuse themselves by moving about the dance floor while tuxedo-clad musicians perform on flutes, cornets, and violins. Fruit does not drop off the trees; it is brought to them on silver trays by servants (presumably other sorts of river creatures). The inhabitants of this city wear finely tailored clothes, and both sexes demonstrate a penchant for expensive jewelry. (The men favor rings with enormous diamonds while the women wear numerous necklaces, bracelets, and diadems ablaze with precious stones.) In addition, Dolphins make liberal use of perfumes. Time and again, both males and females are described as "sweet-smelling," or *cheiroso/a.*[4]

Dolphins' personal fragrance suggests larger and important differences between them and savage (and often notably foul-smelling) forest beings, underscoring the *encantados'* class identity. Not only does perfume have sensuous, exotic connotations, but in a hot climate where the slightest physical exertion causes one to perspire profusely, its use sets apart the laborer from those who lead a life of leisure. Then too, perfume is a manufactured and usually imported product. Unlike the more modest and usually far cheaper *cheiros* distilled from native grasses and flowers, *perfumes* always contain less familiar ingredients that supposedly justify their higher price. While the former often bear names such as "Green Scent" or "Fresh Scent" (*Cheiro Verde*) or "Forest Sigh" (*Suspiro da Mata*), perfumes are called "Paris," "Princess," "Dream of Love."

Residents of the Enchanted City do not sit back on their heels, sleep in

---

4. Fragrant skin appears to be equally important to some indigenous Amazonian groups. Stephen Hugh-Jones notes that Barasana young men "stick sweet-smelling herbs under their G-strings and under the bracelets of black beads they wear on their biceps" and that "the smell of these herbs is said to attract women" (*The Palm and the Pleiades,* p. 110).

threadbare hammocks, or eat from a single pot of fish on a dirt floor.[5] Rather, they perch on elaborate chairs and doze off in beds with soft white sheets that somebody else spends hours ironing. They dine at carefully appointed tables whose linen tablecloths and elaborate place settings contrast with the battered tablespoons or fingers employed by most residents of the interior.

Storytellers, to be sure, express enthusiasm for this privileged existence in which one does not have to lift a finger. "You just sit there all day long and they bring you trays of guavas, pineapple, bananas!" a barber with tired feet exclaims.[6] "The *Encante* is very good," one young man from the interior of Parintins says, deftly tucking a sheet of newspaper about the clump of bananas I have just purchased. "Because here we work a lot, we continually struggle in order to survive, and there, no, they have an easier life. There, the fish leap into the cooking pot; one doesn't have to spend the whole day waiting in the middle of the river, enduring sun and rain."[7]

The variety and richness of the food invites particular comment. "My grandfather was a *sacaca* and on those days when there was no breakfast, he would just dive into the water and come back with a cup of coffee on a silver tray," a retired dock worker in Parintins asserts.[8] "Down there in the *Encante,* they give you breakfast, lunch, a snack, and dinner!" says one woman who became a *rezadeira* after a claimed visit to the river bottom. "The curer who took me there said that we had to return because my mother missed me, but I didn't want to leave!"[9]

As these last remarks suggest, the fantasizing and overt wish fulfillment so obvious in these tales often includes elements of social protest. The atmosphere of magic and promise of the unexpected that pervades the Enchanted City is pointedly at odds with the backbreaking routine that characterizes most storytellers' daily lives.[10] In the following account, a longtime subsistence farmer recently turned carpenter explicitly contrasts

5. The single pot, to be sure, is not simply a reflection of poverty; it is also a symbol of community and the willingness to share.

6. Man, age 44, born Boa Vista (Roraima), lives Manaus (8 years). Married, barber, 3 years school.

7. Man, age 24, interior of Parintins. Single, fruit vendor and farmer, 2 years school.

8. Man, age 67, Parintins. Married, retired dock worker, no formal education.

9. Woman, age 54, born interior of Parintins (Zé Açu), lives Parintins (8 years). Married, housework, no formal education.

10. To the extent that they represent a "temporary liberation from the prevailing truth and from the established order," the Dolphin stories may be considered carnivalesque in the Bakhtinian sense (M. M. Bakhtin, *Rabelais and His World,* p. 10). Rather, however, than turn the social world upside down (i.e., the slave becomes a king), these tales tend to offer exaggerated images of everyday reality (thus, the greedy *branco* becomes a greedy Dolphin).

the Dolphin's carefree existence with his own continuing battle for survival. Not by coincidence, the man is speaking in the presence of his sometime employer, a local priest, who is waiting for him to finish lunch so he can resume work on a churchyard fence. Thus while the man's reference to shouldering a heavy burden has metaphoric overtones, it is also a direct allusion to the pile of posts awaiting him in the midday sun. Recognizing the obvious, if cheerful, dig at him that lies behind this flight of the imagination, the weary priest—who himself would prefer to sleep away the afternoon—grins broadly and points to his watch.

32. The Dolphin,
> he can make a person get sick and die.
> But the person doesn't really die.
> No, no, he's still alive and goes
> > to that perfect city at the river bottom.

> There, they have everything
> —cattle,
> nice houses,
> plenty of chickens and pigs.
> There, everything comes easy,
> > people don't have to work,
> > > they don't have to carry heavy loads
> > > > in the noon sun.
> It's just like this world
> > except that people don't work,
> > > they eat well and stroll about.
> There, everybody takes a little nap after lunch, right?
> [Here he looks meaningfully at the priest, then winks].
> It's a good life.[11]

Storytellers' profound ambivalence toward the *Encante* is particularly obvious in descriptions of the Dolphin as white man. If the *encantados'* ability to indulge their champagne tastes inspires admiration and longing among storytellers, it also elicits envy and resentment, since Dolphins do absolutely nothing to merit their good fortune. Yet worse, they regularly use their power to disrupt the lives of innocent humans. While life in the *Encante* is unquestionably attractive, the *encantados'* happiness relies on the sufferings of those they abduct in order to satisfy their own desires. In the routine indulgence of their own whims at the expense of others, they

11. Male, 66, born interior of Parintins, lives Parintins (2 years). Separated, carpenter and odd jobs, no formal education.

resemble the "very wily" owners of the jute fields in which Dona Marina used to work.

The following storyteller's explicit association of the Dolphin with the once-omnipotent rubber settlement owner underscores the latter's class identity. After comparing the Enchanted City to a turn-of-the-century *seringal* with its great house of imported pine and expensive European furniture, he goes on to suggest that the Dolphin and the *patrão* are alike not only in their immense wealth, but also in their cavalier behavior. Although Dolphins have no interest in expropriating labor, they share the *patrão*'s blithe indifference to the welfare of those who have no power:

33. Look, I think the Dolphin
    is like these old-style bosses.
Because in the past,
    the *seringal* was really beautiful.
The owners brought carpenters from Portugal
    and they built those houses of Oporto pine.
Then, they ordered furniture
    from France and Great Britain.
Even mirrors in pure gold frames arrived here.

Now then, there were some of them who did a lot of harm.
Whoever wouldn't sell his rubber to them
    they had the *capangas* [hired henchmen] string up
        in the noonday sun.
There was one,
    Seu Geraldo, I think his name was,
        who used to make the children climb the guava trees.
Then he would fire on them [for target practice],
    he actually killed them.
And the parents, poor things,
    couldn't say a word.

So then, I think the Dolphin is like this
    —he's very rich
        and also very perverse.
If he wants to carry off a person,
    he carries him off—that's that.
The mother can cry the whole day long
    —it's all the same to him.[12]

12. Man, age 77, born Pernambuco, lives Carauari. Widowed, retired rubber worker, no formal education.

In other accounts, the old-fashioned patriarch becomes a contemporary politician who manipulates public property and other people to his own advantage. Not infrequently, this figure is identified as Gilberto Mestrinho, who appears as a rapacious Dolphin in one of Amazonian novelist Márcio Souza's more devastating political satires.[13] "The Dolphin," one man says, "is like one of these politicians who only lies to people. He's like Gilberto, the one who claims he is a Dolphin, right? But that's just the way it is. Because these Dolphins are very rich, they have their own city that is just like the Hotel Tropical [an opulent tourist hotel in Manaus where a son of the speaker once worked as a bellboy.] There they dance, they drink, they eat, they steal other people's wives. Life is great for them."[14]

If the Dolphin is a *branco,* he is often also a foreigner in a literal as well as metaphoric sense. Even though the term *estrangeiro* refers specifically to persons from countries other than Brazil, many storytellers employ it as a synonym for any perceived outsider, be this individual from São Paulo, Pernambuco, Japan, or Germany. (In some parts of the interior of Amazonas, an *estrangeiro* may even be somebody born and bred in Manaus.) Likewise, despite the Enchanted City's location beneath familiar waters, it remains "another country" or even "another planet." "It's because those people are completely different," asserts Kátia, draping a sheet over her son, who has gone to sleep on the almost-new red vinyl sofa. "They look like human beings but they lead another sort of life."

Dolphins' foreign nature is most obvious in their markedly non-Amazonian appearance: their height and the blue eyes, blond hair, and "white as plastic" skin on which few storytellers fail to comment. A number of people pose direct links between Dolphins and the exterior, insisting that these *encantados* speak a foreign tongue often identified as English or—in Parintins—Italian. (The latter fact unquestionably reflects the city's elevated number of Italian-born clergy.) "How did I know that he was speaking English?" one man who claims to have had an encounter with a Dolphin demanded. "Why, it's the same language that you hear in songs on the radio, of course. 'Hey Baby, light my fire,' right?"[15]

"I think the Dolphin must be an American," says Alzira. "Yes, yes, it's

13. Márcio Souza, *A resistível ascenção do Boto Tucuxi.* Mestrinho later attempted to turn the tables on his critics by defiantly adopting the all-powerful Dolphin as his trademark in a slick television advertising campaign underlying his successful bid to recapture the governorship of Amazonas in 1990.

14. Man, age 65, born interior of Pará, lives Vila Amazonas (13 years). Married, fisherman and farmer, no formal education.

15. Man, age not given, birthplace not given, lives Parintins. Married, sells fishing supplies, educational level unknown.

true. Aren't Americans always tall, strong, rosy-skinned, good-looking? So then, Cândida, they [the Dolphins] look just like you!"

Although Dolphins' non-Amazonian physical appearance reinforces the perception of them as outsiders, other, nonphysical characteristics are ultimately more essential to their foreign, and more specifically *branco*, identity. Chief among these are the *encantados*' shameless cunning, overbearing manner, and insatiable appetite for what belongs to others. In the following account, the Dolphin flashes handfuls of dollars, causing all the women at a country *festa* to give chase. His promises, however, prove as counterfeit as the gleaming necklaces with which he attempts to buy their favors. In the following example, the pockets full of U.S. currency suggest the Dolphin's alliance with the multinational investors who have poured into the Amazon over the last few decades. Not merely a foreigner, this distinctly contemporary *encantado* is an out-and-out opportunist who seduces the gullible with expensive-looking—but ultimately worthless—gifts.

34. The Dolphin, man,
      he goes around chock full of dollars.
Yes, sir, the guy appears in the *festa*
      with those very white, expensive clothes
            and all the country girls go wild for him.
They want to dance with him
      and him alone;
             they no longer give a hoot
                about their boyfriends.
He flashes those dollars
      and they go running after.

But the Dolphin is false-hearted.
He wants to flirt with the prettiest girls,
      he promises them nice things.
But afterward, he disappears
      and what of those promises?
Even his hat isn't a hat—
      it's a stingray, understand?

He gives his girlfriends gold necklaces
      and, next day,
             they turn back to seaweed.

But they aren't at all suspicious of his sweet talk,
no siree![16]

Although most accounts of the Dolphin as *branco* portray him as an exploit-
ative outsider, a smaller, but nonetheless significant number of other tales
credit him with unexpected virtues. In this second group of stories, the
Dolphin is more akin to the white-skinned, godlike beings who have played
a central role in some native Amazonian, and larger South American, traditions. The *Encante* here resembles an aquatic version of the Tupi-Guarani
Land without Evil, in which plants grow by themselves, honey flows in
abundance, and the fair-haired residents devote themselves unceasingly to
joyous celebration.[17]

Although the Dolphins in these narratives still may abduct human beings, their elsewhere capricious, if not downright perverse, actions now
form part of a larger cosmic scheme. The great benevolence which these
good *encantados* display toward their captives and one another prompts
descriptions of them as "more united" (*mais unidos*), "more brotherly" (*mais
irmãos*), and even "more Christian" (*mais cristãos*) than human beings.
"The *encantado* is better than us," a young woman in Zé Açu says. "He is
more generous, more kind, in sum, *more human*" ("O encantado é melhor
do que nós. É mais generoso, mais amável, em fim, *mais humano*") (my
emphasis).[18]

In line with this radical shift in the Dolphin's character, the Enchanted
City is now less an alluring, but ultimately sharply critical, image of upper-
class life than an underwater utopia that provides a dramatic foil to earthly
existence. Distinguished as always by its wealth and beauty, it becomes, in
addition, the epitome of harmony and social justice. "There in the *Encante*,
it is just like here, except that no one has any malice," explains a shamanic
healer. "Everybody there is of a single family" ("Todo mundo lá é de uma
casa só").[19]

Significantly, according to one of Dona Marina's neighbors, the Enchanted City's wealth is not simply an accident of fate, but rather, a direct
result of its inhabitants' eagerness to help one another. Thus, instead of
living off unearned, if not ill-gotten gains, the *encantados* in the following
description enjoy the just deserts of an unfailingly altruistic orientation
largely foreign to human beings. "The life of those in the *Encante*," says

16. Man, age 44, born interior of Parintins (Ilha das Onças), lives Parintins (11 years).
Separated, taxi driver, 1 year grade school and MOBRAL.
17. For a discussion of this primarily Tupi-Guarani utopia see Hélène Clastres, *La terre
sans mal.*
18. Woman, age 19, Zé Açu. Single, housework and school assistant, 5 years school.
19. Man, age 24, Maués. Married, healer, 2 years school.

the neighbor, "is the very same life we live here, but it is superior to ours. The enchanted ones, they are united, they live as friends beneath the waters. When one of them takes sick, everyone tries to help, they all run to get a doctor, they don't let anyone suffer. They have everything we have, they have the same houses, but life there is happier and better."[20]

In at least some Dolphin tales then, the *Encante* is none other than the New Eden, hidden from human beings less by the opaque and shifting waters than by their own selfishness and greed. "The Enchanted City is here," a schoolteacher's assistant in Carauari says, "but we don't see it because we have a lot of sins that blind us. If we didn't have these sins, we would see everything; we would go there beneath the river bottom and be happy like the *encantados*."[21]

"The *Encante* is the same as heaven, except that it's under the waters. But we don't know a lot about it because it is beyond our powers of understanding," comments a young woman in the interior of Parintins.[22]

While the inability to detect the Enchanted City's presence stems from a generalized unworthiness ("a lot of sins") or limits inherent in the human condition ("it is beyond our powers of understanding"), it also may be the result of a more specific exploitation of some human beings by others. That the Dolphins' city is "just like" earthly cities—only better—suggests that life on earth could be very different if the social system in which storytellers find themselves enmeshed were not so egregiously inequitable. "There no one begs for food," says Gerineldo's mother, stirring a spoonful of powdered milk into a cup for the screaming baby. "No one ever begs, because they don't let anyone go hungry. It's not like here, where the rich ignore the poor and only think of money and more money."

This vision of Dolphins as exemplars offers a direct and initially puzzling counter to stories in which they figure as greedy *gringos*. At first glance, there would appear to be not just two Dolphins, but also two narrative traditions with little or nothing in common. Idealized Dolphins are almost certainly linked to older indigenous ideas of a utopia inhabited by superhuman entities, while their self-serving cousins are more apt to be equated with European colonizers, and now, multinationals. And yet, regardless of whether the Enchanted City burlesques upper-class life or shines forth as an underwater paradise, the tales provide a trenchant commentary on the status quo.

20. Woman, age 50, born Faro, lives Parintins (14 years). Widowed, housework, no formal education.
21. Woman, age 28, interior of Carauari, born Carauari (5 years). Married, primary school assistant, 1 year school.
22. Woman, age 15, born interior of Parintins, lives Parintins (3 years). Single, student and domestic employee, 3 years school.

Furthermore, although stories of Dolphins as white man employ elements that reappear in accounts of them as *encantados* and lovers, they are
concerned above all with re-presenting and, in the process, remaking a
society in which the rich openly exploit the poor. "Look," a net maker in
Parintins explains, "the Dolphin can be dangerous. Because he carries off
people, above all, little children. But the most dangerous creature that
exists is man. Because he makes the knife, he makes the bullet, he makes
war upon his brother. He is never content with what he has. The Dolphin,
yes, he can harm people. But there in the *Encante,* no one murders, no one
robs, everybody lives in peace and love."[23]

SHIFTING VISIONS OF THE DOLPHIN

Up to this point, we have considered the various ways in which Dolphins
function as outsiders. Not only do they embody alien and alienating aspects
of a social and economic order in which the great majority of storytellers
find themselves devoid of money, power, and all hope for a better future,
but even those stories that feature impeccably behaved Dolphins still portray them as irrevocably foreign. Thus, regardless of whether they appear
as remarkably bad or remarkably good beings, Dolphins stand apart from
ordinary men and women.

And yet, while most accounts of the Dolphin as white man suggest a
definite insider/outsider dichotomy, the storytellers' relationships to these
enchanted beings are not so fixed or clear as initially might appear. The
encantados' increasingly ambiguous situation in the face of rapid, wide-
scale, and ongoing changes is particularly evident in comparisons between
contemporary Amazonian Indian representations of the white man and
caboclo portrayals of the Dolphin as *branco.* Although the two reveal a
number of common features, they are ultimately very different.

Despite, for instance, the fact that the region's native peoples find themselves in ever closer contact with mainstream Brazilian culture, the white
man remains, on some level, unequivocally other. For the overwhelmingly
mixed-heritage storytellers we have encountered in this study, in contrast,
the Dolphin is often at once hostile invader and defiant symbol of a way
of life under assault. Ironically, those individuals in the second group who
rail most vehemently against the *encantados'* depredations are often the
first to come to their defense.

As noted in an earlier chapter, present-day Dolphin stories recall ele-

23. Man, age 51, born interior of Parintins (Remanso), lives Parintins (11 years). Married,
net maker and fisherman, no formal education.

ments of a still-existing Amazonian Aquatic Seducer tradition, which has necessarily adapted over time. Thus, "one sees an evolution among various native peoples of the western Amazon from the 'raw' Forest Ogres and Aquatic Seducers and the 'rare' Failed Proto-Humans into the Evil Inca, followed by the Stingy White Men and thieving Mestizo."[24] And yet, although the greedy, overbearing, and yet, often inexplicably powerful white protagonist of many contemporary indigenous narratives cannot help but recall the *caboclo* Dolphin, different native groups may treat this supremely alien being in a variety of ways.[25] Furthermore, students of surviving South American Indian cultures have amply documented the deceptive dynamism of apparently timeless oral traditions. Often, these portrayals involve the transformation of preconquest narrative elements and symbolic relations to reflect current social, economic, and political realities.[26]

In addition, a single indigenous group may entertain multiple and apparently competing visions of the white outsider. Waurá presentations of the white man in myth, for instance, differ markedly from those expressed through historical narratives and song poems.[27] In very general terms, however, one can say that present-day indigenous peoples in Amazônia tend to see the white man as an invader whose tremendous power contrasts with his total lack of moral standing. The Shipibo thus find themselves "caught between their admiration of the Westerner's machines and a desire for their wealth and social potency, on the one hand, and their contempt for the Westerner's subhuman, hairy appearance, libidinous (cannibalistic) tendencies, and stingy (anticultural) ways."[28] As a result, their stories tend to metamorphose the figure of the colonizer into dual opposing figures that both fit and challenge traditional mythic categories.

The white man, like the Dolphin, is very rich, yet not quite human. Although enjoying obvious technological prowess, his actions are unpredictable and often destructive. Thus, the Bororo see his material superiority as inextricable from his greed, and the Waúra cannot comprehend this being "whose extraordinary ability to make tools and objects is in bizarre

24. Peter G. Roe, "The Josho Nahuanbo Are All Wet and Undercooked," p. 110.

25. For useful comparisons see Keith Basso's *Portraits of "the Whiteman"*; and Julia Blackburn, *The White Men*.

26. See, for instance, Júlio Cézar Melatti's analysis of three versions of the Shoma Wetsa myth among the Marúbo of the eastern Javari river basin, "A origem dos brancos no mito de *Shoma Wetsa*." Melatti shows how the story may be seen as commentary on the contact of the Marúbo not only with representatives of modern states, but also with pre-Columbian indigenous peoples.

27. Emilienne Ireland, "Cerebral Savage."

28. Roe, "The Josho Nahuanbo," p. 110.

contradiction to his manifest inability to get along with others without constant resort to physical violence or the threat of it."[29] The Kalapalo, for their part, stress white newcomers' careless failure to heed divinely mandated territorial divisions.[30]

Among many indigenous groups, the white man is intimately allied with death and destruction. Hence, the "dark dreams" of the Mehinaku and Tupi-Kagwahiv stories in which the origin of the white man is attributed specifically to an *añang,* one of those ghosts of the dead who "become perverse, antisocial spirits of the wild."[31] The white man's negative characteristics recall the Dolphin in his role as agent of disease and a death synonymous with forced acculturation. Much as the Indian must first renounce his own identity in order to be recreated as a white in these stories, so the person abducted by a Dolphin undergoes a physical as well as psychic metamorphosis into another order of being.

The indigenous white man and the Dolphin-as-*branco* are also similarly incomplete within themselves. Although fabulously wealthy, their riches fail to bring them happiness, leading them to envy in others those qualities they lack. Thus, in the Yekuana myth of Wanadi and Odosha, the culture hero, Wanadi, invents all manner of objects in a futile attempt to satisfy the appetites of his bad-humored half brother, who is explicitly identified with an insatiably greedy white. Finally, an exasperated Wanadi escapes to a distant heaven, leaving Odosha perched atop the heap of radios, tape recorders, clothes, planes, cars, and jukeboxes he mistakenly equates with paradise.[32]

And yet, despite these and other points of contact between the Amerindian white man and the Dolphin, there are nevertheless a number of dissimilarities between the two. Chief among these is the far sharper differentiation between insider and outsider in contemporary Amazonian Indian myths. Although many of these narratives reveal admiration coupled with a deep desire for the white man's goods and power, they also register intense anger and repulsion at his antisocial ways. There is thus no ques-

29. See Charles R. Marsh, "The Indians and the Whites," for the Bororo; and Ireland, p. 160, for the Waúra. The Waúra cannot grasp why "this strange creature, blessed with fabulous quantities of material wealth, does not know how to share and indeed seems to lack ordinary human compassion."

30. The tale of Kwatïngï in Ellen B. Basso, *In Favor of Deceit,* pp. 29–83, explains how Europeans and Indians came into being as culturally distinct peoples.

31. See Thomas Gregor, "Dark Dreams about the Whiteman," for the Mehinaku; Waud Kracke, "Death Comes as the White Man," for the Tupi-Kagwahiv. In other Kagwahiv stories, Indians must die in order to become white men.

32. Marc de Civrieux, *Watunna.*

tion about the *branco*'s profoundly alien, if in some ways perversely attractive, nature.

Indigenous culture heroes, such as the half-human, half-anaconda Unurato of present-day Arapaço narrative, may return from the exterior (in this case, Brasília) in the form of a gigantic submarine crammed with manufactured goods.[33] This Unurato, however, holds himself aloof from, even while he mixes with, the "civilized" Brazilians whose technologies (but not whose values) he appropriates for the benefit of his own people. An insider from the beginning, he goes on to become the ancestor of the Arapaço, who call themselves "Pino Masa, People of the Snake" in deference to him. Whereas in *caboclo* versions of the story, Norato asks a soldier to shoot and thereby disenchant him, Unurato loses his supernatural powers against his will when the white man wrongly shoots. He is thus very different from the Dolphin-like Cobra Norato, the son of a human mother, who seeks through disenchantment to cast off his outsider status and join—not found—the human race. In further contrast to Unurato, who asserts his otherness by actively confronting the white man, Norato renounces his enchanted status. Neither insider nor outsider, he does not fully fit into either world.

The supremely volatile, invariably liminal position of the *encantado* takes on new meaning in the face of the intense changes occurring within Amazônia today. The progressive destruction of the rain forest is an assault on not just the Dolphin's millennial habitat, but also a way of life that, despite its very real inequities and hardships, displays a coherent and distinctive quality that often impels people to affirm it in the face of onslaughts from without. Both the massive inpouring of newcomers from other parts of Brazil and the intense push toward industrialization and bureaucratic centralization that has triggered ongoing migration to the city from the countryside have occasioned rapid and dramatic physical and psychic changes. The once-mighty Dolphin, long the epitome of the intruder, is thus himself under attack from newcomers who do not believe in the enchanted beings and who may reject out of hand the larger complex of beliefs and behaviors of which these stories are, or were, one part.

As a result of these multilevel transformations, the Dolphin's fiercest assailants often find themselves coming to his defense. Not only may they affirm the *encantados'* existence, but they suddenly may begin attributing to these beings positive qualities they themselves had previously ignored or even denied. At stake is far more than whether Dolphins dress up in

33. See Janet M. Chernela, "Righting History in the Northwest Amazon," for one version of the Unurato story with accompanying analysis.

white suits and party dresses to go to country dances or jump into unsuspecting people's hammocks on moonlit nights. Debates about the enchanted beings' precise nature—or, indeed, their mere existence—are above all evaluations of Amazônia's past, present, and future, and impromptu definitions of an at once individual and communal self.

Although many storytellers refer to the Dolphin tales as *lendas* ("legends"), this term has widely different meanings.

In Parintins, where the tremendous growth of the *Boi-Bumbá* festival over the last decade has made residents newly self-conscious about everything that outsiders identify as "folklore," one fairly common definition of a *lenda* is "the kind of story you see [dramatized] in the *Boi*." People may also identify the *lenda* as "folklore" (*folclore*) or "popular culture" (*a cultura do povo*). Pressed for a definition of these terms, they usually looked startled. "I don't know exactly what folklore is," one young woman admits, "but everyone here talks about it."[34] "You mean *you* don't know what culture is?" an older man demands. "I thought for sure you would. Aren't you a teacher?"[35]

Would-be definers may stress quite different aspects of these stories. Whereas, for example, some persons may find the *lenda* to be nothing more than "a pretty story," others associate it with the past. "The *lenda* is a perhaps fictitious fact," says one man, "a story that is passed down from father to son" ("Lenda é um fato talvez fictício, uma história que vai passando de pai para filho").[36] Still others stress the improvisatory quality of these narratives. "A legend," Argemiro says, "is something that appears almost spontaneously, just like the *encantado* pops up when one least expects" ("Lenda é uma coisa que aparece quase de improviso, como o encantado aparece quando a gente menos espera").

As with most narratives that folklorists class as legends, the issue of belief is extremely important in these stories.[37] The *lenda* is "what is in people's heads," says Maurício. "It's what people think is true or, at least, *could* be true" ("Lenda é cabeça do povo, é o que o povo acha é verdade ou, pelo menos, podia ser verdade"). Some storytellers equate the *lenda* with outright fantasy (*pura mentira*) while for others, it is "a true story that happened back in olden times but does not happen any more today" ("his-

34. Woman, age 19, Parintins. Single, manicurist, 5 years school.

35. Man, age 55, born interior of Parintins, lives Parintins (8 years). Married, mechanic, no formal education.

36. Man, age 43, born interior of Monte Alegre, lives Santarém (17 years). Married, taxi driver, MOBRAL literacy program.

37. The question of belief has long been central to legend theorists. See Linda Dégh and Andrew Vázsonyi, "Legend and Belief." For a definition of the genre see Robert A. Georges, "The General Concept of Legend."

tória verídica que aconteceu nos tempos antigos mas que não acontece mais"). Still others agree with Kátia that *lendas* always contain "a drop of truth."[38]

Given these extremely varied definitions, it is not surprising to find a number of storytellers who claim that the Dolphin never existed. For them, continuing belief in the *encantados* is a confirmation of Amazônia's poverty and isolation. Although they themselves may repeat these tales, they emphasize their fictional identity. "Is this story true?" the owner of a corner store asks after enthusiastically describing the antics of one party-going Dolphin. "No, no, not a word of it; it's nothing but invention. Because in those old days, the people were all very innocent, they believed everything they heard."[39]

Persons who deny the Dolphin's existence may equate declining belief in the enchanted beings with progress. "In the past, we were very ignorant," says one woman whose gold miner husband was recently murdered, leaving her to run the dusty corner store where I had gone to buy a pencil. "Today, we are more knowledgeable; almost no one believes any more in this business of the *encantado*. I, at least, have become modern; I have *almost* stopped believing" (my emphasis).[40]

"It was all invention," an older man says firmly as he scrapes the excess plaster off a newly molded garden planter. "Myself, yes, I believed in the Dolphin, I was terribly afraid of the *Cobra Grande*. But with time I came to see that there was nothing to these things."[41]

These sorts of commentaries—familiar today throughout much of Amazônia—serve not only to cast doubt on the existence of the enchanted beings, but, even more, to affirm the teller's own passage from gullible backwoods dweller to citizen of a technologically sophisticated world that has little place and yet less patience for the Dolphin and his fellows. Here, the newfound loyalty to rationalism may have a good deal less to do with

38. Tô Pereira defines *lendas* as "these things that no one knows if they exist, [things] about which everybody talks but which you never saw" ("estas coisas que a gente não sabe se existe, que todo mundo fala mas que você nunca viu"). For Dona Marina, they are "events I never saw happen but which I can nonetheless recount" ("casos que nunca vi passar mas sei contar de todo jeito"). Gerineldo's claim that a *lenda* is "above all, a mystery," underscores the strongly cosmological dimension that separates the *encantado* corpus from many, if not most, tales of the supernatural told today in the United States and Europe. Running through all of these definitions is a stress on the story's communal nature.

39. Woman, age 55, born Óbidos, lives Parintins (47 years). Single, shopkeeper, 6 years school.

40. Woman, age 34, Maués. Widowed, sells sundries, "some" grade school.

41. Man, age 67, born Parintins. Married, makes cement planters, 4 years school "but my father was a cultured man, a Jew from there in Morocco, and he taught me much more than I ever learned in school."

any real commitment to scientific thinking than it does with the desire to identify with the upper classes and the national culture portrayed on radio and television in one's own quest for a better life.[42]

The speaker in the following commentary on changing attitudes toward the *encantados* is the same young man who recounted how the Dolphin Zé Caetano used to appear in his dreams. Although the enchanted beings are usually said to be immortal, the Zé Caetano he describes has aged like any human. In this account, the Dolphin appears in the session of a local *curador* to complain about the soccer players who insist on playing on his beach. However, his threats about what will happen if they ignore his wishes fall upon deaf ears.

35. That older generation that believed in *encantados*
    no longer exists
        —the people have all died,
                or moved to Manaus or Parintins.
  And in their place there is a new generation
    that no longer believes.
  In fact, just to show you how things have changed,
    about three years ago,
        a new beach emerged very near my house
            and a group started playing soccer there.

  So then, people began to say
    that spirits were appearing in that place,
        especially Zé Caetano.
  But it seems that Zé Caetano had grown old,
    at least, that's what people tell me.
  So then, he came and asked them not to play
    any more ball on his land, you see?
  And if they continued to play there after a certain time,
    he would make the beach
        with everyone still on it
           vanish.
  He was mad, Zé Caetano was, you know?

42. "A simplistic model based on rationalism would call for education alone to erase supernatural beliefs, superior scientific explanation replacing inferior traditional wisdom," says Charles Stewart (*Demons and the Devil,* p. 134). "This is not the case. Social forces, particularly hegemony, may better account for shifts that are usually analyzed within the framework of an individualist rationality."

So then, a young man began to tease him.
He said, "Look here, Zé Caetano,
    where are the tortoises?
        They say you have a lot down there—
            send me up a really juicy one, man!"
So then, Zé Caetano got madder and madder,
    but those people kept on making fun of him
        —they no longer believe.

Other storytellers may argue that what passes as progress is simply a new form of exploitation and that the Dolphin is no more illusory than the escapist diversions of contemporary life. "We have passed from the *Boto* to the *Boi*," says one former fisherman, in the midst of arranging a small heap of papayas on a makeshift fruit stand. "But in my opinion neither the one nor the other fills the children's stomachs. Everything is a lie and an illusion. In the past, there was the priest wanting us to believe in the devil so as not to think about the landowner's injustice. And today there are the politicians constructing *Bumbódromos* for the exact same reason."[43]

"Politics makes me angry and disgusted," says one of Gerineldo's schoolmates as the firecrackers set off by various candidates for office pop and twinkle briefly against a very black night sky. "A politician is someone who only tells lies. I consider the most fantastic story of the Dolphin to be truer than any of these fellows' tales."[44]

By affirming the existence of the Dolphin in an irrevocably distant past, still other storytellers justify their own former beliefs and practices while acknowledging the fundamentally different nature of the present. Thus, Argemiro recalls a time in which an enchanted spider (or spider crab) who lived in the Boca do Mocambo caused the river periodically to swell. Today, however, the spider has vanished and the river flows along like any other. "It's that things have changed a lot," he explains. "In that time when I began to fish, at the age of thirteen or fourteen, it was extremely rare to see another boat. We would remain there in the middle of the river, all alone for hours. So then, back in those days, there was this enchanted spider and I myself saw the *Cobra Grande*. But today, almost no one sees them anymore."

"The Dolphin went away and the fields disappeared," asserts Alzira's father, dipping a battered ladle into the large clay water jug which he then

43. Man, age 37, born interior of Pará, lives Parintins (8 years). Married, taxi driver, no formal education "but my mother taught us how to read a little." The *Bumbódromo* is a stadium especially for the *Boi* festival.
44. Boy, age 14, Parintins. Single, student, 4 years school.

covers with a dinner plate. "Oh well, of course, there are still these ordinary dolphins. But that enchanted Dolphin, the one who remained there waiting for young women so he could take them to the river bottom, he has vanished; people say he no longer exists."

Not infrequently, the past itself begins to bear a suspicious resemblance to the *Encante*. Although connected to the present much as the earth is connected to the river bottom, it remains off-limits, strange, and, often, seductively attractive. Nostalgic in the sense that they evoke an inaccessible, and thus on some level unreal, space, descriptions of the *encantados'* former haunts may be at once laments and indictments. Eager for an alternative to his current circumstances, the speaker—a fisherman and noted hunter—puts down the owl he is preparing for that night's dinner and recalls with longing a bygone epoch in which the land yielded a seemingly endless supply of fish and game. "In the old days," he says, "everything existed in abundance, an astounding abundance. No one worried about food. People went down to the river and caught a *tucunaré*, a *tambaqui*, a piranha; the water teemed with fish and we collected lots of turtle eggs upon the beach. Today, no. They have taken all the fish out of the lake; it all goes to Parintins, and we here go hungry. Life is really very hard."[45]

Another man suggests that the *encantado* already has suffered a fate similar to that which the *tracajá* is presently undergoing. The latter, a once-abundant species of river turtle, is now threatened by extinction.[46] "In the past," he asserts as we, his wife, and several children sit together on a balding sofa, watching a badly dubbed U.S. detective movie, "the *tracajá* was the food of the *caboclo*, of the poor man, which people caught and ate every day. Today, we eat *tracajá* only when a friend brings one from the interior. It has become very expensive and in the future, I think there won't be any more at any price. Well then, I think the *tracajá* is like the *encantado*, and that in the next generation people are going to think it just a legend. I'm going to tell my little grandson how I saw the *Cobra Grande* and he's going to say, 'Gosh, Grandad tells more stories!' "[47]

The claim that Dolphins once existed allows individuals to accept the

45. Man, age 33, born interior of Parintins (Zé Açu). Married, fisherman and farmer, no formal education. 29 July 1989. Owls are regarded as ill-omened and, for this reason, usually are not eaten. This man, however, claims that his family is too hungry for him to worry about such superstitions. ("The worst luck one can have is to be born poor," he says dryly.)

46. Early chroniclers, such as Orellana's scribe, Carvajal, describe the turtles choking the rivers and covering the beaches, where they came to lay their eggs. Nineteenth-century travelers observed whole canoes full of turtle eggs, which were crushed for their oil and then left to rot in the sun.

47. Man, age 45, born interior of Parintins, lives Parintins (16 years). Married, taxi driver, 2 years school.

assertions of older people—often their parents and grandparents—without betraying their own, frequently quite different vision of the physical and social world. "I'm of the electronic generation," says a young shoemaker who previously worked for Tô Pereira. "People my age almost don't believe in these things. But I think that, in the past, people really saw these *encantados*. Because there was more forest then, more room for these things."[48]

"My father was born a slave there in Óbidos," a very old man says, rocking gently in his hammock as the morning sunlight streaks the grainy cement floor. "He had a ring in his nose and his owner's brand-mark on his shoulder. But he knew a lot of things; he never lied. So then, if he spoke of *encantados,* then you can be sure they existed *in his time*"[49] (my emphasis).

Insistences on the gulf between past and present also permit younger people to indulge their fondness for (and often, at least half-belief in) the Dolphin stories without fear of mockery. "Myself, for example, I very much like these stories that aren't of my time, that are of an earlier era," says the great-grandson of a now-deceased *sacaca,* toying with the feathers on a crucifix that dangles from a chain of seeds about his neck. "I like to think about them and how they came to be."[50]

Some storytellers affect a studied neutrality in relation to the *encantados.* Unwilling to affirm the Dolphin's existence, they may be equally reluctant to deny these stories' truth. "People invent, but they don't lie" ("O povo inventa, mas não mente"), they may say with a noncommittal shrug. ("I like to describe things I myself have seen," Tô Pereira asserts. "Now then, I can't say something is a lie just because I didn't see it. But I also cannot say that it's true, don't you agree?")

At times, people may admit to being slightly embarrassed by the *encantados.* "You talk about these things and people say to you, 'Look, it doesn't seem you ever went to school.' But there are many things that one can't explain in any other manner," the schoolteacher-daughter of a traditional curer says with a self-conscious laugh as we watch the rain pour down outside the doorway of her bright blue stucco house.[51] Happy to have company at a late hour, the night watchman in a hotel in Parintins yawns and explains that he himself has doubts about the string of stories he has just told me. The watchman says, "I have an Italian *compadre* who always tells me that children believe their parents—that is, they used to in the

48. Man, age 28, born interior of Parintins (Parananema), lives Parintins (14 years). Single, shoemaker, grade-school education.
49. Man, age 87, born interior of Oriximiná, lives Óbidos (47 years). Married, retired butcher, no formal education.
50. Man, age 33, born Parintins. Married, parish worker, 4 years school.
51. Woman, age 33, born Parintins. Married, wife and mother, high-school education.

past! If the father says, 'My son, don't go there in that place, because there are ghosts there,' later on the son will tell his children the same thing. Now then, my *compadre* says there is no such thing as ghosts, there is no *Cobra Grande,* nothing, that all this talk of *encantados* is only fear. I don't know if he is right, but there are certainly a lot of people who talk about these things without ever having seen them."[52] A local writer and folklorist adds that with the advent of electric light and television in even the smallest communities, the Dolphin "feels shame in the *caboclo*'s presence, and the *caboclo* for his part now feels ashamed of him."[53]

Other persons with whom I spoke revealed none of this hesitation, affirming that the *encantados* not only existed, but still exist today. However, virtually no one offered blanket acceptance of the stories, and not a few defended the existence of the Dolphin on a metaphoric, as opposed to strictly literal, level.

Quite frequently, not only residents of the interior, but also urban migrants dissatisfied with their new lives may couple their defense of the Dolphin with a fierce attack upon the city and city ways. Gerineldo's uncle, who lives in the interior, claims that the city is "a kind of hell" for the enchanted beings. "Of course, there are no *encantados* in Parintins," he says scornfully, slapping out the dust from his rubber sandals. "Why would the *encantados* want to come here? There is nothing to attract them; even the people find life bad."

Persons such as Gerineldo's uncle who continue to believe in the Dolphin and his fellows may express *O tempora! O mores!*–type laments for a supposedly better past. "People today make a joke of everything," says a day laborer in Carauari, combing his hair in the kitchen after a backyard bath. "They don't try to find out if something is true, they don't pay attention, they believe in nothing."[54] One of his companions, who has just moved to the city from the same rubber settlement, adds that even curses don't work like they once did. "People say the world is topsy-turvy," he says, "but it is they themselves who are confused, you see. Why, today even curses don't stick! One fellow curses the other and absolutely nothing happens."[55]

At times, these expressions of indignation reveal a conservative or down-

52. Man, age unknown, born Pará, lives Parintins (16 years). Married, night watchman, 3 years school.

53. Man, age 56, Parintins. Married, writer and accountant, high-school education.

54. Man, age 41, born interior of Carauari (Seringal Marabatá), lives Parintins (6 years). Married, day laborer, no formal education.

55. Man, age 55, born interior of Carauari (Seringal Marabatá), lives Carauari (4 months). Married, day laborer, no formal education.

right reactionary tenor. "The Dolphin doesn't pay attention any more to a menstruating woman," says Dona Marina's next-door neighbor as the three of us greedily watch the thin circles of banana turn golden in the frying pan. "Why should he? Today, even little girls are taking tumbles in the bushes. There isn't a corner here in Parintins where one doesn't find them wrapped around their boyfriends."[56] Not infrequently, however, the defense of the Dolphin becomes a sharp attack not just on the city and city ways, but on the capitalist system that is fast making inroads into every corner of Amazônia.

Such attacks are almost always based less on abstract ideological considerations than on personal experience. "I spent some time in Manaus," says a fisherman in the tiny city of Faro, "but I didn't like it. A person needs a lot of money there, and so he spends his whole life working. Here, no, there is more time, one has peace and quiet, and a nice breeze even on the hottest days. In the city, people kill themselves in order to buy a refrigerator. Me, when I get hungry, I go out in my canoe and return with all the fish that I can eat, so what's the need? Of course, the people in the city don't believe in the *encantado*. They don't ever go out on the river. They don't have time to observe nature or anything else—how could they if they spend their whole lives working?"[57]

Opposition to the effects of capitalism, if not the logic underlying it, often finds its way into stories of enchanted beings. It is particularly obvious in accounts of how the *Encante* actively withholds its secrets, thereby resisting conversion into private property. Although the protagonist here finds refuge from injustice within the borders of an enchanted forest, he fails in his attempt to turn its riches to his personal advantage. Furthermore, when he seeks to reenter this privileged domain, it proves impenetrable.

36. The *Encante,*
    it's of the water,
        but it can also be of the forest.
I know a man,
    he went deep into the forest,
        fleeing his *patrão,*
           a very bad sort
              who wanted to kill him
                so as not to have to pay him what he owed.

56. Woman, age 52, born Faro, lives Parintins (13 years). Widowed, housework, no formal education.
57. Man, age 43, born Faro. Married, fisherman, no formal education.

So then, he wandered deep within the forest,
 until he came to a site full of parrots and agouti.
There were also rams
 and a different sort of cattle, more like buffalo.
Well then, he was bedazzled;
 he wanted those cattle for himself.
"Gosh, man, with some animals like these,
 I could really make it big!" he said.

So then, he got all excited and rounded up the cattle.
But just as he was going to leave the forest,
 the cattle completely disappeared.
And so, he left with nothing, absolutely nothing.
And when he tried to return,
 he couldn't find the way.[58]

A similar aversion to the exploitation of the *Encante* for personal profit is obvious in one of the more interesting versions of the Cobra Norato narrative. Although the bulk of the narrative is decidedly conventional, the storyteller closes with a pointed reference to the newly disenchanted Norato's explicit refusal to sell his story to the highest bidder. His experience, the speaker suggests—and indeed, all that pertains to the Enchanted City—belongs to the community and, as such, is not to be exploited for individual gain.[59]

37. Well then,
 once I was traveling by boat to Uaicurapá,
 and there were some people telling this story of Noratinho.
Then, later on,
 a little old man told me
 that he himself was Norato.
Yes, yes!
 —he himself confirmed this
 as we traveled together to Uaicurapá.
A person just like you or me.

58. Man, age 18, born interior of Parintins (Valéria), lives Zé Açu. Single, fisherman and farmer, 4 years grade school.
59. In this resistance to commodification, a number of Brazilian storytellers diverge from those Venezuelan counterparts who portray the *encantados* as happily enmeshed within the new cash economy (see Guss, "The Encantados," pp. 244–45).

He talked about his life at the river bottom,
 he talked about the people there,
  he told me everything.

It was during election time, you see?
 and he was on his way to visit a jute planter.
Now then,
 I don't know where he lives.
He was an old man by this time,
 but when he was young, he played in all the *festas,*
  he was the best musician for miles around.
Now then, if it were another person,
 he would be earning lots of money
  telling his story on the Fantastic [a popular television
program].
He'd get really rich.

But he says he doesn't want to.
That is, he tells the story,
 but not for money.
Because he says these things
 are mysteries of the river bottom
  and not for sale at any price.[60]

Dissatisfaction with the practices and institutions associated with a power-ful new capitalist economic order is equally visible in storytellers' rejections of claims that human beings have visited the moon. (There is a strong correlation between belief in the *encantados* and disbelief in lunar expedi-tions.) Most of the storytellers, one should note, are far less hostile to the notion of scientific research than to what they see as the mass media's manipulation of the news for commercial purposes. "The moon is a planet that God made to light the world," one young man from the interior of Parintins says firmly. "I think this business of man going to the moon is an invention to make money."[61] "I believe in science," asserts Tô Pereira, prompting Gerineldo to nod in agreement. "But there are many persons who only want to profit in its name. Science is one thing and magic [sci-ence-for-money] is another, but often people cannot tell the two apart, and so, the trouble starts."

60. Man, age 22, born Zé Açu. Single, fisherman and farmer, 4 years grade school.
61. Man, age 25, born interior of Parintins (Paraná dos Ramos). Married, fisherman and farmer, no formal education.

"Did I see the man walk on the moon?" asks one older man in Maués as his grandchildren whirl about us in a game of tag. "Of course I did. My niece has television in her house and I watched the whole thing from start to finish. But look, my dear, you can't believe everything you see on television. Because they show many things that only *look* like real."[62]

Not only may belief or disbelief in the *encantados* be selective, but storytellers may underscore the fantastic nature of some narratives in order to support the truth of others that may appear equally, if not more, fantastic to the outsider. ("The *Curupira* does not exist; it's only talk. And ghosts, there is no such thing as ghosts. Now then, the *Cobra Grande* is for real," an individual may affirm.) In like fashion, storytellers may reject or qualify the more fantastic aspects of a given narrative. "My father's grandmother was very brave," notes a small-town pizza parlor employee. "She wore dresses made of seven yards of cloth. She went about with a shotgun, she would leave the house at midnight to tap rubber, and she'd fashion snakes from cloth. She would be sewing while the children played around her and then she'd turn a strip of cloth into a snake and send them all running. Now then, that snake wasn't for real, it only existed in the sight of those children. Because no one makes a snake from cloth; it isn't possible, of course."[63]

In a similar attempt to hang on to deeply rooted ideas and images without appearing ingenuous or backward, a fisherman in Faro takes issue with certain aspects of a friend's version of the hospital story. Unfazed by claims regarding the protagonist's removal of his own harpoon from a wounded Dolphin's side, the man nonetheless is troubled by the friend's alleged trip to the *Encante*. "So that's what this fishing buddy of mine told me, but I didn't believe him," he declares. "It's not that difficult for a person to become enchanted; they [the *encantados*] are enchanted and they transform themselves in order to carry off people to the river bottom. But I found it hard to believe they would invite him to go with them—why couldn't that man pull out the harpoon right here? Why did he have to go there to the river bottom? Look, I believe in the *Encante*. But when people go there, it's for good. They don't return."[64]

By expressing doubts about selected facets of their own or others' stories, people seek to demonstrate a capacity for rational thinking which many equate with modernity and higher social status. "There was a lady there in

62. Man, age 67, born interior of Pará, lives Maués (17 years). Widowed, retired, no formal education.

63. Man, age 42, born interior of Acre, lives Carauari (11 years). Married, works in pizza parlor, no formal education.

64. Man, age 49, born Faro. Married, carpenter and brick maker, 3 years school.

Oriximiná, they say the Dolphin took her to the river bottom," says a young man who has been looking for "almost any job" for over two years now. "And so there must be something to it. But I don't understand it. Because to travel to the river bottom, people must have oxygen. They have to be able to breathe, because if not, one drowns, right? So how can a person breathe there? This is what I want to know."[65]

Other storytellers insist on the factual basis of at least some *encantado* tales. Often, they find support in newspaper, television, and radio reports for the enchanted beings' continuing existence. "My son does not believe in the Dolphin or the *Cobra Grande*," says one man in the interior of Parintins as we sit with various other community members on a log, awaiting the arrival of a boat. "He says they are just inventions. But I have seen many similar things in the films of Jacques Cousteau, many aspects of the river bottom they have shown on television. So I think that the *encantado* is a reality. Hasn't the submarine already filmed the *Encante*'s door?"[66] Storytellers also may cite television soap operas, such as the wildly successful "Pantanal" and the "Canto da Sereia" ("Mermaid's Song") as proof of the *encantados*' existence. "I know that 'Pantanal' is just a story," says one woman. "But you can't tell me these soap opera people are going to spend all that time and money on a mere invention—no, no, there has to be at least a grain of truth."[67]

Younger people are particularly likely to defend the possibility of the *Encante* in the name of a science which represents to them the hope of social ascent and a life very different from that of their parents. "They are always discovering new things," notes one young man in the small city of Maués, "things that in the past many people didn't believe, but that science shows us must be true."[68] He goes on to expound a complicated theory of how the Dolphins' Enchanted City is really the lost Atlantis, which has somehow been transported to beneath the Amazon. "I can't prove it," he says, "but I have read many books, done much research on this problem. And everything indicates that it *could* be true."

And yet, while many people attempt to reconcile traditional beliefs with

---

65. Man, age 18, Parintins. Single, unemployed, 2 years high school.

66. Man, age 57, interior of Parintins (Semeão). Married, fisherman and farmer, no formal education.

67. Woman, age 66, born interior of Parintins, lives Manaus. Widowed, retired, no formal education. The Pantanal is a region of the Brazilian state of Mato Grosso, rich in plant and animal life. One of the characters in the soap opera of the same name was a kind of *encantado* called the *Velho do Lago* or "Old Man of the Lake." Another soap opera, "Amazônia," was launched in 1992.

68. Man, age 27, born interior of Itacoatiara, lives Maués (12 years). Single, bank clerk, high-school education.

their awareness of the growing power of scientific knowledge, a minority ostentatiously rejects these rationalizations. These individuals almost always belong to a more privileged social stratum for whom the *encantados* are intriguing folklore rather than a part of daily life. Thus, the grandson of the founder of one of the wealthiest commercial houses in Amazonas, who has come to Parintins for the *Boi-Bumbá,* relates how none of the pictures he took of *botos* on a recent river expedition revealed their presence. ("You see the river and the trees, but not the slightest trace of them.")

For this young man, unlike for most of the individuals we have seen, the Dolphin is clearly a symbol of a more international New Age consciousness with no direct relationship to everyday Amazonian experience. When I asked if he did not inadvertently put his thumb over the lens or forget to rewind the exposed film, he dismissed these mundane suggestions with a wave of the hand. "Look," he says, "we went out in the middle of the river, and suddenly, fifty, sixty dolphins began to surface for air. I took many pictures, I kept taking pictures from every angle, but later, when I had them developed, you could see nothing except water. For this reason I think that dolphins have something mysterious about them; they are part of a mystic reality no one can explain. People here talk a lot of nonsense but, at times, they say something certain, because the world really is full of incredible things."[69]

Storytellers who did grow up firmly within the *encantado* tradition are more likely to insist on the metaphoric, if not literal, truth of the *Encante.* Even those who express doubts about whether enchanted beings actually emerge from the water to roam moonlit beaches often use these stories to condemn the effects of deforestation and related changes on an older way of life. Thus, after explaining that the *encantados* are withdrawing from populated areas ("I myself am too young ever to have seen a Dolphin or the *Cobra Grande*"), Kátia's sister complains about the short-sighted policies that permit wholesale destruction of the region's riches. "This business of deforestation is very bad," she says. "Everything is money; these government types don't give a damn. In their eyes, everything is fine, they're only interested in filling their own pocket. So then, things go on as always: a rich land in which the people go hungry, in which only the lucky few can find a job. In the past, there was no luxury, everything was more humble. Today there is more luxury but the poor are poorer than ever."[70]

The same growing awareness of a larger world that leads some storytellers to question or reject the Dolphin as a literal reality often prompts them

69. Man, age 25, born Manaus. Single, university student.
70. Woman, age 17, born Rio de Janeiro, Parintins (16 years). Single, high-school student.

to embrace the *encantados* as representatives of their own regional heritage. "I don't like to say that the Dolphin doesn't exist," Maurício says firmly. "Because I think that these things have a basis in truth. Moreover, they are part of a long journey that makes Amazônia different from any other part of Brazil or of the world."

As one might expect, the defense of the Dolphin is often caught up in a defense of the oral tradition as a whole.[71] We have seen that rejections of present-day doubts about the *encantados* often accompany complaints about curses that do not stick and, by extension, the loss of the once-forbidding power of the spoken word. Alzira, herself a graduate of the MOBRAL adult literacy program, notes that "the person who is illiterate doesn't know how to read or write but his memory is surer than that of people who know how to read. Because the person who can read just picks up a book when he wants to remember something while the person who can't read keeps everything right there in his head." Her father, for his part, contrasts the mysterious force of the *Encante* with what he calls *magia estudada* or "book magic," which he defines as "these things that people learn through study and are not a gift of God."

People also may use accounts of the *encantados* to affirm the validity of shamanic healing practices that comprise one part of a more complex cultural whole. "These *caboclos,* they don't believe in doctors, in medicine; they only believe in prayer, in tradition," explains the former head of a rural health assistance program. "And so, if we don't pray, they won't accept our treatment, even if it's free."[72] As if to illustrate this point, a particularly skilled hunter in Zé Açu recalls how he had to sell his only shotgun in order to enter a hospital in Parintins "where all they did was give me pills, just pills!" After three days "just lying in a bed," he walked out the door. "I know how to talk with *brancos*," he asserts defiantly:

38. The doctor wanted to prohibit me from leaving,
     but I told him I was going home
          to die amongst my children.
I wasn't going to remain there to die
     on top of a bed like a dog.

71. For a Yekuana parallel see David M. Guss, "Keeping It Oral," in which the author sees the group's refusal to confide its traditions to writing or tape recordings as a form of resistance to a literate, European culture and its contemporary technologies.

72. Woman, age 41, born Belém, lives Parintins. Married, health service administrator, university education. The speaker goes on to explain that shamanic curers perform a ritual laundering of a new mother's clothes for fourteen days after she gives birth. If state health workers ignore this practice, many mothers will prefer the healer, even if he charges much higher rates and has a poor record in terms of babies' survival.

So then, he told me I was very ill-bred.
And I told him I thought I was very well-bred
    because I wasn't going to stay there in his care,
        no way!
So then, I returned to Zé Açu
    and showed up on the doorstep
        of one of these types who cures with *tauari*.

Look here, *mana*,
    this man charged me nothing.
He saved my life
    but he didn't want to hear of money, see?
Even today when I run into him
    I always give him a little something
        —a bit of game,
        —perhaps an egg,
        —a handful of manioc flour.
He says that I've already given him too much,
    but I don't agree.
Because if I'd stayed there in that hospital,
    I would have died for sure.[73]

THE DOLPHIN AS WHITE MAN

The pull between past and present is nowhere more evident than in stories that portray the enchanted beings seeking disenchantment so that they can live out the rest of their lives in wealth and comfort in Brazil's industrial south. "The Cobra Norato was from here, from Maués," says a young boat repairman, as he and a coworker scrape energetically at a long strip of splintered wood. "He became disenchanted [human] on a beach not far from here, but soon afterward, he left these parts and now he lives in a big apartment house on the beach in Rio."[74] Yet more disconcerting are accounts in which these once most powerful of healers find themselves seeking disenchantment in a series of extra-Amazonian locations. Thus, while in traditional accounts, Cobra Norato asks a local soldier to free him from the *Encante*, a growing number of storytellers portray him turning to alternative, non-native healing sources either within Brazil (Pernambuco, Brasília, São Paulo) or even outside the country (Italy, France, Japan, the United States).

73. Man, age 37, born Zé Açu. Married, fisherman and farmer, no formal education.
74. Man, age 21, Maués. Single, boat repair assistant, 4 years school.

In the following version of the story, told by Argemiro, Norato no longer urges a local resident to shoot him in the forehead or anoint him with the milk of a black cow. ("Those things worked well in the past, but not today," Argemiro explains.) Instead, he journeys abroad in search of treatment with X-rays and "lots of lasers." Norato's eagerness to give himself over to the academy-trained, foreign surgeons is an eloquent admission of a more general loss of faith in native traditions and recalls Maurício's pained reaction to a similar story in which his friend, Paulo, has the *encantado* call on a foreigner to disenchant him ("You want the *gringos* to have everything, man!"). Although once cured, Argemiro's Norato returns home to Amazônia, in other versions of the story, he takes up residence abroad.

39. She, the sister,
        embarked on evil ways.
    But he, Noratinho,
            even though he was transformed into a snake,
                had human feelings.
    Afterward, he wanted to become disenchanted,
            but he couldn't find anyone to disenchant him,
                and so, he had to go abroad.

    So then, he arrived there in one of these really famous clinics
            —I don't know if it was in France
                or California
                    or America
            —he arrived there and the doctors treated him
                with lots of lasers
                        —the word is "laser," right?
                        —and lots of X-rays.

    So then, he ceased to be a snake and became a man,
            he became disenchanted.
    After that, he sent a telegram to say
            he would be returning to Amazonas, to Brazil.

In short, although accounts of Dolphins as white man are as complex and potentially contradictory as others in which they appear as *encantado* and as lover, the undercurrent of protest they reveal is often considerably more conscious and, correspondingly, more explicit. As succeeding waves of migration and urbanization threaten to dislocate the enchanted beings, Dolphins are increasingly a symbol of resistance to the very sort of domination they traditionally have embodied. A *branco* and a foreigner in many stories, the Dolphin, paradoxically, is also today a standard-bearer for people who seek a voice in the larger transformations affecting their own lives. At once profoundly alien and insouciantly familiar, he resembles a wide variety of tricksters who both challenge and affirm a particular set of cultural values currently under assault from within as well as without. "My children almost don't believe in the *Encante*," confesses Argemiro. "They aren't fishermen, they don't go out upon the river, so then, how would they know about these things? The *Cobra Grande* exists, the Dolphin too. Now then, I don't mind so much that they think all of this invention. *That is, just so long as their lives turn out better than my own*" (my emphasis).

9

TRANSFORMATION AND DISENCHANTMENT

O Encante, ele existe. Só não sabemos como ou onde.

(The *Encante,* it exists. We just don't know how or where.)

—*Man, age 35, Parintins*

ncantado, Lover, white man—the Dolphin we have come to know in the preceding pages displays multiple identities. Embodiments of an impersonal natural universe on some occasions, these creatures are eminently social beings on others. Capable of falling head over heels in love with individual men and women, they also may coldly force their will on those less powerful than they. Much like a single body that casts widely different shadows depending on the hour, their significance changes radically in accord with circumstances. And yet, if the aspects we have examined often seem self-contained and even contradictory, all three hinge on paradoxes that offer resistance to definition, and thus, to the paralysis or freezing of a world in flux. Each thus suggests an array of transformations that goes far beyond the extraordinary metamorphosis of dolphins into human beings.

The stories' insistence on the enchanted beings' mysterious power allows their tellers to reject a social and economic order in which they are immersed but that nonetheless largely excludes them. By affirming the fundamental strangeness of the world, *encantados* suggest alternative forms of coherence in a political and economic context where their supporters have little or no power. Although resistance is often equated with a conscious standing firm (the root of the word is *sistere,* "to take a stand" or to exert force in opposition), these tales amply demonstrate how it also may take the form of a refusal to hold still. The Dolphin's dance suggests not only the uneasy boundary between the human and natural spheres, in which the two inevitably impinge upon each other, but also the metaphoric and metaphysical implications of ongoing transformation. The stories are in no way uniform, and their tellers may be reacting to quite different internal as well as external pressures. Nevertheless, their very fluidity ultimately unites them. What looks like breaks and contradictions in these seemingly offhand accounts are often actually marks of the creative and transformative possibilities of a subordinate, but for this reason no less vital, narrative and cultural order.

IDEAS OF AMAZÔNIA

The history of the Amazon as a geographic and sociopolitical reality is inextricable from its existence as a territory of the imagination. Since the arrival of the first European explorers in the sixteenth century, a small number of recurrent images have dominated outsiders' thinking about the region. (These notions, to be sure, have often affected insiders as well.) Glowing portraits of the Amazon as El Dorado, Earthly Paradise, and Last Frontier find a counterbalance in notions of a Land of Warrior Women, Green Hell, and Paradise Lost which reappear in varying guises and admixtures over the course of centuries. Although these ideas apply to some degree to the New World in general, they have attained particular force and tenacity in relation to the Amazon because of the region's immense size, forbidding terrain, and lingering, if increasingly relative, isolation. Particularly obvious in the work of chroniclers, writers, and a variety of artists, they also inform the work of social and natural scientists, shaping statements of public policy as well.[1]

The idea of the Amazon as shimmering El Dorado impelled the first explorers to embark on a series of long and difficult journeys into a forbidding territory. When Gonzalo Pizarro set forth from Quito at the head of a massive expedition in 1540, he was looking for both spices (above all, then-scarce and precious cinnamon) and a fabulously wealthy king said to dust his body each day with a new supply of golden talc. Even as hopes of finding El Dorado proper dimmed, notions of the Amazon as a land of staggering, even mythic, potential, remained very much alive. The rubber tappers of the nineteenth and early twentieth centuries were looking for nothing less than "white gold." Not just the gold boom, but also the land rush of the last few decades offer a reenactment of an abiding dream. Even though its soil has proven far less fertile than imagined, Amazônia still serves as a mecca for both multinational investors and the Brazilian poor.

1. For an exposition of some of these ideas in relation to tropical forests as a whole, see Francis E. Putz and N. Michele Holbrook, "Tropical Rain-Forest Images." In a more specifically Amazonian context see Maria José de Queiroz, "Os itinerários da selva"; and Pedro Maligo, "Symbolic Territory." Mary Louise Pratt suggests the ideological underpinnings of a number of representations of Latin America in her *Imperial Eyes*.

Closely allied to the persistent dream of El Dorado is that of a terrestrial paradise—Columbus's new Eden. Although the garden's spontaneous, unchecked abundance contrasts with the supreme artifice of the Golden City, in both cases the earth's riches—be they in their natural state or, instead, transformed through human intervention—remain the rightful legacy of humankind. The promise of a new beginning inherent in the idea of an American paradise inspired the Jesuits and other Roman Catholic missionaries who played such a major role in colonizing the Amazon.

The great foreign botanists of the late eighteenth and nineteenth centuries—Bates, La Condamine, von Humboldt, and Bonpland, among others—seized on and transformed this dream of a second chance. Although they tended to see paradise as a series of previously uncataloged species of monkeys, palm trees, and horned beetles, their descriptions of the landscape oscillate between a minute analysis of natural phenomena increasingly colored by Darwinism, and a continuing wellspring of extremely lyrical Edenic imagery.[2]

The idea of a New Eden often merges with that of a last frontier in which the Amazon appears as not just a second, but the last, best chance for human beings. Here, unlike most other places, men and women find themselves at liberty—and indeed, under obligation—to complete what God began. While a sense of the Amazon as a world awaiting definition is present in many of the earliest writings, it intensifies with time. Thus, the great turn-of-the-century Brazilian writer Euclides da Cunha identifies an ongoing struggle between civilization and age-old telluric forces within the ever-shifting Amazonian landscape. Long relegated to the sidelines of Brazilian history (some versions of his Amazonian essays appear in a volume entitled *À margem da história* [*On the Margins of History*]; others have been collected in *Um paraíso perdido* [*A Lost Paradise*]), this mute, inchoate territory actively demands voice and form.[3] Notions of the region as a massive work-in-progress bolster related ideas of the Amazon as great ad-

---

2. Bates, for his part, contrasts the slothful civilization of the city with the exuberant nature just beyond its fringes. "It was a mere fancy," he says, "but I thought the mingled squalor, luxuriance and beauty of these [mixed-blood] women were pointedly in harmony with the rest of the scene: so striking, in the view, was the mixture of natural riches and human poverty" (Henry Walter Bates, *The Naturalist on the Rivers Amazons*, p. 3).

3. *Um Paraíso Perdido* was the name da Cunha gave to a work that he did not succeed in finishing before his early, tragic death. *À margem da história,* originally published as a separate work, appears as part of the posthumous edition of *Um Paraíso Perdido* organized by Leandro Tocantins. "There is," da Cunha says, "something extraterrestrial about that amphibious Nature, a mixture of water and land, that conceals itself, completely flattened, in its own grandeur. . . . The people who populate the region carve it out for themselves through courage. They don't cultivate it, beautifying it; rather, they tame it" (*Um Paraíso Perdido,* p. 53, my translation).

venture. Although this image also dates back to the Iberian explorers, it acquires new dimensions in a self-consciously modern age. Thus, one finds that American champion of order and progress, President Theodore Roosevelt, trekking through the Amazonian rain forest alongside the Brazilian colonel Benjamin Rondon. An unforgettable photograph of the two perched high on a rock outcropping from which they sternly survey the River of Doubt serves as frontispiece to Roosevelt's record of his adventures in his best-selling *Through the Brazilian Wilderness* (1914).[4] (The Brazilian government subsequently dispelled the "Doubt" by renaming the river "Teodoro" or "Theodore.") Although Roosevelt himself was not responsible for the pairing, a portion of his notes preface a later English-language edition of the adventure novel *Eight Hundred Leagues on the Amazon,* by nineteenth-century French author Jules Verne.)[5] That Verne and fellow writers, such as Sir Arthur Conan Doyle, could locate their fictions in the Amazon without ever setting foot there emphasizes the region's identity as a glorious space of the imagination as much as a geographical or sociopolitical reality.[6]

Essentially positive images of Amazônia as El Dorado, Earthly Paradise, and Last Frontier find a complement in decidedly darker, if equally enduring visions of the region as Land of Warrior Women, Paradise Lost, and Green Hell. If Orellana did not discover the fabled El Dorado, he nonetheless claimed to have encountered the equally fabled Warrior Women of Greek mythology. These female natives, whom the explorer dubbed the "Amazons" in accord with classical sources, pose an obvious and immediate threat to the scantily armed and ill-provisioned explorers (his scribe, Carvajal, reports that the women's well-aimed arrows made the Spaniards' brigantines resemble porcupines).[7] In addition, their "unnatural" aggressions provided justification for the often brutal exploitation of the native population in the name of a familiar Christian and European order.

Although initially vivid images of bellicose females paled with the massive extermination of the Indians, nature itself remained the supreme Warrior Woman. Particularly prevalent in the late nineteenth and twentieth centuries, notions of the region as Green Hell build on earlier conceptions of the Amazons as wild, and therefore dangerous, beings. Just as the Warrior Women are an extension of an extravagantly luxurious landscape, so

4. Theodore Roosevelt, *Through the Brazilian Wilderness.* The truly striking photograph is by Cherrie, a member of the expedition.
5. Jules Verne, *Eight Hundred Leagues on the Amazon.* The book initially appeared in English as a two-part work entitled *The Giant Raft.*
6. Conan Doyle's *Lost World* has been made into a movie by contemporary Brazilian filmmaker Jorge Bodanzsky.
7. See J. T. Medina, ed., *The Discovery of the Amazon,* p. 214.

this landscape now takes on a life of its own.[8] Enduring notions of the forest as an overpowering, inescapably sexual being underly the work of a host of contemporary artists as diverse as German filmmaker Werner Herzog, and Amazonian novelist Márcio Souza. In Herzog's *Aguirre, Wrath of God* (1972) as well as in his later *Fitzcarraldo* (1981), the forest actively resists the foreign invader.[9] Souza's novel *Mad Maria* depicts an equally lunatic—though historically accurate—endeavor: the construction of a railroad meant to link the rubber fields of southwestern Amazônia with the Atlantic Ocean.[10]

A threat to some, the rain forest's uncontrollable lushness represents a confirmation of lost opportunity for others as human beings now willfully destroy their own collective heritage. The senseless assault upon the natural universe, which will be the theme of numerous twentieth-century writers, finds early expression in W. H. Hudson's *Green Mansions,* in which the fragile and enigmatic Bird-Woman, Rima, disappears in a cataclysmic fire.[11] Significantly, her destroyer is not the imported civilization represented by the impassioned narrator, who vainly attempts to protect her, but rather, a group of savage natives fearful and jealous of her mysterious gifts.

The accelerating assault on the rain forest in the past few decades has given new life to old ideas of Paradise Lost. Although regret for a vanishing Eden dates back to the colonial period—David Sweet's "A Rich Realm of Nature Destroyed" is not about the twentieth, but the seventeenth and eighteenth centuries[12]—the identity of the destroyer has shifted at least partially from savage Indians or greedy colonists to a more impersonal, if no less barbarous, "modernization." An industrialized world's longing for the pristine landscape doomed in large part by its own values and technologies—a phenomenon that Renato Rosaldo has labeled "imperialist nostal-

---

8. Thus, Alberto Rangel's *Inferno verde* (*Green Inferno,* 1914) introduces the unmistakably feminine forest as an "unvarying, full, disordered waste heap of branches and leaves, twisted fronds, caught on hodgepodges of lianas" that remains locked in a constant struggle against itself, and yet which inflicts madness on the human intruders foolhardy enough to assail its "splendid virginity" (Rangel, *Inferno verde,* p. 23, my translation).

9. Aguirre, a somewhat later sixteenth-century explorer whom Herzog conflates with Orellana in his quest for El Dorado, ends the film as a madman, dancing alone on his shipwrecked boat amidst the screech of countless monkeys. Although Fitzcarraldo eventually realizes his dream of transporting an entire opera company into the river's uncharted reaches, his insistence on dragging a mammoth ship over a mountain confirms the insanity of the enterprise.

10. Márcio Souza, *Mad Maria.* For a historical account of the railroad see Manuel Rodrigues Ferreira, *A ferrovia do diabo.*

11. W. H. Hudson, *Green Mansions.*

12. David G. Sweet, "A Rich Realm of Nature Destroyed." The epithet "Rich Realm of Nature" was given to the Amazon by the Portuguese.

gia"—is obvious in a myriad of works as diverse as Claude Lévi-Strauss's *Tristes tropiques,* British filmmaker John Boorman's *The Emerald Forest,* and Brazilian anthropologist Darcy Ribeiro's novel, *Maíra.*[13] While some of these books and films portray the reversal or containment of Western-style progress, others end in death and unmitigated destruction.

THE DOLPHIN TALES WITHIN A FRAMEWORK OF CULTURAL CONFRONTATION

Even this very rapid glance at recurrent images of the Amazon in the work of a variety of educated writers and artists suggests an underlying perspective in dramatic contrast to that informing the great majority of Dolphin tales. Varied on the surface, the notions of New Eden and Green Hell, El Dorado and Paradise Lost, reveal a common emphasis on the landscape as a fixed stage for human action, as well as a moralistic, totalizing vision. All place human beings at the center of the natural universe; all view history as a progression with an ultimate purpose. Regardless of whether the Amazon appears as heaven or hell, it remains a testing ground whose underlying premise is the primacy and perfectability of humankind. Nature is not only separate from, but ultimately subordinate to, men and women who, fashioned in the image of their maker, can rightfully claim dominion over the earth and all within it.

This essential notion of Amazonian nature as both distinct from, and ultimately subject to, the human world is alien to the *encantado* stories. Although individual tales reveal considerable variation, we have seen that the corpus as a whole stresses equilibrium and interdependence. In striking contrast to representations in which human beings are inevitably silhouetted against a natural landscape, the Dolphin stories depict an uneasy continuum. Much as fishermen go out in their canoes to vie for food with other river creatures, so these enchanted beings don white suits and party dresses and show up to dance at country gatherings. While humans and dolphins are fundamentally different, their destiny is ultimately intermingled, if only because the waters belong in some sense to both. Not only is men and women's ability to act upon the universe that encompasses them strictly circumscribed, but the tales' insistence on the life-giving, if supremely enigmatic aspects of the *encantados'* power casts doubt on the notion of history as a unilinear record of human evolution, let alone a moral crusade.

13. Renato Rosaldo, "Imperialist Nostalgia"; Claude Lévi-Strauss, *Tristes tropiques;* and Darcy Ribeiro, *Maíra.*

Furthermore, the sense of self and other underlying the Dolphin stories is distinguished by its profound ambiguity. Much like the Tukanoan Vahti, who leads people astray when they take shortcuts through the forest, the Dolphin is dangerously attractive and suggestive.[14] He, like the Vahti, also looks and acts like a human being. Thus, unlike the other against which the self is defined (the colonizer's quintessential confrontation between civilized and wild man), this far less obvious double may take the form of a spouse, a friend, an aunt, or brother, expressing the very thoughts and desires one struggles hardest to conceal.

Neither their ambiguous, antianthropocentric vision nor the opposition to ideas and institutions imposed from without that underlies many of the Dolphin stories is unique to them. Certainly, the tales we have seen fit a much broader framework of continuing self-assertion through symbolic means that anthropologists, historians, and literary scholars have described for numerous other narrative traditions within the Americas and elsewhere. The tales we have seen reveal a by no means unfamiliar tension between an oral culture with its own history and beliefs, and a self-consciously literate and Christian culture bent on subjugating and radically redefining the world it ostensibly has discovered.[15] Their subtle and sometimes not-so-subtle resistance to outsiders' attempts to impose their own vision of the world upon them underscores the subversive possibilities of superstition and mysticism at play in a wide array of New World rituals and narrative traditions.[16]

Like many outwardly similar tales of transformation and mediation, the Dolphin stories manifest a seemingly unlimited capacity for incorporation

14. See Gerardo Reichel-Dolmatoff, "Some Shortcuts in the Tukanoan Forest of Symbols."

15. Nancy M. Farriss discusses Maya resistance to Spanish rule (*Maya Society under Colonial Rule*), while Patricia Seed presents Atahualpa's failure to marvel at Spanish literacy as a rejection of "textual imperialism" ("Failing to Marvel"). Rolena Adorno shows how the early seventeenth-century Andean writer Felipe Guaman Poma de Ayala includes multiple, frequently competing, voices within a single text (*Guaman Poma*); and Sabine MacCormack documents newly converted Peruvians' ability to find—and create—conceptual links between Andean religion and Christianity (*Religion in the Andes*). Blanca Muratorio analyzes Quichua accommodation and resistance over the past century in *The Life and Times of Grandfather Alonso.*

16. Irene Silverblatt argues that the native women of Peru defied the Spanish Inquisition through practices its representatives denounced as witchcraft (*Moon, Sun, and Witches*). Frank Salomon examines a similar historical phenomenon in "Ancestor Cults and Resistance to the State in Arequipa"; Roger Rasnake demonstrates how the Yura of central Bolivia have reformulated numerous aspects of an original Andean worldview (*Domination and Cultural Resistance*). Michael F. Brown and Eduardo Fernández examine the Asháninka people's reshaping of millennial principles to fight present-day poverty and environmental destruction (*War of Shadows*).

and adaptation that has helped guarantee their survival into the present despite the eradication of associated native institutions.[17] They also reveal a particularly wide range of symbolic possibilities, and a marked capacity to respond to ongoing change. The intensity with which they display these more general characteristics sets them apart from a number of similar narratives, including various accounts of their fellow *encantados*.

Although it is commonplace to speak of "hybrid" cultures in reference to Latin America, the Dolphin stories represent a far more complex intermingling of sources than that associated with the crossing of two separate "races, breeds, varieties, species or genera."[18] While—contrary to the claims of a number of scholars—many of the underpinnings for these narratives are almost certainly native Amazonian, centuries of repeated interaction with a variety of European as well as African sources have effected profound transformations. Successive and ongoing layers of migration have produced narratives more comparable to an unevenly layered, kinetic palimpsest, in which some accretions show through more than others, than they are to a new strain of sugar peas.

Many of the mixtures these tales reveal are decidedly volatile, and while disparate sources often bond—or, at least, tentatively coexist—within individual stories, they do not necessarily reveal the sorts of one-to-one correspondences often indicated by the term "syncretic."[19] Although, for instance, there are storytellers for whom the Dolphin-woman *is* a mermaid or a lesser *orixá*, there are others for whom she bears a limited resemblance to one or both of these entities. Still others would deny any association whatsoever among the three.

The profoundly composite nature of these stories is further complicated by most storytellers' general lack of awareness of—or refusal to accept— Amazônia's, and often their own, cultural legacy (and, sometimes, also their racial and ethnic heritage). Although we have documented a number of indigenous parallels within accounts of enchanted beings, storytellers

17. According to Michael Taussig, "the Spanish conquest in the New World stripped indigenous religion of its formal institutional covering, but by no means destroyed its basis in thought." Instead, religion passed "underground" into "magic," and specifically, healing magic (Taussig, "Folk Healing and the Structure of Conquest in Southwest Colombia," p. 221).

18. This is the first of several dictionary definitions. See *Oxford English Dictionary,* 2d ed., s.v. "hybrid." The figurative meaning of the word is "derived from heterogeneous or incongruous sources; having a mixed character; composed of *two* diverse elements" (my emphasis).

19. The official definition of "syncretism" is "an attempted union or reconciliation of diverse or opposite tenets or practices" (*Oxford English Dictionary,* 2d ed., s.v.). Scholars, however, often use the word more narrowly to indicate a more or less precise equation of two or more different sources.

themselves are rarely cognizant of these. Moreover, we have noted that despite many residents' non-European daily practices—be this their reluctance to hunt or fish more game than they can use in a given period, their way of preparing manioc, or their allegiance to specific alimentary or menstrual taboos—they often reject outright any association between themselves and native peoples. While this rejection owes much to elite conceptions of the latter's inferiority, it also reflects the fact that many of the storytellers are relative newcomers to the region who may have little, if any, Amerindian blood. In this sense, the stories, and the storytellers, present a contrast to the large number of other narrative traditions whose bearers do indeed define themselves on some level as members of—or, at least, sympathizers with—an embattled indigenous or mestizo culture.[20]

Their particular openness to varied influences enhances the stories' symbolic potential. Far more than the *Cavalo Marinho* or the *Cobra Grande,* the humanlike and yet not-quite-human Dolphin invites multiple interpretations. Thus, although the six storytellers to whom we have returned at various points throughout this study have much in common, they do not fail to reveal important differences. While, for instance, from Tô Pereira's viewpoint, the Dolphin's malevolent nature affords an at least partial explanation of otherwise baffling disappointments in his own life, Kátia sees the *encantados* as a far more distant, though still fascinating, puzzle. For Maurício, the Dolphin stories are confirmation of a unique, if embattled, Amazonian identity; Gerineldo considers them part and parcel of an interior to which he hopes to return one day in triumph.

In Alzira and Argemiro's case, the enchanted beings represent an older world to which the two remain emotionally attached, but which they perceive is changing ("After all, not one of my ten children lives in the interior," Alzira observes matter-of-factly.) The enchanted beings provide a bond between Dona Marina and her long-lost mother, as well as a source of self-affirmation in the face of the institutional church's hostility toward traditional healers. If these half dozen individuals, who all live in the same small city, display such varied relationships to the Dolphin, persons from more distant points of this farflung region—Porto Velho and Oiapoque, Benjamin Constant and Araguaia—are likely to reveal equally, if not yet more, diverse perspectives.

Differences among the *encantado* stories underscore not only their complexity as narrative, but also the intricate and fluid nature of those multiple and often contradictory processes frequently subsumed under the catchword "acculturation." Although many pieces of these narratives are similar,

20. For examples of continuing, at least partially conscious, resistance to forced acculturation see the articles in Jonathan D. Hill, ed., *Rethinking History and Myth.*

when not identical, they form a kaleidoscopic string of patterns that are never quite the same. Unlike the kaleidoscope, however, which produces new, always symmetrical constellations in synchronic fashion, these elements and processes regularly overlap in intricate, irregular ways.

The stories' openness to new elements and multiple interpretations makes them especially powerful commentaries on a shifting present. Although other sorts of narratives also reveal this sort of contemporaneity—the native Amazonian accounts of the white man cited in the last chapter are only one example—the Dolphin tales offer a particularly compelling illustration of the extreme plasticity of symbolic forms. While one suspects that the Dolphin always provoked strong and often conflicting emotions, today's rapid transformations have both intensified and reconfigured the debate. Recounted over an immense and extremely varied area by men and women of different ages, occupations, and geographic backgrounds, the stories cast light on the often seemingly autonomous forces that recent development policies have unleashed. Tales of superhuman forces, they also chronicle the looping, jagged course of changes that have touched, and are now partially shaping, millions of individual lives.

Furthermore, if the Dolphin stories reiterate themes played out in numerous instances of cultural confrontation in the Americas and elsewhere, they nonetheless recast these in a unique manner. Although notions of enchantment and disenchantment exist in many, if not most, cultural traditions, the Dolphin stories voice more universal concerns in a distinctive, Amazonian idiom.

ENCHANTMENT AND DISENCHANTMENT

Like its English counterpart, the Portuguese verb *encantar* means "to exert magical influence upon," "to bewitch," "to lay under a spell."[21] We have documented the *encantados'* power to move people deeply—indeed, to *transport* them in both a figurative and literal sense. Few storytellers fail to note the *Encante*'s more attractive aspects: its physical beauty, wondrous ease, and dazzling wealth. Not only do Dolphins and their companions have no need to struggle for survival, but their lives, unlike those of most storytellers, are varied and exciting. Furthermore, the *Encante* brings with it a promise of immortality. Present "since the beginning of time," the enchanted beings need not confront the sickness, aging, and eventual death that is the lot of human beings. Creatures of instinct, they are not morally accountable for their actions.

Enchantment, in the context of the Dolphin stories, is an extremely

---

21. *Oxford English Dictionary,* 2d ed., s.v. "enchant."

ambiguous proposition. As a result, the connotations of the word are considerably more negative than they usually are in contemporary English. (Consider its positive force in expressions such as "Come to New Mexico, Land of Enchantment!" "Some Enchanted Evening," or "What an enchanting smile!") We have seen that to become enchanted is to find oneself suddenly part of another order of being, to become "enclosed in seven layers" ("ficar dentro de sete capas"), in short, to suffer a sea—or, in this case, river—change. The *encantado*'s victims are inevitably torn away against their will or even knowledge. Not just overpowered, but often actively deceived by Dolphins who assume the form of friends and spouses, the enchanted person endures a double violation.

I have suggested elsewhere that to undergo enchantment in these stories is to lose one's social identity, to become foreign to oneself while engaging in admittedly suspect and delicious actions. The person who is enchanted is carried away in every sense. No longer an autonomous subject, but the object of another's desire, these people no longer remember or care about the dreams and obligations that have hitherto defined their individual existence. Significantly, the Dolphin—unlike the Anaconda—spirits off not only those who break or challenge taboos, but also the most innocent community members. Both male and female Dolphins regularly abduct children, and males are said to be particularly attracted to young women with little or no sexual experience.

Newcomers to the Enchanted City acquire riches, power, and a degree of leisure wholly foreign to their lives on earth. We have seen, however, that their new, and apparently superior, status entails a wholesale loss of personal freedom. Although many storytellers are frankly curious about the *Encante* and express a great desire to see its wondrous sights ("If I could, I'd go there this very minute!" exclaims Gerineldo's older brother), very few are actually willing to make the trip. (Recall how Argemiro suddenly declines his *pajé*-boss's invitation after the fifth of seven *tauari* cigars.) "The *encantado* becomes a fish; he becomes another sort of thing," Kátia asserts with a grimace. "Would *you* want to grow gills?" Tô Pereira laughingly demands.

And yet, if the concept of enchantment customarily possesses ambiguous and, often, strongly negative connotations within the Dolphin corpus, the opposing notion of disenchantment traditionally has been largely positive. The Portuguese verb *desencantar* can mean to discover, to find what has previously been lost or unclear. "Go straight down this street, turn left at the green fence on the corner and you are sure to disenchant in that house you're looking for," a person may say. ("Você vai pela rua, dobra no portão verde da esquina, e vai desencantar com certeza, naquela casa.") A lost object, or even a person, can also *desencantar,* or unexpectedly appear.

Likewise, a project that has come to fruition after the surmounting of various obstacles is said to have finally disenchanted. "Puxa, rapaz, aquele seu projeto desencantou por fim!" a person may say. ("Gosh, man, your project turned out in the end!") From this first, distinctively favorable perspective, *desencantar* suggests a capacity not just to locate a tangible object or destination, but also, by extension, to discern with sudden clarity what has been previously hidden or as if under a spell.

To the extent that it is a process involving mysterious and often harrowing procedures, disenchantment in the Dolphin stories constitutes a kind of quest. Unlike many quests, however, disenchantment is never a solitary process, and the restless *encantado*'s first step is always to enlist human assistance. Indeed, one could argue that since the enchanted being is dependent on his or her flesh-and-blood ally performing actions that require considerable courage, disenchantment in these stories presupposes a double test. We have noted that the enchanted individual inevitably appears as a terrifying monster, whom the human partner must first anoint with a series of ritual substances, then coolly proceed to shoot in the eye or forehead. Although the *encantados* promise rich rewards for such assistance and it is usually they alone who bear the risk of failure, most people are reluctant to accede to such frightening demands.

Once the enchanted being has been successfully disenchanted, he or she is literally reborn. Not only do these individuals definitively shed the animal shell, or *capa,* in which they were formerly imprisoned (often, they demand that others burn it), but in most cases, they promptly forget all about their past.[22] "The *encantado*," Dona Marina explains, "is born anew, forgets everything; he doesn't even remember the location of the *Encante.* You ask him anything concerning it and he will not know the answer. It's as if he'd never lived there."[23]

Disenchantment in this initial sense, then, is a distinctly voluntary embracing of the human condition in all its aspects. It is also a return to the most profound sort of transformation—that of life into death and back again—which an immortality marked by mere shape changes not only masks, but actively impedes.[24] For this reason, while different storytellers may disagree on the details of the disenchantment process, they are virtually unanimous in their insistence that the *encantado* must sustain a wound.

22. This destruction of the *encantado*'s former façade is motif D720 in Stith Thompson, *Motif-Index of Folk Literature.*
23. "O encantado renasce, esquece tudo, nem sabe mais onde fica o Encante. Você pergunta qualquer coisa de lá para ele e ele nem sabe responde. É como se tivesse nunca morado lá."
24. The idea of death as part of a regenerative whole occurs in much South American indigenous thought. See Lawrence E. Sullivan, *Icanchu's Drum,* p. 468.

Often a partial blinding that symbolically closes the would-be human's eyes to his or her former existence, the wound inevitably draws blood, itself the supreme symbol of mortality.[25] (Significantly, the verb *sofrer* is always used along with the noun *transformação* in Portuguese, so that one literally "suffers"—instead of simply "undergoing"—a transformation.) The disenchantment process also involves a recognition of the more life-giving impulses that demi-*encantados* carry within them from birth. Thus, although the Cobra Norato is outwardly as much a serpent as his malevolent twin sister, he cannot abide her habit of capsizing boats and gobbling down small children. Increasingly unable to continue living among "those inhuman [river] people" (*aquele povo deshumano*), he knowingly forsakes the Enchanted City's pleasures.

Having opted for humanity, former *encantados* renounce the immortality and imperviousness to physical suffering that marked their former, watery existence. No longer subordinate to impersonal natural forces, they assume responsibility for their own actions. Their decision is binding, their commitment total. Unlike shamanic healers, who regularly move between the human world and that of the *Encante*, disenchanted individuals have no choice but to spend the remainder of their years on earth. "Even if he wants to, he can't go back to that [enchanted state]," explains the owner of a tiny drugstore. "Once disenchanted, that's the end of it, he can't return."[26]

Disenchantment, to be sure, involves a surrender not only of immortality, but also, of the wealth and power that sets apart the enchanted beings. No longer de facto *brancos*, former denizens of the river bottom customarily eke out an existence among people much like the storytellers. "After he became disenchanted, the Cobra Norato came to spend the rest of his life among us," explains the wife of a rubber worker, as we and three of her eight children sit peeling manioc on the doorstep of their wooden shack. "I myself never met him, but my grandmother knew him as a child. He was a very kind old man, a good musician, and a marvelous storyteller."[27]

At the same time, however, that the enchanted being consciously forfeits his or her privileged, if ultimately unenviable, status, the act of disenchantment inevitably enriches the human helper. Most storytellers agree that former *encantados* are extremely generous in their displays of gratitude. "That guy who disenchanted Norato," notes Gerineldo with enthusiasm,

25. Blood is also a manifestation of the individual soul for some Amerindian peoples. See Michael J. Harner, *The Jivaro*, p. 149.

26. "Mesmo querendo, ele não volta para aquilo. Desencantou-se, pronto, não dá mais para voltar." Man, age 64, born Manaus, lives Carauari (55 years). Married, drugstore owner, "a little grade school, but things were hard back in those times, ma'am."

27. Woman, age 27, born Seringal Cupuaí (Amazonas). Married, housework, no formal education.

"he bought two big cattle ranches near Óbidos, plus a very pretty house in Rio de Janeiro, an airplane just for himself, and a whole fleet of riverboats." Furthermore, although it is the individual who reaps the immediate profits of his or her courage, the act of disenchantment sets into circulation riches normally held fast beneath the river.

And yet, if disenchantment traditionally has been perceived as a salutary process, the term is rapidly acquiring a second, more negative sense that approximates its customary English usage. Although the dictionary defines "to disenchant" as "to set free from enchantment, magic spell, or illusion" (and, indeed, this meaning once again holds for children's fairytales), to become disenchanted in common parlance is almost always to be disappointed, to perceive a reality harsher than originally judged.[28] ("I became disenchanted with politician X after he broke his campaign promise," a former supporter may say.)

In recent times, instead of actively affirming their own humanity, the *encantados* are staging a forced retreat from the world of human beings. Linked to the destruction of not just the Amazon rain forest but, even more, the devaluation and dismantling of a once-unifying (if unofficial) vision of men and women's place within the universe, this withdrawal is reminiscent in some aspects of the concept of disenchantment expounded by Max Weber.[29] Despite detailed criticisms and modifications of the model he first proposed in the early part of the twentieth century, it remains implicit in many present-day discussions of the effects of industrialization and postindustrialization, and thus deserves attention in relation to the Dolphin tales.

At its simplest, Weber's "disenchantment of the world" involves the exit of gods and demons from the public arena into a more private sphere. The extraordinary forces of which he speaks are not so much extinguished as rechanneled, thereby freeing that space necessary for cumulative technological rationalization. According to Weber, "precisely the most ultimate and sublime values have retreated from public life either into the transcendental realm of mystic life or into the brotherliness of direct and human relations. It is not accidental that our greatest art is intimate and not monumental, nor is it accidental that today only within the smallest and most intimate circles, in personal human situations, in *pianissimo* that something is pulsating that corresponds to prophetic *pneuma*, which in former times swept through the great communities like a firebrand, welding them together."[30]

28. *Oxford English Dictionary,* 2d ed., s.v. "disenchant."
29. Max Weber, "Religious Rejections of the World and Their Direction." The article originally appeared in German in 1915.
30. Max Weber, "Science as a Vocation," p. 155. The essay was first published in 1918.

Although there may be individuals and particular groups in Amazônia for whom Weber's formula would appear to hold in part or sum, the brand of disenchantment that emerges in contemporary Dolphin stories is generally angrier and far more negative than his description suggests. Bad-humored and initially stubborn in retreat, the *encantados,* once gone, do not reemerge in any guise. Moreover, a loss of faith in these profoundly enigmatic beings does not necessarily indicate a transference of belief to other sources of power or an investiture of personal energies in either mystic life or human relations. Instead, the persons who stop believing in the Dolphin often display a generalized and bitter cynicism.

Not content to slip away into the shrinking forests, let alone the *pianissimo* of interpersonal dealings, Dolphins and their enchanted and unenchanted companions fight back against the growing encroachment upon their domain. "The fisherman's life," says Argemiro, "isn't easy. Sometimes, you are fishing and the wind begins to blow, or a snake or caiman appears. And all of these river beings are increasingly angry at us human beings. There are lakes here where in the summer you can no longer cast a net because they tear everything apart. They are violent, really furious. Before, they weren't like this, such enemies to people."[31]

When they finally do move on, the enchanted beings vent their ire on those who have prompted their departure. Although, for instance, the jeers of unbelievers effectively dislodge the *dono* of the lake in the following story, his exit puts a rapid end to the community. Unlike the Dolphin Zé Caetano, who ineffectually chides the soccer players who refuse to respect his terrain, this sterner-hearted *encantado* makes off with the beach and— for good measure—all the fish. Once gone, no amount of coaxing can convince him to return.

40. But with time,
   the people stopped believing
     in the *dono* of that lake.
"There's no such thing as an *encantado,* man,
   what kind of story is this?"
     the younger people would say, laughing and laughing.
They thought it all a joke.

So then, the *dono* of that place got very angry
   and decided to leave there.

31. In the irreversible quality of their departure, the Brazilian *encantados* diverge from their Venezuelan counterparts. Although the latter are also capable of vengeful actions (disastrous floods, for instance), the water that dries up when they leave begins to flow anew with their return. See Guss, "The Encantados."

And on the day he left,
    that lovely beach just disappeared.
He also took every last fish.
Because beforehand,
    there were always a lot of fish.
But today, my dear,
    you don't see the tiniest
        of tiny fish.

And the people?
Ah no,
    they could do nothing.
They begged him to return,
    but to no avail.
And so,
    they all had to leave.
There isn't anyone who lives there any more.[32]

As this story suggests, the enchanted beings' departure seldom, if ever, benefits the human beings they leave behind. Often marked by catastrophic changes in the natural landscape, their withdrawal strips formerly celebrated healers of those powers on which the community depends for its well-being. "Here in the city," one man in Belém says glumly, "there are no *encantados,* no really good *pajés.* And so, the sick person runs to the pharmacy, runs to the clinic, finds some remedy or other, but it almost never works."[33]

The negative results of the *encantados'* exit extend beyond the sorts of concrete concerns suggested above. In dramatic contrast to the liberation associated with our first type of disenchantment, this second variety entails a generalized diminishment of possibility. This sense of radically diminished potential explains why even those storytellers who complain most bitterly about the Dolphin's misdeeds may actively lament his departure. "The Dolphin can be shameless," Dona Marina remarks, "but he can also do much good. The place he leaves remains abandoned. It no longer has anything; it has no more mystery."

The loss of mystery tends to translate into a depressing sameness. As much as storytellers denounce the *encantados'* capricious and often down-

32. Man, age 46, born interior of Parintins (Semeão). Married, fisherman and farmer, MOBRAL literacy program.
33. Man, age 33, born interior of Macapá, lives Belém (6 years). Married, vegetable vendor, "some" grade school.

right menacing behavior, their presence clearly makes life interesting. Who knows if those handsome strangers twirling around the dance floor are not really Dolphins? How can we be sure that the man who looks just like Carlinhos really *is* Carlinhos who, after all, is supposed to be off visiting his brother in Manaus? In a disenchanted world, there can be no Cobra Norato to enliven a country *festa,* no tours of the river bottom in one's early morning dreams. ("My husband goes to the river bottom [in his sleep] almost every night," explains Maurício's grandmother. "The Dolphins offer him trays full of bananas and guavas, and he strolls around till dawn.")

As a result, even those storytellers who complain the loudest about the Dolphin are rarely eager to exchange the *encantados'* titillating unpredictability for the grinding surety of the crowded bus, the swing shift in the distant factory, the expensive and ill-stocked supermarket, and the landlord's unpaid bill. "The *encantados* are disappearing," says a young motorcycle repair man in Parintins. "Their mystery is disappearing. Because there is no more room in the city for mystery, you see?"[34] His comments bring to mind Bourdieu's observation that "the discovery of labour presupposes the constitution of the common ground of production; i.e., the disenchantment of a natural world henceforth reduced to its economic dimension alone."[35] They also recall Seu João of Terra Preta's implied association of progress with death and disappearance. ("I don't know," he says of an *encantado* said to have inhabited a nearby stretch of beach, "if he has become civilized or died or disappeared.")

It is, of course, not only the *encantados* who abandon humans, but humans who, for various reasons, turn their backs on the enchanted beings. In contrast to Weber's model, which outlines the more or less orderly evolution from Catholic to Protestant Christianity, those persons who have ceased to believe in the enchanted beings often reject transcendence in any shape or form. "I'd like to go there and live at the river bottom," says a manicurist as she briskly sweeps the floor of her half-built house with a makeshift broom. "Because they say the *encantados* are immortal and me, I don't believe this talk of a life after death. To tell you the truth, I don't believe in anything, although I wish I did."[36]

"The *sacaca?*" demands a young fisherman with an exaggerated shrug. "Who knows what happened to him? He doesn't show up here anymore.

---

34. Man, age 18, born interior of Parintins, lives Parintins (4 years). Single, repairs motorcycles, 4 years school.

35. Pierre Bourdieu, *Outline of a Theory of Practice,* p. 176.

36. Woman, age 34, born interior of Manaus, lives Carauari. Separated, manicurist, "a little" grade school.

He died, he was buried. Or, who knows, maybe he went to America. Because there things can only be better than they are here."[37]

In further refutation of the Weberian model, the loss of belief in the supernatural is not necessarily accompanied by an investiture of energies in a newly secularized public space. Even when the rejections of urban life and "progress" that we saw in the last chapter reveal nostalgic or clearly reactionary overtones, they still may underscore many storytellers' perceptions that the new order into which they have been forcibly recruited has little to offer them. Thus, it is not that the past was good, but that the present is definitely bad. "The world," a tired-looking man in the interior of Amapá says, "doesn't get better for the poor man. Oh, one thing or another may change but it doesn't really get better, you see? Look, first there was black-and-white television, and now there is color. But I can't afford one or the other, so what has changed for me?"[38]

"Do I believe that in unity, the poor will achieve liberation? No, of course I don't believe that!" the young godfather of a tiny baby exclaims to his friends once the priest is out of hearing.[39]

"The *encantado* doesn't exist, ghosts don't exist, and there is no resurrection," a milkman in Parintins says firmly as he adjusts the large silver canister strapped to his bicycle. "Why is it that a man who suffers here fifty years on earth, eating only *beiju* [a manioc biscuit] with watery coffee, is going to suffer more in hell? He's already suffered enough. I don't believe in religion. I also don't believe in progress or in politicians. Brazil *isn't* moving forward—it's all a lie, a sham."[40]

The present drama of the Dolphin tales lies in the tension between these two varieties of disenchantment—the voluntary embracing of humanity in all its sorrowful grandeur versus the bitter, often violent loss of possibility. This larger framework subsumes and gives added meaning to the multiple, sometimes conflicting identities we have examined in previous chapters. If individual Dolphin stories offer resistance to specific strictures imposed by institutionalized Christianity, by gender definitions that stereotype both men and women, and by a social and economic hierarchy that inevitably favors the outsider, then the corpus as a whole pits the infinite wealth of the *Encante* against impoverishment in every sense.

---

37. Man, age 27, interior of Parintins (Remanso). Single, fisherman and farmer, no formal education.

38. Man, age 44, Mazagão Velho (Amapá). Married, fisherman and farmer, no formal education.

39. Man, age 24, interior of Parintins (Tracajá). Married, fisherman and farmer ("and sometimes I go to spend a few months there in Manaus where there is more work"), 2 years school.

40. Man, age 62, Parintins. Married, milkman, "some" grade school.

We have seen that the Enchanted City is synonymous with *fartura* or abundance. "There they have everything" ("Lá tem tudo"), "There nothing is lacking" ("Lá não falta nada"), people say time and again. The stories we have examined deal not only with transformation, but also with riches and power. On the most literal level, the term *mistério* refers to the immense and untapped wealth that lies concealed within and beneath the waters of the Amazon—its spectacular flora and fauna, its immense and varied mineral reserves. More or less prosaic statements to the effect that "we live on top of immense riches" ("a gente vive encima de muita riqueza") suggest a sort of subaquatic El Dorado off-bounds to human exploitation, but still a regional legacy. "The *Encante* exists," one young man says. "How could it not exist? The river is so deep, so wide. Look, outside Amazônia everyone admires the *Victoria Regia* [a type of water lily found throughout the Amazon], but here there are so many that we barely notice them."[41]

The *mistério* that lies beneath the surface of virtually all the Dolphin stories, however, also has a more metaphoric and even metaphysical dimension. It applies not only to the submerged treasures that await discovery— "whole heaps of gold and diamonds large as watermelons!"—but also, and above all, to the essential strangeness of the world. "You know," says the old musician who claims to have played the *rabeca* for the marvelously handsome Dolphin couple, "I think that it is we who are the *encantados*. You are here today, tomorrow you will be far away. We are an instrument that doesn't play itself; we think we are free, and yet, we know so little of this world through which we move like strangers."

In the initial pages of this study, I noted that the Dolphin stories may puzzle the people who tell them. Often, they find these tales not just interesting, beautiful, and funny, but also unsettling and, in the end, inexplicable. "The *Encante* exists," storytellers say over and over, "but I can't explain it." Or, "The *Encante*? Just so. It is mystery upon mystery." In the final analysis, there *is* no explanation—logical or otherwise—for the unearthly celebration a fisherman and his family are aghast to discover taking place in their own kitchen on their return home from an extended river trip. Alzira, who tells the haunting story to me and her grown daughter, admits that she does not fully understand it, "but these things happen and you can be sure that it is true." Although the mysterious visitors here are birds insteads of snakes or dolphins, they are clearly *encantados*. ("Mother," says her daughter with an exaggerated shudder, "this story makes me feel so strange!")[42]

41. Man, age 24, born interior of Parintins (Paraná dos Ramos), divides time between Parintins and interior. Single, grade-school teacher (in interior), high-school education.

42. This story's enigmatic quality deeply impressed me. When, two years later, I asked Alzira to repeat it to me, she had completely forgotten it, and I ended up telling it to her.

41. So then, they [the family members] moored the boat
      in the shadow of that big tree
          —there was a lovely moon that night
              —and they climbed up the cliff to their house.
   And look, there were those creatures,
      all dressed in white,
          singing and dancing in the middle of the kitchen
              —there were a lot of them, you see?

   They were creatures,
      birdlike creatures,
          but in the form of people;
              some appeared as people,
                  others were still birds.
   And the kitchen was full of those bird-people, you know?

   So then, when they realized what was happening,
      they went scurrying off into the woods.
   And the men went after them with guns,
      they fell on them with guns, you see?
   And when the men fired on them,
      they fell to the ground in human form.
   But the body would keep shaking
      till it turned back into a bird.

   They killed a lot of those bird-people
      who had been partying in their kitchen.
   This occurred in Sapucaia, near Nhamundá.

Extremely varied, often seemingly contradictory, the stories we have examined suggest an enigmatic commerce between ostensibly separate domains. As such, they are far less about sex-mad Dolphins or human sexual behavior than they are about "alignment, of balancing male and female forces, of conjoining what we would call physical and spiritual constructs into one whole."[43] In them, human beings who have been carried off to the river bottom carve their names on the backs of tortoises who regularly swim up to the surface. Conversely, shamanic healers descend an immense and gleaming staircase that leads down into the opaque, if rainbow-surfaced, water. The Enchanted Island periodically appears in new and

___

43. Regina Harrison, *Signs, Songs, and Memory in the Andes*, p. 171.

unexpected places; the Enchanted Boat steams into port, lights ablaze and streamers fluttering from the mast, and yet, invisible to most. The following account of three Dolphin-men who glide past the speaker's stepfather emphasizes the proximity of an alien world. Transfixed by the beauty of the serpentine canoe upon the moonlit river, the stepfather simply forgets to be afraid:

42. He [the stepfather] smoked *tauari* like a *pajé*.
    He wasn't a *pajé*,
        but he smoked it all the same.

    So then, it happens that one night
        he was in the middle of the lake,
            lying in his hammock, smoking,
                when three men appeared
                    —white clothes, white hat, white skin
                        —in a very long canoe.

    Full moon,
        the water shining in the light,
            and that canoe drawing ever nearer
                without the slightest noise,
                    there wasn't a sound to be heard.

    Well then, those men were *encantados*,
        they were Dolphins, all three.
    So, the canoe halted in mid-river,
        and they looked at him for a long time.
    White people, he could see absolutely everything.

    "Let's not mess with him because he is smoking *tauari*,"
        one of the men said to the others.
    So then, off they went in that long, long canoe.
    They were *encantados* and that canoe was a snake, see?

    So then, they vanished,
        nothing more was ever seen of them.
    My stepfather thought it all so lovely
        that he forgot to be afraid (my emphasis).[44]

44. Man, age 49, born Faro. Married, carpenter and brick maker, 3 years school.

Although shape-changers are associated with boundary definitions in much anthropological literature, the Dolphin stories are concerned far less with setting, than with invalidating, limits. Liberating (and not infrequently, escapist) in the sense that they allow people to express otherwise impossible wishes, the *encantados* and their allies are also pointedly subversive in that the world they inhabit refuses to live by rules.[45] As embodiments of extravagant and essentially promiscuous desire, Dolphins challenge all attempts at governance. Born of, and engendering, ceaseless movement, they and their enchanted fellows defy all dichotomies and, ultimately, all established order. Constantly reinvented, the *encantados* suggest at once the power of tradition and its inherent volatility, revealing both collective pressures and supports. Their taste for ambiguity and fragmentation suggests that they were postmodern many centuries ago. "My great-grandfather was a *sacaca*," says one old man in Parintins. "He spent the day in Manaus, then returned here. Afterward, if he wanted, he would take a spin about Faro. He didn't have a set time to come and go, *he did just as he pleased*" (my emphasis).[46]

On the one hand, the enchanted beings betoken illusion and impermanence, underscoring human fragility and smallness in a landscape that torrential rains continually alter. On the other, their essential slipperiness is an exultant affirmation of the vastness of the world. "I think this business of Dolphins transforming themselves [into humans] is never going to end," says one young woman, as she gently guides a bit of cloth through an ancient sewing machine. "Because it is their nature, there is no way to put a stop to it. That is just the way they are."[47] If the *encantados'* capriciousness and, sometimes, downright malice may limit human action in some cases, their resistance to definition constitutes a safeguard against domination and the accompanying exploitation that has been the recurring theme of so many storytellers' lives. Visitors can scoop up buckets full of diamonds or fill their pockets with *tracajá* eggs in the Enchanted City, but upon returning home, they will discover only air. Fishermen can dance all night on the Enchanted Island, only to fall asleep, then wake to find themselves adrift upon the river. Now and then, an individual may stumble on a wide-open door to the *Encante*. But when he or she returns with witnesses

45. Writers such as Bakhtin and Kristeva stress the subversive possibilities of the carnivalesque, and Foucault underscores the interrogation of established boundaries inherent in transgressive behavior. However, the *encantados'* opposition to the status quo does not necessarily imply an alternate order; indeed, they are fundamentally anarchical.

46. Man, age 67, born interior of Parintins (Mocambo), lives Parintins (44 years). Married, *tacacá* seller, no formal education.

47. Woman, age 19, Carauari. Single, student, 5 years school.

(and, of course, sacks to cart away the riches), the gates are bolted shut.

If, however, the *encantados* continually rebuff incursions by curious and bedazzled humans, they are ultimately dependent on them for their very existence. And, to the extent that they transmute their own deceptions and desires into narratives that make Alzira's daughter and many others "feel strange," the storytellers are as much, or more, the Dolphin's double as is the shamanic healer. Without individual men and women to recount their deeds, the enchanted beings quickly would fall silent. And yet, although dependent on human beings to give voice to their exploits, they quickly take on their own life within these stories, actively producing their own "domains of objects and rituals of truth."[48] Witnesses to (as well as, sometimes, agents of) oppression, their power is no mere reflection of their tellers' often marginal status. Instead, it is a triumphant declaration of a world that does not push back intruders, but rather, artfully evades them at each and every turn. Defiant in the face of a social and economic order that mockingly denies their existence, Dolphins dance on the sidelines, then cartwheel onto center stage before pirouetting off into a river from which they will again emerge when one least expects. Tricksters in whom self and other meet and mingle, they reside both at the river bottom and deep within the human heart.

In the very first chapter of the book of Genesis, God gives humankind dominion "over the fish of the sea, and over the fowl of the air, and over the cattle, and over all the earth, and over every creeping thing that creepeth upon the earth." Although Adam and Eve are later driven out of paradise, the dream of mastery remains. The Dolphin stories, in contrast, suggest a world that men and women do not and cannot control, that reveals itself only momentarily and on its own terms. Those individuals who have found themselves among the revelers on the Enchanted Island have no surety where—or whether—the joyous celebration will resume. There is no way to force or hurry the island's reappearance, no proof of its existence, outside of memory. And memory, to be sure, can betray or fail us, since there is often no way of proving what did—or did not—occur. ("You have seen the river bottom; it's just that you don't remember!" Seu Josias insists when I demur.)

And yet, if the *Encante* consistently eludes definition, at least one thing is certain. "The Dolphin," says Maurício, "like this land, is ours." Cheated and despoiled over the centuries, the tellers of these stories have taken refuge in perpetual motion, countering with a dizzying multiplicity fixed

48. The expression is Michel Foucault's. See his *Power/Knowledge,* p. 98.

hierarchies that would define, and thus control, them. Through their tales of river beings who assume human form in order to dance the night among them, they assert not the kingdom, but the mystery, of this world. "This business of the *Encante*," one man says softly, "I almost don't believe it. Except that I myself have heard the dancers' voices there beneath the water."[49]

49. Man, age 61, born interior of Alenquer (Pará), lives Parintins (16 years). Married, incapacitated, no formal education.

APPENDIX I
GLOSSARY OF SELECTED TERMS

Amazon. The name applied to those parts of the seven Latin American countries drained by the Amazon River and its tributaries (Surinam and French Guiana are also sometimes included), as well as to the river proper. The term comes from the female warriors of classical mythology whom the Spanish explorer Orellana claimed to have encountered in his passage down the river.

Amazônia. The Brazilian Amazon. Without an accent, the term refers to the entire river basin.

benzedor (see *rezador*). A healer who cures through blessing, or praying over, the sick. Female healers are *benzedeiras*.

boato (see *dizque*). Literally, a rumor. Storytellers use this term for tales whose veracity they consider unclear.

Boi-Bumbá. A traditional drama involving the death and resurrection of a prize bull. The spectacle, which has Iberian roots, is known in the Brazilian Northeast as *Bumba-meu-Boi.* It was brought by northeasterners to Amazônia.

boto (also spelled *bouto* or *boutu*). The popular name for the freshwater dolphin of the *Iniidae* family known as *Inia geoffrensis geoffrensis,* found only in the Amazon basin.

branco. Literally a white-skinned person. The term is often applied in an ironic manner to economically and socially privileged individuals of any color.

Cabanagem. An Amazonian rebellion (1835–39), and one of the biggest popular revolts in Brazilian history. The name comes from *cabano,* meaning hut dweller or poor person.

caboclo. A "backwoodsman," "hillbilly," or "half-breed." In some regions of the Amazon, *caboclo* is a synonym for "Indian."

Caboquinho (see *Curupira*). Literally, "little *caboclo*" and often used synonymously with "little Indian" (*indiozinho*). In some parts of the Amazon, the *Curupira* is known as the *Caboquinho.*

cagila. Sexual magnetism. A person who exudes *cagila* is said to be *cagilento.*

caso acontecido. Literally, an event that has occurred. The term for a story believed to be true.

Cavalo Marinho. Sea Horse. Not the miniature marine animal, but rather, a full-size white horse believed to live at the river bottom, who carries off human riders to its enchanted home.

chupa-chupa. Flying saucers (and, sometimes, various others sorts of UFOs). The verb *chupar* ("to suck") suggests these extraterrestrial visitors' vampirelike proclivities.

Cobra Grande. Literally, "Great Snake." Another name for the Anaconda.

Cobra Norato. The protagonist of a story told throughout much of the Amazon region. The son of a human mother and a serpent father, the Cobra Norato does battle with his evil sister, then succeeds in transforming himself permanently into human form.

coisa dos antigos. An old story, generally believed to be true. The *antigos* are the members of past generations.

curador (sometimes *curandeiro.* See also *pajé*). A Portuguese-speaking, usually at least nominally Roman Catholic shamanic healer. Female curers are *cura[n]deiras.*

Curupira. A powerful forest guardian with considerable transformative abilities who often takes the form of a small, dark child with backward-pointing feet.

dizque (see *boato*). Literally "it's said." A synonym for a *boato,* a story of uncertain veracity.

dono (see *mãe*). Owner, protector. Supernatural *donos* are often referred to as mothers or *mães.*
encantado. An entity capable of assuming the form of either an aquatic animal (most often, snakes or dolphins) or a human being. The *encantados* carry off human beings to the river bottom.

Encante. The rich and beautiful city beneath the river, which is home to the *encantados.*

feiticeira (see *macumbeira*). A sorceress or practitioner of the black arts.

feitiço. A spell or evil work directed at a given individual by a shamanic healer who practices the black arts.

festa. A communal celebration. Amazonian *festas* often begin as saint's day commemorations, followed by drinking and dancing.

garimpeiro. A gold miner. There are presently over a million of these individuals in Amazônia.

Juma. A giant, club-wielding forest guardian.

lenda. Literally, a legend. Different storytellers define the term in a variety of ways.

macumbeiro/a (see *feiticeira*). A derogatory term for a practitioner of an African Brazilian religion. The term may be used more widely to indicate anyone believed to be involved with the black arts.

mãe (see *dono*). A protective entity charged with the care of a particular geographical formation or animal species. All living beings and some natural formations are believed to have *mães*.

mano/a. A colloquial term meaning "brother" or "sister." The person to whom it is applied need not be a relative.

Mapinguari. A forest guardian similar to the North American Big Foot, distinguished by its stench and the mouth in its stomach.

Matinta-Perera (also known as *Matins*). A mythical forest creature said to emit maddening chirps in people's ears. Some storytellers distinguish between this generally invisible, birdlike being, and a second sort of *Matinta,* said to be a human being who temporarily assumes nonhuman form.

novidade. Literally, a novelty or new thing. The term refers to stories that are considered news.

orixá. A powerful African Brazilian deity. The *orixás* are often syncretized with Roman Catholic saints.

pajé. An indigenous term frequently used as a synonym for *curador.* Both men and women can be *pajés*.

panema. An incapacity with supernatural causes visited above all on hunters and fishermen.

pauta. A colloquial form of *pacto,* or "pact." Oral contracts between humans and supernatural entities, *pautas* assure the human member success in hunting or fishing during a stipulated period.

peixe-boi. Literally, "fish-bull." The aquatic mammal known as the sea cow or manatee.

puçanga (see *cagila*). A love charm believed to endow its possessor with *cagila.*

quilombo. A community of runaway slaves.

rezador (see *benzedor*). A type of curer who relies primarily on prayers. The female form of the word is *rezadeira.*

sacaca. The most powerful of shamanic healers. *Sacacas* are believed to travel, body and spirit, to the river bottom.

sereia. Mermaid. Considered by some to be a type of *encantado.*

seringal. A rubber colony.

seringalista. The owner of a rubber colony.

seringueiro. A rubber worker.

tauari. Couratari bark. Shamanic healers smoke tobacco wrapped in *tauari* in order to summon the spirits and to enter into trances.

trancoso. Used in the Northeast and Amazon as a synonym for "folktale." The word comes from the name of the sixteenth-century Portuguese author, Gonçalo Fernandes Trancoso, who wrote a series of highly popular moralistic tales.

tucuxi. The colloquial name for the freshwater dolphin, *Sotalia fluviatilis.*

Umbanda. An African Brazilian religious sect with elements of spiritism. In the Amazon, Umbanda and indigenous religions have often exerted a profound influence upon each other.

APPENDIX 2

PORTUGUESE-LANGUAGE ORIGINALS
OF STORIES IN THE TEXT

The following appendix contains the Portuguese versions of stories or pieces of stories quoted in English in the body of this book. Although the humor and, often, real beauty of these narratives is extremely hard to capture, I have attempted to remain faithful to both the sense and spirit of the original. Because the rhythm of the story is so important in Portuguese, I have offered loose instead of literal translations.

Largely for purposes of rhythm, storytellers of both sexes tend to supply unnecessary pronouns (*eu falei* instead of just *falei*), to invert customary sentence order (*logo esse veio* instead of *esse veio logo*), and to employ frequent repetition. Unfortunately for the translator, some of the most effective and poetic of these repetitions sound wooden in English. While, for instance, *puxou, puxou, puxou* moves along the narrative in Portuguese, the equivalent "he pulled, he pulled, he pulled" is hopelessly awkward. In cases of this sort, I often have substituted a rough equivalent such as "he pulled and pulled" or "he kept on pulling and pulling." In addition, I have introduced punctuation marks that do not always correspond to actual pauses in speaking, and occasionally have supplied missing verbs or connectives in brackets.

Because the storyteller often indicates through voice or gesture who is speaking in the case of a dialogue, I sometimes have added a "he said" or "she said" in order to make such shifts equally clear in print. By the same token, I have indicated the identity of the speaker and substituted subjects for pronouns in cases where otherwise there might be doubt. Although the use of the present tense heightens the drama of the action in performance, it may be confusing in the written text, and I occasionally have substituted the past. For the same reason, I also occasionally have recast the past into a future perfect or other tense. Given the almost total absence of *este* ("this") in colloquial speech, I have translated the demonstrative *esse* (technically, "that") as either "this" or "that," depending on the context.

Storytellers frequently use terms such as *né?* ("right?" or "see?"), *sabe?* ("you know?"), and *viu?* ("see?" or "understand?") to involve their listeners in the action. The heavy use of fillers such as *aí* ("and so then"), *então* ("then"), *bem* ("well"), *pois* ("so"), and *agora* ("now then") likewise serve to heighten the listener's sense of anticipation. Although the ubiquity of these terms may come across as monotonous in print, the reader should be aware of their dramatic function.

Sometimes, I have relied on rough equivalents or circumlocutions, such as "right now" for *agorinha* (the diminutive form of "now") or "she started crying all over the place" for *chora para lá, chora para cá* (literally, "she cries here, she cries there"). A number of especially poetic terms which I have found all but impossible to translate are explained in footnotes or brackets within the text. Finally, in order to make the originals accessible to the greatest possible number of readers, many of whom will be able to figure out much of the general sense from Spanish, I have not attempted to imitate the pronunciation of the Portuguese by altering the spelling. However, in no case have I tampered with the actual words or syntax, so that a phrase such as *quando então chegou duas pessoa* or *cheguemos* (either an archaic or hypercorrective form of *chegamos,* "we arrived") remains as it was spoken.

I have broken the stories into lines based largely on breathing spaces in the Portuguese originals and the presence of markers such as *aí.* Stanzas indicate conceptual units, sometimes (though not always) set apart by slightly longer pauses. English lines correspond to Portuguese lines except in a small number of cases where the length of a particular line is significantly longer or shorter than its equivalent in the other language, or where I have changed the word order in English for purposes of clarity or rhythm.

1. Aí, você vê que o boto
     é bem pior do que o tucuxi.

  Olha, foi durante a época
      em que tinha muita castanha lá naquela ilha
       que o pessoal aqui chama Faz-Favor.
     Fica meio longe de casa,
      mas eu fui mais o menino
       —a gente leva bem cinco horas para chegar lá.

  Aí, chegamos
      e fiquei o dia inteiro colhendo castanha
       —puxa, que fartura!
     Dava para encher a canoa,
      até sobrou, que tanto tinha.

  Aí, pela tardezinha,
      resolvi voltar à casa.
     E olha, lá no meio do caminho
      apareceu aquele monte de botos.

Bati neles com o remo,
    joguei alho encima,
        me peguei com todos os santos.
Aí, foram embora, só ficou um.

Mas esse—heh!—era mesmo o diabo,
    só perseguia a canoa.
O menino chorando, chorando,
    e eu com aquele medo tão grande.
Por fim, joguei fora quase toda a castanha
    para poder remar mais ligeiro.
Me deu tanta pena,
    até hoje me dá raiva!

Agora, o tucuxi é bem melhor.
Não judia com a gente desse jeito.

2. Está fazendo uns três anos agora
    que estava lá no lago do Remanso Grande
        quando essa bota apareceu para mim.
Não largava a canoa.
Aí, fiquei com raiva e arpoei ela,
    que me estava atrapalhando, né?

Puxa, tanto de boto que tinha de noite!
Ficaram lá boiando,
    não dava para dormir.
E quando, por fim, dormi, ela veio no meu sonho,
    falou que nunca ia me largar.

Passei três noites assim,
    já pensou?
A mulher queria que eu fosse lá
    com um deles que fuma tauari.
Mas não quis
    —acho crendice—
        pois a bota é só bicho, né?

Mas tenho que lhes dizer,
    eu tinha medo,
        muito medo!
Por fim, peguei tabaco e joguei
    —assim—
        encima da água.

E ela foi embora.
    Nunca mais apareceu por essas bandas,
        graças a Deus!

3. Naquele tempo, minha jovem senhora,
    acontecia muita coisa.
  Olhe, uma vez me pediram para tocar numa festa
    lá num seringal perto de Boca de Acre.
  Aí, eu fui.

  Estava tocando rabeca—festa boa, né?—
    quando então chegou duas pessoa,
      uma moça e um rapaz.
  Mandei a mulher sair pra receber eles.
  Aí, subiram, entraram na sala, dançaram.

  Tem gente aqui que ainda se lembra do que aconteceu,
    que estava também junto com nós naquela hora.
  O rapaz de blusa branca, calça verde,
    e a moça de vestido verde claro e o casaco branco.
  Toquei quase sem parar,
    dançou, dançou
      eles também dançaram muito.

  Aí, depois de passar de onze hora pra meia noite,
    sumiram
      não achemos mais eles.
  Fiquemos todo mundo gritando,
    procuremos em tudo que era canto
      —e nada, nada!
  Tão bonitos eles,
    mas não era gente, não.

4. Ah, dona menina, nós fomos logo atrás dele,
    eu com a poronga,
      e os outros gritando assim,
        "O que é que você quer, seu filho da puta?"
  Quase nós pegamos ele,
    só que ele pulou da ponte
      para a água.
  Era homem em terra,
    mas quando bateu água lá fora,
      era boto—nós vimos tudo, tudo.

Sumiu o homem no instante
  e o que apareceu foi aquele boto grande
    boiando lá fora—Chahhhh!
Que ele queria paquerar aquela moça,
  estava querendo virar cunhado
    dos três irmãos dela, né?
Mas nada feito
  —parece que eles não gostaram da idéia!

5. Aí, quando a festa acabou-se,
    lá pelas três horas da madrugada,
      todo mundo viu aquele homem bonito
        de pé por debaixo da bananeira no luar
          —um tapioca de branco, ele!
  Aí, foi descendo para o rio.

  O pai da menina ficou lá esperando,
    não viu ninguém passar.
  Pois ele [o Boto] já tinha ido
    para a casa do homem!
  "Aquele bicho vai parar na rede de minha filha,"
    ele disse quando se deu conta.
  Aí, pegou a zagaia,
    correu para a casa.

  Mas quando chegou na porta,
    o Boto já vinha saindo da janela.
  Não tinha jeito, não.

  Passaram nove meses,
    então a mulherzinha deu a dor para ter criança.
  Nasceu um botinho perfeito,
    mas perfeito!
      —vi aquele botinho com esses olhos.

6. Aí, ele foi para casa,
    e quando chegou lá,
      chamou a mãe dele e disse,
        "Ah, mamãe, eu sou um assassino."
  "Meu filho, o que é que você está me dizendo?"
  "Sim, matei Antonio, minha mãe."

  "Mas, por quê?"
  "Ele me estava traindo com minha namorada."
    (Era a noiva do cara, né?)

"Meu filho, tens certeza?"
"Tenho.
 Ele entrou na boca da noite,
  só saiu agora.
Furei ele, ele caiu na água."

Aí, a mãe chora para lá, chora para cá, né?
Por fim, ele disse,
 "Vou me entregar na polícia."
Aí, ele deixou mais o dia clarear
 e saiu.

Quando chega aonde estão as canoas
 ele vê um boto vermelhão desses bem grandes,
  morto lá na beira
   com o punhal dele bem nas costas.
Aí, arrancou o punhal.
É verdade,
 aconteceu.

7. Ele estava lá no interior com o pessoal
 naquela passação de gado,
  e quando pararam na beira do Amazonas,
   boiou uma bota perto dele, né?
Então, ele falou assim, "Mulher vem dormir comigo!"
 porque estava lá mais de mês,
  e nada de mulher, né?
Ele falou brincando,
 já tinha escutado várias histórias,
  e aí, falou assim, de brincadeira.

Bom, quando foi a noite, segundo ele contando,
 ele estava já dormindo no motor quando acordou
  e viu uma mulher se aproximar da rede dele.
Então, tentou disfarçar, né?
 mas a mulher veio.
Não teve coragem de fechar os olhos.

Aí, logo que o dia clareou,
 ele saiu de lá desesperado.
Viajou para a cidade, para Manaus,
 ficou lá mais de um mês.
Só que quando por fim criou a coragem de voltar,
 aquela mesma mulher estava lá
  querendo se deitar com ele na rede.

Aí, ele sabia que era aquela bota
    que ele tinha convidado para dormir com ele.
Quem mais podia ser?

8. Esse pescador, ele arpoou um boto velho,
    todo encheado,
        que nem uma pessoa muito velha, né?

Então, parece que os outros começaram perseguir ele
    duma tal forma
        que foi obrigado a matar mais nove.
Que eles fecharam encima,
    e não deixaram ele sair de lá.
Pois tinha matado o vô deles, viu?
    —aí, tinham muita raiva dele.

Bem, depois daquele dia,
    não tinha como poder dormir de noite.
Ia atar o mosquiteiro no escuro
    mas logo quando se deitou na rede,
        diz que ficava claro, claro,
            que nem o dia,
            que nem a luz elétrica, ao redor dele.
E se pegava por fim no sono,
    agarraram no punho da rede
        que não dava nem para dormir nada.

Aí, ele foi para a casa do pai dele,
    que o pai dele sabia de oração.
Aí, mandou chamar uma pessoa que ajudou curar ele
    —tipo sacaca, né?
E esse disse para ele,
    "Olha, mas sempre quando chegar este mês"
        —não sei mais se era novembro ou se era dezembro
        —"todo este mês você não vai dormir direito."

Aí, é mesmo, quando chega aquele mês
    que ele fez esse massacre de Boto,
        aí ele não dorme nadinha.
Até hoje!
Mas quando passa aquele mês,
    pronto,
        ele volta ao normal dele.

9. Pois é, ele não sabia fazer esse curativo.
 Aí, ficou, ficou, ficou, até que um dia
  encontrou quatro ou cinco pretinhos
   jogando bola na mata do Encante.
 E pediu a ajuda deles,
  que aquela ferida não sarava.

 Aí, eles ensinaram o remédio para ele
  —era para ele raspar bem a escama do acara-açu
   e botar várias coisas dentro.
 Esqueço como foi agora,
  mas ensinaram tudo direitinho para ele.
 Bom, aqueles pretinhos eram os tucuxi,
  não sabe?

 Aí, ele fez como lhe tinham ensinado
  e o coronel sarou logo.
 Então deram uma canoa cheia de peixe
  para ele levar.
 Até hoje come bem, esse homem.

10. Pois é, o dia depois da festa,
  apareceu uma velhinha,
   recolhendo os ossinhos do peixe-boi
    e colocando eles num saquinho.
 Parecia ser parente dele, né?
 Falou que aquele povo ia se arrepender
  de ter feito aquilo.

 Aí, todo mundo achou ela doida.
 Só um pescador que ficou de orelha em pé.
 Esse, sim,
  pegou a família dele,
   saiu na hora daquele lugar.

 Os outros, não,
  resolveram fazer outra festa.
 Aí, quando foi de noite,
  estava todo mundo animado,
   todos cantando e comendo,
    quando, naquele instante,
     a terra pegou a mover.
 Fazia um barulho espantoso,
  e a terra ia [a]fundando, [a]fundando,
   até que só ficou uma espécie de ilha submergida.

Até hoje, quem passa nesse lugar
　　ouve aquele barulho de pessoas cantado, conversando.
Você não vê nada mas ouve-se galo cantar,
　　　　　　cachorro ladrar,
　　　　　　criança chorar.
Toca música à toda hora.

Se eu já ouvi aquela música?
Ouvi,
　　sim,
　　　　ouvi.

11. Pois então, essa minha tia
　　tinha dado a luz fazia poucos dias.
Aí, foi para a beira com mais umas pessoas,
　　estava com o nenê nos braços
　　　　quando veio uma onda bem grande.

Naquele momento o esposo dela pediu o menino,
　　ela entregou a criança para ele.
Aí, ela foi embora para a casa cuidar da panela;
　　ele quem ficou lá com o menino.
Só que depois quando ela veio de novo buscar,
　　ele não sabia nada de nada,
　　　　já pensou?
Que ele nem tinha estado lá naquela hora.

Depois, o menino ficou aparecendo no sonho dela.
Aí, o curador mandou batizar
　　com sangue e água benta antes dele fazer dezoito anos,
　　　　antes dele criar guela, né?
Só que depois deixou de aparecer para ela,
　　ela nunca mais viu ele;
Assim que não podia fazer nadinha, coitada!

12. Tinha um Boto que perseguia muito uma criança.
Aí, o pai procurou esse tal de Antonio Sacaca.
Esse foi mesmo sacaca
　　—viajava pelo fundo com o cigarro aceso,
　　　　depois voltava com ele do mesmo jeito, né?

Aí, ele foi lá na beira,
　　chamou o Boto com cachaça e aquelas cantigas,
　　　　aí, logo esse veio.

Ficaram conversando muito tempo lá na beira
    parece que os dois ficaram porres,
        tanta cachaça que tomaram.
Só sei que nunca mais o Boto
    boiou perto da criança.

Que esse Antonio Sacaca, ele era muito bom pajé.
Só que quando se transformava em cobra,
    ninguém queria olhar para ele.
Nossa Senhora, que coisa feia!

13. Aí, quando caíram da canoa,
    uma cobra grande levou eles para o Encante.
E se transformaram em duas cobras, sabe?
    um macho e a outra, mulher.
E esse macho era o Norato.

Então, a mulher,
    ela era muito malvada.
Onde ela encontrasse uma canoa,
    um motor que fosse passando,
        ela metia no fundo sem mais nada.
E o rapaz, o cobra-menino,
    ele não gostava que a irmã dele fizesse isso.
Assim que uma vez, eles traçavam uma briga
    no meio do Amazonas,
        cegou ela.
Aliás, ela cegou ele também.

Depois, esse Norato, ele foi numa festa
    e conversou com cara lá.
Perguntou se o cara
    tinha a coragem de desencantar ele,
        que era só de dar um tiro
            bem na testa da cobra grande
                e ficar esperando ele sair em homem.
E o que trouxesse na mão era para dar de presente para ele.

Aí, o cara foi lá para a beirada
    na hora que tinha marcado.
Deu um tiro bem na testa daquela cobra enorme,
    e dito e feito, dentro de dez minutos,
        vem saindo aquele homem de dentro da pele da cobra
            com uma pedra de diamante na mão.

E o cara pegou o diamante e foi embora,
    até hoje não se sabe
        a história dele.

Agora, esse Norato ainda vive nalgum cantinho
    aqui no interior de Parintins.

14. Esse caso aconteceu em Parintins,
        perto da esquina da General Osório
            onde é agora lugar do guarda da segurança.
    Naquele tempo,
        os homens ainda andavam todo de roupa de paletó,
            chapéu de massa na cabeça,
                bengala na mão.
    Então, justo no momento quando esse homem
        vai passando frente à igreja,
            alguém soltou um grito assim
                —"Matinta-perera!"

Aí, ele pegou a bengala
    e PAH!
        bem na cabeça do bicho, né?
Aí, o Matins sai correndo
    e ele vai para a casa,
        dorme direitinho.
Não pensa mais naquilo.

Só que quando foi o outro dia de manhã,
    o delegado manda chamar ele.
Que parece que ele tinha espancado uma velha,
    sim, era a velha
        que se gerava em Matins.
Aí, estava todo doída
    —não dava mais para ela nem andar!

15. Tinha por aqui um boto
    que ia esculhambando na malhadeira do pescador.
Aí, o cara ficou com raiva,
    disse que ia dar uma lambada naquele sem-vergonha
        se continuasse assim.
Aí, voltou um dia,
    achou o boto bem dentro da malhadeira,
        comendo todo o peixe dele.

Pegou um pau,
    ia dar nele pra valer.
Só que naquele instante
    o boto olha para ele
        e sai correndo da malhadeira.
"Vou embora—
    não volto mais!" ele diz
        e pula para o fundo.

Aí, o cara ficou lá
    sem jeito.
Quer dizer, ia dar lambada no boto,
    mas o boto conseguiu fugir.
Tinha enchido bem o bucho,
    aí, tchau!

16. Foi o meu pai quem fez promessa com o Santo Antonio
    para tirar minha avó do Encante.
Que ela andava procurando um remédio que tem,
    por nome de paracuri,
        lá na beira
            quando viu dois garotinhos daquele lugar.
Só que esses que apareceram para ela
    naquele dia não eram aqueles dois, não
    —eram os encantados
        que tinham se apresentado
            em forma de garoto.

"Dona Claudina, o que é que a senhora está procurando?"
    Ela disse, "Estou procurando paracuri."
        "Sei onde tem uma porção," um deles falou.
E aí, foram caminhando, caminhando,
    cada vez mais para dentro das matas.
Então, deixaram ela presa
    no toco dum pau grande
        e lá ela passou a noite.

A gente procurava, procurava,
    mas embora escutou os gritos,
        não podia responder.
Ela passou a noite inteira lá,
    noite de chuva grossa.
E quando por fim conseguiu sair de lá,
    manhã cedinho, saiu enxuta,
                enxutinha.

Aí, ela mostrou para todo mundo o toco do pau grande
    onde tinha passado a noite.
Ela não foi para o fundo do mar,
    mas foi coisa do Encante.
Os rapazinhos eram do Encante,
    do Encante do fundo do mar.

Bom, depois,
    ficou meio oscilada ela
        —não demorou para morrer.
Mas se meu pai não tivesse feito
    aquela promessa com o santo,
        nunca teria voltado.
Ah não, teriam levado ela naquela hora,
    pronto.

17. E aí, o bicho tinha se transformado
    em forma do pai dela, entende?
Então, levou a menina para o fundo.
Mas ela desconfiou
    porque tudo era muito rico.
Aquelas pessoas que se diziam ser os pais dela
    até tinham carro, levaram ela a passear.

Agora, os pais dela quase enlouqueceram.
Procuraram o sacaca daquele local,
    e esse mandou o Cavalo Marinho buscar ela.

Aí, quando chegou lá,
    ela estava passando bem.
Ficou com medo de montar nele;
    quis ficar.
Mas, por fim,
    acabou levando ela para a casa.
Que os pais estavam com muita saudade dela.

18. Mês de junho,
    o rio muito cheio.
A gente estava levando palha
    para a terra firme.
Aí, pelas onze horas de noite,
    vimos aquele fogo.

Veio, veio, veio,
    era a Cobra Grande.
Iluminava tudo,
    ficou como uma luz elétrica,
        mas bem azul.
A gente tentou fugir,
    mas veio aquela onda enorme.
Todo mundo gritou,
    e eu gritei também.

Aí, a canoa virou,
    tivemos que agarrar
        no capim da beirada.
Só o dono da palha
    —o nome dele era Severo
        —foi quem morreu.
Quer dizer, não morreu de verdade;
    a Cobra Grande que levou ele para o fundo.
Pois depois, veio na banca do curador de lá
    e falou tudo para ele.

19. Eu estava lá na água
    e logo, queria subir
        mas não podia.
Pessoas se aproximaram de mim,
    pessoas que não pertenciam a meu mundo,
        querendo me levar com eles.

Muitas vezes, corria,
    corria e caía,
        mergulhava na água.
Chegou ao ponto
    de eu ficar com medo de ir
        para a beira.

Acho que essas coisas me prejudicaram muito.
Que eu era um de três primos
    e os outros iam crescendo
        e eu, ficando atrás.
Eles com as namoradas, né?
    e eu, ao lado,
        ainda muito garotinho,
        sentadinho, todo mirrado,
        só querendo pegar um calorzinho para mim.

Olha,
   era aquele ambiente
     —eu vivia aquilo.
Todo mundo acreditava nos encantados,
   aí, eu também
     cheguei a acreditar.

20. Aconteceu uma coisa comigo,
   nunca contei para ninguém, né?
Até hoje
   acho meio esquisito.
Que eu ia na beira, né?
   e tinha lá todo um povo
     saindo da água.

Aí, tinha entre eles uma mulher de cabelos bem compridos,
   sempre, sempre que eu ia lá tomar banho,
     ela vinha para mim.
Quase não tinha roupa,
   não tinha roupa mesmo,
     dava par ver o corpo todinho daquela mulher,
       muito perfeito, né?
Era um povo de um vermelho moreno,
   mais ou menos de minha cor,
     todos eles muito bonitos.

Mas era ela que me chamava,
   ela que me dava a mão.
E só eu que enxergava ela,
   mais ninguém.
Falei para meu irmão
   para ir lá comigo na beira uma vez,
     mas ele não viu nada.

Aí, fiquei com medo,
   mas mesmo assim queria ir
     com eles—quer dizer, com ela.

21. Era uma loira muito bonita,
   sempre usava uma roupa branca.
Falava muito,
   dizia tudo da vida dela para mim.
Vinha sempre, sempre no meu sonho;
   depois, me encontrei com ela na praia.

275

Ela me disse que tinha sido encantada
    com os sete anos de idade
        e agora estava querendo se desencantar,
           que ela vinha em forma de uma cobra monstra,
             e era para dar um tiro na cabeça dela.
Depois se desencantava
    e casava comigo,
        e dava muita riqueza para mim.

Olha, achei ela muito bonita.
Queria casar com ela, sim
    —só que depois fiquei com medo.
Fiquei com dúvida, né?
Que eu nunca conheci ninguém
    que fosse lá no fundo.
Ainda hoje não sei o que pensar.

22. Aí, depois do cara chamar a bota,
    ela aparece em forma de mulher,
        tão bonita, tão cheirosa
           que ele só queria se agarrar com ela.
Então ela insistiu
    para ele fazer alguma coisa com ela
        mas ele não conseguiu.
Nada!
Já pensou?
Aí, ela falou para ele
    que era para ele
        nunca mais mexer com ela.

Só depois que ele conseguiu voltar ao normal dele.
Durante dias cheirava aquele perfume de uma flor
    que ele nunca tinha conhecido antes;
        não sabia qual flor era.
O cheiro ficou, ficou,
    deixou ele meio virado da cabeça.

Só o pajé que deu jeito.

23. Tudo, mas tudo,
    começou de uma pescaria.
Joguei a tarrafa,
    ela pegou nela
        e me puxou para o fundo, né?
Aí, me espantei.

Se eu
    não tivesse me espantado
      com a tarrafa,
        nada feito, né?
Mas logo nesse espanto que peguei,
    senti uma dor de cabeça,
      aquela dor fina, sabe?
Vim de lá da beira já com frio.

Aí, procurei camisa,
    procurei lençol.
Deitei na rede,
    mas tremia mesmo.
Tanto do frio que tinha!

24. Olhe, ela me adormecia
    mas eu não estava dormindo de verdade.
Aí,
    queria gritar
      mas a voz não me saía.
E aí,
    ela brincava lá comigo aquelas horas todas,
      só ia embora pela madrugada.

Quando eram seis horas da tarde,
    eu fazia um café
      e me dava uma tristeza bem grande.
Aí,
    eu ficava lá,
      só olhando a imagem do rio.
E aquela tristeza me chegava,
    tristeza de chorar.

Assim que por fim,
    não aguentava mais,
      procurei o curador.
Pois eu achava bom aquela mulher,
    ela fazia com que eu quase morria de gozo.
Mas não aguentava aquela tristeza que me vinha
    sem eu saber de onde.

25. Aí, apareceu lá na beira
    um rapaz muito bonito.

Era Boto, né?
    mas em forma de homem,
        aquele homem bonitão.

Aí, ele queria que eu fosse
    para o fundo com ele.
Queria que eu fosse a mulher dele,
    disse que dava muita riqueza,
        muita coisa boa para mim.
Que ele morava numa casa muitíssimo bonita, né?
Que ele era tipo conde;
    a senhora já ouviu falar em conde, Dona Cândida?

Pois é, ele era conde
    e eu queria,
        queria, sim.
Só que eu tinha os meus filhinhos ainda pequeninhos,
    e não dava para mim.

Então, ele pegou a cantar aquela cantiga
    que já cantei para a senhora, lembra?
Puxa vida, até hoje penso naquele rapaz!

26. Olhe, cada vez eu ia lá na beira,
    apareciam aqueles Botos,
        puxando conversa comigo.
Achei tudo esquisito,
    me davam muito medo.
Me convidaram entrar na água,
    conhecer a cidade deles no fundo.
Logo depois, comecei ter muita dor de cabeça,
    não dava para eu comer,
        não dormia nada.

Até não ligava mais para o nenê,
    —nem sabia mais que eu tinha filho.
Foi o meu esposo que tinha que fazer tudo,
                tudo,
    porque lá não tenho família,
        não tinha quem me ajudasse.

Aí, me levou para o curador daquele lugar,
    passou muito banho,
        muita reza.

Mas não deu jeito,
  aqueles Botos vinham de toda forma.

Por fim,
  ele me levou para um pajé daqui.
Esse falou para ele
  que eu tinha o espírito fraco.
Se eu ficasse lá,
  o Boto me levava
    para o fundo do rio
      e não voltava mais.
Assim que ainda estou aqui em Parintins.

É ruim por uma parte porque meu esposo
  está lá no campo.
Mas a cura é demorada
  —tem que fazer aos poucos
    para ela funcionar, né?

27. Ele vem no meu sonho,
  mas não estou dormindo.
Vem de chapéu de palha,
  vem com flores amarelas.
Ele me manda pegar aquelas flores,
  mas não pego nunca.

Aí, ele me diz,
  "Eu te guardo muito para mim,
    eu te protejo.
  Não sou daqueles
    que vão atrás
      de qualquer rabo de saia.
Eu te respeito,
  não te largo nunca.
Mas eu quero você só para mim.
Nenhum homem vai mexer contigo,
  que você já tem marido.
Vou ficar rezando para ti."

Olhe, ele me traz as samambaias mais bonitas do fundo.
Depois, me leva para a mata.
Ele diz que foi o meu primeiro namorado,
  mas não gosto muito dele.
Se eu gostava muito dele,
  ia me levar com toda certeza.

Ou então ele ia me usar
    e depois me deixar, né?
Pois homem é assim.

E então, todo mundo me arrespeita,
    todo mundo me gosta.
Mas eu não vou atrás de homem, não,
    me dou bem com todo mundo.

28. Aquela senhora morava em Parananema
    e a gente também morava lá.
Aí, adoeceu.
Adoeceu muito, muito,
    e, por fim,
        ficou doidinha.
Eram três homens para aguentar ela
    quando queria correr para a beira.

Bem, um dia deu aquele negócio nela
    e ela falou para mim e uma tia minha,
        "Ah, vou-me embora, que ele veio me buscar"
—O Boto, né?
"Ele veio me buscar numa lancha bem bonita."
Assim falou para nós.

Agora, só tinha nós duas para aguentar ela,
    aí, não houve jeito.
Ela pulou pela janela,
    e quando vínhamos atrás,
        já estava lá no meio do rio.

Agora, não sei como
    ela andava encima daquela água
        —será que ele estava sustentando ela?
Porque lá e muito fundo, né?
    é muito fundo.

Aí,
    um primo meu foi buscar ela.
Mas olha só, ela pulava, pulava,
    que ele não pôde fazer nada.
Aí,
    vieram bem oito homens para segurar ela.

Mas ela ficou pulando lá
   no meio do rio,
      rindo, rindo.

Por fim,
   tiveram que deixar
    —aí, sumiu.
Quer dizer, não sumiu
    —o Boto quem levou.

29. Morava uma mulher no interior,
   o esposo viajava muito.
Deixava ela só
   durante muito tempo.
["Coitada!"]

Aí, um belo dia,
   ele saiu para pescar durante várias semanas.
["É assim mesmo, lá no interior a gente passa muito tempo só."]
Então, todo fim de tarde,
   cantava um pássaro por nome de macucau.
E cada vez que o bicho cantava, ela dizia,
   "Macucau, vem me buscar,
   macucau, vem me buscar,"
      assim.

Então, quando um dia ela estava fazendo
   mingau para os filhos,
      mingau de banana,
         chegou um homem na casa dela,
         ela não sabia de onde vinha.
["Tipo Boto, né?"]
Tipo Boto.
Aí, ela ficou desconfiada,
   mandou os filhos para a beira buscar água.
Só que disse para eles
   ficar esperando ela lá na canoa,
      que ela desconfiava daquele homem.
["Que era bicho, né? Não era nada de homem."]

Então, quando os filhos começavam demorar,
   ela pediu licença daquele senhor
      e foi atrás deles.
Quando chegou na beira,
   pulou na canoa com eles
      e seguiu a viagem rio abaixo.

E quando ela olhou para atrás,
    aquele homem estava na beirada.

Aí gritou para ela,
    "Que te vá, que te vá,
    que se tu não fostes hoje,
      eu ia te levar."

30. Aí, quando a mulher chega lá na beira,
    pula para a canoa, né?
E o homem fica atrás.
Aí, ele começa bater com os braços assim,
    dizendo, "Oba, oba, oba."
"Olha, minha filha," ele disse para ela,
    "vá-te embora agora mesmo!
Pois se não vai agorinha,
    te mostro tudo que tenho aqui
      nesse saco meu."

31. O sogro do meu irmão,
    ele é sacaca.
A mãe dele andava debaixo d'água
    —era sacaca também.
Toda quinta-feira ela ia,
    só voltava na outra semana.
Ela sempre queria que o marido fosse com ela
    —dizia, "Embora, José,
      tu carrega a minha maleta."

Aí, ele carregava a maleta dela.
Quando chegavam lá, ela dizia,
    "Boto bonito, vem buscar ele.
    Boto bonito, vem buscar ele."
Assim, três vezes, viu?
Aí, o boto vinha para deixar ele na beira,
    ela que demorava lá com os peixinhos, né?

Então, o boto deixava ele lá,
    dava tchau para ele
      e o coitado
        tinha que ficar na espera da mulher.
Puxa, aquela senhora curava todo mundo!
Não tinha quem não ficasse bom na mão dela.

32. O Boto,
      ele faz com que a pessoa adoece e morre.
  Mas não morre de verdade.
  Não, não, ainda vive e vai
      para aquela cidade perfeita no fundo.

  Lá tem tudo
    —tem gado,
    tem casa boa,
    tem muito porco e galinha.
  Lá é tudo com facilidade,
      a gente não precisa trabalhar,
          não tem que ficar carregando peso
             no sol de meio-dia.
  É igual a essa terra,
      só que a gente não trabalha,
         come bem e vive passeando.
  Lá todo mundo tira um soninho depois do almoço, né?
  É vida boa.

33. Olhe, acho que o Boto
      é como esses patrões antigos.
  Que nos tempos passados
      o seringal era todo uma beleza.
  Os donos mandaram vir os carpinteiros de Portugal
      e fizeram aquelas casa de pinho do Porto.
  Depois, mandaram vir os móveis
      da França e da Grã-Bretanha.
  Até vinha espelho em marco de ouro.

  Agora, tinha uns deles que fizeram muita malvadeza.
  Quem não vendesse a borracha para eles,
      eles mandavam os capangas pendurar
         no sol do meio-dia.
  Tinha um,
      o Seu Geraldo, parece,
         que mandava os meninos subir na goiabeira.
  Depois, atirava neles,
    matava mesmo.
  E os pais, coitados,
    sem poder dizer nada.

  Assim, acho que o Boto é desse jeito
    —é muito rico
      e também muito perverso.

Querendo levar a pessoa,
    ele leva, pronto.
A mãe pode ficar chorando o dia inteiro
    —para ele, tanto faz.

34. O Boto, rapaz,
    ele anda cheio de dólar.
Sim, senhor, o cara vai lá na festa
    com aquela roupa bem branca, bem cara,
        e todas as caboc[l]as ficam doidinhas por ele.
Querem dançar com ele,
    só com ele;
        não querem saber mais
            do namorado.
Mostra os dólar
    e elas correm atrás.

Só que o Boto é muito falso.
Quer namorar as moças mais bonitas,
    promete muita coisa boa.
Mas depois, vai embora
    e cadê?
Até o chapéu dele não é chapéu—
    é raia, entendeu?

Dá colares de ouro para as namoradas
    e, no outro dia,
        eles viram alga.
Mas elas não desconfiam daquela fala bonita,
    não, senhor.

35. Aquela geração antiga que acreditava no encantado
    não existe mais
        —já morreu,
            ou se mudou para Manaus ou Parintins.
E tem lá no lugar deles uma nova geração
    que não acredita mais.
Inclusive, só para você ver como as coisas já mudaram,
    faz uns três anos
        saiu outra praia bem pertinho de casa,
            e a turma começou a jogar bola lá.

Aí, começaram as pessoas dizer
    que invocava os espíritos,
        principalmente Zé Caetano.

Só parece que Zé Caetano já está idoso,
    o pessoal que me conta.
Aí, ele veio e pediu para eles não jogar
    mais bola encima do terreno dele, sabe?
E se continuassem a jogar depois de determinado tempo,
    ele fazia sumir a praia
        com todo mundo encima.
Estava brabo Zé Caetano, né?

Aí, o rapaz brincou com ele.
Disse, "Olhe, Zé Caetano,
    cadê as tartarugas?
        Dizem que tem muito por lá,
            mande uma bem gostosa para mim, cara!"
Aí, o Zé Caetano ficou cada vez mais muito brabo
    mas o pessoal não deixou de brincadeira
        —não acredita mais.

36. O Encante,
      ele é da água,
          mas também pode ser da mata.
Conheço um homem,
    ele foi lá dentro da mata,
        fugindo do patrão,
            um cara muito ruim
                que queria matar ele
                    para não ter que pagar
                        a grana que estava lhe devendo.

Então, ele varou muito dentro da mata grande
    até dar naquele sítio cheio de arara e agouti.
Também tinha carneiro
    e um gado tudo diferente, tipo búfalo.
Aí, ele ficou deslumbrado;
    queria levar aquele gado para ele.
"Puxa, rapaz, com um gado desses,
    eu ficava bem de vida!"

Aí, ficou tudo animado, aprontou o gado.
Só que quando ia saindo da floresta,
    o gado sumiu por completo.
Assim que ficou com nada, nada.
E quando quis voltar,
    não encontrava o caminho.

37. Pois é,
        uma vez eu ia viajando de motor para Uaicurapá,
          e tinha um pessoal contando essa história do Noratinho.
    Então, mais tarde,
        um velhinho falou para mim
          que era ele mesmo, o Norato.
    Sim, sim!
        —ele mesmo confirmou,
          nós viajando juntos a Uaicurapá.
    Uma pessoa igualmente à gente.
    Ele falou como era a vida dele no fundo,
        falou como era aquele povo,
          me contou tudinho.

    Tempo de eleição, né?
        ele ia visitar um fazendeiro de juta.
    Agora,
        não sei onde ele mora.
    Um senhor já de idade,
        mas quando moço, ele tocava em todas as festas,
          era o melhor músico da região.
    Agora, se fosse outra pessoa,
        ganhava um bom dinheiro
          contando a história dele no Fantástico.
    Enricava mesmo.

    Mas ele diz que não quer.
    Quer dizer, ele conta,
        mas não conta por dinheiro.
    Que ele diz que essas coisas
        são mistério do fundo
          e não se vendem por dinheiro algum.

38. Eu sei falar com tudo que é branco.
    O médico me quis proibir sair,
        mas eu disse para ele que eu ia para casa
          morrer com meus filhos.
    Não ia ficar lá para morrer
        encima da cama feito um cachorro.

    Aí, ele me falou que eu era muito malcriado.
    E eu disse para ele que me achava muito bem-criado
        porque eu não ia ficar ali com ele,
          nem pensar!

Aí, voltei a Zé Açu
 e fui parar na porta
  de um deles que cura com tauarí.

Olhe, mana,
 esse homem não me cobrou nada.
Me salvou a vida
 mas não quis saber de dinheiro, viu?
Até hoje quando lhe vejo,
 sempre lhe dou alguma coisa
  —uma caça,
  talvez um ovo,
  um pouco de farinha.
Ele me diz que já lhe dei demais,
 mas não acho, não.
Que se eu tivesse ficado lá naquele hospital,
 teria morrido, com toda certeza.

39. Ela, a irmã,
 partiu para a malvadeza.
Mas ele, Noratinho,
 mesmo sendo transformado em cobra,
  tinha sentimento.
Depois, queria se desencantar;
 só que não achava aqui quem lhe desencantasse,
 e aí, teve que sair para o exterior.

Aí, chegou lá numa clínica dessas bem famosas
 —não sei se era na França,
  ou na Califórnia,
   ou na América
 —chegou lá e os médicos fizeram tratamento para ele
  com muito laser
   —se chama "laser," né?
   —e muito raio X.

Aí, deixou de ser cobra, virou homem,
 desencantou-se.
Depois mandou um telegrama para dizer
 que voltava para o Amazonas, para o Brasil.

40. Mas com o tempo,
 o pessoal deixou de acreditar
  no dono daquele lago.

"Não tem encantado, rapaz,
    que história é essa?"
        as pessoas mais novas disseram, rindo, rindo.
Acharam graça de tudo.

Aí, o dono de lá ficou com muita raiva,
    resolveu sair de lá.
E no dia que ele foi embora,
    sumiu aquela linda praia.
Também levou o peixe todinho.
Que antes,
    sempre tinha muito peixe lá.
Mas hoje em dia, minha filha,
    você não vê nem um peixinho
        desses bem pequenininhos.

E o povo?
Ah não,
    não puderam nada.
Pediram para ele voltar
    mas nada feito.
E aí,
    foi embora todos.
Não tem mais ninguém que mora lá.

41. Aí, eles encostaram a canoa
    na sombra daquela árvore bem grande
      —noite de luar bonito
        —e subiram para a casa.
E olha, lá tinha aqueles bichos,
    todos vestidos de branco,
      cantando e dançando no meio da cozinha,
        —mas eram muitos, né?

Era bicho,
    tipo pássaro,
      só que engerados em gente;
        uns ainda estavam em pássaro,
          outros já estavam em gente.
E a cozinha estava cheia daquela gente, sabe?

Aí, quando deram fé,
    eles iam correndo pelo meio do mato.
E o pessoal atrás deles com as armas,
    pularam por cima com as armas, né?

E quando eles atiraram neles,
    caíam como pessoa.
Só que o corpo ficava se batendo assim,
    até virar bicho.

Mataram bastante desse povo
    que estavam fazendo festa na cozinha.
Isso no Sapucaia, bandas de Nhamundá.

42. Ele usava o tauari feito um pajé.
    Não era pajé,
        mas usava ele de todo jeito.

Assim que, uma noite,
    ele estava no meio do lago,
        deitado na rede, fumando,
            quando aparecem três homens
                —roupa branca, chapéu branco, pele branca,
                —numa canoa bem comprida.

Noite de lua cheia,
    a água bem brilhosa,
        e aquela canoa que vinha chegando
            sem o menor barulho,
                não se ouvia nada.

Pois bem, aqueles homens eram encantados,
    eram Botos, todos três.
Então, parou a canoa no meio do rio,
    olharam muito tempo para ele.
Gente branca, dava para ele ver tudinho.

"Não vamos mexer com ele porque ele está fumando tauari,"
    um dos homens disse para os outros.
Aí, foram embora naquela canoa comprida, comprida.
Eles eram encantados e a canoa era uma cobra, viu?

Aí, foram embora,
    não se viu deles mais nada.
Meu padrasto achou tudo aquilo tão bonito
    que esqueceu de ter medo.

REFERENCES

I n listing works in Spanish and Portuguese (or translations of these works), I have followed bibliographic convention by alphabetizing the first of multiple Spanish surnames, and the last of multiple Portuguese surnames. Thus, "Juan Santos Ortiz de Villalba" appears under "Santos," while "Luís da Câmara Cascudo" appears under "Cascudo."

Aarne, Antti, and Stith Thompson. *The Types of the Folktale.* 2d ed. rev. Folklore Fellows Communications 184. Helsinki: Suomalainen Tiedakatemia, 1961.

Abu-Lughod, Lila. "The Romance of Resistance: Tracing Transformations of Power through Bedouin Women." *American Ethnologist* 17: 41–55.

Adorno, Rolena. *Guaman Poma: Writing and Resistance in Colonial Peru.* Austin: University of Texas Press, 1986.

Aelian. "The Dolphin Rider." Translated by Charles Doria. In *Mind in the Waters,* edited by Joan McIntyre, pp. 38–40. New York: Scribner, 1974.

Alden, Dauril. "Black Robes versus White Settlers: The Struggle for 'Freedom of the Indians' in Colonial Brazil." In *Attitudes of Colonial Powers toward the American Indian,* edited by Howard Peckham and Charles Gibson, pp. 19–45. University of Utah Publications in the American West 2. Salt Lake City: University of Utah Press, 1969.

de Alencar, José. *Iracema, the Honey-Lips: A Legend of Brazil.* Translated by Isabel Burton. 1886. Reprint. New York: H. Fertig, 1976.

Allen, Ross, and Wilfred T. Neill. "White Whales of the Amazon." *Natural History* 66, no. 6 (1957): 324–31.

Alpers, Anthony. *Dolphins: The Myth and the Mammal.* Boston: Houghton Mifflin Co., 1961.

Amazônia: Bibliografia. Collectanea Bibliographica 1–2. Instituto Brasileiro de Bibliografia e Documentação, 1975.

Amazônia: Bibliografia, 1614–1962. Rio de Janeiro: Instituto Nacional de Pesquisas de Amazônia, 1963.

Bakhtin, M. M. *Rabelais and His World.* Translated by Hélène Iswolsky. Cambridge, Mass.: MIT Press, 1968.

Basso, Ellen B. *In Favor of Deceit: A Study of Tricksters in an Amazonian Society.* Tucson: University of Arizona Press, 1987.

————. *A Musical View of the Universe: Kalapalo Myth and Ritual Performances.* Philadelphia: University of Pennsylvania Press, 1985.

Basso, Keith. *Portraits of "the Whiteman": Linguistic Play and Cultural Symbols among the Western Apache.* New York: Cambridge University Press, 1979.

Bates, Henry Walter. *The Naturalist on the River Amazons: A Record of Adventures, Habits of Animals, and Aspects of Nature under the Equator, during Eleven Years of Travel.* With a preface by Alex Shoumatoff. New York: Penguin Books, 1988.

Ben-Amos, Dan, and Kenneth Goldstein, eds. *Folklore: Performance and Communication.* The Hague: Mouton, 1975.

Benchimol, Samuel. *Amazônia: Um pouco-antes e além depois.* Coleção Amazônia. Manaus: Editora Umberto Calderaro, 1977.

Bersani, Leo. *A Future for Astyanax: Character and Desire in Literature.* New York: Columbia University Press, 1989.

Best, Robin C., and Vera M. F. da Silva. "*Inia geoffrensis.*" *Mammalian Species* 426 (23 April 1993): 1–8.

————. "Preliminary Analysis of Reproductive Parameters of the Boutu, *Inia geoffrensis,* and the Tucuxi, *Sotalia fluviatilis,* in the Amazon River System." *Reports of the International Whaling Commission,* special issue 6 (1984): 361–69.

Bittencourt, Antonio Clemente Ribeiro. *Memórias de Parintins.* Manaus: Livraria Palais Royal, 1924.

Blackburn, Julia. *The White Men: The First Response of Aboriginal Peoples to the White Man.* London: Orbis, 1979.

Blacker, Carmen. "The Snake Woman in Japanese Myth and Legend." In *Animals in Folklore,* edited by J. R. Porter and W. M. S. Russell, pp. 113–25. Totowa, N.J.: Rowman and Littlefield, 1978.

Bopp, Raul. *Cobra Norato e outros poemas.* 16th ed. Coleção Vera Cruz 168. Rio de Janeiro: Civilização Brasileira, 1988.

Bourdieu, Pierre. *Outline of a Theory of Practice.* Translated by Richard Nice. Studies in Social Anthropology 16. 1972. Reprint. Cambridge: Cambridge University Press, 1977.

Brenner, G., and G. Pilleri. "The Dolphin in Ancient Art and Literature." *Investigations on Cetacea* 8 (1978): 295–303.

Brewer, E. Cobham. *A Dictionary of Miracles: Imitative, Dogmatic, and Realistic.* 1884. Reprint. Detroit: Gale Research Co., 1966.

Bronson, Bernard Harris. *The Traditional Tunes of the Child Ballads, with Their Texts, According to Extant Records of Great Britain and America,* vol. 2. Princeton, N.J.: Princeton University Press, 1962.

Brown, Michael F. "Beyond Resistance: A Comparative Study of Utopian Renewal in Amazonia." *Ethnohistory* 38 (1991): 388–413.

————. *Tsewa's Gift: Magic and Meaning in an Amazonian Society.* Smithsonian Series in Ethnographic Inquiry. Washington, D.C.: Smithsonian Institution Press, 1985.

Brown, Michael F., and Eduardo Fernández. *War of Shadows: The Struggle for Utopia in the Peruvian Amazon.* Berkeley: University of California Press, 1991.

Caldwell, Melba C., and David K. Caldwell. "Epimelectic (Care-Giving) Behavior in Cetacea." In *Whales, Dolphins, and Porpoises: First International Symposium on Cetacean Research,* edited by Kenneth S. Norris, pp. 755–89. Berkeley: University of California Press, 1963.

————. "More about the Ugly Dolphin." *Sea Frontiers* 5, no. 6 (1969): 311–17.

————. "The Ugly Dolphin." *Sea Frontiers* 15, no. 5 (1969): 308–14.

Cantanhede, Antonio. *O Amazonas por dentro: Contos, lendas, e narrativas do Amazonas.* Manaus: Sérgio Cardoso e Cia., 1950.

Carvalho, José. *O matuto cearense e o caboclo do Pará: Contribuição ao folclore nacional.* 2d ed. Fortaleza: Imprensa Universitária da Universidade Federal do Ceará, 1973.

de Carvalho, Sílvia Maria S. *Jurupari: Estudos de mitologia brasileira.* São Paulo: Atica, 1979.

Cascudo, Luís da Câmara. *Dicionário do folclore brasileiro,* 5th ed. Clássicos da Cultura Brasileira 4. Belo Horizonte: Itatiaia, 1984.

————. *Geografia dos mitos brasileiros.* 2d ed. Rio de Janeiro: José Olympio/INL, 1976.

Casement, Roger. *Correspondence Respecting the Treatment of British Colonial Subjects and Native Indians Employed in the Collection of Rubber in the Putumayo District, Presented to Both Houses of Parliament by Command of His Majesty, July 12.* London, 1912.

Cerqua, Arcângelo. *Clarões de fé no médio Amazonas.* Manaus: Imprensa Oficial do Estado do Amazonas, 1980.

Chatelain, Heli. *Folk-tales of Angola: Fifty Tales, with Ki-mbundu Texts, Literal English Translation, Introduction, and Notes.* Memoirs of the American Folklore Society 1. Boston: Houghton, Mifflin and Co., 1894.

Chernela, Janet M. "Righting History in the Northwest Amazon: Myth, Structure, and History in an Arapaço Narrative." In *Rethinking History and Myth: Indigenous South American Perspectives on the Past,* edited by Jonathan D. Hill, pp. 35–49. Urbana: University of Illinois Press, 1988.

Chumap Lucía, Aurelio, and Manuel García-Rendueles. *"Duik múun . . .": Universo mítico de los Aguaruna,* 2 vols. Lima: Centro Amazonico de Antropología y Práctica, 1979.

de Civrieux, Marc. "Medatia: A Makiritare Shaman's Tale." Translated by David M. Guss. In *The Language of the Birds: Tales, Texts, and Poems of Interspecies Communication,* edited by David M. Guss, pp. 55–78. San Francisco: North Point Press, 1985.

————. *Watunna: An Orinoco Creation Cycle,* edited and translated by David M. Guss. San Francisco: North Point Press, 1980.

Clastres, Hélène. *La terre sans mal: Le prophetisme tupi-guarani.* Paris: Éditions du Seuil, 1975.

Collins, Mark, ed. *The Last Rain Forests: A World Conservation Atlas.* Foreword by David Attenborough. New York: Oxford University Press, 1990.

da Cunha, Euclides. *Um paraíso perdido: Ensaios, estudos, e pronunciamentos sobre a Amazônia,* edited with notes and introduction by Leandro Tocantins. Rio de Janeiro: José Olympio, 1986.

Dégh, Linda, and Andrew Vázsonyi. "Legend and Belief." In *Folklore Genres,* edited by Dan Ben-Amos, pp. 119–223. Publications of the American Folklore Society Bibliographical and Special Series 26. Austin: University of Texas Press, 1976.

Degler, Carl. *Neither Black nor White: Slavery and Race Relations in Brazil and the United States.* New York: Macmillan, 1971.

Denevan, William M. "The Aboriginal Population of Amazônia." In *The Native Population of the Americas in 1492,* edited by William M. Denevan, pp. 205–34. Madison: University of Wisconsin Press, 1976.

Dicionário Novo Michaelis. 2 vols. 18th ed. São Paulo: Edições Melhoramentos, 1961.

Di Paolo, Pasquale. *Cabanagem: A revolução popular da Amazônia.* Belém: Edições CEJUP, 1986.

Dobkin de Rios, Marlene. "A Psi Approach to Love Magic, Witchcraft, and Psychedelics in the Peruvian Amazon." *Phoenix: New Directions in the Study of Man* 2, no. 1 (1978): 22–27.

Doyle, (Sir) Arthur Conan. *The Lost World.* 1912. Reprint. New York: Pyramid, 1960.

Dwyer, Daisy Hilse. *Images and Self-Images: Male and Female in Morocco.* New York: Columbia University Press, 1978.

Ellis, Richard. *Dolphins and Porpoises.* New York: Alfred A. Knopf, 1982.

Farriss, Nancy M. *Maya Society under Colonial Rule: The Collective Enterprise of Survival.* Princeton, N.J.: Princeton University Press, 1984.

Ferreira, Manuel Rodrigues. *A ferrovia do diabo: História de uma estrada de ferro na Amazônia.* 2d ed. São Paulo: Melhoramentos, 1987.

Figueiredo, Napoleão, and A. Vergolino e Silva. *Festas de santo e encantados.* Belém: Academia Paraense de Letras, 1972.

Foresta, Ronald. *Amazon Conservation in the Age of Development: The Limits of Providence.* Gainesville: University of Florida Press, 1991.

Foucault, Michel. *Power/Knowledge: Selected Interviews and Other Writings, 1972–1977.* Edited by Colin Gordon. Brighton, N.Y.: Pantheon, 1980.

Furneaux, Robin. *The Amazon: The Story of a Great River.* London: Hamish Hamilton, 1969.

Galvão, Eduardo. "Panema: Uma crença do caboclo amazônico." In *Encontro de sociedades: Índios e brancos no Brasil,* pp. 57–62. Coleção Estudos Brasileiros 29. Rio de Janeiro: Paz e Terra, 1979.

———. *Santos e visagens: Um estudo da vida religiosa de Itá, Amazonas.* Brasiliana 284. São Paulo: Editora Nacional, 1955.

Gebhart-Sayer, Angelika. *Die Spitze des Bewußtseins: Untersuchungen zu Weltbild und Kunst der Shipibo-Conibo.* Hohenschäftlarn: Klaus Renner Verlag, 1987.

Georges, Robert A. "The General Concept of Legend: Some Assumptions to be Reexamined and Reassessed." In *American Folk Legend: A Symposium,* edited by Wayland D. Hand. Publications of the UCLA Center for the Study of Comparative Folklore and Mythology 2. Berkeley: University of California Press, 1971.

Gihr, M., and G. Pilleri. "Interspecific Body Length–Body Weight Ratio and Body

Weight–Brain Weight Ratio in Cetacea." *Investigations on Cetacea* 10 (1979): 245–53.

Gilmore, David D., ed. *Honor and Shame and the Unity of the Mediterranean.* Special Publication of the American Anthropological Association 22. Washington, D.C.: American Anthropological Association, 1987.

Ginzberg, Louis. *The Legends of the Jews.* 2 vols. Translated by Henrietta Szold. Philadelphia: Jewish Publication Society of America, 1913.

Girard, René. *Violence and the Sacred.* 6th ed. Translated by Patrick Gregory. Baltimore, Md.: John Hopkins Press, 1989.

Gregor, Thomas. *Anxious Pleasures: The Sexual Lives of an Amazonian People.* Chicago: University of Chicago Press, 1985.

———. "Dark Dreams about the Whiteman." *Natural History* 92, no. 1 (1983): 8–14.

Guss, David M. "The Encantados: Venezuela's Invisible Kingdom." *Journal of Latin American Lore* 8, no. 2 (1982): 223–72.

———. "Keeping It Oral: A Yekuana Ethnology." *American Ethnologist* 13 (1986): 413–29.

———, ed. *The Language of the Birds: Tales, Texts, and Poems of Interspecies Communication.* San Francisco: North Point Press, 1985.

———, trans. "Wiyu and the Man Who Liked to Shoot Dolphins." *Archive Newsletter* (University of California, San Diego) 44 (1990): 15–16.

Hall, Anthony L. *Developing Amazonia: Deforestation and Social Conflict in Brazil's Carajás Programme.* Contemporary Issues in Development Studies. Manchester: Manchester University Press, 1989.

Harner, Michael J. *The Jivaro: People of the Sacred Waterfalls.* Garden City, N.Y.: Doubleday and Co., 1972.

Harrison, Phyllis A. *Behaving Brazilian: A Comparison of Brazilian and North American Social Behavior.* Rowley, Mass.: Newbury House Publishers, 1983.

Harrison, Regina. *Signs, Songs, and Memory in the Andes: Translating Quechua Language and Culture.* Austin: University of Texas Press, 1989.

Harrison, Robert Pogue. *Forests: The Shadow of Civilization.* Chicago: University of Chicago Press, 1992.

Hecht, Susanna, and Alexander Cockburn. *The Fate of the Forest: Developers, Destroyers, and Defenders of the Amazon.* 1989. Reprint. New York: Harper, 1990.

Hemming, John H. *Change in the Amazon Basin.* 2 vols. Manchester: Manchester University Press, 1985.

———. *The Search for El Dorado.* New York: Dutton, 1978.

Herald, Earl S. "Bouto and Tookashee: Amazon Dolphins." *Pacific Discovery* 20, no. 1 (1967): 2–9.

de Heusch, Luc. *The Drunken King; or, The Origin of the State.* Translated by Roy Willis. Bloomington: Indiana University Press, 1982.

Hill, Jonathan D., ed. *Rethinking History and Myth: Indigenous South American Perspectives on the Past.* Urbana: University of Illinois Press, 1988.

Hocquengheim, Anne Marie, and Max Inga. *Los encantos de La Encantada.* Biblioteca

Campesina 7. Piura (Peru): Centro de Investigación y Promoción del Campesinado, 1989.

Hudson, W. H. *Green Mansions: A Romance of the Tropical Forest.* 1904. Reprint. New York: Dover Publications, 1989.

Hugh-Jones, Christine. *From the Milk River: Spatial and Temporal Processes in the Northwest Amazon.* Cambridge: Cambridge University Press, 1979.

Hugh-Jones, Stephen. *The Palm and the Pleiades: Initiation and Cosmology in Northwest Amazonia.* Cambridge Studies in Social Anthropology 24. Cambridge: Cambridge University Press, 1979.

Ireland, Emilienne. "Cerebral Savage: The Whiteman as Symbol of Cleverness and Savagery in Waurá Myth." In *Rethinking History and Myth: Indigenous South American Perspectives on the Past,* edited by Jonathan D. Hill, pp. 157–73. Urbana: University of Illinois Press, 1988.

Ireland, Rowan. *Kingdoms Come: Religion and Politics in Brazil.* Pittsburgh, Pa.: University of Pittsburgh Press, 1991.

Jobes, Gertrude. *Dictionary of Mythology, Folklore, and Symbol.* 2 vols. New York: Scarecrow Press, 1962.

Jobim, Antonio. *Aspectos sócio-geográficos do Amazonas.* Manaus: Sérgio Cardoso e Cia., 1950.

Jordana Laguna, José Luís. *Mitos e historias aguarunas.* Lima: Retablo de Papel, 1974.

Kaplan, Louise J. *Female Perversions: The Temptations of Emma Bovary.* New York: Doubleday, 1991.

Karsten, Rafael. *Studies in the Religion of the South American Indians East of the Andes.* Commentationes Humanarum Litterarum 29, no. 1. Helsinki: Societas Scientiarum Fennica, 1964.

Kracke, Waud. "Death Comes as the White Man: The Conqueror in Kagwahiv Cosmology." Paper presented in the Symposium on Myth Values and Contact in Indigenous South America, American Anthropological Association, Philadelphia, 5 December 1986.

Kristeva, Julia. "Psychoanalysis and the Polis." In *The Politics of Interpretation,* edited by W. J. T. Mitchell, pp. 83–98. Chicago: University of Chicago Press, 1983.

Krushinskaya, N. L. "The Behavior of Cetaceans." *Investigations of Cetacea* 14 (1986): 119–273.

Lacan, Jacques. *Les quatre concepts fundamentaux de la psychanalyse (The Four Fundamental Concepts of Psycho-analysis),* edited by Jacques-Alain Miller. Translated by Alan Sheridan. 1973. Reprint. New York: Norton, 1981.

Lamb, F. Bruce. "The Fisherman's Porpoise." *Natural History* 63, no. 5 (1954): 231–32.

Landy, David, ed. *Culture, Disease, and Healing: Studies in Medical Anthropology.* New York: Macmillan, 1977.

Layne, James N. "Observations on the Freshwater Porpoises in the Upper Amazon." *Journal of Mammalogy* 39, no. 1 (1958): 1–22.

Leacock, Seth, and Ruth Leacock. *Spirits of the Deep: A Study of an Afro-Brazilian Cult.* Garden City, N.Y.: Doubleday, 1972.

Leal, Ondina Fachel. "The Gauchos: Male Culture and Identity in the Pampas." Ph.D. diss., University of California, 1989.

Leite, Serafim. *Suma histórica da Companhia de Jesús no Brasil (assistência de Portugal) 1549–1760*. Lisbon: Junta de Investigações do Ultramar, 1965.

Lévi-Strauss, Claude. *From Honey to Ashes: Introduction to a Science of Mythology*, vol. 2. Translated by John and Doreen Weightman. New York: Harper and Row, 1973.

———. *The Raw and the Cooked: Introduction to a Science of Mythology*, vol. 1. Translated by John Weightman and Doreen Weightman. New York: Harper and Row, 1969.

———. *Tristes tropiques*. Translated by John and Doreen Weightman. 1973. Reprint. New York: Atheneum, 1981.

Lewis, Oscar. *Five Families: Mexican Case Studies in the Culture of Poverty*. New York: Basic Books, 1969.

Lockley, Ronald M. *Whales, Dolphins, and Porpoises*. New York: W. W. Norton and Co., 1979.

Lyotard, Jean-François. *Discours, figure*. Collection d'ésthetique 7. 1971. Reprint. Paris: Klincksieck, 1988.

MacCormack, Sabine. *Religion in the Andes: Vision and Imagination in Early Colonial Peru*. Princeton, N.J.: Princeton University Press, 1991.

MacLachlan, Colin M. "African Slave Trade and Economic Development in Amazônia." In *Slavery and Race Relations in Latin America*, edited by Robert Brent Toplin. Westport, Conn.: Greenwood Press, 1974.

———. "The Indian Labor Structure in the Portuguese Amazon, 1700–1800." In *Colonial Roots of Modern Brazil: Papers of the Newberry Library Conference*, edited by Dauril Alden, pp. 199–230. Berkeley: University of California Press, 1973.

Madriz Galindo, Fernando. "Los encantos, elementos del agua." *Boletín del Instituto de Folklore* 2, no. 2 (1955): 61–65.

Magee, Pennie L. "'The Water Is Our Land': Peasants of the River Tocantins, Brazilian Amazonia." Ph.D. diss., University of Florida, Gainesville, 1990.

Mahar, Dennis J. *Government Policies and Deforestation in Brazil's Amazon Region*. Washington, D.C.: World Bank, 1989.

Mainwaring, Scott. *Grassroots Popular Movements, Identity, and Democratization in Brazil*. Working Paper 84. Notre Dame, Ind.: Helen Kellogg Institute for International Studies, University of Notre Dame, 1986.

Maligo, Pedro. "Symbolic Territory: The Representation of Amazonia in Brazilian Literature." *Centennial Review* 35, no. 2 (1991): 229–48.

Marsh, Charles R., Jr., "The Indians and the Whites: Two Bororo Texts." *Latin American Indian Literatures* 1, no. 1 (1977): 34–36.

Martinello, Pedro. *A 'Batalha da Borracha' na Segunda Guerra Mundial e suas consequências para o Vale Amazônico*. São Paulo: UFAC, 1988.

da Matta, Roberto. *Carnivals, Rogues, and Heroes: An Interpretation of the Brazilian Dilemma*. Translated by John Drury. Notre Dame: University of Notre Dame Press, 1991.

————. "Panema: Uma tentativa de análise estrutural." In *Ensaios de antropologia estrutural*, pp. 202–8. Petrópolis: Vozes, 1973.

Maués, Raymundo Heraldo. *A ilha encantada: Medicina e xamanismo numa comunidade de pescadores*. Coleção Igarapé. Belém: Universidade Federal do Pará, 1990.

Maxwell, Kenneth. "The Mystery of Chico Mendes." *New York Review of Books*, 28 March 1991, pp. 39–48.

————. "The Tragedy of the Amazon." *New York Review of Books*, 7 March 1991, pp. 24–29.

Medina, J. T., ed. *The Discovery of the Amazon According to the Account of Friar Gaspar de Carvajal and Other Documents*. 1934. Reprint. Translated by Bertram T. Lee. New York: Dover, 1988.

Melatti, Júlio Cézar. "A origem dos brancos no mito de *Shoma Wetsa*." *Anuário antropológico* 84 (1985): 109–73.

Menezes, Bruno. *Boi-Bumbá (Auto Popular)*. Belém: n.p., 1958.

Morote Best, Efraín. *Aldeas sumergidas: Cultura popular y sociedad en los Andes*. Biblioteca de la Tradición Andina 9. Cusco: Centro de Estudios Rurales Andinos Bartolomé de las Casas, 1988.

Muratorio, Blanca. *The Life and Times of Grandfather Alonso: Culture and History in the Upper Amazon*. New Brunswick, N.J.: Rutgers University Press, 1991.

Murphy, Yolanda, and Robert Murphy. *Women of the Forest*. New York: Columbia University Press, 1974.

Nery, Frederico José de Santa-Anna. *Folk-lore brésilien: Poésie populaire, contes et légendes, fables et mythes, poésie, musique, danses et croyances des Indiens, accompagné de douze morceaux de musique*. Paris: Perrin, 1889.

Niles, Susan A. *South American Indian Narrative: Theoretical and Analytical Approaches; An Annotated Bibliography*. Garland Folklore Bibliographies 1. New York: Garland Publishing, 1981.

Nimuendaju, Curt. *The Tükuna*, edited by Robert H. Lowie. Translated by William D. Hohenthal. Publications in American Archaeology and Ethnology 45. Berkeley: University of California Press, 1952.

Orico, Osvaldo. *Mitos ameríndios e crendices amazônicos*. Retratos do Brasil 93. Rio de Janeiro: Civilização Brasileira/INL, 1975.

Ortner, Sherry B. "Is Female to Male as Nature Is to Culture?" In *Women, Culture, and Society*, edited by Michelle Zimbalist Rosaldo and Louise Lamphere, pp. 67–87. Stanford: Stanford University Press, 1974.

Ortner, Sherry B., and Harriet Whitehead, eds. *Sexual Meanings: The Cultural Construction of Gender and Sexuality*. New York: Cambridge University Press, 1975.

Parker, Eugene. "Caboclization: The Transformation of the Amerindian in Amazônia, 1615–1800." In *The Amazon Caboclo: Historical and Contemporary Perspectives*, edited by Eugene Parker, pp. 1–49. Studies in Third World Societies 32. Williamsburg, Va.: Department of Anthropology, College of William and Mary, 1985.

Parker, Richard G. *Bodies, Pleasures, and Passions: Sexual Culture in Contemporary Brazil*. Boston: Beacon Press, 1991.

REFERENCES

Parrinder, Geoffrey. *African Traditional Religion.* London: Sheldon Press, 1962.

Péristiany, J. G., ed. *Honour and Shame: The Values of Mediterranean Society.* Chicago: University of Chicago Press, 1966.

Perry, Mary Elizabeth, and Anne J. Cruz, eds. *Cultural Encounters: The Impact of the Inquisition in Spain and the New World.* Berkeley: University of California Press, 1991.

Pescatello, Ann, ed. *Female and Male in Latin America.* 1973. Reprint. Pittsburgh: University of Pittsburgh Press, 1979.

Pilleri, G. "Alexander von Humboldt (1769–1859) and the *Inia* of the Rio Orinoco." *Investigations on Cetacea* 12 (1981): 114–20.

———. "The Chinese River Dolphin (*Lipotes vexillifer*) in Poetry, Literature, and Legend." *Investigations on Cetacea* 10 (1979): 335–49.

———. "Indian River Dolphins in the Moral Edicts of King Asoka and Ancient Indian Literature." *Investigations on Cetacea* 10 (1979): 351–56.

Pinto, Lúcio Flávio. "O Amazonas é Manaus." *Jornal Pessoal* 5, no. 84 (1992).

———. *Amazônia: No rastro do saque.* São Paulo: Hucitec, 1980.

Postma, Minnie. *Tales from the Basotho.* Translated by Susie McDermid, with notes by John Vlach. American Folklore Society Memoir Series 59. Austin: University of Texas Press, 1974.

Pratt, Mary Louise. *Imperial Eyes: Studies in Travel Writing and Transculturation.* New York: Routledge, 1992.

Pryor, Karen, and Kenneth S. Norris, eds. *Dolphin Societies: Discoveries and Puzzles.* Berkeley: University of California Press, 1991.

Putz, Francis E., and N. Michele Holbrook. "Tropical Rain-Forest Images." In *People of the Tropical Rain Forest,* edited by Julie Sloan Denslow and Christine Padoch, pp. 37–52. Berkeley: University of California Press in association with the Smithsonian Institution Traveling Exhibition Service, 1988.

de Queiroz, Maria José. "Os itinerários da selva: Na Amazônia." *Estudos românicos* (Faculdade de Letras, Universidade Federal de Minas Gerais) 1 (1981): 271–81.

Ramos, Alcida R. "Frontier Expansion and Indian Peoples in the Brazilian Amazon." In *Frontier Expansion in Amazônia,* edited by Marianne Schmink and Charles H. Wood, pp. 83–104. Gainesville: University of Florida Press, 1984.

Rangel, Alberto. *Inferno verde: Scenas e scenários do Amazonas.* 2d rev. ed. Famalicão: Typographia Minerva, 1914.

Rasnake, Roger Neil. *Domination and Cultural Resistance: Authority and Power among an Andean People.* Durham, N.C.: Duke University Press, 1988.

Regan, Jaime. *Hacia la tierra sin mal: Estudio sobre la religiosidad del pueblo en la Amazonia,* vol. 2. Iquitos: Centro de Estudios Teológicos de la Amazonia, 1983.

Reichel-Dolmatoff, Gerardo. *Amazonian Cosmos: The Sexual and Religious Symbolism of the Tukano Indians.* Chicago: University of Chicago Press, 1971.

———. "Cosmology as Ecological Analysis: A View from the Rain Forest." *Man* 11 (1976): 307–18.

———. "Some Shortcuts in the Tukanoan Forest of Symbols." Conference paper, Latin American Indigenous Literatures Association International Symposium, San Juan, Puerto Rico, 10 January 1992.

Reis, Arthur Cezar Ferreira. *História do Amazonas*. Manaus: Officinas Typographicas de A. Reis, 1931.

Ribeiro, Darcy. *Maíra*. Translated by E. H. Goodland and Thomas Colchie. New York: Vintage, 1984.

Rodrigues, Manuel Barbosa. "Poranduba amazonense." *Annaes da Bibliotheca Nacional do Rio de Janeiro* 14, no. 2 (1890): 3–85.

Roe, Peter G. *The Cosmic Zygote: Cosmology in the Amazon Basin*. New Brunswick, N.J.: Rutgers University Press, 1982.

———. "The Josho Nahuanbo Are All Wet and Undercooked: Shipibo Views of the Whiteman and the Incas in Myth, Legend, and History." In *Rethinking History and Myth: Indigenous South American Perspectives on the Past*, edited by Jonathan D. Hill, pp. 106–35. Urbana: University of Illinois Press, 1988.

Róheim, Géza. *The Gates of the Dream*. New York: International Universities Press, 1952.

Roosevelt, Theodore. *Through the Brazilian Wilderness*. New York: Charles Scribner's Sons, 1914.

Rosaldo, Renato. "Imperialist Nostalgia." In *Culture and Truth: The Remaking of Social Analysis*, pp. 68–87. Boston: Beacon Press, 1989.

Ross, Eric B. "The Evolution of the Amazon Peasantry." *Journal of Latin American Studies* 10 (1978): 193–218.

Salles, Vicente. *O negro no Pará sob o regime da escravidão*. Rio de Janeiro: Fundação Getúlio Vargas, 1971.

Salomon, Frank. "Ancestor Cults and Resistance to the State in Arequipa, ca. 1749–1754." In *Resistance, Rebellion, and Consciousness in the Andean Peasant World, Eighteenth to Twentieth Centuries*, edited by Steve J. Stern, pp. 148–65. Madison: University of Wisconsin Press, 1987.

Sánchez Ortega, M. Helena, "Sorcery and Eroticism in Love Magic." In *Cultural Encounters: The Impact of the Inquisition in Spain and the New World*, edited by Mary Elizabeth Perry and Anne J. Cruz, pp. 58–92. Berkeley: University of California Press, 1991.

Santos Ortiz de Villalba, Juan. *Sacha Pacha: Mitos, poesías, sueños y refranes de los Quichua Amazónicos*. Colección 500 Años 11. Quito: Ediciones Abya-Yala/ MLAL, 1989.

Saunier, Tonzinho. *O magnífico folclore de Parintins*. Manaus: Casa Civil, 1989.

———. *Várzea e terra firme*. Manaus: Edições Parintintin, 1990.

Schmink, Marianne. "Big Business in the Amazon." In *People of the Tropical Rain Forest*, edited by Julie Sloan Denslow and Christine Padoch, pp. 163–71. Berkeley: University of California Press in association with the Smithsonian Institution Traveling Exhibition Service, 1988.

Schmink, Marianne, and Charles H. Wood, *Contested Frontiers in Amazonia*. New York: Columbia University Press, 1992.

———, eds. *Frontier Expansion in Amazônia*. Gainesville: University of Florida Press, 1984.

Seed, Patricia. "'Failing to Marvel': Atahualpa's Encounter with the Word." *Latin American Research Review* 26, no. 1 (1991): 7–32.

Seljam, Zora A. O. *Iemanjá e suas lendas.* Coleção Atlântica 14. Rio de Janeiro: Record, 1967.

Shoumatoff, Alex. *The Rivers Amazon.* San Francisco: Sierra Club, 1978.

da Silva, Vera F. M. "Botos mitológicos: Hóspedes da Amazônia." *Ciência Hoje* 11, no. 64 (1990): 14–18.

Silverblatt, Irene. *Moon, Sun, and Witches: Gender Ideologies and Class in Inca and Colonial Peru.* Princeton, N.J.: Princeton University Press, 1987.

Simons, Ronald C., and Charles C. Hughes, eds. *The Culture Bound Syndromes: Folk Illnesses of Psychiatric and Anthropological Interest.* Boston: D. Reidel, 1985.

Slater, Candace. *City Steeple, City Streets: Saints' Lives from Granada and a Changing Spain.* Berkeley: University of California Press, 1990.

———. *Stories on a String: The Brazilian 'Literatura de Cordel.'* 1982. Reprint. Berkeley: University of California Press, 1989.

———. *Trail of Miracles: Stories from a Pilgrimage in Northeast Brazil.* Berkeley: University of California Press, 1986.

———. "Transformation Stories from a Changing Amazon: Accounts of *Encantados* by Descendants of Runaway Slaves." In *American Identities: Five Hundred Years after the Conquest,* edited by A. James Arnold. Charlottesville: University of Virginia Press, in press.

Smith, Anthony. *Explorers of the Amazon.* London: Viking, 1990.

de Sousa, Francisco Bernardino. *Lembranças e curiosidades do Valle do Amazonas.* Belém do Pará: Typographia do Futuro, 1873.

de Souza, [Herculano Marquês] Inglês. *Contos amazônicos.* Rio de Janeiro: Laemmert, 1893.

Souza, Márcio. *Emperor of the Amazon.* Translated by Thomas Colchie. 1977. Reprint. New York: Avon Books, 1980.

———. *A resistível ascenção do Boto Tucuxi: Folhetim.* Coleção Histórias do Pau Brasil. Rio de Janeiro: Marco Zero, 1982.

———. *Mad Maria.* Translated by Thomas Colchie. 1980. Reprint. New York: Avon, 1985.

Stahl, Sandra K. D. "The Oral Personal Narrative in Its Generic Context." *Journal of the Folklore Institute* 14, nos. 1–2 (1977): 9–30.

Stewart, Charles. *Demons and the Devil: Moral Imagination in Modern Greek Culture.* Princeton, N.J.: Princeton University Press, 1991.

Sullivan, Lawrence E. *Icanchu's Drum: An Orientation to Meaning in South American Religions.* New York: Macmillan, 1988.

Sweet, David G. "A Rich Realm of Nature Destroyed: The Middle Amazon Valley, 1640–1750." Ph.D. diss., University of Wisconsin, Madison, 1974.

Taggart, James M. *Enchanted Maidens: Gender Relations in Spanish Folktales of Courtship and Marriage.* Princeton, N.J.: Princeton University Press, 1978.

Tagliavini, F., and G. Pilleri. "Occasional Observations on the Distribution and Ecology of the Bufeo (*Inia geoffrensis*) in Ecuadorian Rivers." *Investigations of Cetacea* 16 (1984): 67–76.

Tambiah, Stanley J. "Animals are Good to Think and Good to Prohibit." *Ethnology* 8 (1969): 423–59.

Taussig, Michael T. "Folk Healing and the Structure of Conquest in Southwest Colombia." *Journal of Latin American Lore* 6, no. 2 (1989): 217–78.

———. *Shamanism, Colonialism, and the Wild Man: A Study in Terror and Healing.* Chicago: University of Chicago Press, 1987.

Thompson, Stith. *Motif-Index of Folk Literature: A Classification of Narrative Elements in Folk-tales, Ballads, Myths, Fables, Medieval Romances, Exempla, Fabliaux, Jest-books, and Local Legends.* Rev. ed. 6 vols. Bloomington: Indiana University Press, 1955–58.

Tocantins, Leandro. *Formação histórica do Acre,* 3 vols. Rio de Janeiro: Conquista, 1961.

Urton, Gary, ed. *Animal Myths and Metaphors in South America.* Salt Lake City: University of Utah Press, 1985.

Verger, Pierre. *Orixás: Deuses iorubas na África e no Novo Mundo.* Translated by Maria Aparecida de Nóbrega. Salvador: Corrupio, 1981.

Verne, Jules. *Eight Hundred Leagues on the Amazon.* With a preface by Theodore Roosevelt. New York: Didier, 1954.

———. "The Amazon Caboclo." In *The Amazon Caboclo: Historical and Contemporary Perspectives,* edited by Eugene Parker, pp. vii–xlv. Studies in Third World Societies 32. Williamsburg, Va.: Department of Anthropology, College of William and Mary, 1985.

Wagley, Charles. *Amazon Town: A Study of Man in the Tropics.* 1953. Reprint. Borzoi Books. New York: Alfred A. Knopf, 1964.

Watanabe, John M. *Maya Saints and Souls in a Changing World.* Austin: University of Texas Press, 1992.

Weber, Max. "Religious Rejections of the World and Their Direction." In *From Max Weber: Essays in Sociology,* edited by H. H. Gerth and C. Wright Mills, pp. 252–359. New York: Oxford University Press, 1946.

———. "Science as a Vocation." In *From Max Weber: Essays in Sociology,* edited by H. H. Gerth and C. Wright Mills, pp. 129–56. New York: Oxford University Press, 1946.

Weinstein, Barbara. "The Amazon Rubber Trade, 1850–1920." In *Proletarians and Protest: The Roots of Class Formation in an Industrializing World,* edited by Michael Hanagan and Charles Stephenson, pp. 55–76. Contributions in Labor Studies 17. New York: Greenwood Press, 1986.

Whitten, Norman E., Jr., *Sacha Runa: Ethnicity and Adaptation of Ecuadorian Jungle Quichua.* Urbana: University of Illinois Press, 1976.

Wilbert, Johannes. *Tobacco and Shamanism in South America.* New Haven: Yale University Press, 1987.

Wilbert, Johannes, and Karen Simoneau. *Motif Index of South American Open Lowland Folk Literature.* Los Angeles: Center for Latin American Studies, in press.

Xidieh, Osvaldo Elias. *Narrativas pias populares.* São Paulo: Instituto de Estudos Brasileiros, 1967.

INDEX

Portuguese names are alphabetized under the last surname. Spanish names are alphabetized under the first of multiple surnames.

abduction by Dolphins, 108–9, 163, 176 n. 24, 201, 226; disenchantment and release from, 113–15, 180–81, 231, 243; metamorphosis upon, 214

acculturation, 241–42

adolescents, 170, 177–81

African Brazilian religions, 121, 131; *see also* Roman Catholic religion; deities, 102–3, 102 n. 24, 110 n. 38; influence on *encantado* tradition, 153 n. 38, 157, 157 n. 45; shamanism and, 111–12; Umbanda, 55–56, 56 n. 11, 83, 260

Africans: slaves, 21, 153, 153 n. 38, 260; traditions, 77 n. 51

agriculture, large-scale, 27, 27 nn. 30–31

Aguaruna people, 68, 68 n. 29, 82, 84

Aguirre, Wrath of God, 237, 237 n. 9

Alda, Dona, 55

aldeias labor force, 22

Alencar, José de, 19

alienation, 178–79, 249–50

almas penadas (ghosts), 145

Alzira (storyteller), 164, 172, 195–96, 196–97, 208–9, 229, 241; life of, 51–54

Amazon River, 10, 257

Amazonas (state), 10, 32 n. 46

Amazônia, 10, 167–72, 257; acculturation in, 24–25; as a last frontier, 235–36; books and films on, 236–38; diversity of life in, 31; as earthly paradise, 235–36, 235 nn. 2–3; as El Dorado,

234; government development of, 25–30, 26 nn. 27–29; as Green Hell, 236–37, 237 n. 8, 238; history of, 18–31, 22–31, 234–38; isolation and marginalization of, 18, 172, 235, 255; legal area of, 17–18, 18 n. 4; outsiders' ideas of, 234–38

Amazons, 169, 236

ambiguity: of beliefs about dolphins, 80, 254, 255–56; of enchantment, 242–43, 251

Anaconda boat (Enchanted Boat), 126, 160–61, 160 n. 51, 253

Anacondas, mythic, 67–68, 68 n. 29, 71 n. 33, 94 n. 10, 112, 126, 131, 215; see also *Cobra Grande* (anaconda); Cobra Norato; compared to Dolphins, 160–61

anaconda snakes, 68, 164–65

anatomy, dolphin: human-dolphin sexual encounters and, 85–88; similarity of human and, 81–82; trade in magical parts of, 82–84

animals, 220; *see also* guardians, forest; killing *encantados* as, 103–6, 252; parts as love charms, 82–84, 84 n. 66, 122; shape-changers as, 139–40

animals and humans. *See* bestiality; dolphins as special fish

Animals, Master of (*Vai Mahsë*), 75–76, 75 n. 45, 77 n. 52

anthropomorphism of Dolphins vs. other *encantados,* 156–60, 164

303